Introduction to Functional Programming using Haskell

Second edition

Richard Bird

University of Oxford

Prentice Hall

An imprint of **Pearson Education**

Harlow, England · London · New York · Reading, Massachusetts · San Francisco · Toronto · Don Mills, Ontario · Sydney
Tokyo · Singapore · Hong Kong · Seoul · Taipei · Cape Town · Madrid · Mexico City · Amsterdam · Munich · Paris · Milan

Pearson Education Limited
Edinburgh Gate
Harlow
Essex CM20 2JE, England

Visit us on the World Wide Web at:
http://www.pearsoneduc.com

© Prentice Hall Europe 1998

First published 1988
This second edition published 1988 by
Prentice Hall

Printed and bound in Great Britain by
Redwood Books Ltd, Trowbridge

Library of Congress Cataloging-in-Publication Data

Available from the publisher

British Library Cataloguing in Publication Data

A catalogue record for this book is available from
the British Library

ISBN 0-13-484346-0

10 9 7 6 5 4 3
04 03 02 01 00

Contents

Preface to the second edition

The second edition is a thoroughly reorganised and expanded version of the first. Nevertheless, I have remained true to the aims of the original, as expressed in the opening two paragraphs in the preface to the first edition:

> This is an introductory textbook on programming in general and functional programming in particular. No knowledge of computers or experience in writing programs is assumed. The book is therefore suitable for teaching a course in programming to first-year undergraduates, but it can also be used as an introduction to functional programming for students who are already experienced programmers.
>
> In order to get the most out of the book, the student should know some mathematics, or at least possess a general appreciation of the principles of mathematical reasoning. Our primary aim in writing this book is to convey a view of programming as a mathematical activity, and mathematical reasoning lies at the heart of our subject. Functional programming involves notation and concepts of a kind which should be familiar to anyone with a little mathematical experience. For example, any student who has used the basic trigonometric functions to formulate problems in geometry, and has applied simple trigonometric laws and identities to derive solutions to these problems, will soon appreciate that a similar activity is being suggested for computational problems and their solution by functional programs. It follows that the kind of mathematical understanding required is not very complicated or specialised, just the general ability to follow manipulations of formulae through applying algebraic laws, and the appreciation of why such manipulations can be useful in the task of solving practical problems.

One major change in the present edition has been to use a specific language, Haskell, to express functional programs. At the time the first edition appeared, the design of lazy functional languages was in a state of flux, with a number of closely related but different dialects competing for attention. We tried to take account of the changing state of affairs by using a neutral notation, similar to but not identical with Miranda (Miranda is a trademark of Research Software Limited), one of the more popular lazy functional languages at that time. Ten years later, the situation has stabilised somewhat in that Haskell, a relative of Mark Jones' popular language Gofer, is now widely regarded as the language of choice among lazy functional programmers. In particular, HUGS (the Haskell Users' Gofer System) was designed as a simple interactive system suitable for use on PCs with modest capabilities. References to Haskell and HUGS, and how to get hold of them, are given at the end of Chapter 1. The version of Haskell we use in this book is Haskell 1.3 (and also HUGS 1.3). Haskell itself is currently undergoing modest evolution and standardisation, and it is intended to publish details of Standard Haskell in the summer of 1998. However, since we do not cover all details of Haskell, it is unlikely that any proposed standardisation will affect the text in any significant way.

The second major change concerns the organisation of material. The present edition introduces the idea of defining new datatypes early on. The core of the first part of the book is now devoted to the study of three recursive datatypes: natural numbers, lists, and trees. Each datatype is introduced along with the idea of defining recursive functions over the datatype, and also along with the method of proof by induction to establish properties of these recursively defined functions. Thus, three important ideas are introduced as different aspects of a single coherent whole. The examples and case studies have also been changed or updated. There are completely new chapters on abstract datatypes, efficiency, and monadic functional programming. The bibliography has expanded considerably, and there now are brief chapter notes at the end of each chapter.

The third major change is that, owing to a number of commitments and a change of environment, my co-author Philip Wadler could only give limited assistance in the preparation of the text. He provided detailed comments and suggestions on an early draft of the first six chapters, as well as material that formed the basis of the chapter on monadic programming. Although his major contributions to the understanding of functional programming over the past ten years permeate the book, I alone take responsibility for errors of understanding, mistakes, or inappropriate emphasis. If and when the need for a third edition arises, I hope that we can again join forces to produce it.

Advice to the instructor

The second edition has grown by over a hundred pages, and the material probably cannot be fully covered in a single course. A first course in functional programming can be based on the first six chapters, with Chapter 3 being treated more lightly than the others. In our experience, students only begin to appreciate what a functional style of programming can offer when the subject of lists is broached. The remaining material can be adapted for a second course on programming, emphasising modularity and data structures. The material has also been used for a course on algorithm design and efficiency, as well as courses on the mathematics of program proof and synthesis.

Formal teaching should be supported by laboratory and practical work, and many of the examples and case studies have been used as the basis of practical projects with considerable success. Most of the individual sections also contain a variety of exercises for self study. It is planned to publish answers to these questions on the Web; see the URL

```
http://www.comlab.ox.ac.uk/oucl/publications/books/functional/
```

This web site will also contain many of the programs listed in the text, as well as pointers to Haskell and HUGS, and to additional material.

Acknowledgements

This edition, like the first, took more time than expected. My greatest debt of gratitude is to Phil Wadler. Apart from the reasons cited above, he generously allowed me to complete the text by myself. The second edition was written during a sabbatical year from teaching and administrative duties, and I am truly grateful to the University of Oxford and Lincoln College for supporting hard-pressed academics in this way.

The book has benefited enormously from the continued support, enthusiasm, and constructive advice of colleagues and students, both at Oxford and other universities. The suggestions of colleagues in the Programming Research Group at Oxford have been particularly relevant, since they have been personally responsible for teaching the material to their tutorial students while a lecture course was in progress. Other people who have written or emailed Phil or me with suggestions, or simply to point out typos and silly mistakes in the first edition, include: Nils Andersen, Franklin Chen, Sharon Curtis, Martin Filby, Simon Finn, Jeroen Fokker, Maarten Fokkinga, Jeremy Gibbons, Robert Giegerich, Kevin Hammond, Gerard Huet, Michael Hinchey, Tony Hoare, Iain Houston, John Hughes, Graham Hutton, Stephen Jarvis, Geraint Jones, Mark

Jones, John Launchbury, Paul Licameli, David Lester, Iain MacCullum, Ursula Martin, Lambert Meertens, Erik Meijer, Quentin Miller, Oege de Moor, Chris Okasaki, Oskar Permvall, Simon Peyton Jones, Mark Ramaer, Hamilton Richards, Dan Russell, Don Sannella, Antony Simmons, Deepak D'Souza, John Spanondakis, Mike Spivey, Joe Stoy, Bernard Sufrin, Masato Takeichi, Peter Thiemann, David Turner, Colin Watson, and Stephen Wilson. In particular, Jeremy Gibbons and Rob Hoogerwoord read drafts of the manuscript and suggested a number of corrections.

I would also like to thank Jim Davies for getting my LATEX into shape, and Jackie Harbor of Prentice Hall for continued support. The text was prepared on an Apple Macintosh Powerbook 180, using BBEdit as an editor, and OzTEX as the LATEX processor. All three systems were a delight to use.

Oxford   Richard Bird
December, 1997

Chapter 1

Fundamental concepts

Programming in a functional language consists of building definitions and using the computer to evaluate expressions. The primary role of the programmer is to construct a function to solve a given problem. This function, which may involve a number of subsidiary functions, is described in a notation that obeys normal mathematical principles. The primary role of the computer is to act as an evaluator or calculator; its job is to evaluate expressions and print the results. In this respect the computer acts much like an ordinary pocket calculator. What distinguishes a functional calculator from the humbler variety is the programmer's ability to make definitions to increase its powers of calculation. Expressions that contain occurrences of the names of functions defined by the programmer are evaluated using the given definitions as simplification rules for converting expressions to printable form.

1.1   Sessions and scripts

To illustrate the idea of using a computer as a calculator, imagine we are sitting in front of a terminal screen displaying a prompt sign

?

in a window. We can now type an expression, followed by a newline character, and the computer will respond by displaying the result of evaluating the expression, followed by a new prompt on a new line, indicating that the process can begin again with another expression.

One kind of expression we might type is a number:

?42
42

Here, the computer's response is simply to redisplay the number we typed. The decimal numeral 42 is an expression in its simplest possible form and evaluating it results in no further simplification.

We might type a slightly more interesting kind of expression:

? 6 × 7

42

Here, the computer can simplify the expression by performing the multiplication. In this book we will use common mathematical notations for writing expressions; in particular, the multiplication operator will be denoted by the sign ×, rather than the asterisk * used in Haskell.

We will not elaborate for the moment on the possible forms of numerical and other kinds of expression that can be submitted for evaluation; the important point to absorb now is that one can just type expressions and have them evaluated. This sequence of interactions between user and computer is called a *session*.

The second and intellectually more challenging aspect of functional programming consists of building definitions. A list of definitions is called a *script*. Here is an example of a simple script:

$$\begin{aligned}
square & \quad :: \quad Integer \to Integer \\
square\ x & \quad = \quad x \times x \\
\\
smaller & \quad :: \quad (Integer, Integer) \to Integer \\
smaller\ (x, y) & \quad = \quad \textbf{if}\ x \leq y\ \textbf{then}\ x\ \textbf{else}\ y
\end{aligned}$$

In this script, two functions named *square* and *smaller* have been defined. The function *square* takes an integer as argument and returns its square; the function *smaller* takes a pair of integers as argument and returns the smaller value. The syntax for making definitions follows that of Haskell, the programming language adopted in this book, and will be explained in due course. Notice, however, that definitions are written as equations between certain kinds of expression; these expressions can contain *variables*, here denoted by the symbols x and y. Furthermore, each function is accompanied by a description of its *type*; for example, $(Integer, Integer) \to Integer$ describes the type of functions that take a pair of integers as argument, and deliver an integer as result. Such type descriptions are also called *type assignments* or *type signatures*.

Having created a script, we can submit it to the computer and enter a session. For example, the following session is now possible:

? *square* 3768

14197824

? *square* 14198724

201578206334976

? *square* (*smaller* (5, 3 + 4))

25

Notice, in passing, that *Integer* arithmetic is exact: there is no restriction on the sizes of integers that can be computed.

The purpose of a definition is to introduce a *binding* associating a given name with a given definition. A set of bindings is called an *environment* or *context*. Expressions are always evaluated in some context and can contain occurrences of the names found in that context. The Haskell evaluator will use the definitions associated with these names as rules for simplifying expressions.

Some expressions can be evaluated without having to provide a context. In Haskell a number of operations are given as primitive in the sense that the rules of simplification are built into the evaluator. For example, the basic operations of arithmetic are provided as primitive. Other commonly useful operations are predefined in special scripts, called *preludes* or *libraries*, that can be loaded when we start the computer.

At any stage a programmer can return to the script in order to add or modify definitions. The new script can then be resubmitted to the evaluator to provide a new context and another session started. For example, suppose we return to the above script and change it to read:

$$
\begin{aligned}
square && :: &\quad Float \rightarrow Float \\
square\ x && = &\quad x \times x \\
\\
delta && :: &\quad (Float, Float, Float) \rightarrow Float \\
delta\ (a, b, c) && = &\quad sqrt\ (square\ b - 4 \times a \times c)
\end{aligned}
$$

The type assigned to *square* has been changed to *Float* → *Float*. In Haskell the type *Float* consists of the single-precision floating-point numbers. The function *delta* depends on a predefined function *sqrt* for taking square roots.

Having resubmitted the script, we can enter a new session and type, for example:

? *delta* (4.2, 7, 2.3)

3.2187

To summarise the important points made so far:

- Scripts are collections of definitions supplied by the programmer.

- Definitions are expressed as equations between certain kinds of expression and describe mathematical functions. Definitions are accompanied by type signatures.

- During a session, expressions are submitted for evaluation; these expressions can contain references to the functions defined in the script, as well as references to other functions defined in preludes or libraries.

- In Haskell, at least two different kinds of number can be used in computations: arbitrary-precision integers (elements of *Integer*), and single-precision floating-point numbers (elements of *Float*).

Exercises

1.1.1 Using the function *square*, design a function *quad* that raises its argument to the fourth power.

1.1.2 Define a function *greater* that returns the greater of its two arguments.

1.1.3 Define a function for computing the area of a circle with given radius r (use $22/7$ as an approximation to π).

1.2 Evaluation

The computer evaluates an expression by reducing it to its simplest equivalent form and displaying the result. The terms *evaluation*, *simplification*, and *reduction* will be used interchangeably to describe this process. To give a brief flavour, consider the expression *square* $(3 + 4)$; one possible sequence is

$$square\ (3 + 4)$$

$$=\quad \{\text{definition of } +\}$$

$$square\ 7$$

$$=\quad \{\text{definition of } square\}$$

$$7 \times 7$$

$$=\quad \{\text{definition of } \times\}$$

$$49$$

The first and third steps refer to use of the built-in rules for addition and multiplication, while the second step refers to the use of the rule defining *square* supplied by the programmer. That is to say, the definition *square* $x = x \times x$ is interpreted by the computer simply as a left-to-right rewrite rule for reducing expressions involving *square*. The expression '49' cannot be further reduced, so that is the result displayed by the computer. An expression is said to be *canonical*, or in *normal form*, if it cannot be further reduced. Hence '49' is in normal form.

Another reduction sequence for *square* (3 + 4) is

> *square* (3 + 4)
>
> = {definition of *square*}
>
> (3 + 4) × (3 + 4)
>
> = {definition of + (applied to first term)}
>
> 7 × (3 + 4)
>
> = {definition of +}
>
> 7 × 7
>
> = {definition of ×}
>
> 49

In this reduction sequence the rule for *square* is applied first, but the final result is the same. A characteristic feature of functional programming is that if two different reduction sequences both terminate, then they lead to the same result. In other words, the meaning of an expression is its value and the task of the computer is simply to obtain it.

Let us give another example. Consider the script

> *three* :: *Integer* → *Integer*
> *three x* = 3
>
> *infinity* :: *Integer*
> *infinity* = *infinity* + 1

It is not clear what integer, if any, is defined by the second equation but the computer can nevertheless use the equation as a rewrite rule. Now consider simplification of *three infinity*. If we try to simplify *infinity* first, then we get the reduction sequence

> *three infinity*
>
> = {definition of *infinity*}
>
> *three* (*infinity* + 1)
>
> = {definition of *infinity*}

three ((*infinity* + 1) + 1)

=   {and so on ...}

. . .

This reduction sequence does not terminate. If, on the other hand, we try to simplify *three* first, then we get the sequence

three infinity

=   {definition of *three*}

3

This sequence terminates in one step. So, some ways of simplifying an expression may terminate while others do not. In Chapter 7 we will describe a reduction strategy, called *lazy evaluation*, that guarantees termination whenever termination is possible, and is also reasonably efficient. Haskell is a lazy functional language, and we will explore what consequences such a strategy has in the rest of the book. However, whichever strategy is in force, the essential point is that expressions are evaluated by a conceptually simple process of substitution and simplification, using both primitive rules and rules supplied by the programmer in the form of definitions.

Exercises

1.2.1 In order to evaluate $x \times y$, the expressions x and y are reduced to normal form and then multiplication is performed. Does evaluation of *square infinity* terminate?

1.2.2 How many terminating reduction sequences are there for the expression *square* (3 + 4)?

1.2.3 Imagine a language of expressions for representing integers defined by the syntax rules: (i) *zero* is an expression; (ii) if *e* is an expression, then so are *succ* (*e*) and *pred* (*e*). An evaluator reduces expressions in this language by applying the following rules repeatedly until no longer possible:

$$succ \ (pred \ (e)) \ = \ e$$
$$pred \ (succ \ (e)) \ = \ e$$

Simplify the expression *succ* (*pred* (*succ* (*pred* (*pred* (*zero*))))).

In how many ways can the reduction rules be applied to this expression? Do they all lead to the same final result? Prove that the process of reduction must terminate for all given expressions. (*Hint:* Define an appropriate notion of expression size, and show that each reduction step does indeed reduce size.)

1.2.4 Carrying on from the previous question, suppose an extra syntactic rule is added to the language: (iii) if e_1 and e_2 are expressions, then so is $add(e_1, e_2)$. The corresponding reduction rules are

$$
\begin{aligned}
add\,(zero, e_2) &= e_2 \\
add\,(succ\,(e_1), e_2) &= succ\,(add\,(e_1, e_2)) \\
add\,(pred\,(e_1), e_2) &= pred\,(add\,(e_1, e_2))
\end{aligned}
$$

Simplify the expression $add\,(succ\,(pred\,(zero)), zero)$.

Count the number of different ways the reduction rules can be applied to the above expression. Do they always lead to the same final result?

1.2.5 Now suppose we define the size of an expression by the following rules:

$$
\begin{aligned}
size\,(zero) &= 1 \\
size\,(succ\,(e)) &= 1 + size\,(e) \\
size\,(pred\,(e)) &= 1 + size\,(e) \\
size\,(add\,(e_1, e_2)) &= 1 + 2 \times (size\,(e_1) + size\,(e_2))
\end{aligned}
$$

Show that application of any of the five reduction rules given above reduces expression size. Why does this prove that the process of reduction must always terminate for any given initial expression?

1.3 Values

In functional programming, as in mathematics, an expression is used solely to describe (or *denote*) a *value*. Among the kinds of value an expression may denote are included: numbers of various kinds, truth values, characters, tuples, functions, and lists. All of these will be described in due course. As we will also see, it is possible to introduce new kinds of value and define operations for generating and manipulating them.

It is important to distinguish between values and their representations by expressions. The simplest equivalent form of an expression, whatever that may be, is *not* a value but a representation of it. Somewhere, in outer space perhaps, one can imagine a universe of abstract values, but on earth they can only be recognised and manipulated by concrete representations. There may be many representations for one and the same value. For example, the abstract number forty-nine can be represented by the decimal numeral 49, the roman numeral XLIX, or the expression 7×7. Computers usually operate with the binary representation of numbers in which forty-nine is represented by a certain bit-pattern consisting of a number of 0s followed by 110001.

The evaluator for a functional language prints a value by printing its canonical representation; this representation is dependent both on the syntax given for forming expressions, and the precise definition of the reduction rules.

Some values have no canonical representations, for example function values. It is difficult to imagine a canonical representation for the function *sqrt* :: *Float* → *Float*; one can describe this function in various ways but none of the descriptions can be regarded as canonical. Other values may have reasonable representations, but no finite ones. For example, the number π has no finite decimal representation. It is possible to get a computer to print out the decimal expansion of π digit by digit, but the process will never terminate.

For some expressions the process of reduction never stops and never produces any result. For example, the expression *infinity* defined in the previous section leads to an infinite reduction sequence. Recall that the definition was

$$\begin{aligned} infinity &:: \quad Integer \\ infinity &= \quad infinity + 1 \end{aligned}$$

Such expressions do not denote well-defined values in the normal mathematical sense. As another example, assuming the operator / denotes numerical division, returning a number of type *Float*, the expression 1/0 does not denote a well-defined floating-point number. A request to evaluate 1/0 may cause the evaluator to respond with an error message, such as 'attempt to divide by zero', or go into an infinitely long sequence of calculations without producing any result.

In order that we can say that, without exception, every syntactically well-formed expression denotes a value, it is convenient to introduce a special symbol $\perp$, pronounced 'bottom', to stand for the undefined value of a particular type. In particular, the value of *infinity* is the undefined value $\perp$ of type *Integer*, and 1/0 is the undefined value $\perp$ of type *Float*. Hence we can assert that $1/0 = \perp$.

The computer is not expected to be able to produce the value $\perp$. Confronted with an expression whose value is $\perp$, the computer may give an error message, or it may remain perpetually silent. The former situation is detectable, but the second one is not (after all, evaluation might have terminated normally the moment after the programmer decided to abort it). Thus, $\perp$ is a special kind of value, rather like the special value ∞ in mathematical calculus. Like special values in other branches of mathematics, $\perp$ can be admitted to the universe of values only if we state precisely the properties it is required to have and its relationship with other values.

It is possible, conceptually at least, to apply functions to $\perp$. For example, with the definitions *three x* = 3 and *square x* = $x \times x$, we have

? *three infinity*
3

? *square infinity*
{*Interrupted!*}

In the first evaluation the value of *infinity* was not needed to complete the calculation, so it was never calculated. This is a consequence of the lazy evaluation reduction strategy mentioned earlier. On the other hand, in the second evaluation the value of *infinity* is needed to complete the computation: one cannot compute $x \times x$ without knowing the value of x. Consequently, the evaluator goes into an infinite reduction sequence in an attempt to simplify *infinity* to normal form. Bored by waiting for an answer that we know will never come, we hit the the interrupt key.

If $f \perp = \perp$, then f is said to be a *strict* function; otherwise it is *nonstrict*. Thus, *square* is a strict function, while *three* is nonstrict. Lazy evaluation allows nonstrict functions to be defined, some other strategies do not.

Exercises

1.3.1 Suppose we define *multiply* by

$$\begin{aligned}
multiply && :: && (Integer, Integer) \rightarrow Integer \\
multiply\,(x, y) && = && \textbf{if } x == 0 \textbf{ then } 0 \textbf{ else } x \times y
\end{aligned}$$

The symbol == is used for an equality test between two integers. Assume that evaluation of $e_1 == e_2$ proceeds by reducing e_1 and e_2 to normal form and testing whether the two results are identical. Under lazy evaluation, what would be the value of *multiply* (0, *infinity*)? What would be the value of *multiply* (*infinity*, 0)?

1.3.2 Suppose we define the function h by the equation $h x = f(g x)$. Show that if f and g are both strict, then so is h.

1.4 Functions

Naturally enough, the most important kind of value in functional programming is a function value. Although we cannot display a function value, we can apply functions to arguments and display the results (provided, of course, that the result can be displayed). Mathematically speaking, a function f is a rule of correspondence that associates each element of a given type A with a unique element of a second type B. The type A is called the *source* type, and B the *target* type of the function. We express this information by writing $f :: A \to B$. This formula asserts that the type of f is $A \to B$. In other words, the type expression $A \to B$ denotes a type whenever A and B do, and describes the type of functions from A to B. For example, we have already met the functions

$$
\begin{array}{lll}
three & :: & Integer \to Integer \\
square & :: & Integer \to Integer \\
delta & :: & (Float, Float, Float) \to Float
\end{array}
$$

The definition of *three* describes a rule of correspondence that associates every integer, including the special integer $\perp$, with the single number 3. The definition of *square* associates every well-defined integer with its square, and associates $\perp$ with the undefined integer $\perp$.

A function $f :: A \to B$ is said to take *arguments* in A and return *results* in B. If x denotes an element of A, then we write $f(x)$, or just $f x$, to denote the result of *applying* the function f to x. This value is the unique element of B associated with x by the rule of correspondence for f. The former notation, $f(x)$, is the one normally employed in mathematics to denote functional application, but the parentheses are not really necessary and we will use the second form, $f x$, instead. On the other hand, parentheses are necessary when the argument is not a simple constant or variable. For example, we have to write *square* $(3 + 4)$ (if that is what we mean) because *square* $3 + 4$ means $(square\,3) + 4$. The reason why this is so is because application has a higher *precedence* than $+$ (see below). Similarly, we have to write *square* (*square* 3) and not *square square* 3.

We will be careful never to confuse a function with its application to an argument. In some mathematics texts one often finds the phrase 'the function $f(x)$', when what is really meant is 'the function f'. In such texts, functions are rarely considered as values which may themselves be used as arguments to other functions and the traditional way of speaking causes no confusion. In functional programming, however, functions are values with exactly the same status as all other values; in particular, they can be passed as arguments to other functions and returned as results. Accordingly, we cannot afford to be casual about the difference between a function and the result of applying it to an argument.

1.4.1 Extensionality

Two functions are equal if they give equal results for equal arguments. Thus, $f = g$ if and only if $f x = g x$ for all x. This principle is called the principle of *extensionality*. It says that the important thing about a function is the correspondence between arguments and results, not how this correspondence is described.

For instance, we can define the function which doubles its argument in the following two ways:

$$double, double' \quad :: \quad Integer \rightarrow Integer$$
$$double\ x \qquad\quad = \quad x + x$$
$$double'\ x \qquad\quad = \quad 2 \times x$$

The two definitions describe different *procedures* for obtaining the correspondence, one involving addition and the other involving multiplication, but *double* and *double'* define the same function value and we can assert *double = double'* as a mathematical truth. Regarded as procedures for evaluation, one definition may be more or less 'efficient' than the other, but the notion of efficiency is not one that can be attached to function values themselves. This is not to say, of course, that efficiency is not important; after all, we want expressions to be evaluated in a reasonable amount of time. The point is that efficiency is an *intensional* property of definitions, not an extensional one.

Extensionality means that we can prove $f = g$ by proving that $f\ x = g\ x$ for all x. Depending on the definitions of f and g, we may also be able to prove $f = g$ directly. The former kind of proof is called an *applicative* or *point-wise* style of proof, while the latter is called a *point-free* style. We will see examples of both styles during the course of the book.

1.4.2 Currying

A useful device for reducing the number of parentheses in an expression is the idea of replacing a structured argument by a sequence of simpler ones. To illustrate, consider again the function *smaller* defined earlier:

$$smaller \qquad\quad :: \quad (Integer, Integer) \rightarrow Integer$$
$$smaller\ (x, y) \quad = \quad \text{if } x \leq y \text{ then } x \text{ else } y$$

The function *smaller* takes a single argument consisting of a pair of integers, and returns an integer. Another way of defining essentially the same function is to write

$$smallerc \qquad :: \quad Integer \rightarrow (Integer \rightarrow Integer)$$
$$smallerc\ x\ y \quad = \quad \text{if } x \leq y \text{ then } x \text{ else } y$$

The function *smallerc* takes two arguments, one after the other. More precisely, *smallerc* is a function that takes an integer x as argument and returns a function *smallerc x*; the function *smallerc x* takes an integer *y* as argument and returns an integer, namely the smaller of *x* and *y*.

Here is another example:

$$plus \qquad :: \quad (Integer, Integer) \rightarrow Integer$$
$$plus\ (x, y) \quad = \quad x + y$$

$$plusc \qquad :: \quad Integer \rightarrow (Integer \rightarrow Integer)$$
$$plusc\ x\ y \quad = \quad x + y$$

For each integer *x* the function *pluscx* adds *x* to an integer. In particular, *plusc* 1 is the successor function that increments its argument by 1, and *plusc* 0 is the identity function on integers.

This simple device for replacing structured arguments by a sequence of simple ones is known as *currying*, after the American logician Haskell B. Curry (after whom the programming language Haskell is also named). For currying to work properly in a consistent manner, we require that the operation of functional application associates to the left in expressions. Thus,

$$smallerc\ 3\ 4 \qquad \text{means} \quad (smallerc\ 3)\ 4$$
$$plusc\ x\ y \qquad \text{means} \quad (plusc\ x)\ y$$
$$square\ square\ 3 \quad \text{means} \quad (square\ square)\ 3$$

Although *square square* 3 is a syntactically legal expression, it makes no sense because *square* takes a single integer argument, not a function followed by an integer. In fact, the expression will be rejected by the computer because it cannot be assigned a sensible type. We will return to this point in a later section.

There are two advantages of currying functions. Firstly, currying can help to reduce the number of parentheses that have to be written in expressions. Secondly, curried functions can be applied to one argument only, giving another function that may be useful in its own right. For instance, consider the function *twice* that applies a function twice in succession:

$$twice \qquad :: \quad (Integer \rightarrow Integer) \rightarrow (Integer \rightarrow Integer)$$
$$twice\ f\ x \quad = \quad f\ (f\ x)$$

This is a perfectly legitimate definition in Haskell. The first argument to *twice* is a function (of type *Integer* → *Integer*), and the second argument is an integer. Applying *twice* to the first argument *f*, we get a function *twice f* that applies *f* twice. We can now define, for instance,

$$quad \quad :: \quad Integer \rightarrow Integer$$
$$quad \quad = \quad twice\ square$$

The function *quad* raises its argument to the fourth power. Suppose, on the other hand, that we had defined *twice* by

$$twice \qquad :: \quad (Integer \to Integer, Integer) \to Integer$$
$$twice\,(f, x) \quad = \quad f\,(f\,x)$$

Now there is no way we can name the function that applies a function twice without also mentioning the argument to which the second function is applied. Instead of saying '*quad*, where *quad* = *twice square*', we would have to say '*quad*, where *quad* x = *twice* (*square*, x) for all x'. The second style is clumsier.

If we want to, we can always convert an uncurried function into a curried one. The function *curry* takes an uncurried function and returns a curried version of the same function; its definition is

$$curry \qquad :: \quad ((\alpha, \beta) \to \gamma) \to (\alpha \to \beta \to \gamma)$$
$$curry\,f\,x\,y \quad = \quad f\,(x, y)$$

The type signature of *curry* will be explained in Section 1.6. Note that *curry* is itself an example of a curried function: *curry* takes three arguments, one after the other. We can now refer to *curry f* as the curried version of f. For example, *plusc = curry plus*.

It is left as an exercise to define a function *uncurry* that goes the other way and converts a curried function into a noncurried one.

1.4.3 Operators

Some functions are written between their (two) arguments rather than preceding them. For example, we write

$$3 + 4 \quad \text{rather than} \quad plusc\,3\,4$$
$$3 \le 4 \quad \text{rather than} \quad leq\,3\,4$$

A function written using infix notation is called an *operator*. To remove ambiguity, special symbols are used to denote operators. Occasionally, we will use names rather than symbols for operators, but write them in bold font. For example, we write (15 **div** 4) and (15 **mod** 4), using names in bold font for the operators associated with integer division and remainder. The Haskell convention is to enclose the name in back quotes; for example, in Haskell one would write (15 `div` 4) and (15 `mod` 4).

Enclosing an operator in parentheses converts it to a curried prefix function that can be applied to its arguments like any other function. For example,

$$(+)\,3\,4 \quad = \quad 3 + 4$$
$$(\le)\,3\,4 \quad = \quad 3 \le 4$$

In particular, *plusc* = (+). Like any other name, an operator enclosed in parentheses can be used in expressions and passed as an argument to functions. For example,

$$plus \quad = \quad uncurry \ (+)$$

introduces *plus* as another name for the uncurried version of addition.

1.4.4 Sections

The notational device of enclosing a binary operator in parentheses to convert it into a normal prefix function can be extended: an argument can also be enclosed along with the operator. If $\oplus$ denotes an arbitrary binary operator, then $(x\oplus)$ and $(\oplus x)$ are functions with the definitions

$$(x\oplus)\, y \quad = \quad x \oplus y$$
$$(\oplus y)\, x \quad = \quad x \oplus y$$

These two forms are called *sections*. For example:

$(\times 2)$	is the 'doubling' function
(> 0)	is the 'positive number' test
$(1/)$	is the 'reciprocal' function
$(/2)$	is the 'halving' function
$(+1)$	is the 'successor' function

There is one exception to the rule for forming sections: $(-x)$ is interpreted as the unary operation of negation applied to the number x. Sections are not used heavily in what follows, but on occasion they provide a simple means for describing expressions conveniently and without fuss.

1.4.5 Precedence

When several operators appear together in an expression, certain rules of *precedence* are provided to resolve possible ambiguity. The precedence rules for the common arithmetic operators are absorbed in childhood without ever being stated formally. Their sole purpose in life is to allow one to reduce the number of parentheses in an expression.

In particular, exponentiation, which we will denote by $\uparrow$, takes precedence over multiplication, which in turn takes precedence over addition: for example,

$?\, 1 + 3 \uparrow 4 \times 2$
163

Thus, $1 + 3 \uparrow 4 \times 2 = 1 + ((3 \uparrow 4) \times 2)$. Furthermore, functional application, the operator denoted by a space, takes precedence over every other operator. For example, *square* $3 + 4$ means (*square* 3) $+ 4$.

1.4.6 Association

Another device for reducing parentheses is to provide an order of *association* for an operator. It is clear that when the same operator occurs twice in succession, the rule of precedence is not sufficient to resolve ambiguity. Operators can associate either to the *left* or to the *right*. We have already encountered one example of declaring such a preference: functional application associates to the left in expressions. In arithmetic, operators on the same level of precedence are usually declared to associate to the left as well. Thus $5 - 4 - 2$ means $(5 - 4) - 2$ and not $5 - (4 - 2)$. One operator that associates to the right is the function type operator ($\rightarrow$); thus,

$$A \rightarrow B \rightarrow C \quad \text{means} \quad A \rightarrow (B \rightarrow C)$$

It is not necessary to insist that an order of association be prescribed for every operator. If no preference is indicated, then parentheses must be used to avoid ambiguity. In fact, to avoid complicating a basically simple idea, we will always use parentheses to disambiguate sequences of different operators with the same precedence.

Any declaration of a specific order of association should not be confused with a different, though related, property of operators known as *associativity*. An operator $\oplus$ is said to be associative if

$$(x \oplus y) \oplus z = x \oplus (y \oplus z)$$

for all values x, y, and z of the appropriate type. For example, $+$ and $\times$ are associative operators. For such operators, the choice of an order of association has no effect on meaning.

1.4.7 Functional composition

The composition of two functions f and g is denoted by $f \cdot g$ and is defined by the equation

$$
\begin{aligned}
(\cdot) \quad &:: \quad (\beta \rightarrow \gamma) \rightarrow (\alpha \rightarrow \beta) \rightarrow (\alpha \rightarrow \gamma) \\
(f \cdot g)\, x \quad &= \quad f\,(g\,x)
\end{aligned}
$$

The type signature will be explained in Section 1.6. In words, $f \cdot g$ applied to x is defined to be the outcome of first applying g to x, and then applying f to the result. Not every pair of functions can be composed since the types have to match up: we require that g has type $g :: \alpha \rightarrow \beta$ for some types α and β, and that f has type $f :: \beta \rightarrow \gamma$ for some type γ. Then we obtain $f \cdot g :: \alpha \rightarrow \gamma$. For example, given *square* $:: Integer \rightarrow Integer$, we can define

$$
\begin{aligned}
quad &:: & Integer \rightarrow Integer \\
quad &= & square \cdot square
\end{aligned}
$$

By the definition of composition, this gives exactly the same function *quad* as

$$
\begin{aligned}
quad &:: & Integer \rightarrow Integer \\
quad\, x &= & square\,(square\,x)
\end{aligned}
$$

This example illustrates the main advantage of using functional composition in programs: definitions can be written more concisely. Whether to use a point-free style or a point-wise style is partly a question of taste, and we will see functions defined in both styles in the remainder of the book. However, whatever the style of expression, it is good programming practice to construct complicated functions as the composition of simpler ones.

Functional composition is an associative operation. We have

$$
(f \cdot g) \cdot h \;=\; f \cdot (g \cdot h)
$$

for all functions f, g and h of the appropriate types. Accordingly, there is no need to put in parentheses when writing sequences of compositions.

Exercises

1.4.1 Suppose f and g have the following types:

$$
\begin{aligned}
f &:: & Integer \rightarrow Integer \\
g &:: & Integer \rightarrow (Integer \rightarrow Integer)
\end{aligned}
$$

Let h be defined by

$$
\begin{aligned}
h &:: & \cdots \\
h\,x\,y &= & f\,(g\,x\,y)
\end{aligned}
$$

Fill in the correct type assignment for h.

Now determine which, if any, of the following statements is true:

$$
\begin{aligned}
h &= & f \cdot g \\
h\,x &= & f \cdot (g\,x) \\
h\,x\,y &= & (f \cdot g)\,x\,y
\end{aligned}
$$

1.4.2 Suppose we curry the arguments of the function *delta*, so that we can write *delta a b c* rather than *delta* (a, b, c). What is the type of the curried version?

1.4.3 In mathematics one often uses logarithms to various bases; for example, $\log_2$, $\log_e$, and $\log_{10}$. Give an appropriate type of a function *log* that takes a base and returns the logarithm function for that base.

1.4.4 Describe one appropriate type for the definite integral function of mathematical analysis, as used in the phrase 'the integral of f from a to b'.

1.4.5 Give examples of functions with the following types:

$$(Integer \rightarrow Integer) \rightarrow Integer$$
$$(Integer \rightarrow Integer) \rightarrow (Integer \rightarrow Integer)$$

1.4.6 Which, if any, of the following statements is true?

$$(\times) x = (\times x)$$
$$(+) x = (x+)$$
$$(-) x = (-x)$$

1.4.7 Define a function *uncurry* that converts a curried function into a noncurried version. Show that

$$curry \ (uncurry \ f) \ x \ y = f \ x \ y$$
$$uncurry \ (curry \ f) \ (x, y) = f \ (x, y)$$

for all x and y.

1.5 Definitions

So far, we have seen one or two simple definitions of functions, but definitions of other kinds of value are possible. For example,

$$pi \ :: \ Float$$
$$pi \ = \ 3.14159$$

declares a single-precision approximation to π.

The definition of *smaller* seen earlier made use of a *conditional expression*. Recall that the definition was

$$smaller \ :: \ (Integer, Integer) \rightarrow Integer$$
$$smaller \ (x, y) \ = \ \textbf{if } x \leq y \textbf{ then } x \textbf{ else } y$$

The condition $x \leq y$ evaluates to a *boolean* or truth value, *True* or *False*. Boolean values will be considered in detail in the following chapter.

Another way to express essentially the same definition of *smaller* is to write

$$smaller :: (Integer, Integer) \rightarrow Integer$$
$$smaller\ (x, y)$$
$$\begin{array}{|ll}
x \leq y & = & x \\
x > y & = & y
\end{array}$$

This form of definition uses *guarded equations*. The syntax of guarded equations follows that of Haskell and consists of a sequence of *clauses* delimited by a vertical bar. Each clause consists of a condition, or *guard*, and an expression, which is separated from the guard by an = sign. In the definition of *smaller* (x, y) the guards are $(x \leq y)$ and $(x > y)$, while the associated expressions are x and y.

We will use guarded equations only sparingly in what follows, preferring conditional expressions instead. The main advantage of guarded equations is when there are three or more clauses in a definition. To illustrate, consider the function *signum* that takes an integer argument x and returns -1 if x is negative, 0 if x is zero, and 1 if x is positive. Using guarded equations, we would write

$$signum :: Integer \rightarrow Integer$$
$$signum\ x$$
$$\begin{array}{|ll}
x < 0 & = & -1 \\
x == 0 & = & 0 \\
x > 0 & = & 1
\end{array}$$

Using conditional expressions, we would have to write something like

$$signum \quad :: \quad Integer \rightarrow Integer$$
$$signum\ x \quad = \quad \textbf{if } x < 0 \textbf{ then } -1 \textbf{ else}$$
$$\qquad\qquad\qquad \textbf{if } x == 0 \textbf{ then } 0 \textbf{ else } 1$$

The definition using guarded equations is clearer because the three conditions are made explicit. Note that an equality test is written in the form $x == y$. This is to distinguish it from a definition, which is written in the form $x = y$. Equality and comparison tests are considered further in the following chapter.

1.5.1 Recursive definitions

Definitions can also be *recursive*. Here is a well-known example:

$$fact \quad :: \quad Integer \rightarrow Integer$$
$$fact\ n \ = \ \textbf{if}\ n == 0\ \textbf{then}\ 1\ \textbf{else}\ n \times fact\ (n-1)$$

The function *fact* is the factorial function. Recursive definitions are evaluated like any other definition. For example, one reduction sequence for evaluating *fact* 1 is

       fact 1

=   {definition of *fact*}

     if 1 == 0 **then** 1 **else** 1 × *fact* (1 − 1)

=   {since (1 == 0) evaluates to *False*}

     1 × *fact* (1 − 1)

=   {definition of *fact*}

     1 × (**if** (1 − 1) == 0 **then** 1 **else** (1 − 1) × *fact* ((1 − 1) − 1))

=   {definition of (−)}

     1 × (**if** 0 == 0 **then** 1 **else** (1 − 1) × *fact* ((1 − 1) − 1))

=   {since (0 == 0) evaluates to *True*}

     1 × 1

=   {definition of ×}

     1

There are, of course, other reduction sequences of *fact* 1, but all lead to the same result.

    The above definition of *fact* is not completely satisfactory: if we apply *fact* to a negative integer, then the computation never terminates. For example,

       fact (−1)

=   {definition of *fact*}

     if −1 == 0 **then** 1 **else** (−1) × *fact*(−1 − 1)

=   {since (−1 == 0) evaluates to *False*}

     (−1) × *fact* (−1 − 1)

=   {as before}

$$(-1) \times ((-2) \times fact\ (-1 - 1 - 1))$$

and so on. Although it is the case that *fact x* $=\ \bot$ for negative *x*, we would prefer that the computation terminated with a suitable error message rather than proceeding indefinitely with a futile computation. One way of achieving this is to rewrite the definition as

$$fact :: Integer \rightarrow Integer$$
$$fact\ n$$
$$\begin{array}{lll} n < 0 & = & error\ \text{``negative argument to fact''} \\ n == 0 & = & 1 \\ n > 0 & = & n \times fact\ (n - 1) \end{array}$$

The predefined function *error* takes a string as argument; when evaluated it causes immediate termination of the evaluator and displays the given error message:

? *fact* (−1)
Program error: negative argument to fact

There are other ways to define *fact* and we will discuss them later in the book.

1.5.2 Local definitions

The final piece of notation we will introduce here is called a *local* definition. In mathematical descriptions one often finds an expression qualified by a phrase of the form 'where ...'. For instance, one might find '$f(x, y) = (a + 1)(a + 2)$, where $a = (x + y)/2$'. The same device can be used in a formal definition:

$$f \qquad :: \quad (Float, Float) \rightarrow Float$$
$$f\ (x, y) \quad = \quad (a + 1) \times (a + 2) \quad \textbf{where}\ a = (x + y)/2$$

The special word **where** is used to introduce a local definition whose context (or *scope*) is the expression on the right-hand side of the definition of *f*.

When there are two or more local definitions we can lay them out in one of two styles. For example, one can write

$$f \qquad :: \quad (Float, Float) \rightarrow Float$$
$$f\ (x, y) \quad = \quad (a + 1) \times (b + 2)$$
$$\qquad\qquad\qquad \textbf{where}\ a \quad = \quad (x + y)/2$$
$$\qquad\qquad\qquad\quad\ b \quad = \quad (x + y)/3$$

One can also write

$$f \qquad :: \quad (Float, Float) \to Float$$
$$f(x, y) \quad = \quad (a + 1) \times (b + 2)$$
$$\textbf{where } a = (x + y)/2; \quad b = (x + y)/3$$

In the second form, a semi-colon is used to separate the two definitions. A local definition can be used in conjunction with a definition that relies on guarded equations. Consider the following definition:

$$f :: Integer \to Integer \to Integer$$
$$f\, x\, y$$
$$\begin{array}{l|ll} & x \le 10 & = & x + a \\ & x > 10 & = & x - a \end{array}$$
$$\textbf{where } a = square\,(y + 1)$$

In this definition, the **where** clause qualifies *both* guarded equations.

Exercises

1.5.1 The Fibonacci numbers $f_0, f_1, \ldots$ are defined by the rule that $f_0 = 0$, $f_1 = 1$ and $f_{n+2} = f_n + f_{n+1}$ for all $n \ge 0$. Give a definition of the function *fib* that takes an integer n and returns f_n.

1.5.2 Define a function *abs* :: *Integer* $\to$ *Integer* that returns the absolute value of an integer.

1.6 Types

In functional programming the universe of values is partitioned into organised collections, called *types*. So far, we have mentioned *Integer* and *Float*, but there are also other kinds of number, including *Int* and *Double*, as well as booleans (elements of *Bool*), characters (elements of *Char*), lists, trees, and so on. Moreover, we have already seen how to put types together to make an infinite variety of other types; for example *Integer* $\to$ *Float*, and (*Float, Float*), and so on. In the next chapter we will see how some of these types can be defined, and how to define new types.

Each type has associated with it certain operations which are not meaningful for other types. For instance, one cannot sensibly add a number to a character or multiply two functions together. It is an important principle of many programming languages that every well-formed expression can be assigned a type. Moreover, this type can be deduced from the constituents of the expression alone. In other words, just as the value of an expression depends only on the values of its component expressions, so does its type. This principle is called *strong typing*.

The major consequence of the discipline imposed by strong typing is that any expression which cannot be assigned a sensible type is regarded as not being well formed and is rejected by the computer before evaluation. Such expressions are simply regarded as illegal. We saw one example earlier: the expression *squaresquare*3 is rejected by the computer as not being well formed. Similarly, the script

$$
\begin{array}{lll}
quad & :: & Integer \rightarrow Integer \\
quad\ x & = & square\ square\ x
\end{array}
$$

is rejected by the computer since the expression *square square x* is not well formed.

One great advantage of strong typing is that it enables a range of errors, from simple typographical mistakes to muddled definitions, to be detected before evaluation. The other great advantage is that it steers the programmer into a certain discipline of thought, namely to consider appropriate types for the values being defined before considering the definitions themselves. In other words, adherence to the discipline of strong typing can help significantly in the design of clear and well-structured programs.

There are two stages of analysis when an expression is submitted for evaluation. The expression is first checked to see whether it conforms to the correct syntax laid down for constructing expressions. If it does not, the computer signals a *syntax error*. If it does, then the expression is analysed to see if it possesses a sensible type. If the expression fails to pass this stage, the computer signals a *type error*. Only if the expression passes both stages can the process of evaluation begin. Similar remarks apply to definitions created in a script.

1.6.1 Polymorphic types

Some functions and operations work with many types. For example, suppose

$$
\begin{array}{lll}
square & :: & Integer \rightarrow Integer \\
sqrt & :: & Integer \rightarrow Float
\end{array}
$$

Then the expressions *square · square* and *sqrt · square* are both meaningful and they have the following types:

$$
\begin{array}{lll}
square \cdot square & :: & Integer \rightarrow Integer \\
sqrt \cdot square & :: & Integer \rightarrow Float
\end{array}
$$

However, the two uses of functional composition in these expressions have different types, namely

$$(\cdot) :: (Integer \rightarrow Integer) \rightarrow (Integer \rightarrow Integer) \rightarrow (Integer \rightarrow Integer)$$
$$(\cdot) :: (Integer \rightarrow Float) \rightarrow (Integer \rightarrow Integer) \rightarrow (Integer \rightarrow Float)$$

Thus, the operation of functional composition is assigned different types in different expressions.

The problem of assigning a single type to $(\cdot)$ is solved by introducing *type variables*. The type assigned to $(\cdot)$ is

$$(\cdot) \quad :: \quad (\beta \rightarrow \gamma) \rightarrow (\alpha \rightarrow \beta) \rightarrow (\alpha \rightarrow \gamma)$$

Here, α, β, and γ denote type variables. We will use greek letters to denote type variables. Like other kinds of variable, a type variable can be instantiated to different types in different circumstances. A type containing type variables is called a *polymorphic type*.

Here is another example. Look again the previous definition of *fact*:

fact :: *Integer* $\rightarrow$ *Integer*
fact n

$$\begin{array}{lll} n < 0 & = & error \text{ "negative argument to fact"} \\ n == 0 & = & 1 \\ n > 0 & = & n \times fact\,(n-1) \end{array}$$

Consider the function *error*. It takes a string as argument, so its type is *String* $\rightarrow$ *A* for some type *A*. In the program above it is clear that *A* = *Integer*; only with this type assignment is the program for *fact* well formed. After all, the second and third clauses deliver integers, so the first one should do too. It doesn't matter what integer is delivered, because the sole purpose in evaluating *error* is to abort the computation with an error message. If, however, the general error function had type *error* :: *String* $\rightarrow$ *Integer*, it would have limited usefulness. Instead, the type assigned to *error* is *String* $\rightarrow$ α. Once again, the problem is resolved by making use of type variables.

As a final example for now, consider the function *curry* defined in Section 1.4.2 by the equation

$$curry\ f\ x\ y \quad = \quad f\,(x, y)$$

This function is used to convert functions with type $(A, B) \rightarrow C$ into functions with type $A \rightarrow B \rightarrow C$. No properties of any specific types *A*, *B*, and *C* are required in the definition of *curry*, so it is assigned the polymorphic type

$$curry \quad :: \quad ((\alpha, \beta) \rightarrow \gamma) \rightarrow (\alpha \rightarrow \beta \rightarrow \gamma)$$

The rightmost pair of parentheses could have been omitted, since the type operator ($\rightarrow$) associates to the right, but it is clearer in this case to put them in.

We now have the beginnings of a language of expressions that denote types. This language contains constant expressions, such as *Integer* or *Float*, variables, such as α and β, and functions that take types to other types, such as the function type operator ($\rightarrow$).

1.6.2   Type classes

A careful reading of the first part of this chapter reveals that we have used (curried) multiplication with two different type signatures:

$$(\times) \quad :: \quad Integer \rightarrow Integer \rightarrow Integer$$
$$(\times) \quad :: \quad Float \rightarrow Float \rightarrow Float$$

Like ($\cdot$) and *error*, it seems that ($\times$) should be assigned a polymorphic type, namely

$$(\times) \quad :: \quad \alpha \rightarrow \alpha \rightarrow \alpha$$

But one can argue that this type is too general. For instance, we cannot sensibly multiply two characters or two booleans.

In Haskell the resolution is to group together kindred types into *type classes*. In particular, *Integer* and *Float* belong to the same class, the class of numbers. The type assigned to ($\times$) is

$$(\times) \quad :: \quad Num\ \alpha \Rightarrow \alpha \rightarrow \alpha \rightarrow \alpha$$

The right-hand side should be read as the type $\alpha \rightarrow \alpha \rightarrow \alpha$ restricted to those α that are instances of the type class *Num*.

The same device is used for the numeric constants. For example, 3 can be used to describe a certain floating-point number as well as an integer; accordingly, the type assigned to 3 is $Num\ \alpha \Rightarrow \alpha$. In words, any type, provided it is a number type.

There are other kindred types apart from numbers. For example, there are the types whose values can be displayed, the types whose values can be compared for equality, the types whose values can be enumerated, and so on. A type that is an instance of one type class may also be an instance of another. For example, we can compare numbers for equality and we can also display them. We will explain in the following chapter how type classes can be created and how specific types can be declared to be instances of these classes.

Exercises

1.6.1 Give suitable polymorphic type assignments for the following functions:

$$\begin{cases} const\ x\ y & = & x\ \checkmark \\ subst\ f\ g\ x & = & f\ x\ (g\ x) \\ apply\ f\ x & = & f\ x \\ flip\ f\ x\ y & = & f\ y\ x\ \checkmark \end{cases}$$

1.6.2 Define a function *swap* so that

$$flip\ (curry\ f) \quad = \quad curry\ (f \cdot swap)$$

for all $f :: (\alpha, \beta) \to \gamma$.

1.6.3 Can you find polymorphic type assignments for the following functions?

$$\begin{aligned} strange\ f\ g & = & g\ (f\ g) \\ stranger\ f & = & f\ f \end{aligned}$$

1.6.4 Find a polymorphic type assignment for

$$square\ x \quad = \quad x \times x$$

1.7 Specifications

In computing, a *specification* is a description of what task a program is to perform, while an *implementation* is a program that satisfies the specification. Specifications and implementations serve different purposes: specifications are expressions of the programmer's intent (or client's expectations) and their purpose is to be clear as possible; implementations are expressions for execution by computer and their purpose is to be efficient enough to execute within the time or space available. The link between the two is the requirement that the implementations satisfies, or *meets*, the specification, and the programmer may be obliged to provide a *proof* that this is indeed the case.

A specification for a function is some statement of the intended relationship between arguments and results. A simple example is given by the following specification of a function *increase*:

$$\begin{aligned} increase & \quad :: \quad Integer \to Integer \\ increase\ x & \quad > \quad square\ x, \quad \text{whenever } x \geq 0 \end{aligned}$$

This specification says that the result of *increase* should be strictly greater than the square of its argument, whenever the argument is nonnegative. The specification does not say how *increase* should be computed, but gives only a property that any implementation should have. The specification is *not* part of our programming language, even though it is expressed in a similar style.

One possible implementation is to take *increase* x = *square* $(x + 1)$. The proof that this definition satisfies its specification is as follows:

> *increase* x
>
> =   {definition of *increase*}
>
> *square* $(x + 1)$
>
> =   {definition of *square*}
>
> $(x + 1) \times (x + 1)$
>
> =   {algebra}
>
> $x \times x + 2 \times x + 1$
>
> \>   {since $x \geq 0$ implies $2 \times x + 1 > 0$}
>
> $x \times x$
>
> =   {definition of *square*}
>
> *square* x

The proof format used above will be followed in the rest of the book. Indeed, we have used it already in the discussion of reduction sequences. A reduction sequence is also a kind of proof, albeit one conducted with a very restricted set of reasoning rules. So restricted, in fact, that a computer can be instructed to carry out all the steps in a purely mechanical fashion.

Above, we invented a definition of *increase* first, and then verified that it met its specification. There are many other functions that will satisfy the specification and, since that is the only requirement, all are equally good.

One way of specifying a function is to state the rule of correspondence explicitly. The notation of functional programming can be very expressive, and sometimes the most sensible specification of a function is a legitimate program. The specification can then be executed directly. However, it may prove to be so grossly inefficient that the possibility of execution will be mostly of theoretical interest. Having written an executable specification, the programmer is not necessarily relieved of the burden (or pleasure) of producing an equivalent but acceptably efficient alternative.

As one very simple example of the idea, consider the specification

> *quad*   ::   *Integer* → *Integer*
> *quad* x = $x \times x \times x \times x$

In search of better things, we may calculate:

$$quad\ x$$

$$=\quad \{\text{specification}\}$$

$$x \times x \times x \times x \times x \times x$$

$$=\quad \{\text{since} \times \text{is associative}\}$$

$$(x \times x) \times (x \times x)$$

$$=\quad \{\text{definition of } square\}$$

$$square\ x \times square\ x$$

$$=\quad \{\text{definition of } square\}$$

$$square\ (square\ x)$$

The result is that we can implement *quad* with two multiplications instead of three, a significant saving with arbitrary-precision arithmetic.

In this case, we didn't invent the implementation of *quad* first, but developed it from the specification. The derivation was not entirely mechanical: the creative step was to employ the associativity of multiplication to put in brackets in a clever way. Admittedly, this example is absurdly simple, but we will see other, more convincing, examples of systematic program development, or *program synthesis*, later on in the book.

This paradigm of software development – first write a clear specification, then develop an acceptably efficient implementation – has been the focus of active research over the past twenty years, and should not be taken as a cut-and-dried method applicable in all circumstances. Two potential sources of difficulty are that the formal specification may not match the client's informal requirements, and the proof that the implementation meets the specification may be so large that it cannot be guaranteed to be free of error. Nevertheless, by trying to follow the approach whenever we can, the reliability of programs can be greatly increased.

Exercises

1.7.1 Give another definition of *increase* that meets its specification.

1.8 Chapter notes

The interactive use of a functional language, as described in the text, is provided by the HUGS (Haskell Users Gofer System) environment developed by Mark

Jones of Nottingham University. HUGS is available by FTP from

```
ftp://ftp.cs.nott.ac.uk/haskell/hugs
```

Haskell proper is a non-interactive language. Haskell compilers are available from Chalmers, Glasgow, and Yale Universities, by FTP from

```
ftp://ftp.cs.chalmers.se/pub/haskell
ftp://ftp.dcs.glasgow.ac.uk/pub/haskell
ftp://nebula.cs.yale.edu/pub/haskell
```

The language used in this book follows Haskell 1.3, although not all features of Haskell 1.3 will be covered. Furthermore, normal mathematical symbols are preferred over Haskell ones, which use a restricted character set. For example, Haskell uses * for multiplication. The keywords **if**, **then**, **else**, and **where** are reserved words in Haskell.

Web pages for Haskell, which include an on-line version of the Haskell 1.3 report, extensions to Haskell, and information about Haskell implementations, can be found at the following site:

```
http://www.haskell.org/
```

A tutorial introduction to Haskell is given in Hudak, Fasel, and Peterson (1996). Another elementary text on lazy functional programming that uses Haskell 1.3 is Thompson (1996).

While this text was being prepared there has been another release, Haskell 1.4. Currently the Haskell committee are aiming to move towards a standardisation, Standard Haskell, of the language. None of the changes under discussion is likely to affect the details described in the text.

Other nonstrict functional languages include Gofer and Miranda (Miranda is a trade-mark of Research Software Ltd.). Miranda, which is fairly close to Haskell, is described in Thompson (1995) and Clack, Myers, and Poon (1995). Another popular functional language is ML, which differs from Haskell in that it is strict rather than lazy. ML is described in Paulson (1996).

For further information about the denotational aspects of programming languages, consult Stoy (1977) or Gordon (1979). The implementation of lazy functional languages is covered in Peyton Jones (1987) and Peyton Jones and Lester (1991). The formal derivation of programs from their specifications is the subject of Morgan (1996) and Kaldewaij (1990), although the target programming language is procedural, not functional. For a functional and relational treatment of program derivation in a categorical setting, consult Bird and de Moor (1997). This is an advanced text, suitable for those particularly interested in the mathematics of programming, and can be studied after the present one.

Chapter 2

Simple datatypes

This chapter introduces some basic datatypes, including booleans, characters, tuples, and strings. We will describe how the values of each type are represented and give some useful operations for manipulating them. We will also describe the mechanism for declaring new datatypes, and give an overview of some of the major type classes in Haskell. One class of datatypes not discussed in this chapter consists of numbers in their various manifestations. Numbers will be dealt with in the following chapter. However, it is difficult to give interesting examples of programs that do not make use of numbers in some form or other, so we will just assume for the while that they exist and are available for service.

2.1 Booleans

As we saw in the first chapter, we need truth values in order to define a function using conditional expressions. At the very least we would like to test whether two values are equal and, if the notion makes sense, to see whether one value is smaller or greater than another. There are two truth values, *True* and *False*. These two values comprise the datatype *Bool* of boolean values (named after the nineteenth-century logician George Boole). Notice that the names *True*, *False*, and *Bool* each begin with a capital letter.

The datatype *Bool* can be introduced with a *datatype declaration*:

    data *Bool* = *False* | *True*

This declaration introduces *Bool* for the name of the datatype, and the two values *False* and *True* for its members. Having introduced *Bool*, we can define functions that take boolean arguments by *pattern matching*. For example, the negation function is defined by

$$
\begin{array}{lll}
not & :: & Bool \rightarrow Bool \\
not\ False & = & True \\
not\ True & = & False
\end{array}
$$

The two equations are used by the computer as rewrite rules to simplify expressions of the form *not e*. First *e* is reduced to normal form. If this process terminates and results in *False*, then the first equation is used; if reduction results in *True*, then the second equation is used. If *e* cannot be reduced to normal form, then the value of *not e* is undefined. Thus, *not* $\perp = \perp$ and *not* is a strict function. Notice that the two occurrences of $\perp$ here refer to the undefined boolean value. It follows that there are not two but *three* boolean values, namely *False*, *True*, and $\perp$. In fact, every datatype declaration introduces an extra anonymous value, the undefined value of the datatype.

Two basic functions on booleans are the operations of conjunction, denoted by the binary operator $\wedge$, and disjunction, denoted by $\vee$. These operations can be defined by

$$
\begin{array}{lll}
(\wedge), (\vee) & :: & Bool \rightarrow Bool \rightarrow Bool \\
False \wedge x & = & False \\
True \wedge x & = & x \\
False \vee x & = & x \\
True \vee x & = & True
\end{array}
$$

The definitions use pattern matching on the left-hand argument. For example, in order to simplify expressions of the form $e_1 \wedge e_2$, the computer first reduces e_1 to normal form. If the result is *False*, then the first equation for $\wedge$ is used, so the computer immediately returns the final value *False*. If e_1 reduces to *True*, then the second equation is used, so e_2 is evaluated. It follows from this description of how pattern matching works that

$$
\begin{array}{lll}
\perp \wedge False & = & \perp \\
False \wedge \perp & = & False \\
True \wedge \perp & = & \perp
\end{array}
$$

Thus $\wedge$ is strict in its left-hand argument, but not strict in its right-hand argument. Analogous remarks apply to $\vee$.

We could have defined $\wedge$ and $\vee$ differently. For example, an alternative definition of ∧ is by four equations:

$$
\left.\begin{array}{rcl}
\textit{False} \wedge \textit{False} & = & \textit{False} \\
\textit{False} \wedge \textit{True} & = & \textit{False} \\
\textit{True} \wedge \textit{False} & = & \textit{False} \\
\textit{True} \wedge \textit{True} & = & \textit{True}
\end{array}\right\}
$$

This version uses pattern matching on both arguments, so ∧ is strict in both arguments.

With either definition, ∧ is an associative operation, so there is no need to put in parentheses when writing expressions such as $x \wedge y \wedge z$. Similar remarks apply to ∨. However, it is always good practice to put in parentheses when writing expressions involving both ∧ and ∨. Both operators have a precedence below that of the equality and comparison operators (considered next), so

$$x \le y \wedge y < z \quad \text{means} \quad (x \le y) \wedge (y < z)$$

2.1.1 Equality and comparison operators

There are two equality operators == and ≠. They are defined for boolean arguments by

$$
\begin{array}{rcl}
(==) & :: & \textit{Bool} \rightarrow \textit{Bool} \rightarrow \textit{Bool} \\
x == y & = & (x \wedge y) \vee (\textit{not } x \wedge \textit{not } y)
\end{array}
$$

$$
\begin{array}{rcl}
(\neq) & :: & \textit{Bool} \rightarrow \textit{Bool} \rightarrow \textit{Bool} \\
x \neq y & = & \textit{not } (x == y)
\end{array}
$$

It is important to observe the distinction between == and =. The symbol == is used to denote a computable test for equality, while = is used both in definitions and in its normal mathematical sense. In mathematics, the assertion *double* = *square* is a false statement, and the assertion ⊥ = ⊥ is a true statement, since anything equals itself. However, functions cannot be tested for equality, and the result of evaluating ⊥ == ⊥ is ⊥ not *True*. This is not to say that the evaluator is an unmathematical machine, just that its behaviour is described by a limited set of mathematical rules chosen so that they can be executed mechanically.

The whole purpose of introducing an equality test is to be able to use it with a range of different types, not just elements of *Bool*. In other words, (==) and (≠) are *overloaded* operations. These operations will be defined differently for different datatypes and the proper way to introduce them is first to declare a type class *Eq* consisting of all those types for which (==) and (≠) are to be defined. The declaration of *Eq* takes the form

> **class** *Eq* α **where**
> (==), (≠) :: α → α → *Bool*

This declaration states that the type class *Eq* contains two member functions (or *methods*), namely (==) and (≠). These functions are assigned the type

> (==), (≠) :: *Eq* α ⇒ α → α → *Bool*

To declare that a certain type is an instance of the type class *Eq* we have to give an *instance declaration*. For example,

> **instance** *Eq Bool* **where**
> $(x == y)$ = $(x \land y) \lor (not\ x \land not\ y)$
> $(x \neq y)$ = $not\ (x == y)$

This declares *Bool* to be an equality type by giving specific definitions of (==) and (≠) for boolean arguments. We will see how to give other instances of *Eq* in later sections.

   If we wish, booleans can also be compared with (<), (≤), (≥), and (>). These operations are also overloaded and make sense with elements from a number of different types. Recognising this fact, we can set up another type class *Ord*, which is declared in the following way:

> **class** $(Eq\ \alpha) \Rightarrow Ord\ \alpha$ **where**
> (<), (≤), (≥), (>)   ::   α → α → *Bool*
> $(x \leq y)$ = $(x < y) \lor (x == y)$
> $(x \geq y)$ = $(x > y) \lor (x == y)$
> $(x > y)$ = $not\ (x \leq y)$

The first line says that *Ord* is a *subclass* of *Eq*, that is, only equality types can be ordered. This makes sense since, in any sensible instance definition of (≤), we would expect $x == y$ if and only if $x \leq y$ and $y \leq x$. The last three lines give *default* definitions of the operations (≤), (≥), and (>). Haskell provides for default definitions to save us the trouble of having to repeat them for each instance declaration. It is therefore sufficient to give the definition of (<) for each instance. Note that the default definitions make use of the fact that *Ord* is a subclass of *Eq* since they make use of an equality test (==).

Now we can declare *Bool* to be an instance of *Ord* by writing

> **instance** *Ord Bool* **where**
> *False* < *False* = *False*
> *False* < *True*   = *True*
> *True* < *False*   = *False*
> *True* < *True*   = *False*

The alternative definition, namely $x < y = not\ x \lor y$, doesn't quite work in the way expected (see Exercise 2.1.2).

2.1.2 Example: leap years

Let us now give a couple of examples involving boolean values. First, suppose we want a function to determine whether a year is a leap year or not. In the Gregorian calendar, a leap year is a year that is divisible by 4, except that if it is divisible by 100, then it must also be divisible by 400. We can express this in a number of equivalent ways. One is to define

$$
\begin{cases}
leapyear & :: & Int \to Bool \\
leapyear\ y & = & (y\ \mathbf{mod}\ 4 == 0) \land (y\ \mathbf{mod}\ 100 \neq 0 \lor y\ \mathbf{mod}\ 400 == 0)
\end{cases}
$$

The type *Int* describes the type of limited-precision integers and is considered further in the following chapter. We could have used *Integer* in place of *Int*, but it is unlikely that we would want to consider years with very large numbers of digits. Note that the three occurrences of (==) in the definition of *leapyear* refer to the equality test on *Int*. Number types, including *Int*, are also instances of the type class *Eq*.

Another way of defining *leapyear* is to use a conditional expression:

> *leapyear y*
> = **if** $(y\ \mathbf{mod}\ 100 == 0)$ **then** $(y\ \mathbf{mod}\ 400 == 0)$ **else** $(y\ \mathbf{mod}\ 4 == 0)$

2.1.3 Example: triangles

Next, suppose we want to construct a function, *analyse* say, that takes three positive integers *x*, *y* and *z* in nondecreasing order. These numbers represent the lengths of the sides of a possible triangle. The function *analyse* is to determine whether or not the three sides do in fact form a proper triangle and, if they do, whether the triangle is scalene (three different lengths), isosceles (two equal lengths), or equilateral (three equal lengths). Three sides form a proper triangle if and only if the length of the longest side is less than the sum of the lengths of the other two sides.

Thus, *analyse* is to return one of four distinct values. We could use four distinct numbers for this purpose, but we can also use four values created specially for the purpose:

$$\textbf{data } Triangle \;=\; Failure \;\mid\; Isosceles \;\mid\; Equilateral \;\mid\; Scalene$$

This declaration introduces a new datatype *Triangle* with four values. With that, the program is

$$analyse :: (Int, Int, Int) \rightarrow Triangle$$
$$analyse\,(x, y, z)$$

$$\begin{array}{lcl} x + y \le z & = & Failure \\ x == z & = & Equilateral \\ (x == y) \lor (y == z) & = & Isosceles \\ otherwise & = & Scalene \end{array}$$

The name *otherwise* is bound to the value *True*, so the final condition succeeds whenever the preceding conditions return *False*. This definition of *analyse* is correct only on the assumption that $x \le y \le z$. Note again that the occurrences of $(==)$ and $(\le)$ in this definition refer to comparison operations on values of type *Int*.

Exercises

2.1.1 Define $\land$ and $\lor$ using conditional expressions.

2.1.2 The definition of $(<)$ given in the text for arguments of type *Bool* has *False* < *True*. This reflects the fact that *False* comes before *True* in the declaration of the values of type *Bool*. Naturally, one also expects that both *False* < *False* and *True* < *True* evaluate to *False*.

Now consider the alternative definition $(x < y) = not\ x \lor y$, where $\lor$ is defined by pattern matching on the left argument. Why is this definition of $(<)$ not correct?

2.1.3 In logic, implication, denoted by $\Rightarrow$, is defined by the condition that $x \Rightarrow y$ is false only if x is true and y is false. Give a formal definition of implication as an operation on *Bool*.

2.1.4 Rewrite the declaration of the type class *Eq* by giving a default definition of $(\ne)$.

2.1.5 Rewrite the definition of *analyse* so that the cases in the case analysis do not depend on the order in which they are given.

2.1.6 Define a function *sort3* that sorts three integers into nondecreasing order. Hence define a function, *analyse'* say, that does not depend on the assumption that its arguments are in nondecreasing order.

2.1.7 How many equations would you have to write to define *Triangle* as an instance of the type class *Ord*? (See Section 2.3 for other ways of achieving this end.)

2.1.8 Are there any numbers that can be compared by (==) but cannot sensibly be compared by (<)?

2.1.9 The definition of (==) on a datatype should ensure that this operation is: (i) reflexive, that is, $x == x$ for all x; (ii) transitive, that is, $x == y$ and $y == z$ imply $x == z$; and (iii) symmetric, that is, $x == y$ implies $y == x$. Show that these properties hold for the definition of (==) on *Bool*.

2.1.10 What properties of (<) would you expect to hold in any instance declaration?

2.2 Characters

Mathematicians would be happy if given just numbers and booleans to play with, but computer scientists prefer to fill their terminal screens with more interesting kinds of symbol. The built-in datatype *Char* is provided for this purpose and contains 256 characters, including both visible signs and control characters. Characters are denoted by enclosing them in single quotation marks. For example:

? 'a'
'a'

? '7'
'7'

? ' '
' '

Characters are expressions in their simplest possible forms, so they are simply redisplayed by the evaluator, including the quotation marks. It is important to understand that the character '7' is quite a different entity from the decimal number 7: the former denotes a character, while the latter denotes a number. The third example above shows one way of denoting the space character.

For the purposes of this book, it is convenient to introduce special symbols for denoting the two most important nonvisible control characters: space and newline. The newline character will be denoted by the sign '⁻∤' and the space character by '⊔'.

   Two primitive functions are provided for processing characters, *ord* and *chr*. Their types are

$$
\begin{cases}
ord & :: & Char \to Int \\
chr & :: & Int \to Char
\end{cases}
$$

Recall that *Int* describes the type of limited-precision integers. The function *ord* converts a character *c* to an integer *ord c* in the range $0 \le ord\ c < 256$, and the function *chr* does the reverse, converting an integer back into the character it represents. Thus *chr (ord c) = c* for all characters *c*. For example:

? *ord* 'b'
98

? *chr* 98
'b'

? *chr (ord* 'b' + 1)
'c'

? *ord* '⁻∤'
10

The correspondence between characters and the first 256 nonnegative integers provides an alternative way of describing *Char*. One can think of *Char* as being introduced by a datatype declaration

> **data** *Char* = *Char0* | *Char1* | ... | *Char255*

in which the naming convention for values of *Char* is nonstandard. For example, instead of *Char98* we write 'b', and instead of *Char10* we write '⁻∤'. The integer *ord c* describes the position of character *c* in the enumeration.

   As with *Bool*, it is possible to define functions on *Char* by pattern matching, but the number of patterns is so large that a definition by case analysis is preferable.

   Characters can be compared and tested for equality. We can declare *Char* to be an equality type by writing

> **instance** *Eq Char* **where**
> $(x == y)$ $=$ $(ord\ x == ord\ y)$

This makes use of the fact that *Int* is also an equality type. In a similar vein, we can declare

> **instance** *Ord Char* **where**
> $(x < y)$ = $(ord\ x < ord\ y)$

The linear ordering on letters is, in part, just what one would expect. For example:

? '0' < '9'
True

? 'a' < 'z'
True

? 'A' < 'Z'
True

Upper-case letters precede lower-case letters in the enumeration, so

? 'A' < 'a'
True

Using this information we can define simple functions on characters. For instance, here are three functions for determining whether a character is a digit, a lower-case letter, or an upper-case letter:

> *isDigit*, *isLower*, *isUpper* :: *Char* → *Bool*
> *isDigit c* = ('0' ≤ c) ∧ (c ≤ '9')
> *isLower c* = ('a' ≤ c) ∧ (c ≤ 'z')
> *isUpper c* = ('A' ≤ c) ∧ (c ≤ 'Z')

Next, we can define a function for converting lower-case letters to upper-case:

> *capitalise*   ::   *Char* → *Char*
> *capitalise c* = **if** *isLower c* **then** *chr* (*offset* + *ord c*) **else** *c*
>   **where** *offset* = *ord* 'A' − *ord* 'a'

This definition uses the fact that the lower- and upper-case letters have codes which are in numerical sequence, but do not depend on their actual values. In particular, we can calculate

> *capitalise* 'a'
>
> =   {definition and *isLower* 'a' = *True*}

$$chr \ (offset + ord \ \text{`a'})$$

$$= \quad \{\text{definition of } offset\}$$

$$chr \ ((ord \ \text{`A'} - ord \ \text{`a'}) + ord \ \text{`a'})$$

$$= \quad \{\text{arithmetic}\}$$

$$chr \ (ord \ \text{`A'})$$

$$= \quad \{\text{since } chr \ (ord \ c) = c \text{ for all } c\}$$

$$\text{`A'}$$

In the calculation we do not need to know the codes for 'A' and 'a'.

A list of characters is called a *string*. Strings will be considered in a later section, where it will be shown how they can be used to give complete control over what appears on a terminal screen.

Exercises

2.2.1 Define a function *nextlet* that takes a letter of the alphabet and returns the letter coming immediately after it. Assume that letter 'A' follows 'Z'.

2.2.2 Define a function *digitval* that converts a digit character to its corresponding numerical value.

2.3 Enumerations

We have seen in the case of *Bool* and *Char* that one way to define a new datatype is by explicit enumeration of its values. Here is another example. Suppose we are interested in a problem that deals with the days of the week. We can introduce a new type *Day* with the declaration

$$\textbf{data } Day \ = \ Sun \ | \ Mon \ | \ Tue \ | \ Wed \ | \ Thu \ | \ Fri \ | \ Sat$$

The effect of this definition is to bind the name *Day* to a new type that consists of eight distinct values, seven of which are represented by the constants *Sun*, *Mon*, and so on, and the eighth by the ubiquitous $\perp$, which is assumed to be a value of every type. The seven new constants are called the *constructors* of the datatype *Day*. By convention, constructor names are distinguished from other kinds of name by beginning them with an upper-case letter. The name of a declared datatype also begins with an upper-case letter.

It is possible to compare elements of type *Day*, so *Day* can be declared as an instance of the type classes *Eq* and *Ord*. However, a definition of (==) and (<) based on pattern matching would involve a large number of equations. A better idea is to code elements of *Day* as integers, and use integer comparisons instead. Since the same idea can be employed with other enumerated types, we introduce a new type class *Enum* that describes types whose elements can be enumerated. The declaration is

> **class** *Enum* α **where**
>   *toEnum*   :: $\alpha \rightarrow Int$
>   *fromEnum* :: $Int \rightarrow \alpha$

A type is declared an instance of *Enum* by giving definitions of *toEnum* and *fromEnum*, functions that convert between elements of the type and *Int*. In instance declarations, *fromEnum* should be a *left-inverse* to *toEnum*, that is to say,

> *fromEnum* (*toEnum x*)   = x

for all x. This requirement, like the requirement that $(<)$ be a transitive relation for *Ord*, cannot be expressed in Haskell. The specification of *fromEnum* as a left-inverse of *toEnum* is nonconstructive and does not provide a default definition. It is the task of the programmer to give a constructive definition of *fromEnum* that meets the specification.

Now we can declare *Day* to be a member of *Enum* with the instance declaration

> **instance** *Enum Day* **where**
>   *toEnum Sun*   =   0
>   *toEnum Mon*   =   1
>   *toEnum Tue*   =   2
>   *toEnum Wed*   =   3
>   *toEnum Thu*   =   4
>   *toEnum Fri*   =   5
>   *toEnum Sat*   =   6

The function *fromEnum* can also be defined by seven equations, as we will see in the following chapter when we discuss pattern matching with natural numbers.

Exactly the same idea of associating values of an enumerated type with integers was used in the discussion of *Char*. In fact, we can declare

> **instance** *Enum Char* **where**
>   *toEnum*   =   *ord*
>   *fromEnum* =   *chr*

Given the function *toEnum* on *Day*, we can now declare

> **instance** *Eq Day* **where**
> $(x == y)$ = $(toEnum\ x == toEnum\ y)$

> **instance** *Ord Day* **where**
> $(x < y)$ = $(toEnum\ x < toEnum\ y)$

Here are some simple examples of the use of the type *Day*. First, we might define

> *workday*   :: *Day* → *Bool*
> *workday d* = $(Mon \le d) \wedge (d \le Fri)$

> *restday*   :: *Day* → *Bool*
> *restday d*   = $(d == Sat) \vee (d == Sun)$

Next, we can use *toEnum* and *fromEnum* to define a function *dayAfter* that returns the day after a given day:

> *dayAfter*   :: *Day* → *Day*
> *dayAfter d* = *fromEnum* $((toEnum\ d + 1) \bmod 7)$

In particular, *dayAfter Sat* = *Sun*.

2.3.1 Automatic instance declarations

We have now met three type classes, *Eq*, *Ord*, and *Enum*. The instance declarations for *Bool*, *Char*, and *Day* are in each case the obvious ones: the order in which elements are presented in the datatype declaration gives all the necessary information. Haskell allows a shortcut to save the programmer the bother of writing out these instances directly. For instance, one can declare *Day* by writing

> **data** *Day* = *Sun* | *Mon* | *Tue* | *Wed* | *Thu* | *Fri* | *Sat*
>   **deriving** (*Eq, Ord, Enum*)

The **deriving** clause causes the evaluator to generate instance declarations of the named type classes automatically, and these instances will be the ones we have seen above. An automatically derived instance declaration of *Enum* is possible only for a datatype that is declared by listing its values explicitly.

Exercises

2.3.1 Define a function *dayBefore* that returns the day before a given day.

2.3.2 Define a datatype *Direction* whose values describe the four major points of the compass, and define a function *reverse* for reversing direction.

2.3.3 Declare *Bool* as a member of the type class *Enum* by giving an explicit instance declaration.

2.4 Tuples

One way of combining types to form new ones is by pairing them. For example, the type (*Integer, Char*) consists of all pairs of values (x, c) for which x is an arbitrary-precision integer, and c is a character. In particular, $(3, \text{'a'})$ and $(1765341, \text{'+'})$ are both values of this type. The type (A, B) corresponds to the cartesian product operation of set theory, where the notation $A \times B$ is more often seen.

The polymorphic type (α, β) is, in effect, the same as the datatype *Pair* $\alpha \beta$ introduced by the datatype declaration

   data *Pair* $\alpha \beta$ = *MkPair* $\alpha \beta$

The datatype *Pair* $\alpha \beta$ has a single constructor *MkPair*. Unlike the constructors of *Bool* and *Char*, this constructor is a function; its type is

   MkPair :: $\alpha \to \beta \to$ *Pair* $\alpha \beta$

What distinguishes *MkPair* $x y$ from (x, y) is simply that the latter form employs a special and more traditional syntax.

Two basic functions on pairs are *fst* and *snd*, defined by

   fst   :: $(\alpha, \beta) \to \alpha$
   fst (x, y) = x

   snd   :: $(\alpha, \beta) \to \beta$
   snd (x, y) = y

The definitions of *fst* and *snd* use pattern matching: the expression (x, y) on the left of the equations is a pattern that is matched by any pair of values. Thus *fst* e is evaluated by reducing e to the form (x, y) for some x and y, and then returning x.

Like other types, the type (α, β) contains an additional value, namely the undefined value $\perp$. In particular, *undefined* $= \perp$, where

$$\begin{array}{lcl} undefined & :: & (\alpha, \beta) \\ undefined & = & undefined \end{array}$$

The value $(\perp, \perp)$ is different from $\perp$. To see why, consider the definition

$$\begin{array}{lcl} test & :: & (\alpha, \beta) \rightarrow Bool \\ test\ (x, y) & = & True \end{array}$$

Since *test* is defined by pattern matching, we have *test* $\perp = \perp$. On the other hand, *test* $(\perp, \perp) = True$. In the evaluation of *test p*, pattern matching is required to reduce p to the form (x, y), but it is not required to determine the values of x and y. Since $\perp \neq True$ it follows that $(\perp, \perp) \neq \perp$.

More generally, if α is instantiated to an enumerated type with m declared constructors, and similarly β is instantiated to an enumerated type with n declared constructors, then (α, β) will have $1 + (m + 1) \times (n + 1)$ values in total.

We can also define functions that take pairs of functions as arguments; for example,

$$\begin{array}{lcl} pair & :: & (\alpha \rightarrow \beta, \alpha \rightarrow \gamma) \rightarrow \alpha \rightarrow (\beta, \gamma) \\ pair\ (f, g)\ x & = & (f\ x, g\ x) \end{array}$$

$$\begin{array}{lcl} cross & :: & (\alpha \rightarrow \beta, \gamma \rightarrow \delta) \rightarrow (\alpha, \gamma) \rightarrow (\beta, \delta) \\ cross\ (f, g) & = & pair\ (f \cdot fst, g \cdot snd) \end{array}$$

The word *cross* comes from category theory, where the notation $f \times g$ is used instead of *cross* (f, g). Note that *cross* $(f, g) \perp = (f \perp, g \perp)$, which we can see by arguing:

$$\begin{array}{ll} & cross\ (f, g)\ \perp \\ = & \{\text{definition of } cross\} \\ & pair\ (f \cdot fst, g \cdot snd)\ \perp \\ = & \{\text{definition of } pair\} \\ & ((f \cdot fst)\ \perp, (g \cdot snd)\ \perp) \\ = & \{\text{definition of composition}\} \\ & (f\ (fst\ \perp), g\ (snd\ \perp)) \\ = & \{\text{since both } fst \text{ and } snd \text{ are strict}\} \\ & (f\ \perp, g\ \perp) \end{array}$$

Contrast this with the following definition of *cross*:

$$cross' \ (f, g) \ (x, y) \quad = \quad (f \ x, g \ y)$$

The value $\perp$ fails to match the pattern (x, y), so $cross' \ (f, g) \perp = \perp$ and so *cross'* is a strict function. The function *cross* is 'lazier' than *cross'* and is to be preferred because it can deliver additional results.

The functions *pair* and *cross* form part of a group of general-purpose functions that can be used in an alternative, point-free style of programming. For instance, the function $leq = uncurry \ (\leq)$, the uncurried version of $(\leq)$ on an enumerated datatype, can be defined in terms of the same function *leqInt* on *Int* by

$$
\begin{aligned}
leq \quad &:: \quad (Enum \ \alpha) \Rightarrow (\alpha, \alpha) \to Bool \\
leq \quad &= \quad leqInt \cdot cross \ (toEnum, toEnum)
\end{aligned}
$$

As another example, the function *workday* of the previous section can also be defined by

$$workday \quad = \quad uncurry \ (\wedge) \cdot pair \ ((Mon \leq), (\leq Fri))$$

This point-free style works best when binary operators are typed as uncurried functions. Since Haskell assigns curried types to operators, we have to uncurry them explicitly.

The functions *pair* and *cross* satisfy a number of properties that are useful in point-free calculations:

$$
\begin{aligned}
fst \cdot pair \ (f, g) \quad &= \quad f \\
snd \cdot pair \ (f, g) \quad &= \quad g \\
pair \ (f, g) \cdot h \quad &= \quad pair \ (f \cdot h, g \cdot h) \\
cross \ (f, g) \cdot pair \ (h, k) \quad &= \quad pair \ (f \cdot h, g \cdot k)
\end{aligned}
$$

Here is a proof of the fourth equation, which uses the other three:

$$
\begin{aligned}
&\quad cross \ (f, g) \cdot pair \ (h, k) \\
= &\quad \{\text{definition of } cross\} \\
&\quad pair \ (f \cdot fst, g \cdot snd) \cdot pair \ (h, k) \\
= &\quad \{\text{third property}\} \\
&\quad pair \ (f \cdot fst \cdot pair \ (h, k), g \cdot snd \cdot pair \ (h, k)) \\
= &\quad \{\text{first and second properties}\} \\
&\quad pair \ (f \cdot h, g \cdot k)
\end{aligned}
$$

The calculation is conducted entirely with functions, and there is no appeal to the principle of extensionality described in Section 1.4. In Chapter 12 we will construct a program that performs such proofs automatically.

As well as forming pairs of values, we can also form triples, quadruples and so on. Note, however, that each of the types $(\alpha, (\beta, \gamma))$, $((\alpha, \beta), \gamma)$, and (α, β, γ) is distinct from the others: the first is a pair whose second component is also a pair, the second is a pair whose first component is a pair, and the third is a triple. Pairs, triples, quadruples, and so on, all belong to different types.

For completeness, Haskell also provides a *nullary* tuple. By definition, the *unit* expression () has type (). The type () has just two members, $\perp$ and (). One use of () is to turn constants into functions; for example,

$$
\begin{aligned}
&pifun &&::& &() \rightarrow Float \\
&pifun\,() &&=& &3.14159
\end{aligned}
$$

By lifting constants to the function level, one can move even further along the path to a point-free style of programming. For instance, one can write

$$square \cdot square \cdot pifun \quad \text{instead of} \quad (square \cdot square)\, pi$$

The expression on the left is the composition of three functions, while the expression on the right consists of the composition of two functions applied to an argument. With lifted constants we do not need to mix composition with application.

Finally, as a practical example in the use of tuples, here is a function that returns a pair of numbers, the two real roots of a quadratic equation with coefficients (a, b, c):

$$
\begin{aligned}
&roots :: (Float, Float, Float) \rightarrow (Float, Float) \\
&roots\,(a, b, c) \\
&\qquad \left|
\begin{aligned}
&a == 0 &&=&& error\ \text{``not quadratic''} \\
&e < 0 &&=&& error\ \text{``complex roots''} \\
&otherwise &&=&& ((-b - r)/d, (-b + r)/d)
\end{aligned}
\right. \\
&\qquad\quad \mathbf{where}\ r\ =\ sqrt\ e \\
&\qquad\qquad\qquad d\ =\ 2 \times a \\
&\qquad\qquad\qquad e\ =\ b \times b - 4 \times a \times c
\end{aligned}
$$

The local definition defines three values, whose scope is the whole equation for *roots*.

2.4.1 Comparison operations

We can compare elements of (α, β) for equality only if the elements of both α and β can themselves be compared for equality. Here is the appropriate instance declaration:

> **instance** $(Eq\ \alpha, Eq\ \beta) \Rightarrow Eq\ (\alpha, \beta)$ **where**
> $(x, y) == (u, v)\quad =\quad (x == u) \wedge (y == v)$

Similarly, we can declare pairs to be an ordered type:

> **instance** $(Ord\ \alpha, Ord\ \beta) \Rightarrow Ord\ (\alpha, \beta)$ **where**
> $(x, y) < (u, v)\quad =\quad (x < u) \vee (x == u \wedge y < v)$

This particular way of ordering pairs of values is called the *lexicographic* ordering. In particular,

? $(1, undefined) < (2, undefined)$
True

? $(undefined, 1) < (undefined, 2)$
{Interrupted!}

The first computation terminates because $\vee$ is defined by pattern matching on the left argument. Hence

$$(1, \perp) < (2, \perp) = (1 < 2) \vee (1 == 2 \wedge \perp < \perp) = True$$

On the other hand, the second computation fails to terminate, so we interrupt it.

Exercises

2.4.1 Prove that $cross\ (f, g) \cdot cross\ (h, k) = cross\ (f \cdot h, g \cdot k)$.

2.4.2 Give a datatype declaration of a type *Triple* that corresponds to triples.

2.4.3 Suppose a date is represented by a triple (d, m, y) of three integers, where d is the day, m is the month, and y the year. Define a function *age* that takes two dates, the first being the current date, and the second being the birthdate of some person P, and returns the age of P as a whole number of years.

2.4.4 Is it possible to declare (α, β) as a member of the type class *Enum*, given that both α and β are instances of *Enum*?

2.5 Other types

As well as declaring a type by listing its constants, we can also declare types whose values depend on those of other types. For example,

> **data** *Either* = *Left Bool* | *Right Char*

This declares a type *Either* whose values are denoted by expressions of the form *Left b*, where *b* is a boolean, and *Right c*, where *c* is a character. There are three boolean values (including $\perp$) and 257 characters (including $\perp$), so there are 261 distinct values of the type *Either*; these include *Left* $\perp$, *Right* $\perp$, and $\perp$. When they are functions, the constructors of a type are nonstrict, so *Left* $\perp \neq \perp$ and *Right* $\perp \neq \perp$.

The type *Either* combines booleans and characters into a single type. We can generalise the idea, and define

> **data** *Either* $\alpha \beta$ = *Left* α | *Right* β

With this generalisation the previous type is described by *Either Bool Char*.

The names *Left* and *Right* introduce two constructors for building values of type *Either*; these constructors are nonstrict functions with types

> *Left* :: $\alpha \rightarrow$ *Either* $\alpha \beta$
> *Right* :: $\beta \rightarrow$ *Either* $\alpha \beta$

There are two key properties that distinguish constructors such as *Left* and *Right* from other functions. First of all, there is no associated definition: constructors just construct. For example, *Left* 3 is an expression in its simplest possible form:

? *Left* 3
Left 3

The second property is that expressions involving *Left* and *Right* can appear as patterns on the left-hand side of definitions. For example,

> *case* :: $(\alpha \rightarrow \gamma, \beta \rightarrow \gamma) \rightarrow$ *Either* $\alpha \beta \rightarrow \gamma$
> *case* (f, g) $(Left\ x)$ = $f\ x$
> *case* (f, g) $(Right\ y)$ = $g\ y$

Using *case* we can define *plus* by

> *plus* :: $(\alpha \rightarrow \beta, \gamma \rightarrow \delta) \rightarrow$ *Either* $\alpha \beta \rightarrow$ *Either* $\gamma \delta$
> *plus* (f, g) = *case* $(Left \cdot f, Right \cdot g)$

The word *plus* comes from category theory, where the notation $f + g$ is used instead of *plus* (f, g).

The algebraic properties of *case* and *plus* are dual to those of *pair* and *cross* described in the previous section:

$$
\begin{aligned}
case\,(f, g) \cdot Left &= f \\
case\,(f, g) \cdot Right &= g \\
h \cdot case\,(f, g) &= case\,(h \cdot f, h \cdot g) \\
case\,(f, g) \cdot plus\,(h, k) &= case\,(f \cdot h, g \cdot k)
\end{aligned}
$$

The proof of the last equation is left as an exercise.

Assuming that values of types α and β can be compared, we can define comparisons on the type *Either* $\alpha\,\beta$. The instance declarations are

instance $(Eq\;\alpha, Eq\;\beta) \Rightarrow Eq\;(Either\;\alpha\,\beta)$ **where**

$$
\begin{aligned}
Left\ x == Left\ y &= (x == y) \\
Left\ x == Right\ y &= False \\
Right\ x == Left\ y &= False \\
Right\ x == Right\ y &= (x == y)
\end{aligned}
$$

instance $(Ord\;\alpha, Ord\;\beta) \Rightarrow Ord\;(Either\;\alpha\,\beta)$ **where**

$$
\begin{aligned}
Left\ x < Left\ y &= (x < y) \\
Left\ x < Right\ y &= True \\
Right\ x < Left\ y &= False \\
Right\ x < Right\ y &= (x < y)
\end{aligned}
$$

We could also have installed these instances automatically by writing

> **data** *Either* $\alpha\,\beta$ = *Left* α | *Right* β
> **deriving** (Eq, Ord)

Except for one important point we have now covered the main details of how new datatypes are declared. The remaining point is the fact that datatype declarations can be *recursive*. Recursive datatypes will be dealt with in the following chapters.

Exercises

2.5.1 Define a function with source type *Either Bool Char* that behaves differently on the three arguments *Left* $\bot$, *Right* $\bot$, and $\bot$.

2.5.2 Prove that $case\,(f, g) \cdot plus\,(h, k) = case\,(f \cdot h, g \cdot k)$.

2.6 Type synonyms

Before proceeding, it is convenient to introduce a simple notational device for giving alternative names for types, names that are more suggestive of the purposes for which they are intended. The device is called a *type synonym* declaration. We will introduce the idea through a couple of simple examples.

First, recall the function *roots* of Section 2.4 which was assigned the type

$$roots \quad :: \quad (Float, Float, Float) \rightarrow (Float, Float)$$

As an alternative to this type description we can introduce two type synonyms

> **type** *Coeffs* = (*Float, Float, Float*)
> **type** *Roots* = (*Float, Float*)

These declarations do not introduce new types but merely alternative names for existing types. The type of *roots* can now be described in the equivalent form

$$roots \quad :: \quad Coeffs \rightarrow Roots$$

The new type description is shorter and more informative.

As another example, suppose we want to define a function, *move* say, that takes a number, representing a distance, an angle and a pair consisting of a coordinate position, and moves to a new position as indicated by the angle and distance. We can introduce type synonyms for these values as follows:

> **type** *Position* = (*Float, Float*)
> **type** *Angle* = *Float*
> **type** *Distance* = *Float*

Note that both *Angle* and *Distance* are introduced as synonyms for *Float*. We can now define *move* by

$$move \qquad\qquad :: \quad Distance \rightarrow Angle \rightarrow Position \rightarrow Position$$
$$move\ d\ a\ (x,y) \quad = \quad (x + d \times \cos a, y + d \times \sin a)$$

The trigonometric functions *cos* and *sin* are predefined. As with the type assignment of *roots*, the type assignment of *move* is both short and helpful in understanding what *move* does.

Type synonyms can be parameterised with one or more type variables, just like datatype definitions. For example, all of the following are valid synonym declarations:

> **type** *Pairs* α   =   (α, α)
> **type** *Automorph* α   =   α → α
> **type** *Flag* α   =   (α, *Bool*)

Two type synonyms cannot be declared in terms of each other since every synonym must be expressible in terms of existing types. On the other hand, it is legitimate to declare a synonym in terms of another synonym. For example,

> **type** *Bools*   =   *Pairs Bool*

There is no circularity here since *Bools* is a type synonym for *Pairs Bool*, which in turn is a synonym for (*Bool, Bool*). For the same reason, one can mix synonyms and declarations; for example,

> **data** *OneTwo* α   =   *One* α | *Two* (*Pairs* α)

2.6.1 New types

It is important to emphasise that type synonyms, not being new types, inherit whatever class instances are declared for the underlying type: one cannot give new instance declarations. For example, (==) is defined on *Bools* because it is defined on the underlying type (*Bool, Bool*). Similarly, the meaning of (==) on *Angle* is just the meaning of (==) on *Float*. In practice, this may not be what we want. For example, one might want to declare equality on *Angle* to be equality modulo a multiple of 2π. We can always use a specially defined function for this purpose, but if we want to use (==), then we have to declare *Angle* to be a new datatype and not a type synonym:

> **data** *Angle*   =   *MkAngle Float*

> **instance** *Eq Angle* **where**
>   *MkAngle x* == *MkAngle y*   =   *normalise x* == *normalise y*

> *normalise* :: *Float* → *Float*
> *normalise x*
> | $x < 0$ =   *normalise* (*x* + *rot*)
> | $x \geq rot$ =   *normalise* (*x* − *rot*)
> | *otherwise*   =   *x*
>   **where** *rot* = 2 × *pi*

The function *normalise* returns an angle θ in the range $0 \leq \theta < 2\pi$.

The price paid for using the above definition of equality on angles is that elements of *Angle* have to be 'wrapped' with a constructor *MkAngle* to give a new datatype. This has two disadvantages. One is that operations to construct and examine angles have to be continually unwrapped and rewrapped. This adds to the running time of the operations. Secondly, in declaring a new datatype we also declare possibly unwanted elements. For example, *MkAngle* ⊥ is also an element of *Angle*. In other words, *Angle* and *Float* are not *isomorphic*.

Recognising this, Haskell provides an alternative mechanism for creating new types. The declaration

newtype *Angle* = *MkAngle Float*

introduces *Angle* as a new type whose representation is exactly the same as *Float*. It differs from the type synonym in that a new type is constructed, one that can have new class instances declared for it. It differs from a **data** declaration in two ways. Firstly, wrapping and unwrapping with *MkAngle* does not add to the execution time; although occurrences of *MkAngle* have to appear in the text of a program, they can be eliminated before evaluation begins. The values of a new type are systematically replaced by the corresponding values of the underlying type. The second difference, necessary for the safe elimination described above, is that *MkAngle* is a *strict* constructor, so *MkAngle* ⊥ and ⊥ denote the same value. Hence the values of *Angle* and *Float* are in exact one-to-one correspondence.

Exercises

2.6.1 Suppose you wanted to treat two distances as equal if they were less than 10 miles apart. Can you define an equality test on *Distance*, when *Distance* is a type synonym? If you can, can you call it (==)?

2.6.2 Consider the declarations

data *Jane*   = *MkJane Int*
newtype *Dick* = *MkDick Int*

By defining appropriate functions, demonstrate that *Jane* and *Dick* are different from one another.

2.7 Strings

A list of characters is called a *string*. The type *String* is a synonym type:

type *String* = [*Char*]

The datatype [α] of lists of type α will be studied in Chapter 4. Strings are denoted with a special syntax: the characters comprising the string are enclosed in double quotation marks. The difference between 'a' and "a" is that the former is a character, while the latter is a list of characters that happens to contain only one element. For example,

? "a"
"a"

? "Hello World"
"Hello World"

? "This sentence contains ‾↓a newline."
"This sentence contains ‾↓a newline."

Strings, being a type synonym and not a separate datatype, cannot be declared separately as instances of *Eq* and *Ord*. They inherit whatever instances are declared for general lists:

> **instance** *Eq* α $\Rightarrow$ *Eq* [α] **where**
>   . . .
> **instance** *Ord* α $\Rightarrow$ *Ord* [α] **where**
>   . . .

The missing instance definitions will be given in Chapter 4. Comparisons on strings follow the normal lexicographic ordering since that will be the ordering defined for lists. For example,

? "hello" < "hallo"
False

? "Jo" < "Joanna"
True

Most often, we want to print strings *literally*, which means that (i) the double quotation marks do not appear in the output; and (ii) special characters, such as '↓', are printed as the actual character they represent. Other effects we might want could be printing a string to a file, or reading a string from a file. The subject of input and output will be dealt with in Chapter 10; for now it is sufficient to observe that Haskell provides a primitive *command* for printing strings. The command is called *putStr* and its type is

> *putStr* :: *String* → *IO* ()

Evaluating the command *putStr* causes the string to be printed literally. For example,

? *putStr* "Hello World"
Hello World

? *putStr* "This sentence contains ⁻↓a newline."
This sentence contains
a newline.

In fact, every request to show a value at the terminal involves an explicit or implicit application of *putStr* as we will now see.

2.7.1 The type class *Show*

Depending on the application, a programmer may want to produce tables of numbers, pictures of various kinds, or formatted text. In order to achieve these effects in a consistent fashion, Haskell provides a special type class *Show*, which is declared by

> **class** *Show* α **where**
> $\quad$ *showsPrec* $\quad$ :: $\quad$ *Int* $\rightarrow$ α $\rightarrow$ *String* $\rightarrow$ *String*

The function *showsPrec* is provided for displaying values of type α. This function is designed for flexibility and efficiency, but it is a little complicated and we will not describe the purpose of each argument here (but see Sections 5.3 and 7.3 where more details are given). It is sufficient to say that, using *showsPrec*, it is possible to define a simpler function

> *show* :: *Show* α $\Rightarrow$ α $\rightarrow$ *String*

The function *show* takes a value and converts it to a string. For example, *Bool* is declared to be a member of *Show* and *show* is defined for booleans so that

> *show False* $\quad$ = $\quad$ "False"
> *show True* $\quad$ = $\quad$ "True"

A request to evaluate a boolean expression and display the result at the terminal involves a silent application of the function *putStr · show*. The boolean value is converted into a string via *show* and the result is printed via *putStr*. We can make this application explicit:

? *putStr* (*show True*)
True

Previous requests to evaluate and print values of type α have depended on a declaration that α is an instance of *Show*. The types *Char* and *String* are also instances of *Show* and, for example,

$$show \text{ 'a'} \quad = \quad \text{" 'a' "}$$

Applying *putStr* to the last expression on the right removes the outer pair of double quotation marks and results in the three characters 'a' being printed.

Some instances of *Show* are provided as primitive. For example, integers are printable and the value *show n* for an element *n* of type *Integer* is the list of characters that make up the decimal representation of *n*. The same is true of other number types. For example,

$$
\begin{aligned}
show\ 42 \quad &= \quad \text{"42"} \\
show\ (42.73) \quad &= \quad \text{"42.73"}
\end{aligned}
$$

Use of *show* enables us to control layout. In the following examples, the operation ++ concatenates two lists and is described in detail in Chapter 4.

? *putStr* ("The year is␣" ++ *show* (3×667))
The year is 2001

? *putStr* (*show* 100 ++ "⁻⌄" ++ *show* 101 ++ "⁻⌄" ++ *show* 102)
100
101
102

If we do not declare, for example, *Day* to be a member of the type *Show*, then the values of *Day* cannot be printed. Thus,

? *Mon*
Error: cannot find definition of *show* for *Day*

Fortunately, we do not have to provide an explicit declaration of *Day* as a member of *Show*. It is sufficient to declare *Day* by

> **data** *Day* = *Sun* | *Mon* | *Tue* | *Wed* | *Thu* | *Fri* | *Sat*
> **deriving** (*Eq*, *Ord*, *Enum*, *Show*)

The *Show* class can be derived automatically for datatypes.

On the other hand, the derived definitions may not be exactly what we want. For example, in Section 5.3 we will want to install a certain datatype as a member of *Show*, but do not want the visible appearance of elements to be that given by the derived definition. Hence we will need to give an instance declaration explicitly.

It is also useful to be able to introduce datatypes whose values should *not* be printed, even though they could be by including *Show* in a **deriving** clause for the datatype. We will explain this further in Chapter 8.

Finally, if we want to design a particular way of printing the elements of a datatype, then we can always do so by setting up a specific function for the purpose. We do not have to make use of the function *show*. To illustrate this point, let us show how to customise the printing of elements of the datatype

> **data** *Data*   =   *Pair Bool Int*

If we had asked for it, the derived instance of *Show* would lead to the following way of printing elements of *Data*:

? Pair True $(3 + 4)$
Pair True 7

There is, however, nothing to prevent us defining

> *showData*   ::   *Data* $\rightarrow$ *String*
> *showData* (*Pair b n*)
>   =   **if** *b* **then** "+" ++ *show n* **else** "−" ++ *show n*
> *putData*   =   *putStr* · *showData*

For example,

? putData (*Pair True* $(3 + 4)$)
+7

The definition of *showData* makes use of the function *show* for *Int*, but does not provide a function *show* for *Data*. In other words, *Data* is not made a fully paid-up member of *Show* just because we have provided a way of printing its elements. Nor does non-membership imply a second-class status for *Data*: type classes are there simply for our convenience and to provide standard methods for handling the predefined types in Haskell. New datatypes do not have to join if we don't want them to.

Exercises

2.7.1 Put the following strings in ascending order: "McMillan", "Macmillan", and "MacMillan".

2.7.2 What are the values of the following expressions?

> *show* (*show* 42)
> *show* 42 ++ *show* 42
> *show* "ᵗ"

2.7.3 Suppose a date is represented by a triple (d, m, y) of three *Int* integers, where d is the day, m the month, and y the year. Define a function *showDate* that takes a date and prints the corresponding date. For example,

> *showDate* (10, 12, 1997)   prints as   "10 December, 1997"

As a more complicated version, revise the definition so that

> *showDate* (10, 12, 1997)   prints as   "10th December, 1997"
> *showDate* (31, 12, 1997)   prints as   "31st December, 1997"

2.8 Chapter notes

Boole (1847) introduced a calculus for reasoning about truth-valued expressions, though he wrote $x + y$ for $x \vee y$ and xy for $x \wedge y$. Modern accounts of boolean algebra and logic, suitable for computing scientists, include Ben-Ari (1993), Burke and Foxley (1996), Gries and Schneider (1995).

Haskell uses the syntax **&&** for $\wedge$, and **||** for $\vee$. The Haskell syntax for == and ≠ is == and /=. The comparison operators $\leq$ and $\geq$ are written <= and >=.

The Haskell character set is based on the ISO Unicode standard 8859-1. In common with most other languages, Haskell uses escape sequences for denoting control characters. For example, a newline character is denoted by \n, tab by \t, and backspace by \b. See the Haskell 1.3 report, or ISO (1989), for further details on the representation of control codes and other nonstandard characters.

The theoretical foundations of type classes are studied in Wadler and Blott (1989) and Jones (1992, 1995). The standard type classes of Haskell have evolved through various versions of the language.

The notations $f \times g$ and $f + g$ are used in a branch of mathematics called *category theory*, which from one point of view can be regarded as a foundation for functional programming. Suitable texts for computing scientists include Barr and Wells (1995), Pierce (1991), Bird and de Moor (1997).

Chapter 3

Numbers

We have already mentioned three distinct types of number: arbitrary-precision integers (elements of *Integer*), limited-precision integers (elements of *Int*), and single-precision floating-point numbers (elements of *Float*). Other types of number one might wish to use include double-precision floating-point numbers, rational numbers, and complex numbers. The definitions of the arithmetic operations are different for different kinds of number; for example, integer division is quite different from real division, and one cannot compare complex numbers by ($<$). Haskell provides a sophisticated hierarchy of type classes for describing various kinds of number, and we will give a simplified account of the system in Section 3.4.

   Although (some) numbers are provided as primitive datatypes, it is theoretically possible to introduce them through suitable datatype declarations. We will begin by seeing how this is done. The discussion serves to introduce three important ideas: recursive datatypes, recursive definitions, and proof by induction. These three ideas, which constitute the holy trinity of functional programming, will be a major theme of the following three chapters as well.

3.1   Natural numbers

The natural numbers are the numbers 0, 1, 2, and so on, used for counting. The type *Nat* is introduced by the declaration

    data *Nat*   =   *Zero* | *Succ Nat*

Nat is our first example of a *recursive* datatype declaration. The definition says that *Zero* is a value of *Nat*, and that *Succ n* is a value of *Nat* whenever *n* is. In particular, the constructor *Succ* (short for 'successor') has type *Nat* → *Nat*. For example, each of

$$Zero, \quad Succ \; Zero, \quad Succ \; (Succ \; Zero)$$

is an element of *Nat*. As an element of *Nat* the number 7 would be represented
by

$$Succ \; (Succ \; (Succ \; (Succ \; (Succ \; (Succ \; (Succ \; Zero))))))$$

Every natural number is represented by a unique value of *Nat*. On the other
hand, not every value of *Nat* represents a well-defined natural number. In fact,
Nat also contains the values $\perp$, $Succ \perp$, $Succ \; (Succ \perp)$, and so on. These additional values will be discussed later.

Let us see how to program the basic arithmetic and comparison operations
on *Nat*. Addition can be defined by

$$
\begin{array}{lll}
(+) & :: & Nat \to Nat \to Nat \\
m + Zero & = & m \\
m + Succ \; n & = & Succ \; (m + n)
\end{array}
$$

This is a recursive definition, defining + by pattern matching on the second
argument. Since every element of *Nat*, apart from $\perp$, is either *Zero* or of the
form *Succ n* where *n* is an element of *Nat*, the two patterns in the equations for
+ are disjoint and cover all numbers apart from $\perp$.

Here is how $Zero + Succ \; (Succ \; Zero)$ would be evaluated:

$$
\begin{array}{ll}
& Zero + Succ \; (Succ \; Zero) \\
= & \{\text{second equation for } +\} \\
& Succ \; (Zero + Succ \; Zero) \\
= & \{\text{second equation for } +\} \\
& Succ \; (Succ \; (Zero + Zero)) \\
= & \{\text{first equation for } +\} \\
& Succ \; (Succ \; Zero)
\end{array}
$$

This calculation shows why it is not a practical proposition to introduce natural
numbers through the datatype *Nat*: arithmetic would be just too inefficient. In
particular, calculating $m + n$ would require $(n + 1)$ evaluation steps. On the
other hand, counting on your fingers is a good way to understand addition.

Given +, we can define × by

$$
\begin{aligned}
&(\times) && :: && Nat \to Nat \to Nat \\
&m \times Zero && = && Zero \\
&m \times Succ\ n && = && (m \times n) + m
\end{aligned}
$$

Given ×, we can define exponentiation (↑) by

$$
\begin{aligned}
&(\uparrow) && :: && Nat \to Nat \to Nat \\
&m \uparrow Zero && = && Succ\ Zero \\
&m \uparrow Succ\ n && = && (m \uparrow n) \times m
\end{aligned}
$$

The definitions of +, ×, and ↑ follow a similar pattern, and Section 3.3 contains a discussion of how this common pattern can be exploited.

We can define *Nat* to be a member of the type class *Eq* with the instance declaration

instance *Eq Nat* **where**
$$
\begin{aligned}
&Zero == Zero && = && True \\
&Zero == Succ\ n && = && False \\
&Succ\ m == Zero && = && False \\
&Succ\ m == Succ\ n && = && (m == n)
\end{aligned}
$$

This is also a recursive definition, using pattern matching on both arguments. Similarly, we can define *Nat* to be a member of *Ord* with the declaration

instance *Ord Nat* **where**
$$
\begin{aligned}
&Zero < Zero && = && False \\
&Zero < Succ\ n && = && True \\
&Succ\ m < Zero && = && False \\
&Succ\ m < Succ\ n && = && (m < n)
\end{aligned}
$$

We can print elements of *Nat* by defining a function *showNat*:

$$
\begin{aligned}
&showNat && :: && Nat \to String \\
&showNat\ Zero && = && \text{“Zero”} \\
&showNat\ (Succ\ Zero) && = && \text{“Succ Zero”} \\
&showNat\ (Succ\ (Succ\ n)) && = && \text{“Succ}_\sqcup\text{(”} \mathbin{+\!\!+} showNat\ (Succ\ n) \mathbin{+\!\!+} \text{“)”}
\end{aligned}
$$

The definition of *showNat* makes use of three patterns, namely *Zero*, *Succ Zero*, and *Succ (Succ n)*. These patterns are different from one another and together cover all the elements of *Nat*, apart from ⊥. There are three patterns in the definition of *showNat* because the first two natural numbers are shown without parentheses.

Alternatively, we could have introduced *Nat* with the declaration

data *Nat* = *Zero* | *Succ Nat*
                deriving (*Eq*, *Ord*, *Show*)

With this declaration, *Nat* is installed automatically as a member of each of the type classes *Eq*, *Ord*, and *Show*. In particular, the function *show* for *Nat* gives the same function as *showNat*. As we will see later, all number types are equality types and are instances of *Show*. However, not all numbers can be compared by ($<$).

The remaining arithmetic operation common to all numbers is subtraction ($-$). However, subtraction is a *partial* operation on natural numbers. The definition is

$$
\begin{array}{lcl}
(-) & :: & Nat \rightarrow Nat \rightarrow Nat \\
m - Zero & = & m \\
Succ\ m - Succ\ n & = & m - n
\end{array}
$$

This definition uses pattern matching on both arguments; taken together, the patterns are disjoint but not exhaustive. For example,

$$Succ\ Zero - Succ\ (Succ\ Zero)$$

=   {second equation for ($-$)}

$$Zero - Succ\ Zero$$

=   {case exhaustion}

$$\perp$$

The hint 'case exhaustion' in the last step indicates that no equation for ($-$) has a pattern that matches (*Zero* $-$ *Succ Zero*). More generally, $m - n = \perp$ if $m < n$. The partial nature of subtraction on the natural numbers is the prime motivation for introducing the *integer* numbers; over the integers ($-$) is a *total* operation. On the other hand, we can always define a total operation $\ominus$ on natural numbers so that $m \ominus n = m - n$ if $m \geq n$ and $m \ominus n = Zero$ if $m < n$. The definition of $\ominus$ is left as an exercise.

Finally, here are two more examples of programming with *Nat*. The factorial function is defined by

$$
\begin{array}{lcl}
fact & :: & Nat \rightarrow Nat \\
fact\ Zero & = & Succ\ Zero \\
fact\ (Succ\ n) & = & Succ\ n \times fact\ n
\end{array}
$$

The Fibonacci function is defined by

fib	::	*Nat → Nat*
fib Zero	=	*Zero*
fib (Succ Zero)	=	*Succ Zero*
fib (Succ (Succ n))	=	*fib (Succ n) + fib n*

The definition of *fib* uses the same three patterns as in *showNat*.

3.1.1 Partial numbers

Let us now return to the point about there being extra values in *Nat*. The values

$$\bot,\quad Succ\ \bot,\quad Succ\ (Succ\ \bot),\ \ldots$$

are all different and each is also an element of *Nat*. That they exist is a consequence of three facts: (i) $\bot$ is an element of *Nat* because every datatype declaration introduces at least one extra value, the undefined value of the type; (ii) constructor functions of a datatype are assumed to be nonstrict; and (iii) *Succ n* is an element of *Nat* whenever *n* is.

To appreciate why these extra values are different from one another, suppose we define *undefined :: Nat* by the equation *undefined = undefined*. Then

? Zero < undefined
{Interrupted!}

? Zero < Succ undefined
True

? Succ Zero < Succ undefined
{Interrupted!}

? Succ Zero < Succ (Succ undefined)
True

One can interpret the extra values in the following way: $\bot$ corresponds to the natural number about which there is absolutely no information; *Succ* $\bot$ to the natural number about which the only information is that it is greater than *Zero*; *Succ (Succ* $\bot$) to the natural number about which the only information is that it is greater than *Succ Zero*; and so on.

There is also one further value of *Nat*, namely the 'infinite' number:

$$Succ\ (Succ\ (Succ\ (Succ\ \ldots)))$$

This number can be defined by

$$infinity \quad :: \quad Nat$$
$$infinity \quad = \quad Succ\ infinity$$

It is different from all the other numbers because it is the only number x for which $Succ\ m < x$ returns $True$ for all finite numbers m. In this sense, $infinity$ is the largest element of Nat. If we request the value of $infinity$, then we obtain

? $infinity$

$Succ\ (Succ\ (Succ\ (Succ\ (Succ\{Interrupted!\})$

The number $infinity$ satisfies other properties, in particular $n + infinity = infinity$ for all numbers n. The dual equation $infinity + n = infinity$ holds only for finite numbers n. We will see how to prove assertions such as these in the next section.

To summarise this discussion, we can divide the values of Nat into three classes:

- The *finite* numbers, those that correspond to well-defined natural numbers.

- The *partial* numbers, $\perp$, $Succ\ \perp$, and so on.

- The *infinite* numbers, of which there is just one, namely $infinity$.

We will see that this classification holds true of *all* recursive types. There will be the *finite* elements of the type, the *partial* elements, and the *infinite* elements. Although the infinite natural number is not of much use, the same is not true of the infinite values of other datatypes.

Exercises

3.1.1 Construct the positive numbers as a recursive datatype.

3.1.2 Define a function $convert :: Nat \rightarrow Integer$ that converts a natural number to an integer.

3.1.3 Define versions of $+$ and $\times$ that use pattern matching on the first argument. Can the same be done for $\uparrow$?

3.1.4 How many evaluation steps does it take to evaluate $m \times n$?

3.1.5 Define a total version $\ominus$ of subtraction so that $m \ominus n = Zero$ if $m < n$.

3.2 Induction

In order to reason about the properties of recursively defined functions over a recursive datatype, we can appeal to a principle of *structural induction*. In the case of *Nat* the principle of structural induction can be stated as follows: in order to show that some property $P(n)$ holds for each finite number n of *Nat*, it is sufficient to show:

Case (*Zero*). That $P(Zero)$ holds.

Case (*Succ n*). That if $P(n)$ holds, then $P(Succ\ n)$ holds also.

Induction is valid for the same reason that recursive definitions are valid: every finite number is either *Zero* or of the form *Succ n* where n is a finite number. If we prove the first case, then we have shown that the property is true for *Zero*; if we also prove the second case, then we have shown that the property is true for *Succ Zero*, since it is true for *Zero*. But now, by the same argument, it is true for *Succ* (*Succ Zero*), and so on.

The principle needs to be extended if we want to assert that some proposition is true for *all* elements of *Nat*, but we postpone discussion of this point to the following section.

As an example, let us prove that $Zero + n = n$ for all finite numbers n. In words, *Zero* is a *left unit* of +. Recall that + is defined by the two equations

$$m + Zero\quad =\quad m$$
$$m + Succ\ n\quad =\quad Succ\ (m + n)$$

The first equation asserts that *Zero* is a *right unit* of +. In general, e is a left unit of $\oplus$ if $e \oplus x = x$ for all x, and a right unit if $x \oplus e = x$ for all x. If e is both a left unit and a right unit of an operator $\oplus$, then it is called *the* unit of $\oplus$. The terminology is appropriate since only one value can be both a left and right unit. So, by proving that *Zero* is a left unit, we have proved that *Zero* is the unit of +.

Proof. The proof is by induction on n. More precisely, we take for $P(n)$ the assertion $Zero + n = n$. This equation is referred to as the *induction hypothesis*.

Case (*Zero*). We have to show $Zero + Zero = Zero$, which is immediate from the first equation defining +.

Case (*Succ n*). We have to show that $Zero + Succ\ n = Succ\ n$, which we do by simplifying the left-hand expression:

> $Zero + Succ\ n$
>
> =   {second equation for +}
>
> $Succ\ (Zero + n)$
>
> =   {induction hypothesis}
>
> $Succ\ n$

□

This example shows the format we will use for inductive proofs, laying out each case separately and using a □ to mark the end. The very last step made use of the induction hypothesis, which is allowed by the way induction works.

As a more complicated example, let us prove the well-known law that for all finite natural numbers x, m, and n,

$$x \uparrow (m + n)\ =\ (x \uparrow m) \times (x \uparrow n)$$

For the proof we will need the definitions of $\times$ and $\uparrow$ from the previous section, repeated here for easy reference:

> $m \times Zero\quad =\quad Zero$
> $m \times Succ\ n\quad =\quad (m \times n) + m$
>
> $m \uparrow Zero\quad =\quad Succ\ Zero$
> $m \uparrow Succ\ n\quad =\quad (m \uparrow n) \times m$

Proof. The proof is by induction on n, taking the induction hypothesis to be

$$x \uparrow (m + n)\ =\ (x \uparrow m) \times (x \uparrow n)$$

It is important to state the variable we are doing the induction on, since there are three possible choices, namely x, m, and n.

Case (*Zero*). The idea is to substitute *Zero* for n in the hypothesis, and then to simplify both sides independently.

For the left-hand side we reason

> $x \uparrow (m + Zero)$
>
> =   {first equation for +}
>
> $x \uparrow m$

For the right-hand side we reason

$$(x \uparrow m) \times (x \uparrow Zero)$$

= {first equation for ↑}

$$(x \uparrow m) \times Succ\ Zero$$

= {second equation for ×}

$$(x \uparrow m) + (x \uparrow m) \times Zero$$

= {first equation for ×}

$$(x \uparrow m) + Zero$$

= {first equation for +}

$$x \uparrow m$$

The two sides simplify to the same result, so they are equal. The simplification of the right-hand side is the more complicated of the two because it involves proving that *Succ Zero* is a right unit of multiplication.

Case (*Succ n*). Again, the idea is to substitute *Succ n* for *n* in the hypothesis, and to simplify both sides separately.

First, the left-hand side:

$$x \uparrow (m + Succ\ n)$$

= {second equation for +}

$$x \uparrow Succ\ (m + n)$$

= {second equation for ↑}

$$(x \uparrow (m + n)) \times x$$

= {induction hypothesis}

$$((x \uparrow m) \times (x \uparrow n)) \times x$$

Now, the right-hand side:

$$(x \uparrow m) \times (x \uparrow Succ\ n)$$

= {second equation for ↑}

$$(x \uparrow m) \times ((x \uparrow n) \times x)$$

The two sides simplify to two different expressions, which are equal under the assumption that × is associative. The proof of this claim involves another induction argument and is left as an exercise.

□

Apart from one decision, the proof follows a fairly automatic sequence of steps: in each case there is a substitution into both sides of the equation, and each side is then simplified; each simplification step is determined by the shape of the current expression in a fairly obvious way.

The one inventive part consists of deciding what choice of variable to do the induction on. In this example, there were three possible choices, but only two reasonable ones, namely m and n. What would happen if we did the induction on m? Let us see by doing the proof again:

Proof. The proof is by induction on m.

Case (*Zero*). For the left-hand side we reason

$$x \uparrow (Zero + n)$$
$$= \quad \{\text{claim: } Zero + n = n \text{ for all } n\}$$
$$x \uparrow n$$

For the right-hand side we reason

$$(x \uparrow Zero) \times (x \uparrow n)$$
$$= \quad \{\text{first equation for } \uparrow\}$$
$$Succ\ Zero \times (x \uparrow n)$$
$$= \quad \{\text{claim: } Succ\ Zero \times n = n \text{ for all } n\}$$
$$x \uparrow n$$

The two claims are that *Zero* is a left unit of +, and *Succ Zero* is a left unit of ×. The proofs of the claims are left as exercises.

Case (*Succ m*). For the left-hand side we reason

$$x \uparrow (Succ\ m + n)$$
$$= \quad \{\text{claim: } Succ\ m + n = Succ\ (m + n)\}$$
$$x \uparrow Succ\ (m + n)$$
$$= \quad \{\text{second equation for } \uparrow\}$$
$$(x \uparrow (m + n)) \times x$$

$=$ {induction hypothesis}

$((x \uparrow m) \times (x \uparrow n)) \times x$

For the right-hand side we reason

$(x \uparrow Succ\ m) \times (x \uparrow n)$

$=$ {second equation for $\uparrow$}

$((x \uparrow m) \times x) \times (x \uparrow n)$

Now we need an extra assumption, namely that $\times$ is commutative as well as associative; that is, $x \times y = y \times x$. The two sides are equal under these two assumptions.

$\square$

The second proof is more complicated than the first in that it involves no fewer than four additional assumptions, all of which themselves have to be proved by induction. The lesson here is that the choice of variable on which to do induction (if there is a choice, of course) can be crucial. It seemed sensible to start out by doing an induction on n because + is defined by recursion on its second argument; then at least the first step of simplification on the left-hand side is known to be a simple one. Fortunately, the rest of the proof was simpler too.

3.2.1 Full induction

In the form given above, the induction principle for *Nat* suffices only to prove properties of the *finite* members of *Nat*. If we want to show that a property P also holds for every *partial* number, then we have to prove three things:

Case ($\bot$). That $P(\bot)$ holds.

Case (*Zero*). That $P(Zero)$ holds.

Case (*Succ n*). That if $P(n)$ holds, then $P(Succ\ n)$ holds also.

We can omit the second case, but then we can conclude only that $P(n)$ holds for every partial number. The reason the principle is valid is that every partial number is either $\bot$ or of the form *Succ n* for some partial number n.

To illustrate, let us prove the somewhat counterintuitive result that $m + n = n$ for all numbers m and all partial numbers n.

Proof. The proof is by partial number induction on n.

Case (⊥). The equation $m + \perp = \perp$ follows at once by case exhaustion in the definition of +. That is, ⊥ does not match either of the patterns *Zero* or *Succ n*.

Case (*Succ n*). For the left-hand side we reason

$$m + Succ\ n$$

$$=\quad \{\text{second equation for } +\}$$

$$Succ\ (m + n)$$

$$=\quad \{\text{induction hypothesis}\}$$

$$Succ\ n$$

Since the right-hand side is also *Succ n*, we are done.

□

The omitted case, namely $m + Zero = Zero$, is false, which is why the assertion does not hold for finite numbers.

So, it is easy to extend induction to apply to partial numbers. What we also obtain as a bonus is that, having proved that an equation holds for all partial numbers, we can assert that it holds for the infinite number *infinity* too. See Exercise 3.2.7 for elaboration on this point. In particular, we can now assert that $m + infinity = infinity$ for all numbers *m*.

3.2.2 Program synthesis

In the proofs above we defined some functions and then used induction to prove a certain property. We can also view induction as a way to *synthesise* definitions of functions so that they satisfy the properties we want.

Let us illustrate with a simple example. Suppose we *specify* subtraction of natural numbers by the condition

$$(m + n) - n\quad =\quad m$$

for all *m* and *n*. The specification does not give a constructive definition of $(-)$, merely a property that it has to satisfy. However, we can do an induction proof on *n* of the equation above, but view the calculation as a way of generating a suitable definition of $(-)$. Unlike previous proofs, we reason with the equation as a whole, since simplification of both sides independently is not possible if we do not know what all the rules of simplification are.

Case (*Zero*). We reason

$$(m + Zero) - Zero = m$$

$\equiv$ {first equation for +}

$$m - Zero = m$$

Hence we can take $m - Zero = m$ to satisfy the case. The symbol $\equiv$ is used to separate steps of the calculation since we are calculating with mathematical assertions, not with values of a datatype.

Case (*Succ n*). We reason

$$(m + Succ\ n) - Succ\ n = m$$

$\equiv$ {second equation for +}

$$Succ\ (m + n) - Succ\ n = m$$

$\equiv$ {hypothesis $(m + n) - n = m$}

$$Succ\ (m + n) - Succ\ n = (m + n) - n$$

Replacing $m + n$ in the last equation by m, we can take $Succ\ m - Succ\ n = m - n$ to satisfy the case. Hence we have derived

$$m - Zero \qquad = \quad m$$
$$Succ\ m - Succ\ n \quad = \quad m - n$$

This is the program for $(-)$ seen earlier.

Exercises

3.2.1 Prove that *Succ Zero* is a left unit of $\times$.

3.2.2 Prove that if $\oplus$ has a left unit a and a right unit b, then $a = b$.

3.2.3 Does the law $x \uparrow (m + n) = (x \uparrow m) \times (x \uparrow n)$ hold for *all* natural numbers x, m, and n?

3.2.4 Prove that + is associative, that is, $(m + n) + p = m + (n + p)$ for all natural numbers m, n, and p.

3.2.5 Prove that $\times$ distributes over +, that is,

$$k \times (m + n) \quad = \quad (k \times m) + (k \times n)$$

for all natural numbers k, m, and n.

3.2.6 Define $\sqcap$ by

$$
\begin{aligned}
Zero \sqcap n &= Zero \\
Succ\ m \sqcap Zero &= Zero \\
Succ\ m \sqcap Succ\ n &= Succ\ (m \sqcap n)
\end{aligned}
$$

What operation on integers does $\sqcap$ correspond to? Prove that $m \sqcap infinity = m$ for all elements m of *Nat*, finite, partial, or infinite.

3.2.7 The claim made in the text is that if $P(n)$ is an equation that holds for all partial numbers n, then $P(infinity)$ holds as well. Any free variables in P are required to be universally quantified. For instance, we can take $P(n)$ to be any of the propositions

(for all x and m) $x \uparrow (m + n) = (x \uparrow m) \times (x \uparrow n)$

(for all m) $(m + n) - n = m$

However, we cannot in general take $P(n)$ to be an equation that involves an existentially quantified variable. Consider, for instance, the proposition $P(n)$ given by

(for some finite number m) $n \ominus m = \bot$

where $\ominus$ is the total version of subtraction, satisfying $n \ominus m = Zero$ if $n < m$. Show by induction that $P(n)$ holds for all partial numbers n. Prove, also by induction, that $infinity \ominus m = infinity$ for all finite numbers m.

3.3 The fold function

Many of the recursive definitions seen so far have a common pattern, exemplified by the following definition of a function f:

$$
\begin{aligned}
f &\quad :: \quad Nat \to A \\
f\ Zero &= c \\
f\ (Succ\ n) &= h\ (f\ n)
\end{aligned}
$$

Here, A is some type, c is an element of A, and $h :: A \to A$. Observe that f works by taking an element of *Nat* and replacing *Zero* by c and *Succ* by h. For example, f takes

$$Succ\ (Succ\ (Succ\ Zero)) \quad \text{to} \quad h\ (h\ (h\ c))$$

The two equations for f can be captured in terms of a single function, *foldn*, called the *fold* function for *Nat*. The definition is

$$
\begin{array}{lll}
\textit{foldn} & :: & (\alpha \to \alpha) \to \alpha \to \textit{Nat} \to \alpha \\
\textit{foldn } h \, c \, \textit{Zero} & = & c \\
\textit{foldn } h \, c \, (\textit{Succ } n) & = & h \, (\textit{foldn } h \, c \, n)
\end{array}
$$

In particular, we have

$$
\begin{array}{lll}
m + n & = & \textit{foldn Succ } m \, n \\
m \times n & = & \textit{foldn } (+m) \, \textit{Zero } n \\
m \uparrow n & = & \textit{foldn } (\times m) \, (\textit{Succ Zero}) \, n
\end{array}
$$

It follows also that the identity function *id* on *Nat* satisfies *id* = *foldn Succ Zero*. A suitable fold function can be defined for every recursive type, and we will see other fold functions in the following chapters.

In the examples above, each instance of *foldn* also returned an element of *Nat*. In the following two examples, *foldn* returns an element of $(\textit{Nat}, \textit{Nat})$:

$$
\begin{array}{lll}
\textit{fact} & :: & \textit{Nat} \to \textit{Nat} \\
\textit{fact} & = & \textit{snd} \cdot \textit{foldn } f \, (\textit{Zero}, \textit{Succ Zero}) \\
& & \textbf{where } f \, (m, n) = (\textit{Succ } m, \textit{Succ } m \times n)
\end{array}
$$

$$
\begin{array}{lll}
\textit{fib} & :: & \textit{Nat} \to \textit{Nat} \\
\textit{fib} & = & \textit{fst} \cdot \textit{foldn } g \, (\textit{Zero}, \textit{Succ Zero}) \\
& & \textbf{where } g \, (m, n) = (n, m + n)
\end{array}
$$

The function *fact* computes the factorial function, and *fib* computes the Fibonacci function. Each program works by first computing a more general result, namely an element of $(\textit{Nat}, \textit{Nat})$, and then extracts the required result. In fact,

$$
\begin{array}{lll}
\textit{foldn } f \, (\textit{Zero}, \textit{Succ Zero}) \, n & = & (n, \textit{fact } n) \\
\textit{foldn } g \, (\textit{Zero}, \textit{Succ Zero}) \, n & = & (\textit{fib } n, \textit{fib } (\textit{Succ } n))
\end{array}
$$

These equations can be proved by induction. The program for *fib* is more efficient than a direct recursive definition. The recursive program requires an exponential number of + operations, while the program above requires only a linear number. We will discuss efficiency in more detail in Chapter 7, where the programming technique that led to the invention of the new program for *fib* will be studied in a more general setting.

There are two advantages of writing recursive definitions in terms of *foldn*. Firstly, the definition is shorter; rather than having to write down two equations, we have only to write down one. Secondly, it is possible to prove general properties of *foldn* and use them to prove properties of specific instantiations. In other words, rather than having to write down many induction proofs, we have only to write down one.

3.3.1 Fusion

To illustrate, let us prove the following *fusion* law for *Nat*. It states that

$$f \cdot foldn\, g\, a \;=\; foldn\, h\, b$$

under certain assumptions on the variables involved. The law is called a fusion law because the computation of f is fused with the computation of *foldn g a*. Fusion laws can lead to a significant increase in efficiency; instead of processing an element of a datatype and then processing the result, we can sometimes combine the two processing steps into one.

Rather than state at the outset what the assumptions are that make fusion work, let us use the induction proof to bring them to the surface.

Proof. We prove that $f\,(foldn\,g\,a\,n) = foldn\,h\,b\,n$ by full induction on n, deriving the required assumptions along the way.

Case ($\perp$). For the left-hand side we reason

$$f\,(foldn\,g\,a\,\perp)$$

$$= \quad \{\text{case exhaustion in definition of } foldn\}$$

$$f \perp$$

For the right-hand side we reason

$$foldn\,h\,b\,\perp$$

$$= \quad \{\text{case exhaustion in definition of } foldn\}$$

$$\perp$$

These two results have to be the same, so we have our first assumption, namely that f is a strict function.

Case (*Zero*). For the left-hand side we reason

$$f\,(foldn\,g\,a\,Zero)$$

$$= \quad \{\text{first equation for } foldn\}$$

$$f\,a$$

For the right-hand side we reason

$$foldn\ h\ b\ Zero$$

= {first equation for *foldn*}

$$b$$

These two results have to be the same, so we have our second assumption, namely that $f\ a = b$.

Case (*Succ n*). For the left-hand side we reason

$$f\ (foldn\ g\ a\ (Succ\ n))$$

= {second equation for *foldn*}

$$f\ (g\ (foldn\ g\ a\ n))$$

For the right-hand side we reason

$$foldn\ h\ b\ (Succ\ n)$$

= {second equation for *foldn*}

$$h\ (foldn\ h\ b\ (Succ\ n))$$

= {induction hypothesis}

$$h\ (f\ (foldn\ g\ a\ n))$$

These two results have to be the same, which follows if $f \cdot g = h \cdot f$.

$\square$

Since an equation that holds for all partial numbers also holds for the infinite number, we have proved

Fusion theorem for *foldn*. If f is strict, $f\ a = b$, and $f \cdot g = h \cdot f$, then

$$f \cdot foldn\ g\ a\ \ =\ \ foldn\ h\ b$$

3.3.2 Examples

Let us now use the fusion theorem to prove that *Zero* is a left unit of +; in symbols, $Zero + n = n$ for all numbers n. Since $n = foldn\ Succ\ Zero\ n$, our obligation is to prove that

$$(Zero\ +) \cdot foldn\ Succ\ Zero\ \ =\ \ foldn\ Succ\ Zero$$

An appeal to the fusion law says that this equation holds provided

$$A \begin{cases} Zero + \bot & = & \bot \\ Zero + Zero & = & Zero \\ Zero + Succ\ n & = & Succ\ (Zero + n) \end{cases}$$

All three equations are immediate from the definition of $+$.

As a second example, let us show that *Succ Zero* is a left unit of $\times$. By an appeal to fusion, exactly as in the previous case, we have three conditions to check:

$$\begin{array}{rcl} Succ\ Zero \times \bot & = & \bot \\ Succ\ Zero \times Zero & = & Zero \\ Succ\ Zero \times Succ\ n & = & Succ\ (Succ\ Zero \times n) \end{array}$$

The first two are immediate from the definition of $\times$, and the third is proved as follows:

$$\begin{array}{rl} & Succ\ Zero \times Succ\ n \\ = & \{\text{definition of } \times\} \\ & (Succ\ Zero \times n) + Succ\ Zero \\ = & \{\text{definition of } +\} \\ & Succ\ ((Succ\ Zero \times n) + Zero) \\ = & \{\text{definition of } +\} \\ & Succ\ (Succ\ Zero \times n) \end{array}$$

Neither of these two results was proved using induction explicitly. The single use of induction was in the proof of the fusion law.

Exercises

3.3.1 Prove that *foldn Succ Zero n* $= n$ for all elements n of *Nat*, finite, partial, or infinite.

3.3.2 Use the fusion law to prove that $+$ is commutative.

3.3.3 Division of natural numbers can be specified by the condition that $(n \times m)/n = m$ for all positive n and all m. Construct a program for division and prove that it meets the specification.

3.3.4 The function *log* can be specified by the condition that $log\ (2 \uparrow m) = m$ for all m. Construct a program for *log* and prove that it meets the specification.

3.4 Haskell numbers

There are three kinds of integer: positive integers, zero, and negative integers. Therefore we could declare *Integer* by a datatype declaration

> **data** *Integer* = *Neg Positive* | *Zero* | *Pos Positive*
> **data** *Positive* = *One* | *Succ Positive*

The type *Positive* delivers the positive natural numbers, and the type *Integer* delivers a signed positive number, or zero. Having constructed the integers, we could construct the rationals as pairs of integers, and the complex rationals as pairs of rationals. We could also construct suitable approximations of the real numbers as sequences of decimal digits. The bottom line is that we can recreate all of arithmetic from scratch without appealing to anything more than purely symbolic computation.

However, every computer possesses a built-in arithmetic unit, capable of performing limited-precision integer arithmetic at least. In many computers there is also a floating-point unit, and for those computers that do not have such a device, floating-point arithmetic is coded efficiently as low-level software routines. It is far more efficient to make use of these facilities than to rely on symbolic alternatives.

Numbers are dealt with differently in different languages. For example, in Miranda there is a single type *num* that contains both the arbitrary-precision integers and limited-precision floating-point numbers. Haskell, on the other hand, divides the numbers up into distinct types. In this book we will follow the Haskell naming conventions and refer to the following types:

> *Int*   single-precision integers
> *Integer* arbitrary-precision integers
> *Float*   single-precision floating-point numbers
> *Double*   double-precision floating-point numbers

There are other Haskell number-types, including the type *Rational*, but we will not make use of them (the following section shows one way of defining rational numbers). Nor will we say exactly what 'single-precision' and 'double-precision' mean, because the meanings can differ depending on the available hardware, although there is a standard to which most computers adhere. We will see one way of implementing arbitrary-precision arithmetic in Section 5.3. Arithmetic with *Int* is the fastest of all; arithmetic with *Integer* is appreciably slower. However, where *Integer* arithmetic is exact, *Int* arithmetic is not; beyond a certain range *integer overflow* occurs and the computer may either give an error message or simply return incorrect results.

Note that there is no type *Nat* of natural numbers in Haskell. Nevertheless, the ghost of natural numbers is present in the integers because we can still make use of pattern matching. For example, we can define

$$
\begin{array}{lcl}
\textit{fact} & :: & \textit{Integer} \rightarrow \textit{Integer} \\
\textit{fact } 0 & = & 1 \\
\textit{fact } (n+1) & = & (n+1) \times \textit{fact } n
\end{array}
$$

This mirrors the recursive definition seen earlier, when we wrote *Zero* instead of 0 and *Succ n* instead of $n+1$. Pattern matching with integers is restricted to the subclass of natural numbers. Thus, the pattern $(n+1)$ matches only a positive integer. Even though we could avoid pattern matching by using a case analysis (or, better, by using a new version of *foldn*), there are many examples where pattern matching is the clearest method of definition. Furthermore, the use of pattern matching parallels the cases in an induction proof.

There is one crucial difference between the constructor *Succ* of *Nat* and the function $(+1)$ on integers: whereas *Succ* is a nonstrict function, $(+1)$ is strict. Hence there are no partial numbers in built-in arithmetic.

3.4.1   The numeric type classes

The same symbols, $+$, $\times$, and so on, are used for arithmetic on each numeric type, even though these operators denote different operations on different types. In other words, $+$, $\times$, and so on, are overloaded functions like $==$ and $<$. Haskell uses a sophisticated system of type classes for describing the various types of number and we will not give details in this book. Instead, we will describe a simplified scheme that is intended to capture the essential ideas.

All Haskell number types are instances of the type class *Num* defined by

$$
\begin{array}{ll}
\textbf{class } (Eq\ \alpha,\ Show\ \alpha) \Rightarrow Num\ \alpha\ \textbf{where} & \\
\quad (+), (-), (\times) \quad :: \quad \alpha \rightarrow \alpha \rightarrow \alpha & \\
\quad \textit{negate} \qquad\quad :: \quad \alpha \rightarrow \alpha & \\
\quad \textit{fromInteger} \quad :: \quad \textit{Integer} \rightarrow \alpha & \\
& \\
\quad x - y \qquad\qquad = \quad x + \textit{negate } y &
\end{array}
$$

The class *Num* provides a default definition of $(-)$ in terms of *negate*. All numbers can be compared for equality and have printable representations. All numbers can be added, subtracted, and multiplied. Finally, there is a conversion function *fromInteger* for dealing with constants. An integer constant, such as

3 or 65472233, represents the application of *fromInteger* to the appropriate *Integer* value. Hence

$$65472233 \ :: \ Num\ \alpha \Rightarrow \alpha$$

Integer numeric constants are defined in this indirect way so that they may be interpreted as values of any appropriate numeric type.

Not all numbers can be compared by $(<)$; for example, complex numbers cannot be. The type class *Real* captures those kinds of computable number for which $<$ is a meaningful operation:

> **class** $(Num\ \alpha, Ord\ \alpha) \Rightarrow Real\ \alpha$ **where**
>   *toRational* $::\ \ \alpha \rightarrow Rational$

The type *Rational* consists of pairs of *Integer* numbers and is discussed further in the following section. The new function *toRational* captures the idea that every finite-precision real number can be expressed as the ratio of two arbitrary-precision integers. The remaining type classes we will mention are *Integral* and *Fractional*. The type class *Integral* is declared by

> **class** $(Real\ \alpha, Enum\ \alpha) \Rightarrow Integral\ \alpha$ **where**
> $(\textbf{div}), (\textbf{mod})\ \ ::\ \ \alpha \rightarrow \alpha \rightarrow \alpha$
>   *toInteger* $::\ \ \alpha \rightarrow Integer$

The members of *Integral* are the two primitive types *Int* and *Integer*. For each type, the operators **div** and **mod** are provided as primitive. If x and y are integers, and y is not zero, then $x\ \textbf{div}\ y = \lfloor x/y \rfloor$, where $\lfloor x \rfloor$, pronounced the 'floor' of x, is the largest integer n satisfying $n \leq x$. In particular, $\lfloor 13.8 \rfloor = 13$ and $\lfloor -13.8 \rfloor = -14$. We will discuss how to compute $\lfloor x \rfloor$ in Section 3.6. The value $x\ \textbf{mod}\ y$ is defined by the equation

$$x\ =\ (x\ \textbf{div}\ y) \times y + (x\ \textbf{mod}\ y)$$

The number y in $(x\ \textbf{mod}\ y)$ is called the *modulus*. In most applications the modulus is positive. For positive y we have $0 \leq x\textbf{mod}\,y < y$. In fact, for positive y the values $x\ \textbf{div}\ y$ and $x\ \textbf{mod}\ y$ are the unique integers q and r satisfying the condition

$$x = q \times y + r \quad \text{and} \quad 0 \leq r < y$$

When y is negative, we have $y < x\ \textbf{mod}\ y \leq 0$.

The type class *Fractional* captures those kinds of numbers for which division is meaningful and contains the floating-point number types *Float* and *Double*:

```
class (Num α) ⇒ Fractional α where
  (/)          ::  α → α → α
  fromRational ::  Rational → α
```

The conversion function *fromRational* is used for floating-point constants. A constant, such as 2.1414, stands for an application of *fromRational* to the appropriate value of type *Rational*. Thus,

$$2.1414 \quad :: \quad Fractional\ \alpha \Rightarrow \alpha$$

Floating-point constants are defined in this indirect way so that they can be interpreted as values of the appropriate numeric types.

Exercises

3.4.1 What is the value of 3 **mod** (-4)?

3.4.2 Show that when y is negative, $y < x \bmod y \le 0$.

3.4.3 Is it the case that $\lfloor \lfloor x \rfloor \rfloor = \lfloor x \rfloor$?

3.5   Example: the rationals

A rational number is a pair (x, y) of integers that represents the number x/y. For example, $(1, 7)$, $(3, 21)$, and $(168, 1176)$ all denote the fraction $1/7$, and $(-1, 3)$, $(1, -3)$ both denote the fraction $-(1/3)$. However, only fractions (x, y) with $y \ne 0$ represent well-defined values.

Since there is an infinite number of ways to represent one and the same rational, it is sensible to choose a *canonical* representation. A fraction can always be represented uniquely by a pair (x, y) in which $y > 0$ and $gcd(x, y) = 1$, where $gcd\ (x, y)$, the greatest common divisor of x and y, is defined below. In particular, the unique representation of 0 satisfying these conditions is $(0, 1)$.

Our aim in this section is to install the rationals as a Haskell number type. First, we introduce *Rational* as a datatype:

```
newtype Rational  =  Rat Integer Integer
```

The function *mkRat* takes a pair of integers and returns an element of *Rational* in canonical form:

$$
\begin{aligned}
mkRat &\quad :: \quad (Integer, Integer) \rightarrow Rational \\
mkRat\ (x, y) &\quad = \quad Rat\ (u\ \mathbf{div}\ d)\ (v\ \mathbf{div}\ d) \\
&\qquad\qquad \mathbf{where}\ u \quad = \quad (signum\ y) \times x \\
&\qquad\qquad\qquad\quad v \quad = \quad abs\ y \\
&\qquad\qquad\qquad\quad d \quad = \quad gcd\ (u, v)
\end{aligned}
$$

We will build rational numbers only through the use of *mkRat*, thereby guaranteeing all rational numbers are in canonical form.

The type *Rational* is declared as a new type rather than simply a type synonym for (*Integer*, *Integer*) because the equality and comparison operations on *Rational* are different from the corresponding operations on pairs. For example, $(2, 1) < (3, 2)$ on pairs, but as rationals we want $2 > 3/2$. Accordingly, we define

> **instance** *Eq Rational* **where**
> $Rat\ x\ y\ == Rat\ u\ v \quad = \quad (x \times v) == (v \times y)$

> **instance** *Ord Rational* **where**
> $Rat\ x\ y < Rat\ u\ v \quad = \quad (x \times v) < (y \times u)$

The definition of $(<)$ is correct only if both $Rat\ x\ y$ and $Rat\ u\ v$ are in canonical form.

We can show a rational number by defining a special function *showRat*:

> $showRat\ (Rat\ x\ y)$
> $\quad = \quad$ **if** $y == 1$ **then** *show* x **else** *show* $x\ +\!\!+\ $ "/" $+\!\!+\ $ *show* y

This definition makes use of the primitive *show* function for the type *Integer*, and also the operator $+\!\!+$ for concatenating two strings (discussed in the following chapter). Provided its argument is a rational in canonical form, *showRat* prints a sensible result.

The problem with *showRat* is that it does not declare *Rational* as a member of the type class *Show*. Such a declaration is needed if we want to install *Rational* as a proper number type. One can use the default definition by including a deriving clause in the declaration of *Rational*, but the result is a function *show* that is different from *showRat*. This point aside, we can declare *Rational* to be a member of *Num* by declaring

instance *Num Rational* **where**

$$Rat\ x\ y + Rat\ u\ v\ =\ mkRat\ (x \times v + u \times y, y \times v)$$
$$Rat\ x\ y - Rat\ u\ v\ =\ mkRat\ (x \times v - u \times y, y \times v)$$
$$Rat\ x\ y \times Rat\ u\ v\ =\ mkRat\ (x \times u, y \times v)$$
$$negate\ (Rat\ x\ y)\ =\ mkRat\ (-x, y)$$
$$fromInteger\ x\ =\ mkRat\ (x, 1)$$

It remains to define *gcd*. There are two slightly different ways that the function *gcd* can be specified. One is to say that *gcd* (x, y) is the largest positive integer *d* that divides both *x* and *y*. The other way is to say that *gcd* (x, y) = *d* if and only if (i) *d* divides both *x* and *y*; and (ii) for all *e*, if *e* divides both *x* and *y*, then *e* divides *d*. Under the first specification we have *gcd* $(0, 0)$ = $\perp$ because every positive integer divides 0, so there is no largest one; under the second specification we have *gcd* $(0, 0)$ = 0. Apart from this one case, the two definitions are equivalent. With the second specification, *gcd* can be computed recursively by Euclid's algorithm:

$$gcd\ \ ::\ \ (Integer, Integer) \to Integer$$
$$gcd\ (x, y)\ =\ \textbf{if}\ y = 0\ \textbf{then}\ x\ \textbf{else}\ gcd\ (y, x\ \textbf{mod}\ y)$$

For example, since $0 \bmod 3 = 0$, $(-6) \bmod 4 = 2$, and $(-3) \bmod 1 = 0$, we obtain

$$gcd\ (0, 3) = gcd\ (3, 0) = 3$$
$$gcd\ (-6, 4) = gcd\ (4, 2) = gcd\ (2, 0) = 2$$
$$gcd\ (-3, 1) = gcd\ (1, 0) = 1$$

Finally, we can declare *Rational* as an instance of the type class *Fractional* by

instance *Fractional Rational* **where**
$$fromRational\ =\ id$$

$$Rat\ x\ y / Rat\ u\ v$$
$$\left| \begin{array}{lll} u < 0 & = & mkRat\ (-x \times v, -y \times u) \\ u == 0 & = & error\ \text{“division by 0”} \\ u > 0 & = & mkRat\ (x \times v, y \times u) \end{array} \right.$$

Exercises

3.5.1 Using the fact that for positive integers *x* and *y*, if *x* divides *y* and *y* divides *x*, then *x* = *y*, prove that each rational number has a unique representation

(x, y) with $y > 0$ and $gcd\,(x, y) = 1$.

3.5.2 An integer x can be represented by a pair of integers (y, z) with $x = 10 \times y + z$. For example, 27 can be represented by $(2, 7)$, $(3, -3)$, and $(1, 17)$, among others. Among possible representations we can choose one in which $abs\,z < 5$ and $abs\,y$ is as small as possible (subject to $abs\,z < 5$). Show that each integer has a unique representation of this form, and define a function *repint* so that *repint x* returns this canonical representation.

3.6 Example: linear and binary search

The function $\lfloor - \rfloor$, taking an arbitrary real number and returning an integer, is more primitive than **div**, but it cannot be implemented in Haskell which can represent only limited-precision real numbers. Nevertheless, it is instructive to see how *floor* :: *Float* → *Integer* can be programmed. The problem isn't as simple as one might think, so we will develop a program in a systematic manner. In fact, we will develop two programs, one much more efficient than the other. The two strategies behind the two programs are called *linear* and *binary* search. The section ends with a second application of searching to the problem of computing square roots.

Let us begin with the specification:

$$floor \qquad :: \quad Float \to Integer$$
$$floor\ x = n \quad \equiv \quad n \le x < n + 1$$

Thinking about what shape the program for *floor* might take, it is tempting to plunge immediately into a case analysis, considering what to do if x is positive, what to do if it is negative, and, possibly, what to do if it is zero. But the specification does not mention cases and, since programs that avoid case analyses are clearer and simpler than those that do, we should try not to mention cases either.

We will have to search for n, and the specification suggests at least one way that the search might be conducted: we can search for an n satisfying $n \le x$ and then increase n until the condition $x < n + 1$ also holds. Dually, of course, we could first search for an n such that $x < n + 1$ and then decrease n until the condition $n \le x$ hold as well. The idea of searching until some condition holds can be encapsulated in a function *until*, defined by

$$until \qquad :: \quad (\alpha \to Bool) \to (\alpha \to \alpha) \to \alpha \to \alpha$$
$$until\ p\ f\ x \quad = \quad \textbf{if}\ p\ x\ \textbf{then}\ x\ \textbf{else}\ until\ p\ f\ (f\ x)$$

To search for an n satisfying $n \le x$, where x is some fixed number, we can begin with any integer we like, and then decrease it until the condition holds. For example, the search

$$lower \quad :: \quad Integer \rightarrow Integer$$
$$lower \quad = \quad until \ (\leq x) \ decrease, \quad \textbf{where} \ decrease \ n = n - 1$$

applied to any starting value will do the job. The search will terminate because for every real number x there is an integer n with $n \leq x$.

The integer n found by the first search may be far too small, so we need a second search to increase n until the condition $x < n + 1$ is satisfied as well. We need to increase n in steps of 1 to ensure that the condition $n \leq x$ is maintained. The second search can be written in two ways, either as

$$until \ (> (x - 1)) \ increase \quad \textbf{where} \ increase \ n = n + 1$$

or as $decrease \cdot upper$, where

$$upper \quad = \quad until \ (> x) \ increase \quad \textbf{where} \ increase \ n = n + 1$$

In the second solution, $upper$ is dual to $lower$. The function $decrease \cdot upper$ will be applied to the result of the first search. The complete program can now be expressed as

$$floor \quad :: \quad Float \rightarrow Integer$$
$$floor \ x \quad = \quad searchFrom \ 0$$
$$\textbf{where} \ searchFrom \quad = \quad decrease \cdot upper \cdot lower$$
$$lower \quad = \quad until \ (\leq x) \ decrease$$
$$upper \quad = \quad until \ (> x) \ increase$$
$$decrease \ n \quad = \quad n - 1$$
$$increase \ n \quad = \quad n + 1$$

An attempt has been made to make this program as clear as possible. The names $searchFrom$, $increase$ (rather than the equivalent $succ$), and $decrease$ (rather than $pred$) have been chosen to bring out the contributions of the associated parts of the definition, and the functions $lower$ and $upper$ have been defined to be as dual to each other as possible. Finally, the various subsidiary functions have been made local to the main definition. The program is surprisingly short, owing mainly to the absence of a case analysis on the sign of x. It is easy to see how the two cases are treated: if $0 \leq x$, then the first loop terminates at once, and the second loop does the real work; while if $x < 0$ it is the other way around.

The above program is not very efficient, since it takes about $abs \ x$ steps to find the answer. A better method is first to find two integers m and n such that

$m \leq x < n$, and then to bring m and n closer together, so that eventually the condition $m + 1 = n$ also holds. The advantage of decoupling the two searches is that we can make use of larger steps. More precisely, consider the pair of searches

$$
\begin{aligned}
lower &= until\ (\leq x)\ double \\
upper &= until\ (> x)\ double
\end{aligned}
$$

where $double\ n = 2 \times n$. Provided *lower* is applied to a negative number, and *upper* is applied to a positive one, the two searches are guaranteed to find a pair (m, n) with $m \leq x < n$ in a number of steps proportional to $\log_2 (abs\ x)$. These two searches have to be supplemented with a third search that brings the pair (m, n) closer together until $m + 1 = n$. We can choose either to increment m in steps of 1, or similarly decrement n in steps of 1. But we can do better. Consider the integer $p = (m + n)$ **div** 2 that is halfway between m and n. More precisely, if $m + 1 < n$, then $m < p < n$. If $p \leq x$, then we can increase m to the value p; dually, if $x < p$, then we can decrease n to p. The result is the new program

$$
\begin{aligned}
floor\ x \\
&=\ searchFrom\ (-1, 1) \\
&\quad \textbf{where}\ searchFrom && =\ fst \cdot middle \cdot cross\ (lower, upper) \\
&\quad\quad\ lower && =\ until\ (\leq x)\ double \\
&\quad\quad\ upper && =\ until\ (> x)\ double \\
&\quad\quad\ middle && =\ until\ done\ improve \\
&\quad\quad\ done\ (m, n) && =\ (m + 1 = n) \\
&\quad\quad\ improve\ (m, n) && =\ \textbf{if}\ p \leq x\ \textbf{then}\ (p, n)\ \textbf{else}\ (m, p) \\
&\quad\quad && \quad\ \textbf{where}\ p = (m + n)\ \textbf{div}\ 2
\end{aligned}
$$

The function *cross* was defined in Section 2.4. The new program takes a number of steps proportional to $\log_2 (abs\ x)$. For example, with $x = 17.3$, we get $lower\ (-1) = -1$ and $upper\ 1 = 32$. The third search produces the intermediate values

$$(-1, 32) \rightarrow (15, 32) \rightarrow (15, 23) \rightarrow (15, 19) \rightarrow (17, 19) \rightarrow (17, 18)$$

and returns 17. With $x = -17.3$, we get $lower\ (-1) = -32$ and $upper\ 1 = 1$. The third search produces the intermediate values

$$(-32, 1),\ (-32, -16),\ (-24, -16),\ (-20, -16),\ (-18, -16),\ (-18, -17)$$

and returns -18. The strategy behind this program is called *binary search*. Rather than bring two integers together in steps of 1, while maintaining a certain relationship between them, it is sometimes possible to cut the gap to half the size.

3.6.1 Example: computing square roots

Let us give a second example of searching. Our aim is to construct a definition of the function *sqrt* for computing the (nonnegative) square root of a nonnegative number. The mathematical specification of *sqrt* is that

$$sqrt\ x \geq 0 \quad \text{and} \quad square\ (sqrt\ x) = x,$$

whenever $x \geq 0$. The specification is rather strong in that it does not make allowances for the limited precision of arithmetic operations on actual computers. For example, it requires that

$$sqrt\ 2 = 1.4142135623\ldots$$

be computed exactly. As we will see in Chapters 4 and 9, it is quite possible to design a function that returns an infinite list of digits, though the process of printing this list will never terminate. The programmer can then show that *sqrt* meets its specification by proving that the list of digits, if continued for long enough, will approximate the answer to any required degree of accuracy. However, for the purposes of the present example we will weaken the specification to require only that *sqrt :: Float → Float* should satisfy

$$sqrt\ x \geq 0 \quad \text{and} \quad abs\ (square\ (sqrt\ x) - x) < eps$$

for a suitably small number $eps > 0$.

To illustrate the revised specification, suppose we take $eps = 0.0001$ and $x = 2$. We require:

$$abs\ (square\ (sqrt\ 2) - 2) < 0.0001$$

and since

$$
\begin{aligned}
1.4141 \times 1.4141 &= 1.99967881 \\
1.4142 \times 1.4142 &= 1.99996164 \\
1.4143 \times 1.4143 &= 2.00024449
\end{aligned}
$$

the value *sqrt* 2 = 1.4142 is an acceptable answer.

In order to construct *sqrt* we will use Newton's method for finding the roots of a given function. This is an iterative method that repeatedly improves approximations to the answer until the required degree of accuracy is achieved. In the case of square roots, Newton's method says that if y_n is an approximation to $\sqrt{x}$, then

$$y_{n+1} = (y_n + x/y_n)/2$$

is a better approximation. For example, taking $x = 2$ and $y_0 = x$, we have

$$
\begin{array}{lllll}
y_0 & & & = & 2 \\
y_1 & = & (2 + 2/2)/2 & = & 1.5 \\
y_2 & = & (1.5 + 2/1.5)/2 & = & 1.4167 \\
y_3 & = & (1.4167 + 2/1.4167) & = & 1.4142157
\end{array}
$$

and so on. By iterating this process we can determine $\sqrt{2}$ to any required degree of accuracy, subject to the limitations of computer arithmetic.

Using the search function *until* introduced above, we can implement *sqrt* with the program

```
sqrt    ::  Float → Float
sqrt x  =   until done improve x
            where done y    =   abs (y × y − x) < eps
                  improve y =   (y + x/y)/2
```

Exercises

3.6.1 Justify the claim that the second program for *floor x* takes $2 \log_2 (abs\, x)$ steps.

3.6.2 Let $p = (m + n)$ **div** 2. Show that $m < p < n$ provided $m + 1 < n$. What happens if $m + 1 = n$?

3.6.3 In Newton's method, the test for determining whether an approximation y to $\sqrt{x}$ is good enough was taken to be $abs (y × y − x) < eps$. Another test is

$$abs (y × y − x) < eps × x$$

Rewrite the *sqrt* function to use this test.

3.6.4 Yet another test for convergence is to stop when two successive approximations y and y' are sufficiently close:

$$abs (y − y') < eps × abs\, y$$

Rewrite the definition of *sqrt* to use this new test. Give reasons why these new tests are likely to be superior in practice.

3.7 Church numbers

We end this chapter on numbers with an exercise in theoretical fancy; the material is not used anywhere else and can safely be omitted by those wishing to pursue more practical programming topics.

We have seen that it is not necessary to assume that numbers are built-in, because we can always introduce them through datatype declarations. Now we will see that datatypes are not necessary either: everything can be done with functions alone! In fact, one can get away with functions as the sole primitive mathematical entity; once we understand functions, we understand everything. This was part of the programme that Alonzo Church set himself in the 1940s when he was working on the λ-calculus, the formal mathematical system that underpins much of today's research on functional programming.

Let us begin, not with numbers, but with *Bool*. What are the truth values actually for? Basically, one might answer, they are there to make decisions, to help us choose between two alternatives. We can capture this impression by defining them as functions:

$$
\begin{array}{lll}
\textit{true, false} & :: & \alpha \to \alpha \to \alpha \\
\textit{true}\, x\, y & = & x \\
\textit{false}\, x\, y & = & y
\end{array}
$$

The function *true* chooses the first alternative; the function *false* chooses the second. Thus, Church booleans are a synonym for a certain kind of function type:

type *Cbool* α $=$ $\alpha \to \alpha \to \alpha$

The definition of negation with Church booleans is

$$
\begin{array}{lll}
\textit{not} & :: & \textit{Cbool}\,(\textit{Cbool}\,\alpha) \to \textit{Cbool}\,\alpha \\
\textit{not}\, x & = & x\,\textit{false}\,\textit{true}
\end{array}
$$

Similarly, conjunction and disjunction with Church booleans are defined by

$$
\begin{array}{lll}
\textit{and, or} & :: & \textit{Cbool}\,(\textit{Cbool}\,\alpha) \to \textit{Cbool}\,\alpha \to \textit{Cbool}\,\alpha \\
\textit{and}\, x\, y & = & x\, y\, \textit{false} \\
\textit{or}\, x\, y & = & x\, \textit{true}\, y
\end{array}
$$

In each case, the Church boolean x selects appropriate alternatives. This function takes Church booleans as arguments, which explains the type signatures of *not*, *and*, and *or*.

In a similar spirit, one can ask the question: what are the natural numbers actually for? The answer, one might say, is for counting things, for controlling the number of times that something is done. Again, we can capture this impression by defining the natural numbers as functions:

$$
\begin{array}{lll}
\textit{zero, one, two} & :: & (\alpha \to \alpha) \to \alpha \to \alpha \\
\textit{zero } f & = & \textit{id} \\
\textit{one } f & = & f \\
\textit{two } f & = & f \cdot f
\end{array}
$$

and so on. The function *zero f* applies *f* no times to its argument, the function *one f* applies *f* once, and so on. Thus, Church numbers are a synonym type too:

$$
\textbf{type } \textit{Cnum } \alpha \;\; = \;\; (\alpha \to \alpha) \to (\alpha \to \alpha)
$$

Instead of having to write down each number explicitly, we can make use of the successor function, defined by

$$
\begin{array}{lll}
\textit{succ} & :: & \textit{Cnum } \alpha \to \textit{Cnum } \alpha \\
\textit{succ cn } f & = & f \cdot \textit{cn } f
\end{array}
$$

In words, *succ cn f* applies *f* first *cn* times, and then once more.

Here is a program that turns natural numbers into Church numbers and back again:

$$
\begin{array}{lll}
\textit{church} & :: & \textit{Int} \to \textit{Cnum Int} \\
\textit{church} & = & \textit{foldn succ zero} \\
\\
\textit{natural} & :: & \textit{Cnum Int} \to \textit{Int} \\
\textit{natural cn} & = & \textit{cn } (+1)\, 0
\end{array}
$$

The function *foldn* was defined for *Nat* in Section 3.3. The value *natural cn* is computed by using *cn* to apply the function $(+1)$ exactly *cn* times to the number 0. Note the types of *church* and *natural*. The source type of *natural* is required to be *Cnum Int* because its argument is applied to an *Int* → *Int* function on the right-hand side. The target type of *church* is chosen to be the same to ensure that *church* and *natural* are each other's inverse.

We can also do arithmetic with Church numbers. In fact, there is more than one way to implement the basic arithmetic operations, though not all of them can be assigned the type *Cnum* $\alpha \to$ *Cnum* $\alpha \to$ *Cnum* α.

One legitimate definition of *plus* is

$$plus1 \quad :: \quad Cnum\, \alpha \rightarrow Cnum\, \alpha \rightarrow Cnum\, \alpha$$
$$plus1\, cn\, dn\, f \quad = \quad cn\, f \cdot dn\, f$$

This defines *plus1 cn dn* to be the result of doing *f* first *dn* times, and then doing it *cn* times more. An even briefer definition of *plus* is to write

$$plus2 \quad :: \quad Cnum\, (Cnum\, \alpha) \rightarrow Cnum\, \alpha \rightarrow Cnum\, \alpha$$
$$plus2\, cn \quad = \quad cn\, succ$$

The function *plus2 cn dn* applies *succ* exactly *cn* times to *dn*. The first argument of *plus2* is a Church number that takes *succ* :: $Cnum\, \alpha \rightarrow Cnum\, \alpha$ as argument. This explains the change in type.

Multiplication can also be given a brief definition:

$$times1 \quad :: \quad Cnum\, \alpha \rightarrow Cnum\, \alpha \rightarrow Cnum\, \alpha$$
$$times1\, cn\, dn \quad = \quad cn \cdot dn$$

The function *times1 cn dn f* applies *dn f* exactly *cn* times. An alternative definition is

$$times2 \quad :: \quad Cnum\, (Cnum\, \alpha) \rightarrow Cnum\, \alpha \rightarrow Cnum\, (\alpha \rightarrow \alpha)$$
$$times2\, cn \quad = \quad cn \cdot plus1$$

The function *times2 cn dn* applies *plus1 dn* exactly *cn* times. We can replace *plus1* by *plus2* in the definition of *times2* to obtain a third version of multiplication. The type signatures of these functions are getting complicated, and we will not attempt to justify them. In fact, they were deduced with the help of the Haskell type inference system.

Finally, one version of exponentiation is

$$arrow1\, cn \quad = \quad cn \cdot times1$$

There is a switch of arguments here: the expression *arrow1 m n* means n^m. The function *arrow1 cn dn* applies *times1 dn* exactly *cn* times. An even briefer definition is

$$arrow2\, cn\, dn \quad = \quad cn\, dn$$

We leave it as an exercise to explain why this version works.

Exercises

3.7.1 Write a definition of *isZero* :: $Cnum\, \alpha \rightarrow CBool\, \alpha$ that determines whether its argument is *zero* or not.

3.7.2 Consider the definition $arrow2\, m\, n = m\, n$. Why does this give the Church number for n^m? What is the type of $arrow2$?

3.7.3 Use a computer to discover the type of $arrow1$.

3.7.4 Define a Church version of *Either $\alpha\,\beta$*.

3.8   Chapter notes

A full discussion of computer arithmetic can be found in Knuth (1981). Linear and binary search are fundamental programming techniques and are covered in Morgan (1996) and Kaldewaij (1990).   The properties of floors, as well as many other useful numerical functions, are given in Graham, Knuth, and Pata- shnik (1990). Church numerals are presented in Church (1941) and discussed in Gordon (1994).

Chapter 4

Lists

The datatype of lists is the workhorse of functional programming. Lists can be used to fetch and carry data from one function to another; they can be taken apart, rearranged, and combined with other lists; lists of numbers can be summed and multiplied; lists of characters can be read and printed; and so on. The list of useful operations on lists is a long one. The purpose of this chapter is to introduce the more important functions on lists, giving their names and definitions, simple examples of how they are used, and the properties they satisfy. We also describe the principle of induction over lists for proving such properties. More extended programming examples in the use of lists are given in Chapter 5; this material is arranged so that it can be studied in parallel with the present chapter.

4.1 List notation

A finite list is denoted using square brackets and commas. For example, $[1, 2, 3]$ is a list of three numbers and ["hallo", "goodbye"] is a list of two strings. All the elements of a list must have the same type. The empty list is written as [ ] and a singleton list, containing just one element x, is written as $[x]$. In particular, [[ ]] is a singleton list, containing the empty list as its only member.

If the elements of a list all have type α, then the list itself will be assigned the type $[\alpha]$ (pronounced 'list of α'). For example, all of the following are valid type assignments:

$$
\begin{aligned}
[1, 2, 3] &:: [Int] \\
['h', 'a', 'l', 'l', 'o'] &:: [Char] \\
[[1, 2], [3]] &:: [[Int]] \\
[(+), (\times)] &:: [Int \to Int \to Int]
\end{aligned}
$$

On the other hand, [1, "fine day"] is not a well-formed list because its elements have different types. Strings, introduced in Chapter 2, are simply lists of characters written with a special syntax. Thus, "hallo" is just a convenient additional syntax for the particular list ['h', 'a', 'l', 'l', 'o']. Every generic operation on lists is therefore also applicable to strings.

Unlike a set, a list may contain the same value more than once. For example, [1, 1] is a list of two elements, both of which happen to be 1, and is distinct from the list [1], which contains only one element. Two lists are equal if and only if they contain the same values in the same order.

4.1.1   Lists as a datatype

A list can be constructed from scratch by starting with the empty list and successively adding elements one by one. One can add elements to the front of the list, or to the rear, or to somewhere in the middle. In the following datatype declaration, nonempty lists are constructed by adding elements to the front of a list:

data *List* α =   *Nil* | *Cons* α (*List* α)

For another view of lists, see Exercise 4.1.4. The constructor *Cons* (short for 'construct' – the name goes back to the programming language LISP) adds an element to the front of a list. For example, the list [1, 2, 3] would be represented as the following element of *List Int*:

Cons 1 (*Cons* 2 (*Cons* 3 *Nil*))

In functional programming, lists are defined as elements of *List* α. The syntax [α] is used instead of *List* α, the constructor *Nil* is written as [ ], and the constructor *Cons* is written as an infix operator (:). Moreover, (:) associates to the right, so

$$[1, 2, 3]   =   1 : (2 : (3 : [\,])) = 1 : 2 : 3 : [\,]$$

In other words, the special syntax on the left can be regarded as an abbreviation for the syntax on the right, which is also special but only by virtue of the fact that the constructors are given nonstandard names.

Like functions over other datatypes, functions over lists can be defined by pattern matching. For example, the following class instance declaration defines

(==) over lists:

```
instance (Eq α) ⇒ Eq [α] where
  [ ] == [ ]              =  True
  [ ] == (y : ys)        =  False
  (x : xs) == [ ]        =  False
  (x : xs) == (y : ys)   =  (x == y) ∧ (xs == ys)
```

Notice the names given to list variables. By convention, we will use the letters x, y, z, and so on, to denote elements of lists, and the names xs, ys, zs, and so on, to denote the lists themselves. The convention can be extended, writing xss, yss, zss, and so on, to describe lists whose elements are themselves lists. This convention is not enforced by Haskell, but is simply a useful aid to comprehension.

It seems obvious that if one wants to test elements of $[\alpha]$ for equality, then one needs an equality test on α. But there is one case where this is not true: testing equality with the empty list. The function *null*, defined by

```
null             ::  [α] → Bool
null [ ]         =  True
null (x : xs)    =  False
```

does not require α to be an equality type; see Exercise 4.1.3.

4.1.2 Induction over lists

Recall from Section 3.2 that, for the datatype *Nat* of natural numbers, structural induction is based on three cases: every element of *Nat* is either ⊥, or *Zero*, or else has the form *Succ n* for some element n of *Nat*. Similarly, structural induction on lists is also based on three cases: every list is either the undefined list ⊥, the empty list [ ], or else has the form $(x : xs)$ for some x and list xs. To show by induction that a proposition $P(xs)$ holds for all lists xs it suffices therefore to establish three cases:

Case (⊥). That $P(⊥)$ holds.

Case ([ ]). That $P([\,])$ holds.

Case $(x : xs)$. That if $P(xs)$ holds, then $P(x : xs)$ also holds for every x.

If we prove only the second two cases, then we can conclude only that $P(xs)$ holds for every finite list; if we prove only the first and third cases, then we can conclude only that $P(xs)$ holds for every partial list. If P takes the form of an equation, as all of our laws do, then proving the first and third cases is sufficient to show that $P(xs)$ holds for every infinite list. Partial lists and infinite lists are described in the following section. Examples of induction proofs are given throughout the remainder of the chapter.

Exercises

4.1.1 Give an example of an expression that contains two occurrences of the empty list, the first occurrence having type [*Bool*] and the second having type [*Char*].

4.1.2 Complete the following instance declaration:

> **instance** (*Ord* α) $\Rightarrow$ *Ord* [α] **where**
>
>   . . .

Recall from Chapter 2 that, for the particular type [*Char*], the ordering on strings is lexicographic. The general definition of $\leq$ on lists should be lexicographic too.

4.1.3 Consider the following two definitions of the function *last* that returns the last element of a nonempty list:

> *last* ($x : xs$)   =   **if** *null xs* **then** x **else** *last xs*
> *last'* ($x : xs$)   =   **if** xs == [ ] **then** x **else** *last' xs*

The difference between *last* and *last'* is that they have slightly different types:

> *last*   ::   [α] $\rightarrow \alpha$
> *last'*   ::   (*Eq* α) $\Rightarrow$ [α] $\rightarrow \alpha$

Since the definition of *last'* involves an explicit equality test, its type is restricted to lists whose elements are drawn from an equality type. Give an expression e such that the evaluator responds differently to *last e* and *last' e*.

4.1.4 The dual view of lists is to construct them by adding elements to the end of the list:

> **data** *Liste* α =   *Nil* | *Snoc* (*Liste* α) α

Snoc, of course, is just *Cons* backwards. With this view of lists, [1, 2, 3] would be represented as an element of *Liste Int* by

> *Snoc* (*Snoc* (*Snoc Nil* 1) 2) 3

Exactly the same information is provided by the two views, but it is organised differently. For example, the function *head*, which returns the first element of a nonempty list, is easy to define with the datatype $[\alpha]$, but more complicated with *Liste* α. Give the definitions of *head* for the two types. Give a function

$$convert \quad :: \quad Liste\ \alpha \rightarrow [\alpha]$$

for converting from one datatype to the other.

4.2 List operations

This section introduces some of the most commonly used functions and operations on lists. For each function we will give the definition, illustrate its use, and state some of its properties. We will also appeal to structural induction over lists to prove these properties.

4.2.1 Concatenation

Two lists can be concatenated to form one longer list. This function is denoted by the binary operator + (pronounced 'concatenate'). As two simple examples, we have

? $[1, 2, 3] + [4, 5]$
$[1, 2, 3, 4, 5]$

? $[1, 2] + [\ ] + [1]$
$[1, 2, 1]$

The formal definition of + is

$$
\begin{array}{lll}
(+) & :: & [\alpha] \rightarrow [\alpha] \rightarrow [\alpha] \\
[\ ] + ys & = & ys \\
(x : xs) + ys & = & x : (xs + ys)
\end{array}
$$

Concatenation takes two lists, both of the same type, and produces a third list, again of the same type. Hence the type assignment. The definition of + is by pattern matching on the left-hand argument; the two patterns are disjoint and cover all cases, apart from the undefined list $\bot$. It follows by case exhaustion that $\bot + ys = \bot$.

However, it is not the case that $xs + \bot = \bot$. For example,

? $[1, 2, 3] + undefined$
$[1, 2, 3\{Interrupted!\}$

The list $[1, 2, 3] +\!\!\!+ \perp$ is a *partial* list; in full form it is the list $1 : 2 : 3 : \perp$. The evaluator can compute the first three elements, but thereafter it goes into a nonterminating computation, so we interrupt it.

The second equation for $+\!\!\!+$ is very succinct and requires some thought. Once one has come to grips with the definition of $+\!\!\!+$, one has understood a good deal about how lists work in functional programming. Note that the number of steps required to compute $xs +\!\!\!+ ys$ is proportional to the number of elements in xs. For example,

$$[1, 2] +\!\!\!+ [3, 4, 5]$$

$= \quad$ {notation}

$$(1 : (2 : [\,])) +\!\!\!+ (3 : (4 : (5 : [\,])))$$

$= \quad$ {second equation for $+\!\!\!+$}

$$1 : ((2 : [\,]) +\!\!\!+ (3 : (4 : (5 : [\,]))))$$

$= \quad$ {second equation for $+\!\!\!+$}

$$1 : (2 : ([\,] +\!\!\!+ (3 : (4 : (5 : [\,])))))$$

$= \quad$ {first equation for $+\!\!\!+$}

$$1 : (2 : (3 : (4 : (5 : [\,]))))$$

$= \quad$ {notation}

$$[1, 2, 3, 4, 5]$$

Concatenation is an associative operation with unit $[\,]$:

$$
\begin{aligned}
(xs +\!\!\!+ ys) +\!\!\!+ zs &= xs +\!\!\!+ (ys +\!\!\!+ zs) \\
xs +\!\!\!+ [\,] &= [\,] +\!\!\!+ xs = xs
\end{aligned}
$$

Let us now use induction over lists to prove that $+\!\!\!+$ is associative.

Proof. The proof is by induction on xs.

Case ($\perp$). For the left-hand side we reason

$$(\perp +\!\!\!+ ys) +\!\!\!+ zs$$

$= \quad$ {case exhaustion}

$$\perp +\!\!\!+ zs$$

$= \quad$ {case exhaustion}

$$\perp$$

The right-hand side simplifies to $\perp$ as well, establishing the case.

Case ([ ]). For the left-hand side we reason

$$([\,] +\!\!+ ys) +\!\!+ zs$$

$=$ {first equation for $+\!\!+$}

$$ys +\!\!+ zs$$

The right-hand side simplifies to $ys +\!\!+ zs$ as well, establishing the case.

Case $(x : xs)$. For the left-hand side we reason

$$((x : xs) +\!\!+ ys) +\!\!+ zs$$

$=$ {second equation for $+\!\!+$}

$$(x : (xs +\!\!+ ys)) +\!\!+ zs$$

$=$ {second equation for $+\!\!+$}

$$x : ((xs +\!\!+ ys) +\!\!+ zs)$$

$=$ {induction hypothesis}

$$x : (xs +\!\!+ (ys +\!\!+ zs))$$

For the right-hand side we reason

$$(x : xs) +\!\!+ (ys +\!\!+ zs)$$

$=$ {second equation for $+\!\!+$}

$$x : (xs +\!\!+ (ys +\!\!+ zs))$$

The two sides are equal, establishing the case.

$\square$

The reader should consider why the induction in this proof is on xs rather than on ys or zs. Note that associativity is proved for *all* lists, finite, partial, or infinite. Hence we can assert that $+\!\!+$ is associative without qualification. The reader should compare the proof above with a similar proof that $+$ is an associative operation on the type *Nat* of the previous chapter.

Let us now prove a result that is true for partial and infinite lists, but not for finite lists. The claim is that $xs +\!\!+ ys = xs$ for all partial lists xs. The assertion is an equation, so it also holds for all infinite lists xs.

Proof. The proof of the claim $xs +\!\!+ ys = xs$ is by partial induction on xs.

Case ($\perp$). Immediate by case exhaustion with $+\!+$.

Case ($x : xs$). We reason

$$(x : xs) +\!+ ys$$

$=$ {second equation for $+\!+$}

$$x : (xs +\!+ ys)$$

$=$ {induction hypothesis}

$$x : xs$$

$\square$

The reader should compare this claim with a similar one in the previous chapter that $m + n = n$ for all partial elements n of *Nat*.

To illustrate the result, consider the function *from* that returns an infinite list of integers:

$$from \quad :: \quad (Integral\ \alpha) \Rightarrow \alpha \to [\alpha]$$
$$from\ n \quad = \quad n : from\ (n + 1)$$

Evaluation of *from n* will not terminate, so

? *from* 0
$[0, 1, 2, 3, 4, 5, 6, 7, \{Interrupted!\}$

Now consider

? *from* 0 $+\!+$ [0]
$[0, 1, 2, 3, 4, 5, 6, 7, \{Interrupted!\}$

Both evaluations, if continued for long enough, will produce only the elements of the infinite list $[0, 1, \ldots]$, which is exactly what the result predicts.

4.2.2 Concat

Concatenation performs much the same function for lists as the union operator $\cup$ does for sets. A companion function is *concat*, which concatenates a list of lists into one long list. This function, which roughly corresponds to the big-union operator $\bigcup$ for sets of sets, is defined by

$$concat \quad :: \quad [[\alpha]] \to [\alpha]$$
$$concat\ [\,] \quad = \quad [\,]$$
$$concat\ (xs : xss) \quad = \quad xs +\!+ concat\ xss$$

For example:

? concat $[[1,2],[\,],[3,2,1]]$
$[1,2,3,2,1]$

? putStr (*concat* ["We", "␣", "like", "␣", "lists."])
We like lists.

A basic property of *concat* is that

$$concat\ (xss + yss)\quad =\quad concat\ xss + concat\ yss$$

for all lists *xss* and *yss*. This property can be proved by induction on *xss* and is left as an exercise.

4.2.3 Reverse

Another basic function on lists is *reverse*, the function that reverses the order of elements in a finite list. For example:

? reverse "Madam, I'm Adam."
".madA m'I ,madaM"

The definition is

$$
\begin{aligned}
reverse &\quad::\quad [\alpha] \to [\alpha]\\
reverse\ [\,] &\quad=\quad [\,]\\
reverse\ (x:xs) &\quad=\quad reverse\ xs + [x]
\end{aligned}
$$

In words, to reverse a list $(x:xs)$ one reverses *xs* and then adds *x* to the end. As a program, the above definition is not very efficient: on a list of length *n* it will need a number of reduction steps proportional to n^2 to deliver the reversed list. The first element will be appended to the end of a list of length $(n-1)$, which will take about $(n-1)$ steps, the second element will be appended to a list of length $(n-2)$, taking $(n-2)$ steps, and so on. The total time is therefore about

$$(n-1) + (n-2) + \cdots 1 = n(n-1)/2\ \text{steps}$$

A more precise analysis is given in Chapter 7, and a more efficient program for *reverse* is given in Section 4.5.

Let us now prove by induction that

$$reverse\ (reverse\ xs)\quad =\quad xs$$

for all finite lists *xs*. The proof is instructive because it requires an auxiliary result. Rather than give the auxiliary result first, we will start the induction proof and see what is needed to complete it.

Proof. The proof is by induction on *xs*.

Case ([ ]). For the left-hand side we reason

$$reverse\,(reverse\,[\,])$$

= {first equation for *reverse*}

$$reverse\,[\,]$$

= {first equation for *reverse*}

$$[\,]$$

The result is the right-hand side.

Case (*x* : *xs*). For the left-hand side we reason

$$reverse\,(reverse\,(x : xs))$$

= {second equation for *reverse*}

$$reverse\,(reverse\,xs \mathbin{+\!\!+} [x])$$

There is nothing more we can do to the left-hand side, so we turn to the right-hand side:

$$x : xs$$

= {induction hypothesis}

$$x : reverse\,(reverse\,xs)$$

The two sides have simplified to two different expressions. We are left with the task of showing that

$$reverse\,(reverse\,xs \mathbin{+\!\!+} [x]) \;=\; x : reverse\,(reverse\,xs)$$

for all finite lists *xs*. Trying to prove this result directly by induction does not work, as the reader may verify. Instead, we have to *generalise* the equation to read

$$reverse\,(ys \mathbin{+\!\!+} [x]) \;=\; x : reverse\,ys$$

for all finite lists *ys*. By taking the special case *ys = reverse xs*, and making use of the fact that *reverse xs* is a finite list if *xs* is, we can complete the proof of the main result.

To prove the auxiliary result we need a second induction argument. Here is the induction step:

Case (*y* : *ys*). For the left-hand side we reason

$$reverse\,((y : ys) \mathbin{+\!\!+} [x])$$

= {definition of $\mathbin{+\!\!+}$}

$$reverse\,(y : (ys \mathbin{+\!\!+} [x]))$$

= {second equation for *reverse*}

$$reverse\,(ys \mathbin{+\!\!+} [x]) \mathbin{+\!\!+} [y]$$

= {induction hypothesis}

$$(x : reverse\,ys) \mathbin{+\!\!+} [y]$$

= {definition of $\mathbin{+\!\!+}$}

$$x : (reverse\,ys \mathbin{+\!\!+} [y])$$

= {second equation for *reverse*}

$$x : reverse\,(y : ys)$$

The result is the right-hand side, establishing the case and the proof.

□

Since similar situations arise in many induction proofs, it is worth reiterating how the proof of the main result was achieved. First we simplified both sides of the equation in the inductive case, arriving at two different expressions. To prove that these two expressions were equal, we needed to resort to a second induction proof. However, before doing so, it was necessary to generalise the auxiliary result to something more manageable. One might expect that this would make the proof harder, but the reverse is the case. The induction hypothesis of the generalised equation, being stronger, can carry more weight from one side of the equation to the other.

4.2.4 Length

The length of a list is the number of elements it contains:

$$
\begin{aligned}
length & :: \quad [\alpha] \to Int \\
length\,[\,] & = \quad 0 \\
length\,(x:xs) & = \quad 1 + length\,xs
\end{aligned}
$$

The nature of the list elements is irrelevant when computing the length of a list, whence the type assignment. For example,

? length [undefined, undefined]
2

However, not every list has a well-defined length. In particular, the partial lists $\bot, x:\bot, x:y:\bot$, and so on, have an undefined length. Only finite lists have well-defined lengths. The list $[\bot, \bot]$ is a finite list, *not* a partial list because it is the list $\bot:\bot:[\,]$, which ends in $[\,]$ not $\bot$. The computer cannot produce the elements, but it can produce the length of the list.

Like *concat*, the function *length* satisfies a distribution property:

$$
length\,(xs \mathbin{+\!\!+} ys) \quad = \quad length\,xs + length\,ys
$$

The proof is left as an exercise.

4.2.5 Head and tail, init and last

The function *head* selects the first element of a nonempty list, and *tail* selects the rest:

for

$$
\left\{
\begin{aligned}
head & :: \quad [\alpha] \to \alpha \\
head\,(x:xs) & = \quad x \\[1ex]
tail & :: \quad [\alpha] \to [\alpha] \\
tail\,(x:xs) & = \quad xs
\end{aligned}
\right.
$$

These are constant-time operations, since they deliver their results in one reduction step.

The companion functions, *last* and *init*, which select the last element of a nonempty list and what remains after the last element has been removed, cannot be implemented so efficiently. One short definition of *last* is

4

$$
\left\{
\begin{aligned}
last & :: \quad [\alpha] \to \alpha \\
last & = \quad head \cdot reverse
\end{aligned}
\right.
$$

However, the analogous definition of *init*, namely

$$
1 \begin{cases} init & :: \quad [\alpha] \to [\alpha] \\ init & = \quad reverse \cdot tail \cdot reverse \end{cases}
$$

defines *init xs* $= \perp$ for all partial and infinite lists *xs* (see Exercise 4.2.6). A superior definition of these two functions is

$$
2 \begin{cases} last\ (x : xs) & = \quad \textbf{if } null\ xs \textbf{ then } x \textbf{ else } last\ xs \\ init\ (x : xs) & = \quad \textbf{if } null\ xs \textbf{ then } [\,] \textbf{ else } x : init\ xs \end{cases}
$$

With this definition, *init xs* = *xs* for all infinite lists *xs*.

Since $[x]$ is an abbreviation for $x : [\,]$, and can be used as a pattern on the left of definitions, one might be tempted to write the definitions of *last* and *init* in the form

$$
\begin{aligned}
last\ [x] & = \quad x \\
last\ (x : xs) & = \quad last\ xs \\[6pt]
init\ [x] & = \quad x \\
init\ (x : xs) & = \quad x : init\ xs
\end{aligned}
$$

However, there is a serious danger of confusion with these particular definitions. The patterns $[x]$ and $(x : xs)$ are *not* disjoint because the second includes the first as a special case. Although the definitions are valid in many languages, including Haskell, they depend on an understanding that patterns are matched 'top to bottom', that is, from the first equation downwards. If we had reversed the order of the equations, writing, say,

$$
\begin{aligned}
last'\ (x : xs) & = \quad last'\ xs \\
last'\ [x] & = \quad x
\end{aligned}
$$

then the definition of *last'* would simply be incorrect. In fact, *last' xs* $= \perp$ for all *xs*. It is not good practice to write definitions that depend critically on the order in which we put the equations.

The difficulties can be resolved with yet a third definition:

$$
\begin{aligned}
last\ [x] & = \quad x \\
last\ (x : y : ys) & = \quad last\ (y : ys)
\end{aligned}
$$

The first pattern $[x]$ matches only singleton lists, and the pattern $x : y : ys$ matches only lists that have at least two elements. Hence the two patterns cover disjoint cases and everything in the garden is fine.

4.2.6 Take and drop

The functions *take* and *drop* each take a nonnegative integer *n* and a list *xs* as arguments. The value *take n xs* consists of the first *n* elements of *xs*, and *drop n xs* is what remains. For example,

? *take* 3 "functional"
"fun"

? *take* 3 [1, 2]
[1, 2]

The definitions are

$$
\begin{array}{lcl}
take & :: & Int \rightarrow [\alpha] \rightarrow [\alpha] \\
take\ 0\ xs & = & [\ ] \\
take\ (n+1)\ [\ ] & = & [\ ] \\
take\ (n+1)\ (x:xs) & = & x:take\ n\ xs \\
\\
drop & :: & Int \rightarrow [\alpha] \rightarrow [\alpha] \\
drop\ 0\ xs & = & xs \\
drop\ (n+1)\ [\ ] & = & [\ ] \\
drop\ (n+1)\ (x:xs) & = & drop\ n\ xs
\end{array}
$$

These definitions use a combination of pattern matching with natural numbers and lists. Note that the patterns are disjoint and cover all possible cases: every natural number is either zero (first equation) or the successor of a natural number; in the latter case we distinguish between an empty list (second equation) and a nonempty list (third equation).

Since there are two arguments on which pattern matching is performed, it is important to know which argument gets matched first. As we have said, pattern matching is performed on the clauses of a definition in order from first to last. Within each clause, pattern matching is performed from left to right. Hence in *take* and *drop* the numeric pattern is matched first. In particular, *take* $0 \perp = [\ ]$ and *take* $\perp [\ ] = \perp$.

We could have written the definition of *take* in the form

$$
\begin{array}{lcl}
take'\ n\ [\ ] & = & [\ ] \\
take'\ 0\ (x:xs) & = & [\ ] \\
take'\ (n+1)\ (x:xs) & = & x:take'\ n\ xs
\end{array}
$$

However, the definition of *take'* is subtly different from that of *take*. This time, pattern matching with the first equation gives *take'* $\perp [\ ] = [\ ]$, and pattern matching with the second equation gives $take'\ 0\ \bot = \bot$.

The definition of *take'* is less satisfactory than that of *take* because the order in which the equations are written is significant. Suppose *take''* is defined by switching the first two equations for *take'*:

$$take''\ 0\ (x : xs) \quad = \quad [\ ]$$
$$take''\ n\ [\ ] \quad\quad\quad = \quad [\ ]$$
$$take''\ (n + 1)\ (x : xs) \quad = \quad x : take''\ n\ xs$$

We have $take''\ \bot\ [\ ] = \bot$ because of the numeric pattern in the first equation. Hence $take'' \neq take'$. But also $take'' \neq take$ because $take''\ 0\ \bot = \bot$.

The functions *take* and *drop* satisfy a number of useful laws, including the basic relationship

$$take\ n\ xs \mathbin{+\!\!+} drop\ n\ xs \quad = \quad xs$$

for all (finite) natural numbers n and all lists xs. The proof is instructive because it uses a combination of induction on the natural numbers and case analysis.

Proof. The proof is an induction on n with a case analysis on xs.

Case (0, xs). For the left-hand side we reason

$$take\ 0\ xs \mathbin{+\!\!+} drop\ 0\ xs$$

$$= \quad \{\text{first equations for } take \text{ and } drop\}$$

$$[\ ] \mathbin{+\!\!+} xs$$

$$= \quad \{\text{first equation for } \mathbin{+\!\!+}\}$$

$$xs$$

Case $(n + 1, \bot)$. For the left-hand side we reason

$$take\ (n + 1)\ \bot \mathbin{+\!\!+} drop\ (n + 1)\ \bot$$

$$= \quad \{\text{case exhaustion with } take \text{ and } drop\}$$

$$\bot \mathbin{+\!\!+} \bot$$

$$= \quad \{\text{case exhaustion with } \mathbin{+\!\!+}\}$$

$$\bot$$

Case $(n + 1, [\ ])$. For the left-hand side we reason

$$take\ (n + 1)\ [\ ] \mathbin{+\!\!+} drop\ (n + 1)\ [\ ]$$

$=$ {definition of *take* and *drop*}

[ ] ++ [ ]

$=$ {definition of ++}

[ ]

Case $(n + 1, x : xs)$. For the left-hand side we reason

$take \ (n + 1) \ (x : xs) \ ++ \ drop \ (n + 1) \ (x : xs)$

$=$ {definition of *take* and *drop*}

$(x : take \ n \ xs) \ ++ \ drop \ n \ xs$

$=$ {definition of ++}

$x : (take \ n \ xs \ ++ \ drop \ n \ xs)$

$=$ {induction hypothesis}

$x : xs$

$\square$

The proof is straightforward but there are two points of interest. First, the proof can be viewed as an induction argument on n with a case analysis on xs. The various cases match the patterns in the definition of *take* and *drop*; indeed, that is precisely why the patterns were chosen in the way they were. The proof of the additional case $(n + 1, \perp)$ is necessary if we want to assert that the equation holds without restriction on xs.

The second point to note is that the equation fails to hold in the case $n = \perp$ because

$take \perp xs \ ++ \ drop \perp xs \ \ = \ \ \perp \ ++ \ \perp \ \ = \ \ \perp, \ \ not \ xs$

In a similar fashion, one can prove a number of additional laws about *take* and *drop*, including

$$take \ m \cdot take \ n \ \ = \ \ take \ (m \ \mathbf{min} \ n)$$
$$drop \ m \cdot drop \ n \ \ = \ \ drop \ (m + n)$$
$$take \ m \cdot drop \ n \ \ = \ \ drop \ n \cdot take \ (m + n)$$

The expression $(m \ \mathbf{min} \ n)$ denotes the smaller of m and n.

In a number of situations the value $(take \ n \ xs, drop \ n \ xs)$ is required, and Haskell provides a standard function for computing it. The function *splitAt* is specified by

$$splitAt \quad :: \quad Int \rightarrow [\alpha] \rightarrow ([\alpha],[\alpha])$$
$$splitAt \, n \, xs \quad = \quad (take \, n \, xs, drop \, n \, xs)$$

However, *splitAt* is implemented by the equations

$$splitAt \, 0 \, xs \qquad\qquad = \quad ([\,],xs)$$
$$splitAt \, (n+1) \, [\,] \qquad = \quad ([\,],[\,])$$
$$splitAt \, (n+1) \, (x:xs) \quad = \quad (x:ys,zs)$$
$$\textbf{where} \, (ys,zs) = splitAt \, n \, xs$$

It is easy to derive the second version, and we leave details as an exercise. As we will see in Chapter 7, the alternative program is more efficient in the use of space because the argument list is traversed only once. The difference in time between the two versions is marginal.

4.2.7 List index

A list *xs* can be indexed by a natural number *n* to find the element appearing at position *n*. This operation is denoted by $xs \, !! \, n$. For example,

? $[1,2,3,4] \, !! \, 2$
3

? $[1,2,3,4] \, !! \, 0$
1

Indexing begins at 0, which for most purposes is a better choice than beginning at 1.

The operator (!!) is defined by

$$(!!) \qquad\qquad\qquad :: \quad [\alpha] \rightarrow Int \rightarrow \alpha$$
$$(x:xs) \, !! \, 0 \qquad\quad = \quad x$$
$$(x:xs) \, !! \, (n+1) \quad = \quad xs \, !! \, n$$

Indexing a list corresponds to the mathematical device of using subscripts and so seems a very natural and useful operation. However, indexing is a fairly expensive operation in functional programming, since $xs \, !! \, n$ takes a number of reduction steps proportional to *n*, and should be avoided whenever there is a suitable alternative. On the other hand, there are situations when indexing a list is appropriate and Section 5.1, which depends only on the material presented so far, contains one such example.

Exercises

4.2.1 Which of the following equations are true for all xs and which are false?

$$[\,]:xs \;=\; xs$$
$$[\,]:xs \;=\; [[\,],xs]$$
$$xs:[\,] \;=\; xs$$
$$xs:[\,] \;=\; [xs]$$
$$xs:xs \;=\; [xs,xs]$$

4.2.2 Which of the following equations are true for all xs and which are false?

$$[[\,]] \mathbin{+\!\!+} xs \;=\; xs$$
$$[[\,]] \mathbin{+\!\!+} xs \;=\; [xs]$$
$$[[\,]] \mathbin{+\!\!+} xs \;=\; [[\,],xs]$$
$$[[\,]] \mathbin{+\!\!+} [xs] \;=\; [[\,],xs]$$
$$[xs] \mathbin{+\!\!+} [\,] \;=\; [xs]$$
$$[xs] \mathbin{+\!\!+} [xs] \;=\; [xs,xs]$$

4.2.3 Prove by induction that $xs \mathbin{+\!\!+} [\,] = xs$ for all lists xs.

4.2.4 Prove that $concat\,(xss \mathbin{+\!\!+} yss) = concat\,xss \mathbin{+\!\!+} concat\,yss$.

4.2.5 Prove that $length\,(xs \mathbin{+\!\!+} ys) = length\,xs + length\,ys$.

4.2.6 Prove that $reverse\,xs = \bot$ for all infinite lists xs, and show that $init\,xs = \bot$ for all infinite lists xs, where $init = reverse \cdot tail \cdot reverse$.

4.2.7 Consider again the assertion $reverse\,(reverse\,xs) = xs$. Since

$$reverse\,(reverse\,\bot) = reverse\,\bot = \bot$$

it seems that the assertion is proved for all lists, not just the finite ones. But one cannot reverse an infinite list (see the previous exercise), so what has gone wrong?

4.2.8 Using pattern matching with $(:)$, define a function $rev2$ that reverses all lists of length 2, but leaves others unchanged. Ensure that the patterns are exhaustive and disjoint.

4.2.9 Give an informal characterisation of those finite lists xs and ys which satisfy $xs \mathbin{+\!\!+} ys = ys \mathbin{+\!\!+} xs$.

4.2.10 What is the value of $[head\,xs] \mathbin{+\!\!+} tail\,xs$ when $xs = [\,]$?

4.2.11 Is it the case that $(drop\,m\,xs)\,!!\,n = xs\,!!\,(m+n)$ for all finite lists xs and all natural numbers m and n?

4.2.12 Prove that

$$(xs \mathbin{+\!\!+} ys) \,!!\, k \quad = \quad \textbf{if } k < n \textbf{ then } xs \,!!\, k \textbf{ else } ys \,!!\, (k - n)$$
$$\textbf{where } n = length\, xs$$

4.2.13 Since concatenation seems such a basic operation on lists, we can try to construct a datatype that captures concatenation as primitive. For example,

> **data** *CatList* α $=$ *Nil* | *Wrap* α | *Cat* (*CatList* α) (*CatList* α)

The intention is that *Nil* represents [ ], and *Wrap x* represents [*x*], and *Cat xs ys* represents *xs* $\mathbin{+\!\!+}$ *ys*. However, since $\mathbin{+\!\!+}$ is an associative operation, the expressions

> *Cat xs* (*Cat ys zs*)   and   *Cat* (*Cat xs ys*) *zs*

should be regarded as equal. Define appropriate instances of *Eq* and *Ord* for *CatList*.

4.3 Map and filter

Two useful functions on lists are *map* and *filter*. The function *map* applies a function to each element of a list. For example,

? *map square* [9, 3]
[81, 9]

? *map* (< 3) [1, 2, 3]
[*True, True, False*]

? *map nextLetter* "HAL"
"IBM"

The definition is

> *map* $\quad$ :: $\quad (\alpha \to \beta) \to [\alpha] \to [\beta]$
> *map f* [ ] $\quad = \quad$ [ ]
> *map f* (*x* : *xs*) $\quad = \quad$ *f x* : *map f xs*

As another example, suppose we want to compute the sum of the squares of the integers from 1 up to 100. The functions *sum* and *upto* can be defined by

> *sum* $\quad$ :: $\quad (Num\, \alpha) \Rightarrow [\alpha] \to \alpha$
> *sum* [ ] $\quad = \quad$ 0
> *sum* (*x* : *xs*) $\quad = \quad$ *x* + *sum xs*

$$upto \quad :: \quad (Integral\ \alpha) \Rightarrow \alpha \rightarrow \alpha \rightarrow [\alpha]$$
$$upto\ m\ n \ = \ \textbf{if } m > n \textbf{ then } [\,] \textbf{ else } m : upto\ (m+1)\ n$$

Now we have

? *sum* (*map square* (*upto* 1 100))
338700

The use of *map* is neatly illustrated by the previous example: the English phrase 'the sum of the squares of the integers from 1 up to 100' can be translated virtually word for word into a simple formal expression.

The function *upto*, and the related function *from*, crop up frequently in computations, and Haskell provided a special and more convenient syntax. The forms [*m* .. *n*] and [*m* ..] are defined by

$$[m\,..\,n] \ = \ upto\ m\ n$$
$$[m\,..\,] \quad = \ from\ m$$

The special forms can be used with enumeration types other than *Int* or *Integer*, though we will not do so in this book.

There are a number of useful algebraic identities concerning *map*. Two basic facts are that

$$\begin{cases} map\ id & = & id \\ map\ (f \cdot g) & = & map\ f \cdot map\ g \end{cases}$$

The first equation says that applying the identity function to every element of a list leaves the list unchanged. The two occurrences of *id* in the first equation have different types; on the left *id* :: $\alpha \rightarrow \alpha$, and on the right *id* :: $[\alpha] \rightarrow [\alpha]$. The second equation says that applying *g* to every element of a list, and then applying *f* to each element of the result, gives the same result as applying *f* · *g* to the original list. Read from right to left, the equation says that two traversals of a list can be replaced by one, with a corresponding gain in efficiency. The proofs of both laws use induction over lists and are left as exercises. In category theory, functions like *map* that satisfy the two basic properties above are called *functors*, and we will use the word functor when referring to the two properties in calculations.

Here is a list of additional laws, all of which have a common theme:

$$\begin{cases} f \cdot head & = & head \cdot map\ f \\ map\ f \cdot tail & = & tail \cdot map\ f \\ map\ f \cdot reverse & = & reverse \cdot map\ f \\ map\ f \cdot concat & = & concat \cdot map\ (map\ f) \end{cases}$$

The first equation holds only if f is a strict function, but the other three hold for arbitrary f. If we apply both sides of the first equation to [ ], then

$$f \,(head\,[\,]) = head\,(map\,f\,[\,]) = head\,[\,]$$

Hence, since $head\,[\,] = \bot$, we require f to be strict.

Each equation has a simple interpretation. For example, the last equation says that one can either concatenate a list of lists and apply f to each element of the result, or apply $map\,f$ to every component list and then concatenate the result.

Since $concat\,[xs, ys] = xs +\!\!+ ys$, a special case of the last result is that

$$map\,f\,(xs +\!\!+ ys) = map\,f\,xs +\!\!+ map\,f\,ys$$

for all lists xs and ys. In words $map\,f$ distributes over $+\!\!+$ for all f. In fact, the special case is needed as an auxiliary result in the proof by induction of the more general one.

The common theme behind each of these equations, and many others like them, concerns the types of the functions involved:

$$
\begin{array}{lcl}
head & :: & [\alpha] \to \alpha \\
tail & :: & [\alpha] \to [\alpha] \\
reverse & :: & [\alpha] \to [\alpha] \\
concat & :: & [[\alpha]] \to [\alpha]
\end{array}
$$

The point about these functions is that they do not depend in any way on the nature of the list elements; they are simply combinators that shuffle, rearrange, or extract elements from lists. That is why they have polymorphic types. It follows that we can either 'rename' the list elements (via $map\,f$) and then do the operation, or do the operation and then rename the elements. This is exactly what each equation above says. In category theory, such equations are called *naturality* conditions, and we will use this terminology in calculation hints.

4.3.1 Filter

The second function, *filter*, takes a boolean function p and a list xs and returns that sublist of xs whose elements satisfy p. For example,

? *filter even* $[1, 2, 4, 5, 32]$
$[2, 4, 32]$

? $(sum \cdot map\,square \cdot filter\,even)\,[1 \,..\, 10]$
220

The last example asks for the sum of the squares of the even integers in the range 1 to 10.

The definition of *filter* is

$$
\begin{array}{lll}
\textit{filter} & :: & (\alpha \rightarrow \textit{Bool}) \rightarrow [\alpha] \rightarrow [\alpha] \\
\textit{filter } p \, [\,] & = & [\,] \\
\textit{filter } p \, (x : xs) & = & \textbf{if } p \, x \textbf{ then } x : \textit{filter } p \, xs \textbf{ else } \textit{filter } p \, xs
\end{array}
$$

Like *map*, there are a number of useful identities concerning *filter*, including the basic fact that

$$
\textit{filter } p \cdot \textit{filter } q \;\; = \;\; \textit{filter } (p \textbf{ and } q)
$$

where $(p \textbf{ and } q) \, x = p \, x \wedge q \, x$. This equation is valid only if p and q are strict functions. Another law is

$$
\textit{filter } p \cdot \textit{concat} \;\; = \;\; \textit{concat} \cdot \textit{map} \, (\textit{filter } p)
$$

which is valid for any p.

4.3.2 List comprehensions

Haskell, in common with some other functional languages, provides an alternative notation, called a *list comprehension*, for describing computations involving *map* and *filter*. Here is an example:

$$
? \, [x \times x \mid x \leftarrow [1 .. 5], \textit{odd } x]
$$
$$
[1, 9, 25]
$$

This reads: the list of squares of odd numbers in the range 1 to 5.

Formally, a list comprehension takes the form $[e \mid Q]$ where e is an expression and Q is a *qualifier*. A qualifier is a possibly empty sequence of *generators* and *guards*, separated by commas. A generator takes the form $x \leftarrow xs$, where x is a variable or tuple of variables, and xs is a list-valued expression. A guard is a boolean-valued expression. The qualifier Q may be empty, in which case we just write $[e]$. Otherwise we define

$$
\begin{array}{lll}
[e \mid x \leftarrow xs, Q] & = & \textit{concat} \, (\textit{map } f \, xs) \quad \textbf{where } f \, x = [e \mid Q] \\
[e \mid p, Q] & = & \textbf{if } p \textbf{ then } [e \mid Q] \textbf{ else } [\,]
\end{array}
$$

The first equation is called the *generator rule*, and the second is called the *guard rule*. Using these rules, we can calculate

$$
[x \times x \mid x \leftarrow [1 .. 5], \textit{odd } x]
$$

$=$ {generator rule}

    concat (*map f* [1 .. 5])   **where** $f\,x = [x \times x \mid odd\,x]$

$=$ {guard rule}

    concat (*map f* [1 .. 5])   **where** $f\,x =$ **if** *odd* x **then** $[x \times x]$ **else** [ ]

$=$ {map}

    concat [[1], [ ], [9], [ ], [25]]

$=$ {concat}

    [1, 9, 25]

Here are some more examples:

? $[(a, b) \mid a \leftarrow [1 .. 3],\ b \leftarrow [1 .. 2]]$
$[(1, 1), (1, 2), (2, 1), (2, 2), (3, 1), (3, 2)]$

? $[(a, b) \mid b \leftarrow [1 .. 2],\ a \leftarrow [1 .. 3]]$
$[(1, 1), (2, 1), (3, 1), (1, 2), (2, 2), (3, 2)]$

Later generators can depend on the variables introduced by earlier ones:

? $[(i, j) \mid i \leftarrow [1 .. 4],\ j \leftarrow [i + 1 .. 4]]$
$[(1, 2), (1, 3), (1, 4), (2, 3), (2, 4), (3, 4)]$

We can freely intersperse generators with guards:

? $[(i, j) \mid i \leftarrow [1 .. 4],\ even\,i,\ j \leftarrow [i + 1 .. 4],\ odd\,j]$
$[(2, 3)]$

Here is an example where the generator takes the form $(x, y) \leftarrow xs$. First, define

     pairs $=$ $[(i, j) \mid i \leftarrow [1 .. 2],\ j \leftarrow [1 .. 3]]$

Then we have

? $[i + j \mid (i, j) \leftarrow pairs]$
$[2, 3, 4, 3, 4, 5]$

As a more interesting example, here is a program to list all pythagorean triads in a given range. These are triples of numbers (x, y, z) such that $x^2 + y^2 = z^2$. We define *triads* by

     triads   :: $Int \rightarrow [(Int, Int, Int)]$
     triads n $=$ $[(x, y, z) \mid (x, y, z) \leftarrow triples\,n,\ pyth\,(x, y, z)]$

$$triples \quad :: \quad Int \rightarrow [(Int, Int, Int)]$$
$$triples \ n \quad = \quad [(x, y, z) \mid x \leftarrow [1 .. n], \ y \leftarrow [1 .. n], \ z \leftarrow [1 .. n]]$$

$$pyth \quad\quad :: \quad (Int, Int, Int) \rightarrow Bool$$
$$pyth \ (x, y, z) \quad = \quad (x \times x + y \times y = z \times z)$$

For example:

? *triads* 5
$[(3, 4, 5), (4, 3, 5)]$

Since *triads* generates essentially the same triad in two different ways, the following definition of *triples* is a better one:

$$triples \ n \quad = \quad [(x, y, z) \mid x \leftarrow [1 .. n], \ y \leftarrow [x .. n], \ z \leftarrow [y .. n]]$$

In the new definition, the value of y is restricted to the range $x \leq y \leq n$, and the value of z to the range $y \leq z \leq n$. Since z must be at least as big as the larger of x and y, all triads will still be found, but no triad will be found more than once. For example,

? *triads* 5
$[(3, 4, 5)]$

4.3.3 Reasoning about list comprehensions

List comprehensions provide an attractive alternative to a combinatorial style based on *map*, *filter*, and *concat*. There are also a number of derived rules for reasoning about list comprehensions, including the following:

$$[f \ x \mid x \leftarrow xs] \quad\quad = \quad map \ f \ xs$$
$$[x \mid x \leftarrow xs, \ p \ x] \quad\quad = \quad filter \ p \ xs$$
$$[e \mid Q, P] \quad\quad\quad = \quad concat \ [[e \mid P] \mid Q]$$
$$[e \mid Q, x \leftarrow [d \mid P]] \quad = \quad [e[x := d] \mid Q, P]$$

In the last equation $e[x := d]$ denotes the expression that results when occurrences of x in the expression e are replaced by the expression d. The last two rules can be proved by induction on the structure of the qualifier Q.

On the other hand, the combinatory style has some advantages too. One is that the algebraic properties of *map* and *filter* are easier to state and to use. The fair conclusion is that the choice as to whether to use list comprehensions or a combinatory style is mostly a matter of personal preference. The same is true about a point-wise style versus a point-free style.

Exercises

4.3.1 Evaluate *map* (*map square*) [[1, 2], [3, 4, 5]].

4.3.2 What is the value of *map f* ⊥? What is the value of *map* ⊥ [ ]?

4.3.3 What is the type of *map map*?

4.3.4 Prove that *map f* (*xs* ++ *ys*) = *map f xs* ++ *map f ys*. Hence prove that *map f* · *concat* = *concat* · *map* (*map f*).

4.3.5 The function *inits* computes the list of initial segments of a list; its type is *inits* :: [α] → [[α]]. What is the appropriate naturality condition for *inits*?

4.3.6 The function *filter* can be defined in terms of *concat* and *map*:

$$filter\ p\ =\ concat \cdot map\ box$$
$$\textbf{where}\ box\ x = \ldots$$

Give the definition of *box*.

4.3.7 The useful functions *takeWhile* and *dropWhile* are similar to *take* and *drop* except that they both take a boolean function as first argument instead of a natural number. In this respect, they are both similar to *filter* too. The value *takeWhile p xs* is the longest initial segment of *xs* all of whose elements satisfy *p*. For example

$$takeWhile\ even\ [2, 4, 6, 1, 5, 6]\ =\ [2, 4, 6]$$

The value *dropWhile p xs* gives what remains; for example,

$$dropWhile\ even\ [2, 4, 6, 1, 5, 6]\ =\ [1, 5, 6]$$

Give recursive definitions of *takeWhile* and *dropWhile*.

4.3.8 Under what conditions on *xs* and *ys* does the following equation hold?

$$[x \mid x \leftarrow xs,\ y \leftarrow ys] = [x \mid y \leftarrow ys,\ x \leftarrow xs]$$

4.3.9 Define a function *pairs* so that *pairs n* is a list of all distinct pairs of integers $1 \le x, y \le n$.

4.3.10 Write a program to find all essentially distinct quadruples (a, b, c, d) in the range $0 < a, b, c, d \le n$ such that $a^2 + b^2 = c^2 + d^2$.

4.3.11 Convert the following list comprehensions to combinatory style:

$$[(x, y) \mid x \leftarrow [1 .. n],\ odd\ x,\ y \leftarrow [1 .. n]]$$
$$[(x, y) \mid x \leftarrow [1 .. n],\ y \leftarrow [1 .. n],\ odd\ x]$$

Are they equal? Compare the costs of evaluating the two expressions.

4.4 Zip

The function *zip* takes two lists and returns a list of pairs of corresponding elements. For example,

? *zip* [0 .. 4] "hallo"
[(0, 'h'), (1, 'a'), (2, 'l'), (3, 'l'), (4, 'o')]

? *zip* [0, 1] "hallo"
[(0, 'h'), (1, 'a')]

As the second example shows, if the two lists do not have the same length, then the length of the zipped list is the shorter of the lengths of the two arguments. The full definition of *zip* is

$$
\begin{array}{lll}
zip & :: & [\alpha] \to [\beta] \to [(\alpha, \beta)] \\
zip\ [\ ]\ ys & = & [\ ] \\
zip\ (x:xs)\ [\ ] & = & [\ ] \\
zip\ (x:xs)\ (y:ys) & = & (x, y) : zip\ (xs, ys)
\end{array}
$$

The pattern matching in this definition parallels that of *take* and *drop*. Matching on the left-hand argument is performed first, so $zip \perp [\ ] = \perp$ and $zip\ [\ ] \perp = [\ ]$.

The function *zip* has many uses. For example, the scalar product of two vectors x and y is defined by $\sum_{i=1}^{n} x_i \times y_i$. The function *sp*, for computing scalar products, can be defined by

$$
\begin{array}{lll}
sp & :: & (Num\ \alpha) \Rightarrow [\alpha] \to [\alpha] \to \alpha \\
sp\ xs\ ys & = & sum\ (map\ times\ (zip\ xs\ ys)) \\
& & \textbf{where}\ times\ (x, y) = x \times y
\end{array}
$$

The function *times* is the uncurried version of $\times$; in fact, *times = uncurry* ($\times$).

As a second example, suppose we want to define a function *nondec* for determining whether a sequence $[x_0, \ldots, x_{n-1}]$ is nondecreasing. Thus, we want to determine whether $x_k \le x_{k+1}$ for all k in the range $0 \le k \le n - 2$. The type of *nondec* is

$$
nondec\ ::\ (Ord\ \alpha) \Rightarrow [\alpha] \to Bool
$$

It is easy to give a direct recursive definition of *nondec*, but the following definition also works:

$$
\begin{array}{ll}
nondec\ xs\ = & and\ (map\ leq\ (zip\ xs\ (tail\ xs))) \\
& \textbf{where}\ leq\ (x, y) = (x \le y)
\end{array}
$$

The function *and* takes a list of booleans and returns *True* if all the elements are *True*, and *False* otherwise:

$$and \qquad\qquad :: \quad [Bool] \rightarrow Bool$$
$$and\,[\,] \qquad\quad = \quad True$$
$$and\,(x:xs) \quad = \quad x \wedge and\,xs$$

The expression *zip xs (tail xs)* returns the list of adjacent pairs of elements in *xs*. In particular,

$$zip\,[\,]\,(tail\,[\,]) \quad = \quad zip\,[\,] \perp \,=\, [\,]$$
$$zip\,[x]\,(tail\,[x]) \quad = \quad zip\,[x]\,[\,] \,=\, [\,]$$

Note also that *leq = uncurry* ($\leq$).

As a third example, consider the problem of building a function *position* with the property that *position x xs* denotes the position of the first occurrence of *x* in *xs* (counting from 0), and -1 if *x* does not appear in *xs*. Thus *position* has type

$$position \quad :: \quad (Eq\,\alpha) \Rightarrow \alpha \rightarrow [\alpha] \rightarrow Int$$

This is an instructive problem because the best way to tackle it is to solve a more general problem first, namely to compute *all* positions at which *x* appears in *xs*. The definition, which uses a list comprehension, is

$$positions \qquad :: \quad (Eq\,\alpha) \Rightarrow \alpha \rightarrow [\alpha] \rightarrow [Int]$$
$$positions\,x\,xs \quad = \quad [i\,|\,(i,y) \leftarrow zip\,[0\,..\,]\,xs,\ x == y]$$

The expression *zip* [0 ..] *xs* pairs each element of *xs* with its position in *xs*. Although [0 ..] is an infinite list, *zip* [0 ..] *xs* will return a finite list whenever *xs* is a finite list. We can now define *position* by

$$position\,x\,xs \quad = \quad head\,(positions\,x\,xs + \!\!\!+ [-1])$$

It turns out that the simplicity of this definition is achieved at no increase in the cost of evaluation. In order to calculate the head of a list, it is not necessary to determine the value of every element of the list.

These examples illustrate that combinations of *map*, *filter*, and *zip* can be put to a variety of uses. In order to make the definitions shorter, we can introduce the function *zipWith*, defined by

$$zipWith \qquad\qquad :: \quad (\alpha \rightarrow \beta \rightarrow \gamma) \rightarrow ([\alpha] \rightarrow [\beta] \rightarrow [\gamma])$$
$$zipWith\,f\,xs\,ys \quad = \quad map\,(uncurry\,f)\,(zip\,xs\,ys)$$

For example,

$$sp \; xs \; ys \quad = \quad sum \; (zipWith \; (\times) \; xs \; ys)$$
$$nondec \; xs \quad = \quad and \; (zipWith \; (\leq) \; xs \; (tail \; xs))$$

For greater brevity we can introduce noncurried versions of *zip* and *zipWith*:

$$zipp \quad :: \quad ([\alpha], [\beta]) \rightarrow [(\alpha, \beta)]$$
$$zipp \quad = \quad uncurry \; zip$$

$$zippWith \quad :: \quad (\alpha \rightarrow \beta \rightarrow \gamma) \rightarrow ([\alpha], [\beta]) \rightarrow [\gamma]$$
$$zippWith \; f \quad = \quad map \; (uncurry \; f) \cdot zipp$$

For example, with *spp* denoting the uncurried version of *sp*, we have

$$spp \quad = \quad sum \cdot zippWith \; (\times)$$
$$nondec \quad = \quad and \cdot zippWith \; (\leq) \cdot pair \; (id, tail)$$

The new definition of *nondec* uses the function

$$pair \; (f, g) \; x \quad = \quad (f \; x, g \; x)$$

defined in Section 2.4. It will be seen from the new definitions that a point-free style of definition is possible only if some functions are given in noncurried form. Haskell, in common with Miranda and some other functional languages, defines all binary operators as curried functions, and also *zip* as a curried function; consequently, the conversion to noncurried forms has to be made explicit.

4.4.1   Unzip

The function *unzip* takes a list of pairs and unzips it into two lists:

$$unzip \quad :: \quad [(\alpha, \beta)] \rightarrow ([\alpha], [\beta])$$
$$unzip \quad = \quad pair \; (map \; fst, map \; snd)$$

For example,

? *unzip* $[(1, True), (2, True), (3, False)]$
$([1, 2, 3], [True, True, False])$

The functions *zipp* (the noncurried version of *zip*) and *unzip* are related by the equation

$$zipp \; (unzip \; xys) \quad = \quad xys$$

for all lists *xys* of well-defined pairs (see Exercise 4.4.1 for the reason for the restriction to well-defined pairs).

Since *zip* and *unzip* have polymorphic types, we might expect that they satisfy appropriate naturality conditions of the kind described in the previous section. For instance, to rename elements of the target type of *unzip* we need two functions, a function *map f* to rename the first component, and a function *map g* to rename the second. The function that does both renamings is *cross* (*map f*, *map g*), where *cross* is given by

$$cross\ (f, g) \quad = \quad pair\ (f \cdot fst, g \cdot snd)$$

This function was also introduced in Section 2.4. To rename elements of the source type of *unzip* we need to map with a single function, and it is not hard to see that the function *map* (*cross* (*f*, *g*)) does the job. Hence we should expect that

$$cross\ (map\ f, map\ g) \cdot unzip \quad = \quad unzip \cdot map\ (cross\ (f, g))$$

Indeed, this equation does hold. The proof is left as Exercise 4.4.3. The dual result

$$zipp \cdot cross\ (map\ f, map\ g) \quad = \quad map\ (cross\ (f, g)) \cdot zipp$$

also holds.

A more extended programming exercise in the use of *zip* is given in Section 5.2. This exercise also uses material from the following section.

Exercises

4.4.1 What is *unzip* $[\bot]$? Using the fact that $(\bot, \bot) \neq \bot$, construct a list *xys* such that *zipp* (*unzip xys*) $\neq$ *xys*.

4.4.2 Does the converse equation *unzip* $\cdot$ *zipp* = *id* hold?

4.4.3 Provided certain other laws are assumed, the equation

$$cross\ (\underline{map\ f, map\ g}) \cdot \underline{unzip} \quad = \quad unzip \cdot map\ (cross\ (f, g))$$

can be proved by simple calculation with functions. The necessary additional laws are

$$
\begin{array}{lcl}
map\ (f \cdot g) & = & map\ f \cdot map\ g \\
cross\ (f, g) \cdot pair\ (h, k) & = & pair\ (f \cdot h, g \cdot k) \\
pair\ (f, g) \cdot h & = & pair\ (f \cdot h, g \cdot h) \\
fst \cdot cross\ (f, g) & = & f \cdot fst \\
snd \cdot cross\ (f, g) & = & g \cdot snd
\end{array}
$$

Use these laws, together with the definition of *unzip*, to prove the required result.

4.5 The fold functions

We have seen in the case of the datatype *Nat* that many recursive definitions can be expressed very succinctly using a suitable fold operator. Exactly the same is true of lists. Consider the following definition of a function *h*:

$$h \,[\,] \quad = \quad e$$
$$h \,(x : xs) \quad = \quad x \oplus h \, xs$$

The function *h* works by taking a list, replacing [ ] by *e* and (:) by $\oplus$, and evaluating the result. For example, *h* converts the list

$$x_1 : (x_2 : (x_3 : (x_4 : [\,])))$$

to the value

$$x_1 \oplus (x_2 \oplus (x_3 \oplus (x_4 \oplus e)))$$

Since (:) associates to the right, there is no need to put in parentheses in the first expression. However, we do have to put in parentheses in the second expression because we do not assume that $\oplus$ associates to the right.

The pattern of definition given by *h* is captured in a function *foldr* (pronounced 'fold right') defined as follows:

$$foldr \qquad\qquad :: \quad (\alpha \to \beta \to \beta) \to \beta \to [\alpha] \to \beta$$
$$foldr \, f \, e \,[\,] \quad = \quad e$$
$$foldr \, f \, e \,(x : xs) \quad = \quad f \, x \,(foldr \, f \, e \, xs)$$

We can now write $h = foldr\,(\oplus)\,e$. The first argument of *foldr* is a binary operator that takes an α-value on its left and a β-value on its right, and delivers a β-value. The second argument of *foldr* is a β-value. The third argument is of type $[\alpha]$, and the result is a value of type β. In many cases, α and β will be instantiated to the same type, for instance when $\oplus$ denotes an associative operation.

The single function *foldr* can be used to define almost every function on lists that we have met so far. Here are just some examples:

$$concat \quad :: \quad [[\alpha]] \to [\alpha]$$
$$concat \quad = \quad foldr\,(\!+\!\!+)\,[\,]$$

$2\left\{\begin{array}{ll}\text{reverse} & :: & [\alpha] \rightarrow [\alpha] \\ \text{reverse} & = & \text{foldr snoc } [\,] \\ & & \textbf{where } \text{snoc } x \text{ } xs = xs \mathbin{+\!\!+} [x]\end{array}\right.$

$3\left\{\begin{array}{ll}\text{length} & :: & [\alpha] \rightarrow \text{Int} \\ \text{length} & = & \text{foldr oneplus } 0 \\ & & \textbf{where } \text{oneplus } x \text{ } n = 1 + n\end{array}\right.$

$4\left\{\begin{array}{ll}\text{sum} & :: & \text{Num } \alpha \Rightarrow [\alpha] \rightarrow \alpha \\ \text{sum} & = & \text{foldr } (+) \text{ } 0\end{array}\right.$

$5\left\{\begin{array}{ll}\text{and} & :: & [\text{Bool}] \rightarrow \text{Bool} \\ \text{and} & = & \text{foldr } (\wedge) \text{ True}\end{array}\right.$

$6\left\{\begin{array}{ll}\text{map} & :: & (\alpha \rightarrow \beta) \rightarrow [\alpha] \rightarrow [\beta] \\ \text{map } f & = & \text{foldr } (\text{cons} \cdot f) \text{ } [\,] \\ & & \textbf{where } \text{cons } x \text{ } xs = x : xs\end{array}\right.$

$7\left\{\begin{array}{ll}\text{unzip} & :: & [(\alpha, \beta)] \rightarrow ([\alpha], [\beta]) \\ \text{unzip} & = & \text{foldr conss } ([\,], [\,]) \\ & & \textbf{where } \text{conss } (x, y) \text{ } (xs, ys) = (x : xs, y : ys)\end{array}\right.$ $8 : filter$

In some of these definitions the operator $\oplus$ that replaces (:) is associative, and the constant c that replaces $[\,]$ is the unit of $\oplus$. For example, $(\mathbin{+\!\!+}, [\,])$, $(+, 0)$, $(\wedge, \text{True})$, and so on. In other definitions, $\oplus$ is not associative; indeed, $\oplus$ may not even have a type appropriate for an associative operator, namely $\alpha \rightarrow \alpha \rightarrow \alpha$.

Not every function on lists can be defined as an instance of *foldr*. For example, *zip* cannot be so defined. Even for those that can, an alternative definition may be more efficient. To illustrate, suppose we want a function *decimal* that takes a list of digits and returns the corresponding decimal number; thus

$$\text{decimal } [x_0, x_1, \ldots, x_n] = \sum_{k=0}^{n} x_k 10^{(n-k)}$$

It is assumed that the most significant digit comes first in the list. One way to compute *decimal* efficiently is by a process of multiplying each digit by ten and adding in the following digit. For example,

$$\text{decimal } [x_0, x_1, x_2] \quad = \quad 10 \times (10 \times (10 \times 0 + x_0) + x_1) + x_2$$

This decomposition of a sum of powers is known as *Horner's rule*. Suppose we define $\oplus$ by $n \oplus x = 10 \times n + x$. Then we can rephrase the above equation as

$$decimal\ [x_0, x_1, x_2] \quad = \quad ((0 \oplus x_0) \oplus x_1) \oplus x_2$$

This is almost like an instance of *foldr*, except that the grouping is the other way round, and the starting value appears on the left, not on the right. In fact, the computation is dual: instead of processing from right to left, the computation processes from left to right.

This example motivates the introduction of a second fold operator, called *foldl* (pronounced 'fold left'). Informally,

$$foldl\ (\oplus)\ e\ [x_0, x_1, \ldots, x_{n-1}] \quad = \quad (\cdots ((e \oplus x_0) \oplus x_1) \cdots) \oplus x_{n-1}$$

The parentheses group from the left, which is the reason for the name. The full definition of *foldl* is

$$
\begin{aligned}
&foldl &&:: &&(\beta \rightarrow \alpha \rightarrow \beta) \rightarrow \beta \rightarrow [\alpha] \rightarrow \beta \\
&foldl\ f\ e\ [\,] &&= &&e \\
&foldl\ f\ e\ (x : xs) &&= &&foldl\ f\ (f\ e\ x)\ xs
\end{aligned}
$$

For example,

$$
\begin{aligned}
&&&foldl\ (\oplus)\ e\ [x_0, x_1, x_2] \\
&=&&foldl\ (\oplus)\ (e \oplus x_0)\ [x_1, x_2] \\
&=&&foldl\ (\oplus)\ ((e \oplus x_0) \oplus x_1)\ [x_2] \\
&=&&foldl\ (\oplus)\ (((e \oplus x_0) \oplus x_1) \oplus x_2)\ [\,] \\
&=&&((e \oplus x_0) \oplus x_1) \oplus x_2
\end{aligned}
$$

If $\oplus$ is associative with unit e, then *foldr* $(\oplus)$ e and *foldl* $(\oplus)$ e define the same function on finite lists, as we will see in the following section.

As another example of the use of *foldl*, consider the following definition:

$$
\begin{aligned}
&reverse' &&:: &&[\alpha] \rightarrow [\alpha] \\
&reverse' &&= &&foldl\ cons\ [\,] \quad \textbf{where } cons\ xs\ x = x : xs
\end{aligned}
$$

Note the order of the arguments to *cons*; we have *cons* = *flip* (:), where the standard function *flip* is defined by *flip f x y = f y x*. The function *reverse'* reverses a finite list. For example,

$$
\begin{aligned}
&&&reverse'\ [x_0, x_1, x_2] \\
&=&&cons\ (cons\ (cons\ [\,]\ x_0)\ x_1)\ x_2 \\
&=&&cons\ (cons\ [x_0]\ x_1)\ x_2 \\
&=&&cons\ [x_1, x_0]\ x_2 \\
&=&&[x_2, x_1, x_0]
\end{aligned}
$$

One can prove that *reverse'* = *reverse* by induction, or as an instance of a more general result to be described in the following section. Of greater importance than the mere fact that *reverse* can be defined in a different way, is that *reverse'* gives a much more efficient program: *reverse'* takes time proportional to n on a list of length n, while *reverse* takes time proportional to n^2.

There are a number of important laws concerning *foldr* and its relationship to *foldl*, but we will postpone discussion to the following section.

4.5.1 Fold over nonempty lists

Say we wish to find the maximum element in a finite list of elements drawn from an ordered type. We would like to do this by defining

$$maxlist \quad :: \quad (Ord \; \alpha) \Rightarrow [\alpha] \rightarrow \alpha$$
$$maxlist \quad = \quad foldr \; (\textbf{max}) \; e$$

where ($x \; \textbf{max} \; y$) returns the greater of x and y. But what should we choose as the value of e? In other words, what is *maxlist* [ ]? The choice is not arbitrary because we naturally want *maxlist* $[x] = x$, and the definition gives ($x \; \textbf{max} \; e$) instead. So e has to be smaller than any other value in the type α. Such a value may not exist. In Haskell there is a type class *Bounded* whose instances are types possessing maximum and minimum elements:

$$\textbf{class} \; Bounded \; \alpha \; \textbf{where}$$
$$minBound, maxBound \quad :: \quad \alpha$$

Hence one solution is to redefine *maxlist* to

$$maxlist \quad :: \quad (Ord \; \alpha, Bounded \; \alpha) \Rightarrow [\alpha] \rightarrow \alpha$$
$$maxlist \quad = \quad foldr \; (\textbf{max}) \; minBound$$

An alternative solution that does not make use of *Bounded* is to introduce a new fold function, one that works on nonempty lists. In fact, there are two such functions, *foldr1* and *foldl1*. The definitions are

$$foldr1 \quad :: \quad (\alpha \rightarrow \alpha \rightarrow \alpha) \rightarrow [\alpha] \rightarrow \alpha$$
$$foldr1 \; f \; (x:xs) \quad = \quad \textbf{if} \; null \; xs \; \textbf{then} \; x \; \textbf{else} \; f \; x \; (foldr1 \; f \; xs)$$

$$foldl1 \quad :: \quad (\alpha \rightarrow \alpha \rightarrow \alpha) \rightarrow [\alpha] \rightarrow \alpha$$
$$foldl1 \; f \; (x:xs) \quad = \quad foldl \; f \; x \; xs$$

For example,

$$foldr1 \; (\oplus) \; [x_0, x_1, x_2, x_3] \quad = \quad x_0 \oplus (x_1 \oplus (x_2 \oplus x_3))$$
$$foldl1 \; (\oplus) \; [x_0, x_1, x_2, x_3] \quad = \quad ((x_0 \oplus x_1) \oplus x_2) \oplus x_3$$

Now we can solve the problem by defining

$$maxlist \quad = \quad foldr1 \ (\mathbf{max})$$

Of course, since **max** is associative, we could equally well have defined *maxlist* in terms of *foldl1*.

4.5.2 Scan left

Sometimes it is convenient to apply a *foldl* operation to every initial segment of a list. This is done by a function *scanl*, pronounced 'scan left'. For example,

$$scanl \ (\oplus) \ e \ [x_0, x_1, x_2] \quad = \quad [e, e \oplus x_0, (e \oplus x_0) \oplus x_1, ((e \oplus x_0) \oplus x_1) \oplus x_2]$$

In particular, *scanl* $(+)$ 0 computes the list of accumulated sums of a list of numbers, and *scanl* $(\times)$ 1 $[1..n]$ computes a list of the first n factorial numbers. More substantial examples of the use of *scanl* are given in Sections 5.2 and 5.3. We will give two programs for *scanl*; the first is the clearest, while the second is more efficient.

For the first program we will need the function *inits* that returns the list of all initial segments of a list. For example,

$$inits \ [x_0, x_1, x_2] \quad = \quad [[\ ], [x_0], [x_0, x_1], [x_0, x_1, x_2]]$$

The empty list has only one segment, namely the empty list itself; a list $(x : xs)$ has the empty list as its shortest initial segment, and all the other initial segments begin with x and are followed by an initial segment of xs. Hence

$$A \left\{ \begin{array}{lll} inits & :: & [\alpha] \to [[\alpha]] \\ inits \ [\ ] & = & [[\ ]] \\ inits \ (x : xs) & = & [\ ] : map \ (x :) \ (inits \ xs) \end{array} \right.$$

The function *inits* can be defined more succinctly as an instance of *foldr*:

$$B \left\{ \begin{array}{l} inits \ = \ foldr \ f \ [[\ ]] \quad \textbf{where} \ f \ x \ xss = [\ ] : map \ (x :) \ xss \end{array} \right.$$

Now we define

$$C \left\{ \begin{array}{lll} scanl & :: & (\alpha \to \beta \to \beta) \to \beta \to [\alpha] \to [\alpha] \\ scanl \ f \ e & = & map \ (foldl \ f \ e) \cdot inits \end{array} \right.$$

This is the clearest definition of *scanl* but it leads to an inefficient program. The function f is applied k times in the evaluation of *foldl* $f \ e$ on a list of length k and, since the initial segments of a list of length n are lists with lengths $0, 1, \ldots, n$, the function f is applied about $n^2/2$ times in total.

Let us now synthesise a more efficient program. The synthesis is by an induction argument on *xs* so we lay out the calculation in the same way.

Case ([ ]). Here we get *scanl f e* [ ] = [*e*]. The details are routine and are left as an exercise.

Case (*x* : *xs*). We calculate

> *scanl f e* (*x* : *xs*)
>
> =   {definition of *scanl*}
>
> *map* (*foldl f e*) (*inits* (*x* : *xs*))
>
> =   {definition of *inits*}
>
> *map* (*foldl f e*) ([ ] : *map* (*x* :) (*inits xs*))
>
> =   {second equation for *map*}
>
> *foldl f e* [ ] : *map* (*foldl f e*) (*map* (*x* :) (*inits xs*))
>
> =   {first equation for *foldl*}
>
> *e* : *map* (*foldl f e*) (*map* (*x* :) (*inits xs*))
>
> =   {since *map* is a functor}   *map f* · *map g* = *map* (*f*·*g*)
>
> *e* : *map* (*foldl f e* · (*x* :)) (*inits xs*)
>
> =   {claim: *foldl f e* · (*x* :) = *foldl f* (*f e x*)}   ⟹ prove
>
> *e* : *map* (*foldl f* (*f e x*)) (*inits xs*)
>
> =   {definition of *scanl*}
>
> *e* : *scanl f* (*f e x*) *xs*

The claim is left as a short exercise. In summary, we have derived

> *scanl f e* [ ]   =   [*e*]
> *scanl f e* (*x* : *xs*)   =   *e* : *scanl f* (*f e x*) *xs*

This program is more efficient in that the function *f* is applied exactly *n* times on a list of length *n*.

4.5.3   Scan right

The dual computation is given by *scanr*, defined by

> *scanr f a*   =   *map* (*foldr f a*) · *tails*

The function *tails* returns the tail segments of a list. For example,

$$tails\,[x_0, x_1, x_2] \quad = \quad [[x_0, x_1, x_2], [x_1, x_2], [x_2], [\,]]$$

Note that while *inits* produces a list of initial segments in increasing order of length, *tails* produces the tail segments in decreasing order of length. We can define *tails* by

$$
\begin{array}{lll}
tails\,[\,] & = & [[\,]] \\
tails\,(x:xs) & = & (x:xs) : tails\,xs
\end{array}
$$

The corresponding efficient program for *scanr* is given by

$$
\begin{array}{lll}
scanr\,f\,a\,[\,] & = & [a] \\
scanr\,f\,a\,(x:xs) & = & f\,x\,(head\,ys) : ys \\
& & \mathbf{where}\ ys = scanr\,f\,a\,xs
\end{array}
$$

We will leave the synthesis of the more efficient version as an exercise.

4.5.4 Scans over nonempty lists

We can also define two further scan functions, *scanl1* and *scanr1*. We have

$$
\begin{array}{lll}
scanl1\,f & = & map\,(foldl1\,f) \cdot inits1 \\
scanr1\,f & = & map\,(foldr1\,f) \cdot tails1
\end{array}
$$

where *inits1* and *tails1* return the nonempty initial and final segments of a nonempty list. For example,

$$inits1\,(x:xs) \quad = \quad map\,(x:)\,(inits\,xs)$$

Using $foldl1\,f \cdot (x:) = foldl\,f\,x$, we obtain

$$
\begin{array}{lll}
scanl1 & :: & (\alpha \to \alpha \to \alpha) \to [\alpha] \to [\alpha] \\
scanl1\,f\,(x:xs) & = & scanl\,f\,x\,xs
\end{array}
$$

The efficient version of *scanr1* is left as an exercise.

Exercises

4.5.1 Define *filter p* as an instance of *foldr*.

4.5.2 Consider the two functions *takeWhile* and *dropWhile*, which were discussed in Exercise 4.3.7. Define *takeWhile* as an instance of *foldr*. Can *dropWhile* be defined as an instance of a fold function?

4.5.3 Which, if either, of the following equations is true?

$$foldl \ (-) \ x \ xs \ = \ x - sum \, xs$$
$$foldr \ (-) \ x \ xs \ = \ x - sum \, xs$$

4.5.4 Consider the following definition of a function *insert*:

$$insert \ x \ xs \ = \ takeWhile \ (\leq x) \ xs \ {+}\mkern-8mu{+}\ [x] \ {+}\mkern-8mu{+}\ dropWhile \ (\leq x) \ xs$$

Show that if *xs* is in nondecreasing order, then so is *insert x xs* for all *x*. Use *insert* to define a function *isort* for sorting a list into nondecreasing order. Use *foldr*.

4.5.5 The function *remdups* removes adjacent duplicates from a list. For example, *remdups* $[1, 2, 2, 3, 3, 3, 1, 1] = [1, 2, 3, 1]$. Define *remdups* using either *foldl* or *foldr*.

4.5.6 Given a list $xs = [x_1, x_2, \ldots, x_n]$ of numbers, the sequence of successive maxima *ssm xs* is the longest subsequence $[x_{j_1}, x_{j_2}, \ldots, x_{j_m}]$ such that $j_1 = 1$ and $x_j < x_{j_k}$ for $j < j_k$. For example, the sequence of successive maxima of $[3, 1, 3, 4, 9, 2, 10, 7]$ is $[3, 4, 9, 10]$. Define *ssm* in terms of *foldl*.

4.5.7 Prove that *scanl f e* $[\,] = [e]$.

4.5.8 Justify the efficient program for *scanr*.

4.5.9 What list does *scanl* $(/) [1 .. n]$ produce?

4.5.10 The mathematical constant *e* is defined by $e = \sum_{n=0}^{\infty} 1/n!$. Write down an expression that can be used to evaluate *e* to some reasonable measure of accuracy.

4.5.11 Consider the datatype *Liste α* defined in Exercise 4.1.4. The fold function for this datatype is defined by

$$
\begin{array}{lll}
folde & :: & (\beta \to \alpha \to \beta) \to \beta \to Liste \ \alpha \to \beta \\
folde \ f \ e \ Nil & = & e \\
folde \ f \ e \ (Snoc \ xs \ x) & = & f \ (folde \ f \ e \ xs) \ x
\end{array}
$$

The type assigned to *folde* is very nearly the same type as that assigned to *foldl*, the only difference being that $[\alpha]$ is replaced by *Liste α*. In fact,

$$folde \ f \ e \ = \ foldl \ f \ e \cdot convert$$

where *convert* :: $[\alpha] \to Liste \ \alpha$. Define the function *convert* and prove by induction that the above equation holds.

4.5.12 Derive an efficient program for *scanr1*.

4.6 Laws of fold

There are a number of important laws concerning *foldr* and its relationship
with *foldl*. As we saw in Section 3.3, instead of having to prove a property of
a recursively defined function over a recursive datatype by writing down an
explicit induction proof, one can often phrase the property as an instance of
one of the laws of the fold operator for the datatype.

4.6.1 Duality theorems

The first three laws are called *duality theorems* and concern the relationship
between *foldr* and *foldl*. The *first duality theorem* is as follows:

First duality theorem. Suppose $\oplus$ is associative with unit e. Then

$$foldr \ (\oplus) \ e \ xs \ = \ foldl \ (\oplus) \ e \ xs$$

for all finite lists xs.

For example, we could have defined

$$A \left\{ \begin{array}{lcl} sum & = & foldl \ (+) \ 0 \\ and & = & foldl \ (\wedge) \ True \\ concat & = & foldl \ (+\!\!+) \ [\ ] \end{array} \right.$$

However, as we will elaborate in Chapter 7, it is sometimes more efficient to
implement a function using *foldl*, and sometimes more efficient to use *foldr*.
   The *second duality theorem* is a generalisation of the first.

Second duality theorem. Suppose $\oplus$, $\otimes$, and e are such that for all x, y, and z
we have

$$B \left\{ \begin{array}{lcl} x \oplus (y \otimes z) & = & (x \oplus y) \otimes z \\ x \oplus e & = & e \otimes x \end{array} \right.$$

In other words, $\oplus$ and $\otimes$ associate with each other, and e on the right of $\oplus$ is
equivalent to e on the left of $\otimes$. Then

$$foldr \ (\oplus) \ e \ xs \ = \ foldl \ (\otimes) \ e \ xs$$

for all finite lists xs.

Proof. The proof of the second duality theorem is by induction on xs.

Case ([ ]). Both sides simplify to e.

Case $(x : xs)$. For the left-hand side we reason

$$foldr \ (\oplus) \ e \ (x : xs)$$

$=$ {definition of *foldr*}

$$x \oplus foldr \ (\oplus) \ e \ xs$$

$=$ {induction hypothesis}

$$x \oplus foldl \ (\otimes) \ e \ xs$$

For the right-hand side we reason

$$foldl \ (\otimes) \ e \ (x : xs)$$

$=$ {definition of *foldl*}

$$foldl \ (\otimes) \ (e \otimes x) \ xs$$

$=$ {assumption}

$$foldl \ (\otimes) \ (x \oplus e) \ xs$$

The two sides have simplified to two different expressions. To show that they are equal we have to resort to a second induction proof. However, if one takes as the second induction hypothesis the obvious assertion that

$$x \oplus foldl \ (\otimes) \ e \ xs \quad = \quad foldl \ (\otimes) \ (x \oplus e) \ xs$$

for all x and finite lists xs, then the induction doesn't work. The only way to appreciate this fact is to try it, a task we leave as an exercise. What is needed is a *stronger* hypothesis, namely

$$x \oplus foldl \ (\otimes) \ y \ xs \quad = \quad foldl \ (\otimes) \ (x \oplus y) \ xs$$

for all x, y, and finite lists xs. As we saw in Section 4.2 in the discussion of *reverse*, making an induction hypothesis stronger can often simplify a proof.

Case $([\ ])$. Both sides simplify to $x \oplus a$.

Case $(z : xs)$. (Note the use of z to avoid confusion with the variable x already present in the assertion.) For the left-hand side we reason

$$x \oplus foldl \ (\otimes) \ y \ (z; \ xs)$$

$$= \quad \{\text{definition}\}$$

$$x \oplus foldl \ (\otimes) \ (y \otimes z) \ xs$$

$$= \quad \{\text{induction hypothesis}\}$$

$$foldl \ (\otimes) \ (x \oplus (y \otimes z)) \ xs$$

$$= \quad \{\text{assumption}\}$$

$$foldl \ (\otimes) \ ((x \oplus y) \otimes z) \ xs$$

For the right-hand side we reason

$$foldl \ (\otimes) \ (x \oplus y) \ (z : xs)$$

$$= \quad \{\text{definition}\}$$

$$foldl \ (\otimes) \ ((x \oplus y) \otimes z) \ xs$$

$$\square$$

The second duality theorem has the first duality theorem as a special case, namely when $(\oplus) = (\otimes)$.

To illustrate the second duality theorem, consider the following definitions of *length* and *reverse*:

$$
\begin{cases}
length & = & foldr \ oneplus \ 0, & \text{where } oneplus \ x \ n = 1 + n \\
length & = & foldl \ plusone \ 0, & \text{where } plusone \ n \ x = n + 1 \\
\\
reverse & = & foldr \ snoc \ [\,], & \text{where } snoc \ x \ xs = xs \mathbin{+\!\!+} [x] \\
reverse & = & foldl \ cons \ [\,], & \text{where } cons \ xs \ x = x : xs
\end{cases}
$$

The functions *oneplus*, *plusone*, and 0 meet the conditions of the second duality theorem, as do *snoc*, *cons*, and [ ]. We leave the verification as an exercise. Hence the two definitions of *length* and *reverse* are equivalent on all finite lists. It is not obvious whether there is any practical difference between the two definitions of *length*, but the second program for *reverse* is the more efficient of the two,

The proof of the *third duality theorem* is left as an exercise.

Third duality theorem. For all finite lists xs,

$$foldr \ f \ e \ xs \quad = \quad foldl \ (flip \ f) \ e \ (reverse \ xs)$$

where $flip \ f \ x \ y = f \ y \ x$.

To illustrate the third duality theorem, consider

$$foldr \ (:) \ [\,] \ xs \quad = \quad foldl \ (flip \ (:)) \ [\,] \ (reverse \ xs)$$

define

Since $foldr\ (:)\ [\ ] = id$ and $foldl\ (flip\ (:))\ [\ ] = reverse$, we obtain

$$xs\ =\ reverse\ (reverse\ xs)$$

for all finite lists xs, a result we have already proved directly.

4.6.2 Fusion

The duality theorems deal with the relationship between the two kinds of fold operator on lists; the fusion theorems deal with one kind of fold operator only. The fusion theorems for *foldr* and *foldl* are as follows.

Fusion theorem for *foldr*. If f is strict, $f\ a = b$, and $f\ (g\ x\ y) = h\ x\ (f\ y)$ for all x and y, then

$$f \cdot foldr\ g\ a\ =\ foldr\ h\ b$$

Fusion theorem for *foldl*. If f is strict, $f\ a = b$, and $f\ (g\ x\ y) = h\ (f\ x)\ y$ for all x and y, then

$$f \cdot foldl\ g\ a\ =\ foldl\ h\ b$$

The proof of the fusion theorem for *foldr* is very similar to the one in the previous chapter for *foldn*, and is left as an exercise. The proof of the fusion theorem for *foldl* is trickier, and is explored in Exercise 4.6.3.

The fusion law is very general, and there are useful special cases. Four of these are considered next.

4.6.3 Fold-map fusion

Recall that $map\ g = foldr\ (cons \cdot g)\ [\ ]$, where $cons\ x\ xs = x : xs$. Consider what conditions ensure that

$$foldr\ f\ a \cdot map\ g\ =\ foldr\ h\ b$$

Looking at the conditions of the fusion theorem for *foldr*, we have that *foldr f a* is a strict function, and the second condition is satisfied by taking $a = b$. The third condition expands to

$$foldr\ f\ a\ ((cons \cdot g)\ x\ xs) = h\ x\ (foldr\ f\ a\ xs)$$

$\equiv$ {definition of *cons*}

$$foldr\ f\ a\ (g\ x : xs) = h\ x\ (foldr\ f\ a\ xs)$$

$\equiv$ {definition of *foldr*}

$$f\,(g\,x)\,(foldr\,f\,a\,xs) = h\,x\,(foldr\,f\,a\,xs)$$

$$\Leftarrow \quad \{\text{generalisation}\}$$

$$f\,(g\,x)\,y = h\,x\,y$$

The symbol $\Leftarrow$ is pronounced 'follows from'. Since $h\,x\,y = f\,(g\,x)\,y$ if and only if $h\,x = f\,(g\,x)$ if and only if $h = f \cdot g$, we get the result that

$$foldr\,f\,a \cdot map\,g \quad = \quad foldr\,(f \cdot g)\,a$$

In words, a fold after a map can always be expressed as a single fold. We will call this law the *fold-map fusion* law.

4.6.4 Fold-concat fusion

As a second example, recall that $concat = foldr\,(+\!\!+)\,[\,]$. Consider what conditions ensure that

$$foldr\,f\,a \cdot concat \quad = \quad foldr\,h\,b$$

Again, looking at the conditions for fusion, we have that $foldr\,f\,a$ is strict, and the second condition is satisfied by taking $a = b$. The third condition expands to

$$foldr\,f\,a\,(xs +\!\!+ ys) = h\,xs\,(foldr\,f\,a\,ys)$$

$$\equiv \quad \{\text{claim: } foldr\,f\,a\,(xs +\!\!+ ys) = foldr\,f\,(foldr\,f\,a\,ys)\,xs\}$$

$$foldr\,f\,(foldr\,f\,a\,ys)\,xs = h\,xs\,(foldr\,f\,a\,ys)$$

Hence we can take $h\,xs\,y = foldr\,f\,y\,xs$ or, more shortly, $h = flip\,(foldr\,f)$. The proof of the claim is left as an exercise. Hence we have shown that

$$foldr\,f\,a \cdot concat \quad = \quad foldr\,(flip\,(foldr\,f))\,a$$

We will call this the *fold-concat fusion* law.

4.6.5 Bookkeeping law

As a third example, consider what conditions on f and a ensure that

$$foldr\,f\,a \cdot concat \quad = \quad foldr\,f\,a \cdot map\,(foldr\,f\,a)$$

We will call this particular equation the *bookkeeping* law. The special instance $sum \cdot concat = sum \cdot map\,sum$ is exploited by every bookkeeper who sums each individual day's accounts, and then gets the year's total by summing the sums.

We can use the fold-concat and fold-map fusion laws to rewrite the book-keeping law in the form

$$foldr \ (flip \ (foldr \ f)) \ a \ = \ foldr \ (f \cdot foldr \ f \ a) \ a$$

This equation holds if $flip \ (foldr \ f) = f \cdot foldr \ f \ a$. Applying both sides to xs and then y, we get

$$foldr \ f \ y \ xs \ = \ f \ (foldr \ f \ a \ xs) \ y$$

This equation holds if f is associative with unit a, a proof we will leave as an exercise.

In summary, the bookkeeping law is valid whenever the arguments to $foldr$ are an associative operation and its unit. For example, since $sum = foldr \ (+) \ 0$, the bookkeeper's accounting method is justified. As another example,

$$concat \cdot concat \ = \ concat \cdot map \ concat$$

This equation says that flattening a list of lists of lists into one long list can be done by concatenating outside-in or inside-out.

4.6.6 Fold-scan fusion

Consider the equation

$$1 + x_0 + x_0 \times x_1 + x_0 \times x_1 \times x_2 \ = \ 1 + x_0 \times (1 + x_1 \times (1 + x_2))$$

The equation generalises to an arbitrary list of numbers and can be expressed in the form

$$foldr1 \ (+) \cdot scanl \ (\times) \ 1 \ = \ foldr \ (\odot) \ 1$$

where $x \odot y = 1 + x \times y$. This leads to a more general question: when does the law

$$foldr1 \ (\oplus) \cdot scanl \ (\otimes) \ e \ = \ foldr \ (\odot) \ e$$

hold, where $x \odot y = e \oplus (x \otimes y)$?

Under the assumption that $\otimes$ is associative and e is the unit of $\otimes$, we can express $scanl$ as an instance of $foldr$:

$$scanl \ (\otimes) \ e \ = \ foldr \ g \ [e] \quad \text{where } g \ x \ xs = e : map \ (x\otimes) \ xs$$

The proof is left as an exercise. Having rewritten $scanl$ as an instance of $foldr$, we can see that the required law is yet another instance of the fusion law for *foldr*. The first two conditions are immediate, and the third expands to

$$foldr1 \ (\oplus) \ (g \ x \ xs) = x \odot (foldr1 \ (\oplus) \ xs)$$

$\equiv$ \quad {definition of g}

$$foldr1 \ (\oplus) \ (e : map \ (x\otimes) \ xs) = x \odot (foldr1 \ (\oplus) \ xs)$$

$\equiv$ \quad {definition of *foldr1* and $\odot$}

$$e \oplus foldr1 \ (\oplus) \ (map \ (x\otimes) \ xs) = e \oplus (x \otimes foldr1 \ (\oplus) \ xs)$$

$\Leftarrow$ \quad {substitution}

$$foldr1 \ (\oplus) \cdot map \ (x\otimes) = (x\otimes) \cdot foldr1 \ (\oplus)$$

The last equation holds if $\otimes$ distributes over $\oplus$, that is, if

$$x \otimes (y \oplus z) \quad = \quad (x \otimes y) \oplus (x \otimes z)$$

for all x, y, and z. The proof is left as an exercise.

In summary, if $\otimes$ is associative with unit e, and $\otimes$ distributes over $\oplus$, then *foldr1* $(\oplus) \cdot scanl \ (\otimes) \ e = foldr \ (\odot) \ e$ where $x \odot y = e \oplus (x \otimes y)$. We will call this the *fold-scan* fusion law.

In the remainder of this section we will give an example of how these laws can be used in the synthesis of efficient programs.

4.6.7 Example: the maximum segment sum

The maximum segment sum problem is a famous one and its history is described in J. Bentley's *Programming Pearls* (1987). Given a sequence of numbers it is required to compute the maximum of the sums of all segments in the sequence. For example, the sequence

$$[-1, 2, -3, 5, -2, 1, 3, -2, -2, -3, 6]$$

has maximum sum 7, the sum of the segment $[5, -2, 1, 3]$. On the other hand, the sequence $[-1, -2, -3]$ has a maximum segment sum of zero, since the empty sequence $[\ ]$ is a segment of every list and its sum is zero. It follows that the maximum segment sum is always nonnegative. (The exercises deal with a variant problem in which the empty sequence is excluded, so the maximum segment sum can be negative.)

The problem can be specified formally by

$$mss \ :: \ [Int] \to Int$$
$$mss \ = \ maxlist \cdot map \ sum \cdot segs$$

where *segs* returns a list of all segments of a list. This function can be defined in a number of ways, including

$$segs \quad = \quad concat \cdot map\ inits \cdot tails$$

This definition corresponds to the process of taking all the initial segments of all the tail segments. For example,

$$segs\ \text{"abc"} \quad = \quad [\text{""}, \text{"a"}, \text{"ab"}, \text{"abc"}, \text{""}, \text{"b"}, \text{"bc"}, \text{""}, \text{"c"}, \text{""}]$$

The empty sequence appears four times in this list, once for every tail segment of "abc".

Direct evaluation of *mss* will take a number of steps proportional to n^3 on a list of length n. There are about n^2 segments, and summing them all takes about n^3 steps. It is not obvious that we can do better than cubic time for this problem.

However, let us see what we can achieve with some calculation. Installing the definition of *segs* in *mss*, we have to compute

$$maxlist \cdot map\ sum \cdot concat \cdot map\ inits \cdot tails$$

The only thing we can do with this expression (apart from going backwards) is to use the law $map\ f \cdot concat = concat \cdot map\ (map\ f)$ to replace the second and third terms, obtaining

$$maxlist \cdot concat \cdot map\ (map\ sum) \cdot map\ inits \cdot tails$$

There are two things we can do now: we can either apply the bookkeeping law to the first two terms, or apply the law $map\ (f \cdot g) = map\ f \cdot map\ g$ to the third and fourth terms. Of course, we can also do both these steps at once, in which case the result will be

$$maxlist \cdot map\ maxlist \cdot map\ (map\ sum \cdot inits) \cdot tails$$

For the next step we can apply the *map* law once more and obtain

$$maxlist \cdot map\ (maxlist \cdot map\ sum \cdot inits) \cdot tails$$

The term $map\ sum \cdot inits$ can be replaced by a *scanl*, a substitution that could have been done one step earlier:

$$maxlist \cdot map\ (maxlist \cdot scanl\ (+)\ 0) \cdot tails$$

Since $maxlist = foldr1\ (\mathbf{max})$ and $(+)$ distributes over $(\mathbf{max})$, the fold-scan fusion law now gives

$$maxlist \cdot map\ (foldr\ (\odot)\ 0) \cdot tails$$

where $x \odot y = 0 \, \textbf{max} \, (x + y)$. Finally, the last two terms can be replaced by a *scanr*, and we obtain

$$mss \;\; = \;\; maxlist \cdot scanr \, (\odot) \, 0$$

The result is a linear-time program for the maximum segment sum.

Exercises

4.6.1 Prove the third duality theorem.

4.6.2 Prove the fusion theorem for *foldr*.

4.6.3 The fusion theorem for *foldl* states that $f \cdot foldl \, g \, a = foldl \, h \, b$ provided f is strict, $f \, a = b$, and $f \, (g \, x \, y) = h \, (f \, x) \, y$ for all x and y.
In the induction proof the case $(x : xs)$ requires us to show that

$$f \, (foldl \, g \, (g \, a \, x) \, xs) \;\; = \;\; foldl \, h \, (h \, (f \, a) \, x) \, xs$$

To do this we need a second induction hypothesis, namely that

$$f \, (foldl \, g \, (g \, x \, y) \, zs) \;\; = \;\; foldl \, h \, (h \, (f \, x) \, y) \, zs$$

for all x and y and for all lists zs. Prove this equation and complete the proof of the fusion law.

4.6.4 Prove the equations

$$\begin{aligned} foldr \, f \, a \, (xs \mathbin{+\!\!+} ys) &= foldr \, f \, (foldr \, f \, a \, ys) \, xs \\ foldl \, f \, a \, (xs \mathbin{+\!\!+} ys) &= foldl \, f \, (foldl \, f \, a \, xs) \, ys \end{aligned}$$

What restrictions on xs and ys are necessary, if any?

4.6.5 Prove that $scanl \, (\otimes) \, e$ can be written as a *foldr* if $\otimes$ is associative with unit e. Can $scanl \, (\otimes) \, e$ be written as a *foldl* without any assumptions on $\otimes$ and e?

4.6.6 Prove that if $\otimes$ distributes over $\oplus$, then

$$foldr1 \, (\oplus) \cdot map \, (x \otimes) \;\; = \;\; (x \otimes) \cdot foldr1 \, (\oplus)$$

4.6.7 It is tempting to try to push the calculation of the maximum segment sum one step further and use the fold-scan fusion law to replace $maxlist \cdot scanr \, (\odot) \, 0$ by a *foldl*. Why doesn't this work? (See Exercise 4.6.10 for a version of fold-scan fusion that does work.)

4.6.8 Give a fusion law for *foldr1* and use it to give conditions on f, g, and h so that the law

$$foldr1\ f \cdot scanl1\ g \quad = \quad foldr1\ h$$

is valid.

4.6.9 Define *segs1* by *segs1* = *concat* · *map inits1* · *tails1*, where *inits1* returns the nonempty initial segments of a list, and *tails1* the nonempty tail segments. Use this version to state and solve a version of the maximum segment sum problem that leaves out empty segments.

4.6.10 There is a version of the fold-scan fusion law that does not depend on any properties of the operators involved. The law is

$$foldl1\ (\oplus) \cdot scanl\ (\otimes)\ e \quad = \quad fst \cdot foldl\ (\odot)\ (a, a)$$

with $(x, y) \odot z = (x \oplus t, t)$, where $t = y \otimes z$. Prove this version of fold-scan fusion.

4.7 Chapter notes

Haskell provides many more standard functions on lists than we have described in this chapter. For full details, consult the Haskell standard prelude and the library of list functions.

A great deal of work has been done on automatic or machine-aided generation of induction proofs; see, for example, Boyer and Moore (1979), Gordon, Milner, and Wadsworth (1979), Paulson (1983), Martin and Nipkow (1990).

The relationship between polymorphic functions and naturality conditions is explored in Wadler (1989); see also Bird and de Moor (1997).

The fusion laws for fold operators were systematised in Malcolm (1990), Fokkinga (1992), Jeuring (1993), and Meijer (1992).

The maximum segment sum problem is described in Bentley (1987). The derivation recorded in this chapter was first given in Bird (1989).

Chapter 5

Examples

The examples of list processing dealt with in the present chapter come from a variety of sources and cover both numeric and symbolic applications. In particular, we will build a simple package for doing arithmetic with arbitrary precision integers, design some useful functions for handling text, and show how to print a calendar. We begin with a simple problem in which list indexing plays a central role.

5.1 Converting numbers to words

Sometimes we need to write numbers in words. For instance, to fill out a cheque or cash transfer correctly, not only must the amount appear in figures, it must also be written in words. Suppose, for simplicity, that the given number is an integer greater than zero but less than one million. We want to design a function *convert* so that, provided *n* is in the stated range, the value of *convert n* is the list of characters corresponding to the usual English formulation of the whole number *n*.

The informal specification above assumes we know exactly what 'the usual English formulation' of a number is. In fact, different rules and conventions are adopted in different places. The rules we shall follow are illustrated by the following examples:

? *convert* 308000
"three hundred and eight thousand"

? *convert* 369027
"three hundred and sixty-nine thousand and twenty-seven"

? *convert* 369401
"three hundred and sixty-nine thousand four hundred and one"

Notice the dash in the phrases "twenty-seven" and "sixty-nine", and the connecting word "and" which appears: (i) after the word "hundred" if the tens part is nonzero; and (ii) after the word "thousand" if the hundreds part is zero but the tens part is not.

A good way to tackle such problems is to consider a simpler problem first. There is, of course, no guarantee that solutions obtained for simpler problems can be used directly in the problem that inspired them; they may only serve to familiarise the solver with some of the features and difficulties involved. Even so, the work is not wasted; familiarity with a problem is one of our most important tools for solving it. And often we will be able to use the solution directly or by adapting it.

An obvious place to begin is to suppose that the number n belongs to a smaller interval, say $0 < n < 100$. In this case n has one or two digits. These digits are going to be needed, so we start with the definition

$$
\begin{array}{lll}
convert2 & :: & Int \rightarrow String \\
convert2 & = & combine2 \cdot digits2 \\[4pt]
digits2 & :: & Int \rightarrow (Int, Int) \\
digits2\ n & = & (n \ \mathbf{div}\ 10, n \ \mathbf{mod}\ 10)
\end{array}
$$

In order to define *combine2*, we will need the English names for the simplest numbers. These can be given as lists of strings:

$$
\begin{array}{lll}
units, teens, tens & :: & [String] \\
units & = & [\text{"one", "two", "three", "four", "five",}] \\
 & & [\text{"six", "seven", "eight", "nine"}] \\
teens & = & [\text{"ten", "eleven", "twelve", "thirteen", "fourteen",}] \\
 & & [\text{"fifteen", "sixteen", "seventeen", "eighteen", "nineteen"}] \\
tens & = & [\text{"twenty", "thirty", "forty", "fifty",}] \\
 & & [\text{"sixty", "seventy", "eighty", "ninety"}]
\end{array}
$$

The definition of *combine2* uses these lists by extracting appropriate elements, depending on the digits:

$$
\begin{array}{lll}
combine2 & :: & (Int, Int) \rightarrow String \\
combine2\ (0, u + 1) & = & units\ !!\ u \\
combine2\ (1, u) & = & teens\ !!\ u \\
combine2\ (t + 2, 0) & = & tens\ !!\ t \\
combine2\ (t + 2, u + 1) & = & tens\ !!\ t\ \mathbin{+\!\!+}\ \text{"-"}\ \mathbin{+\!\!+}\ units\ !!\ u
\end{array}
$$

Recall that list-indexing begins at 0, not 1. The patterns on the left are mutually disjoint, so the order of the equations is not important. However, no value is specified for the pattern $(0, 0)$.

The case $0 < n < 100$ yielded easily enough, so now let us investigate the range $0 < n < 1000$ when n can have up to three digits. We would like to make use of *convert2*, as well as to exploit the simple structure of its definition, so we define

$$
\begin{array}{lll}
\textit{convert3} & :: & \textit{Int} \rightarrow \textit{String} \\
\textit{convert3} & = & \textit{combine3} \cdot \textit{digits3} \\[4pt]
\textit{digits3} & :: & \textit{Int} \rightarrow (\textit{Int}, \textit{Int}) \\
\textit{digits3 } n & = & (n \textbf{ div } 100, n \textbf{ mod } 100) \\[4pt]
\textit{combine3} & :: & (\textit{Int}, \textit{Int}) \rightarrow \textit{String} \\
\textit{combine3 } (0, t + 1) & = & \textit{convert2 } (t + 1) \\
\textit{combine3 } (h + 1, 0) & = & \textit{units} \mathbin{!!} h \mathbin{+\!\!+} \text{``\textvisiblespace hundred''} \\
\textit{combine3 } (h + 1, t + 1) & = & \textit{units} \mathbin{!!} h \mathbin{+\!\!+} \text{``\textvisiblespace hundred and\textvisiblespace ''} \\
& & \mathbin{+\!\!+} \textit{convert2 } (t + 1)
\end{array}
$$

This step is the crucial one as far as the design of the overall algorithm is concerned. We split n into digits in two stages: first into a hundreds part h and a part t less than a hundred; and then, in the definition of *convert2*, split t into a tens part and a part less than ten.

Now we are ready to tackle the next and final step in which n lies in the range $0 < n < 1000000$ and so can have up to 6 digits. In a similar spirit to before, we split n into two numbers m and h, where m is the thousands part and h is the part less than a thousand. There will be a connecting "and" between the words for m and h only in the case that $m > 0$ and $0 < h < 100$. Hence we have

$$
\begin{array}{lll}
\textit{convert6} & :: & \textit{Int} \rightarrow \textit{String} \\
\textit{convert6} & = & \textit{combine6} \cdot \textit{digits6} \\[4pt]
\textit{digits6} & :: & \textit{Int} \rightarrow (\textit{Int}, \textit{Int}) \\
\textit{digits6 } n & = & (n \textbf{ div } 1000, n \textbf{ mod } 1000) \\[4pt]
\textit{combine6} & :: & (\textit{Int}, \textit{Int}) \rightarrow \textit{String} \\
\textit{combine6 } (0, h + 1) & = & \textit{convert3 } (h + 1) \\
\textit{combine6 } (m + 1, 0) & = & \textit{convert3 } (m + 1) \mathbin{+\!\!+} \text{``\textvisiblespace thousand''} \\
\textit{combine6 } (m + 1, h + 1) & = & \textit{convert3 } (m + 1) \mathbin{+\!\!+} \text{``\textvisiblespace thousand''} \\
& & \mathbin{+\!\!+} \textit{link } (h + 1) \mathbin{+\!\!+} \textit{convert3 } (h + 1) \\[4pt]
\textit{link} & :: & \textit{Int} \rightarrow \textit{String} \\
\textit{link } h & = & \textbf{if } h < 100 \textbf{ then } \text{``\textvisiblespace and\textvisiblespace ''} \textbf{ else } \text{``\textvisiblespace ''}
\end{array}
$$

The required function *convert* is just the function *convert6*, so we are done. As well as being a good illustration of the use of ++ and !!, this example also demonstrates the advantages of pattern matching over a definition using conditional expressions. Each case is expressed clearly and concisely, and it is easier to check that all cases are covered.

Exercises

5.1.1 Modify the solution so that a full-stop character is printed after a number.

5.1.2 Generalise the solution to handle positive numbers up to one billion.

5.1.3 Show how the solution can be adapted to handle negative numbers and zero.

5.1.4 Write a similar program to convert a whole number of pence into words. For example, the number 3649 should convert to "thirty-six pounds and forty-nine pence".

5.1.5 As a much more difficult exercise, write a program which will do the inverse of *convert*. In other words, the input is the English formulation of a number and the output is the corresponding decimal representation.

5.2   Producing a class list

Consider the problem of processing examination marks to produce a final class list. There are two inputs to the problem, both of them nonempty lists. One list, known only to the examiner, consists of an alphabetical list of candidate names together with candidate identification numbers. For example,

```
ANDERSON    101372
BAYLIS      101369
CARTER      101370
DENNIS      101371
EDWARDS     101373
```

The second list, produced by the marker for the examination, consists of an ordered list of candidate identification numbers and the marks. For example,

```
101369    62
101370    75
101371    62
101372    30
101373    50
```

The task of the examiner is to use these two lists to produce an alphabetical class list of candidates, their marks, and their final ranking. It is also required to print the result in a suitably attractive form. For example,

```
Name         Mark   Rank
ANDERSON      30      5
BAYLIS        62      2
CARTER        75      1
DENNIS        62      2
EDWARDS       50      4
```

Before starting to think about the problem, we introduce some appropriate type synonyms:

$$\begin{array}{lll} \textbf{type } Name & = & String \\ \textbf{type } Iden & = & Integer \\ \textbf{type } Mark & = & Int \\ \textbf{type } Rank & = & Int \end{array}$$

For brevity, we also introduce

$$\begin{array}{lll} \textbf{type } Codes & = & [(Name, Iden)] \\ \textbf{type } Marks & = & [(Iden, Mark)] \\ \textbf{type } Ranks & = & [(Name, Mark, Rank)] \end{array}$$

The two functions we have to implement are

$$\begin{array}{lll} classlist & :: & (Codes, Marks) \rightarrow Ranks \\ display & :: & Ranks \rightarrow String \end{array}$$

Defining *classlist* as a noncurried function means that we can exploit a compositional style.

Let us concentrate first on *classlist*. It is sensible to construct this function in two phases: collating marks with candidate names, and producing the ranking. Hence we define

$$classlist = rank \cdot collate$$

The types of the subsidiary functions are

$$\begin{array}{lll} collate & :: & (Codes, Marks) \rightarrow [(Name, Mark)] \\ rank & :: & [(Name, Mark)] \rightarrow Ranks \end{array}$$

We will deal with each of these functions separately.

5.2.1 Collating

In the construction of *collate* we can assume that the list of codes is in alphabetical order of *Name* and the list of marks is in numerical order of *Iden*. Furthermore, no two candidates have the same name or the same identification number, and the two lists have equal length. The result has to be a list in alphabetical order of *Name*.

There is one fairly obvious way to construct *collate*: sort the first list by identification numbers, zip with the second list, remove the identification numbers, and sort the result by candidate name. Here is the definition, which is a faithful transcription of the previous sentence:

$$collate \;=\; sortby\; name \cdot remove \cdot zipp \cdot cross\,(sortby\; iden, id)$$
$$\textbf{where } name\,(xn, xm) \;=\; xn$$
$$iden\,(xn, xi) \;\;=\; xi$$

Recall from Section 4.4 that *zipp* is the noncurried version of *zip*. The function *remove* is defined by

$$remove \;\;::\;\; [((\alpha, \beta), (\beta, \gamma))] \;\rightarrow\; [(\alpha, \gamma)]$$
$$remove \;\;=\;\; map\,(cross\,(fst, snd))$$

The function *sortby* has type

$$sortby \;\;::\;\; Ord\,\beta \Rightarrow (\alpha \rightarrow \beta) \rightarrow [\alpha] \rightarrow [\alpha]$$

The specification of *sortby f xs* is that it returns a permutation *ys* of *xs* satisfying

$$and\,[f\;x \le f\;y \mid (x, y) \leftarrow zip\; ys\,(tail\; ys)]$$

In particular, the function *sortby id* sorts a list into ascending order. We will give a definition of *sortby* at the end of the section. For now we mention only that, assuming *f* takes constant time, *sortby f* can be implemented to run in time proportional to $n \log n$ steps on a list of length n.

The program for *collate* can be written in an alternative form. Recall the naturality condition

$$map\,(cross\,(f, g)) \cdot zipp \;\;=\;\; zipp \cdot cross\,(map\,f, map\,g)$$

discussed in Section 4.4. Using this law, we obtain

$$remove \cdot zipp \;\;=\;\; zipp \cdot cross\,(map\,fst, map\,snd)$$

Now recall the law

$$cross\ (f, g) \cdot cross\ (h, k) \quad = \quad cross\ (f \cdot h, g \cdot k)$$

proved in Section 2.4. Using this law, we obtain

$$cross\ (map\ fst, map\ snd) \cdot cross\ (sortby\ iden, id)$$
$$= \quad cross\ (map\ fst \cdot sortby\ iden, map\ snd)$$

Putting these two facts together, we obtain

$$collate \quad = \quad sortby\ name \cdot zipp \cdot cross\ (map\ fst \cdot sortby\ iden, map\ snd)$$

5.2.2 Computing rank

Now let us turn to the second problem, that of computing *rank*. What, precisely, does it mean to say that a candidate A has rank n? We might answer that it means that A comes in position n (counting from 1) in the list of candidates in descending order of mark, but that is not quite correct. Two candidates can have the same marks, and therefore the same rank, but they cannot both be in the same position. The right answer is that A has rank n if and only if there are exactly $(n - 1)$ candidates with higher marks. One way of defining *rank* is therefore to count, for each candidate, the number of candidates with better marks:

$$
\begin{array}{lll}
rank & :: & [(Name, Mark)] \rightarrow Ranks \\
rank\ xs & = & map\ (score\ xs)\ xs \\
score\ xs\ (xn, xm) & = & (xn, xm, 1 + length\ (filter\ (beats\ xm)\ xs)) \\
beats\ xm\ (yn, ym) & = & xm < ym
\end{array}
$$

Provided the class list is reasonably small, examiners do tend to use exactly this method for computing *rank*. It is easy to see that computing *score* takes about n steps on a list of size n, so computing the ranks of all candidates takes about n^2 steps. This is fine for small n, but classes are getting bigger these days; in any case, most examiners can use computers to help them, so we should not be restricted to a method that is easy to perform only by hand.

The problem of computing *rank* would be a lot easier if the marks were in descending order. We could then assign ranks in a single pass through the list. This suggests redefining *rank* by

$$
\begin{array}{ll}
rank \quad = & sortby\ name \cdot assign \cdot reverse \cdot sortby\ mark \\
\textbf{where}\ mark\ (xn, xm) & = \quad xm \\
\quad\quad\quad\ name\ (xn, xm, xr) & = \quad xn
\end{array}
$$

To define *assign* we can attach an initial rank of *n* to the *n*th candidate (counting from 1), and then reduce it if a candidate has the same mark as the immediately preceding candidate. The rank is reduced to that of the preceding candidate. This method requires us to traverse the list from left to right. The following implementation of *assign* uses the function *scanl1*. Recall from Section 4.5 that

$$scanl1 \ (\oplus) \ [x1, x2, x3] \quad = \quad [x1, x1 \oplus x2, (x1 \oplus x2) \oplus x3]$$

The definition of *assign* is

$$
\begin{array}{lll}
assign & :: & [(Name, Mark)] \rightarrow Ranks \\
assign \ xs & = & scanl1 \ reduce \cdot initialise
\end{array}
$$

$$
\begin{array}{lll}
initialise & :: & [(Name, Mark)] \rightarrow Ranks \\
initialise \ xs & = & zipWith \ mktriple \ xs \ [1 \ .. \ ] \\
& & \textbf{where} \ mktriple \ ((xn, xm), xr) = (xn, xm, xr)
\end{array}
$$

The function *reduce* is defined by

$$
\begin{array}{l}
reduce \ (xn, xm, xr) \ (yn, ym, yr) \\
\quad = \quad \textbf{if} \ ym = xm \ \textbf{then} \ (yn, ym, xr) \ \textbf{else} \ (yn, ym, yr)
\end{array}
$$

Each candidate therefore gets the same rank as any previous candidate with the same mark, or the rank initially assigned if there is no such previous candidate.

It is clear that, on an input of length *n*, the function *assign* takes time proportional to *n*. The result is a program for *rank* that takes about the time required to carry out two sorting procedures. As we mentioned above, the implementation of *sortby* takes time proportional to *n* log *n* on a list of length *n*, so the revised definition of *rank* can lead to a big saving.

At this point, we have obtained the following definition of *classlist*:

$$
\begin{array}{ll}
classlist \quad = & sortby \ name \cdot assign \cdot reverse \cdot \\
& sortby \ mark \cdot sortby \ name' \cdot zipp \cdot \\
& cross \ (map \ fst \cdot sortby \ iden, map \ snd)
\end{array}
$$

The two definitions of *name* are slightly different (see above), which is why the second occurrence is decorated with a prime. But it is easy to see that

$$sortby \ f \cdot sortby \ g \quad = \quad sortby \ f$$

In other words, there is no point in sorting the same list twice. Hence the term *sortby name'* in the above expression for *classlist* is redundant.

5.2.3   Printing the class list

The implementation of *display* :: *Ranks* → *String* is straightforward as we are not required to do anything sophisticated. The simplest method is to build a list of the lines of the output and then flatten the result to a single string:

$$display \quad :: \quad [(Name, Mark, Rank)] \to String$$
$$display \quad = \quad unlines \cdot (heading :) \cdot map\ line$$

The definition of *unlines* is similar to *concat* except that newline characters are inserted before concatenating:

$$unlines \quad :: \quad [String] \to String$$
$$unlines \quad = \quad foldr1\ join \quad \textbf{where}\ join\ xs\ ys = xs \mathbin{+\!\!+} \text{``}\bar{\mathsf{f}}\text{''} \mathbin{+\!\!+} ys$$

The string *heading* and the function *line* depend on how many columns should be allocated to the names of candidates, the length of the identification numbers, and the size of the marks in decimal notation. For concreteness we take

$$heading$$
$$= \quad ljustify\ 12\ \text{``Name''} \mathbin{+\!\!+} rjustify\ 4\ \text{``Mark''} \mathbin{+\!\!+} rjustify\ 6\ \text{``Rank''}$$
$$line\ (xn, xm, xr)$$
$$= \quad ljustify\ 12\ xn \mathbin{+\!\!+} rjustify\ 4\ (show\ xm) \mathbin{+\!\!+} rjustify\ 6\ (show\ xr)$$

The functions *ljustify* and *rjustify* are defined as follows:

$$ljustify, rjustify \quad :: \quad Int \to String \to String$$
$$ljustify\ n\ xs \quad = \quad xs \mathbin{+\!\!+} spaces\ (n - length\ xs)$$
$$rjustify\ n\ xs \quad = \quad spaces\ (n - length\ xs) \mathbin{+\!\!+} xs$$

In particular, *ljustify n xs* is the string *xs* padded with extra spaces on the right to make a string of total length *n*. The definition of *spaces* is left as an exercise.

5.2.4   Sorting

It remains to implement the function *sortby*. We will give two implementations, one is simple and the other is efficient.

The simple method is to insert elements of the list one by one in the correct order:

$$sortby \quad :: \quad (Ord\ \beta) \Rightarrow (\alpha \to \beta) \to [\alpha] \to [\alpha]$$
$$sortby\ f \quad = \quad foldr\ (insertby\ f)\ [\ ]$$

$$insertby \quad :: \quad (Ord\ \beta) \Rightarrow (\alpha \rightarrow \beta) \rightarrow \alpha \rightarrow [\alpha] \rightarrow [\alpha]$$
$$insertby\ f\ x \quad = \quad insert \cdot span\ test$$
$$\mathbf{where}\ insert\ (xs, ys) \quad = \quad xs + [x] + ys$$
$$test\ y \qquad\qquad = \quad (f\ y < f\ x)$$

The function *span* can be defined by

$$span \qquad :: \quad (\alpha \rightarrow Bool) \rightarrow [\alpha] \rightarrow ([\alpha], [\alpha])$$
$$span\ p\ xs \quad = \quad (takeWhile\ p\ xs, dropWhile\ p\ xs)$$

The functions *takeWhile* and *dropWhile* were considered in Exercise 4.3.7. The way to write a more efficient program for *span* is discussed in Chapter 7.

The problem with the above method of sorting is that it can take time proportional to n^2 steps on a list of length n. A more efficient method for computing *sortby* is to use a *divide and conquer* strategy: if the list has length at most one, then it is already sorted; otherwise, divide it into two equal halves, recursively sort each half, and then merge the two sorted halves together. This idea leads to the following algorithm:

$$sortby\ f\ [\ ] \qquad\qquad = \quad [\ ]$$
$$sortby\ f\ [x] \qquad\qquad = \quad [x]$$
$$sortby\ f\ (x : y : xs) \quad = \quad mergeby\ f\ (divide\ (x : y : xs))$$

The function *divide* allocates each element of the list to one of two lists in strict alternation:

$$divide \quad :: \quad [\alpha] \rightarrow ([\alpha], [\alpha])$$
$$divide \quad = \quad foldr\ allocate\ ([\ ], [\ ]) \quad \mathbf{where}\ allocate\ x\ (ys, zs) = (zs, x : ys)$$

For an alternative definition of *divide*, see Exercise 5.2.3.

The function *mergeby* is defined as follows:

$$mergeby \qquad\qquad\qquad :: \quad Ord\ \beta \Rightarrow (\alpha \rightarrow \beta) \rightarrow ([\alpha], [\alpha]) \rightarrow [\alpha]$$
$$mergeby\ f\ ([\ ], ys) \qquad = \quad ys$$
$$mergeby\ f\ (x : xs, [\ ]) \quad = \quad x : xs$$

$$mergeby\ f\ (x : xs, y : ys)$$
$$\left|\ \begin{array}{ll} f\ x \leq f\ y & = \quad x : mergeby\ f\ (xs, y : ys) \\ otherwise & = \quad y : mergeby\ f\ (x : xs, ys) \end{array}\right.$$

Assuming f takes constant time, this program for *sortby* f takes time proportional to $n \log n$ steps on a list of length n. We will prove this fact in Chapter 7.

As well as being a good illustration of a compositional style of programming, the problem of producing a class list also demonstrates the importance of being able to sort a list efficiently. The complete program is dominated by the time to sort various lists. If there are n candidates, then the class list can be produced in time proportional to $n \log n$ steps. The naive method that examiners do by hand can take time proportional to n^2 steps.

Exercises

5.2.1 In the list of candidate–identification pairs where was the assumption used that the list was sorted in alphabetical order?

5.2.2 Assume that *sortby f* takes at most $cn \log n$ steps on a list of length n, and that *mergeby f* takes at most cn steps when the result is a list of length n. Prove that *sortby f* takes at most $2cn \log(2n)$ on a list of length $2n$.

5.2.3 Give an alternative (though not equivalent) definition of *divide* that makes use of the standard function *splitAt* defined in Section 4.2. The definition of *divide* given in the text makes one traversal of the list. Does yours?

5.2.4 The equation *reverse · zipp* = *zipp · cross* (*reverse, reverse*) holds on pairs of lists of equal length. Use this fact, together with

$$reverse \cdot map\, f \quad = \quad map\, f \cdot reverse$$

to rewrite the definition of *classlist*.

5.2.5 It could fairly be argued that the function *sortby* is not as useful as a more general function *sortwith* with type

$$sortwith \quad :: \quad (\alpha \rightarrow \alpha \rightarrow Bool) \rightarrow [\alpha] \rightarrow [\alpha]$$

The specification of *sortwith compare xs* is that it returns a permutation *ys* of *xs* satisfying

$$and\, [compare\, x\, y \mid (x, y) \leftarrow zip\, ys\, (tail\, ys)]$$

Rewrite the class list algorithm using *sortwith*. Show why there is no need to reverse lists with the new algorithm.

5.2.6 The examination might have been for an optional course, so some candidates will not appear on the marks list. How would you tackle this refinement of the problem?

5.3 Arbitrary-precision arithmetic

The aim of this section is to show how arbitrary-precision arithmetic, the arithmetic of *Integer*, can be implemented in terms of arithmetic on limited-precision integers, the arithmetic of *Int*. The full installation of a new class of integral numbers in Haskell is a significant task, so we will go only part of the way.

   An arbitrary-precision integer will be represented as a list of digits in some given base *base*. Each digit *d* will lie in the range $0 \leq d < base$, except possibly for the first one, which will lie in the range $-1 \leq d < base$. An initial digit of -1 will signify a negative integer. The representation of negative numbers is considered later on; for the moment, assume that arbitrary-precision integers are nonnegative.

   The declaration

> **newtype** *ArbInt*   =   *Norm* [*Digit*]
> **type** *Digit*   =   *Int*

introduces *ArbInt* as a new type rather than a type synonym because we are going to install *ArbInt* as a member of the class *Num*, and so will need instances of *Show* and *Ord* that are different from the generic instantiations of these classes for lists. For simplicity, elements of *ArbInt* will be referred to as *numerals*.

   The conversion function

> *digits*   ::   *ArbInt* → [*Digit*]
> *digits* (*Norm* xs)   =   xs

returns the digits of a numeral. Numerals will be represented with the most significant digit first. This representation is the one used with ordinary decimals and, in the absence of a compelling reason to the contrary, is the sensible one to adopt for our arithmetic package. Thus, an integer *x* is represented by a sequence $[x_0, x_1, \ldots, x_{n-1}]$ of digits, where

$$x = x_0 \times base^{n-1} + x_1 \times base^{n-2} + \cdots + x_{n-1} \times base^0$$

The major criterion influencing the choice of base is that we want digit-by-digit multiplications to be performed by the built-in multiplication provided by *Int* without danger of going out of range. On the other hand, we would like our digits to be reasonably large in order to keep the representation of numerals reasonably small. For concreteness, we will take

> *base, baseSize*   ::   *Int*
> *base*   =   10000
> *baseSize*   =   4

This choice supposes that all numbers up to 10^8 lie within the permitted range of limited-precision arithmetic. The quantity *baseSize* is needed for printing numerals. To illustrate the choice of *base*, observe that

$$[1, 2345, 89] \quad \text{represents} \quad 123450089$$
$$[1, 2, 3] \quad \text{represents} \quad 100020003$$

These representations are not unique, since an arbitrary number of leading zeros can be added to a numeral without changing its value.

We can normalise a numeral by applying a function *norm* to strip off nonsignificant zeros. In particular, the number 0 will be represented by the empty list. All numerals will be built using *norm*, so we can suppose in the definition of the operations to come that numeral arguments are in normal form. It will be convenient, however, to define *norm* as a more general function, one that converts an arbitrary list of integers, rather than just a list of digits, into a numeral. Thus, the type assigned to *norm* will be $norm :: [Int] \rightarrow ArbInt$.

To specify *norm*, define

$$convert \quad :: \quad [Int] \rightarrow Integer$$
$$convert \quad = \quad foldl\, (\oplus)\, 0 \quad \textbf{where}\ n \oplus d = base \times n + d$$

Then *norm* is specified by two conditions. Firstly,

$$convert \cdot digits \cdot norm \quad = \quad convert$$

This condition states that *norm* does not change the value of the represented integer. Secondly, *norm* should return a value *Norm xs*, where *xs* is a list of digits x in the range $0 \le x < base$, except possibly for the first digit, which will be in the range $-1 \le x < base$.

To implement *norm*, we process the list of integers from right to left, reducing each digit modulo *base* after adding in a carry from the previous step. The initial carry is 0. For example, supposing $base = 10$, the list $[11, 9, 16]$ is normalised by beginning with a carry 0, reducing 16 to the digit 6 and a carry of 1, reducing $9 + 1$ to the digit 0 and a carry of 1, reducing $11 + 1$ to the digit 2 and a carry of 1, and finally adding in this carry to give the normalised number $[1, 2, 0, 6]$.

If the final carry c is not in the required range $-1 \le c < base$, then it has to be processed further. For example, again supposing $base = 10$ the list $[987]$ is normalised to $[7]$ with a carry of 98. This carry is not in the required range, so it is reduced to the digit 8 and another carry of 9.

The process can be described in terms of *foldr*. Define

type *Carry*   =   *Int*

carry   ::   *Digit* → (*Carry*, [*Digit*]) → (*Carry*, [*Digit*])
carry x (*c*, *xs*)   =   ((*x* + *c*) **div** *base*, (*x* + *c*) **mod** *base* : *xs*)

Then *norm* is defined by

norm   ::   [*Int*] → *ArbInt*
norm   =   *Norm* · *dropWhile* (== 0) · *addCarry* · *foldr carry* (0, [ ])

The term (0, [ ]) ensures that normalisation starts off with an initial carry of 0,
the term *addCarry* adds in the final carry as one or more new most significant
digits, and *dropWhile* (== 0) removes leading zeros. The definition of *dropWhile*
was given in Exercise 4.3.7. The final list of digits is converted to a numeral by
applying the constructor *Norm*. The definition of *addCarry* is

addCarry   ::   (*Carry*, [*Digit*]) → [*Digit*]
addCarry (*c*, *xs*)   =   **if** (−1 ≤ *c*) ∧ (*c* < *base*) **then** *c* : *xs*
                             else *addCarry* (*c* **div** *base*, *c* **mod** *base* : *xs*)

We will leave it as an exercise to show that *addCarry* terminates and that *norm*
satisfies the first condition of its specification. It is clear by construction that
norm returns a list of digits in the required range.

5.3.1   Comparison operations

Given our choice of representation, which has the most significant digit first,
comparison operations on numerals can be based on the standard lexicographic
ordering on lists. We first have to align the two lists by adding nonsignificant
zeros to the shorter one. For example, 57 is less than 126 because 057 is
lexicographically less than 126. We can align two lists of digits by

align :: ([*Digit*], [*Digit*]) → ([*Digit*], [*Digit*])
align (*xs*, *ys*)
    | *n* > 0   =   (*replicate n* 0 ++ *xs*, *ys*)
    | *n* ≤ 0   =   (*xs*, *replicate* (−*n*) 0 ++ *ys*)
    where *n* = *length ys* − *length xs*

The function *replicate* can be defined by

replicate   ::   *Int* → α → [α]
replicate n x   =   [*x* | *k* ← [1 .. *n*]]

The comparison functions can now be introduced by

> **instance** *Eq ArbInt* **where**
> $\quad (==) \quad = \quad translate\,(==)$

> **instance** *Ord ArbInt* **where**
> $\quad (<) \quad = \quad translate\,(<)$

> $translate :: ([Digit] \rightarrow [Digit] \rightarrow Bool) \rightarrow (ArbInt \rightarrow ArbInt \rightarrow Bool)$
> $translate\ op\ x\ y \quad = \quad op\ xs\ ys$
> $\qquad\qquad\qquad\qquad\;$ **where** $(xs, ys) = align\,(digits\ x, digits\ y)$

The test for zero can also be implemented directly by

> $isZero \quad :: \quad ArbInt \rightarrow Bool$
> $isZero \quad = \quad null \cdot digits$

This uses the assumption that the argument is a numeral in normal form.

5.3.2 Addition and subtraction

The functions $(+)$ and $(-)$ for doing arbitrary-precision addition and subtraction are easily defined. We can align the two lists of digits, do the operation digit by digit, and then normalise the result. For example, suppose we want to add the numbers $[7, 3, 7]$ and $[4, 6, 9]$, where, temporarily, we suppose that $base = 10$. The digit-by-digit addition of these numbers is $[11, 9, 16]$ and, as we saw above, the normalised result is $[1, 2, 0, 6]$.

The addition and subtraction operations can be introduced with their conventional names, by declaring *ArbInt* as an instance of the class *Num*:

> **instance** *Num ArbInt* **where**
> $x + y \qquad = \quad norm\,(zippWith\,(+)\,(align\,(digits\ x, digits\ y)))$
> $x - y \qquad = \quad norm\,(zippWith\,(-)\,(align\,(digits\ x, digits\ y)))$
> $x \times y \qquad = \quad \ldots$
> $negate\ x \quad = \quad \ldots$

The definition of $(\times)$ and *negate* is considered later on. Recall that *zippWith* is the noncurried version of *zipWith*. The type class *Num* has both *Eq* and *Show* as a superclass, so the installation of *ArbInt* as a *Num* type is incomplete until *ArbInt* is declared as an instance of the *Show* class. This task is postponed to the end of the section.

The interesting point about subtraction is what happens when the second argument is greater than the first, so the answer is a negative number. For example, again supposing *base* = 10, subtracting $[3, 7, 5]$ from $[1, 0, 6]$ gives the list $[-2, -7, 1]$ after digit-by-digit subtraction, and normalisation yields *Norm* $[-1, 7, 3, 1]$. These digits represent the number

$$-1 \times 10^3 + 7 \times 10^2 + 3 \times 10^1 + 1 \times 10^0 \quad = \quad -269$$

The answer is correct since $106 - 375 = -269$. After normalisation, a negative number is indicated by a leading digit of -1. The absolute value of a negative number can be obtained by negating all the digits in the representation and normalising. It follows that we can define the predicate *negative*, which tests whether the result of subtraction is negative, and the function *negate* for negating a number by

$$
\begin{array}{lll}
\textit{negative} & :: & \textit{ArbInt} \rightarrow \textit{Bool} \\
\textit{negative} \, (\textit{Norm} \, \textit{xs}) & = & \textit{not} \, (\textit{null} \, \textit{xs}) \wedge (\textit{head} \, \textit{xs} < 0) \\
\\
\textit{negate} & :: & \textit{ArbInt} \rightarrow \textit{ArbInt} \\
\textit{negate} & = & \textit{norm} \cdot \textit{map} \, \textit{neg} \cdot \textit{digits} \quad \textbf{where} \, \textit{neg} \, x = -x
\end{array}
$$

This method of representing negative numbers is called *signed-complement* notation. Signed-complement representation is convenient both for arithmetic and comparison operations, since no special measures have to be taken for negative arguments and results. We leave the proof that the comparison operations work without modification for negative numbers as an exercise.

Another representation of negative numbers is the one normally used with decimal calculations done by hand. This is called *signed-magnitude* notation. Here, a number is denoted by its absolute value, together with an indication of whether the number is positive or negative. Arithmetic with signed-magnitude representation requires case analyses on the sign of the number.

5.3.3 Multiplication

Next, we define $(\times)$ over the type *ArbInt*. The straightforward definition is a translation of the school book method, whereby the multiplicand is multiplied by each digit of the multiplier and the partial sums are added together, shifting appropriately. The list of partial sums, in decreasing order of significance, is returned by the function *sums*, where

$$
\begin{array}{lll}
\textit{sums} & :: & \textit{ArbInt} \rightarrow \textit{ArbInt} \rightarrow [\textit{ArbInt}] \\
\textit{sums} \, x \, y & = & \textit{map} \, (\textit{mult1} \, x) \, (\textit{digits} \, y)
\end{array}
$$

$$mult1 \quad :: \quad ArbInt \rightarrow Digit \rightarrow ArbInt$$
$$mult1 \, x \, d \quad = \quad norm \, (map \, (\times d) \, (digits \, x))$$

The function *mult1* multiplies a numeral by a single digit. To do the shifting and adding, let *splus* be defined by

$$splus \quad :: \quad ArbInt \rightarrow ArbInt \rightarrow ArbInt$$
$$splus \, x \, y \quad = \quad shift \, x + y$$

$$shift \quad :: \quad ArbInt \rightarrow ArbInt$$
$$shift \, (Norm \, xs) \quad = \quad \textbf{if} \, null \, xs \, \textbf{then} \, Norm \, [\,] \, \textbf{else} \, Norm \, (xs \, +\!\!+ \, [0])$$

The definition of *shift* does not use *norm*, but if *xs* is normalised and nonempty, then so is $xs +\!\!+ [0]$. Now we can define

$$x \times y \quad = \quad foldl \, splus \, (Norm \, [\,]) \, (sums \, x \, y)$$

The reader should consider why *foldl* is used here instead of *foldr* or *foldl1*.

5.3.4 Division

Finally, we turn to the division of one integer by another. As every schoolchild knows, division is the hardest of the arithmetic operations to get right; not only is the algorithm complicated, it also involves a certain amount of guesswork. In fact, the following algorithm for division is probably the most complicated program in this book. We will define division only for nonnegative integers, leaving the extension to negative integers as an exercise. Our aim is to define a function

$$quotrem \quad :: \quad ArbInt \rightarrow ArbInt \rightarrow (ArbInt, ArbInt)$$

for returning the quotient and remainder of the division of a nonnegative numeral by a positive numeral. We will not, however, install *ArbInt* as an instance of the type class *Integral*, so the use of the names **div** and **mod** are denied us. Haskell has a hierarchy of type classes above *Integral*, including *Real* and *Enum*, and we do not want to complicate matters by going into a discussion of this hierarchy.

Before tackling the full algorithm, let us consider a simpler problem first, namely to compute the quotient and remainder when a numeral is divided by a single digit. The corresponding function is

$$quotrem1 \quad :: \quad ArbInt \rightarrow Digit \rightarrow (ArbInt, Digit)$$

For example, consider dividing 5 into 369. The steps of the process are learned by rote in childhood: we divide 5 into 3 giving a quotient of 0 and a remainder of 3; we then divide 5 into 36 giving a quotient of 7 and a remainder of 1; finally, we divide 5 into 19 to give a quotient of 3 and a final remainder of 4. The final quotient is 073.

In general, suppose $x = Norm\,[x_0, x_1, \ldots, x_{n-1}]$ is the numeral, and d the digit. The (unnormalised) digits $[q_0, q_1, \ldots, q_{n-1}]$ of the quotient can be computed by setting an initial remainder $r_0 = 0$ and evaluating, for $0 \le i < n$,

$$q_i = (base \times r_i + x_i) \ \textbf{div}\ d$$
$$r_{i+1} = (base \times r_i + x_i) \ \textbf{mod}\ d$$

The single-digit remainder is r_n. We can implement this scheme using the function $scanl$. Recall that

$$scanl\ (\oplus)\ e\,[x_0, x_1, \ldots] \ =\ [e, e \oplus x_0, (e \oplus x_0) \oplus x_1, \ldots]$$

We can define

$$quotrem1 \qquad :: \quad ArbInt \to Digit \to (ArbInt, Digit)$$
$$quotrem1\ x\ d \ = \ finish1\ (scanl\ (step1\ d)\ (0,0)\ (digits\ x))$$

$$step1 \qquad\quad :: \quad Digit \to (Digit, Digit) \to Digit \to (Digit, Digit)$$
$$step1\ d\ (q, r)\ x \ = \ (y\ \textbf{div}\ d, y\ \textbf{mod}\ d) \quad \textbf{where}\ y = base \times r + x$$

$$finish1 \qquad :: \quad [(Digit, Digit)] \to (ArbInt, Digit)$$
$$finish1\ qrs \ = \ (norm\ (map\ fst\ qrs), snd\ (last\ qrs))$$

The function $finish1$ finishes off the computation by normalising the quotient digits and extracting the final remainder.

For the full algorithm we will start with exactly the same structure. Later on we will need to revise it slightly. Hence we take

$$quotrem \qquad :: \quad ArbInt \to ArbInt \to (ArbInt, ArbInt)$$
$$quotrem\ x\ y \ = \ finish\ (scanl\ (step\ y)\ (0, Norm\,[\,])\ (digits\ x))$$

$$finish \qquad :: \quad [(Digit, ArbInt)] \to (ArbInt, ArbInt)$$
$$finish\ qrs \ = \ (norm\ (map\ fst\ qrs), snd\ (last\ qrs))$$

The difference between $quotrem$ and $quotrem1$ is that, in the former, the remainder at each step is not necessarily a single digit. The functions $finish$ and $finish1$ differ only in their types.

The remaining function *step* has type

$$step \quad :: \quad ArbInt \to (Digit, ArbInt) \to Digit \to (Digit, ArbInt)$$

Evaluation of *step y* (q, r) *d* involves dividing the numeral *y* into the numeral $x = splus1\ r\ d$, where

$$
\begin{aligned}
splus1 \quad &:: \quad ArbInt \to Digit \to ArbInt \\
splus1\ r\ d \quad &= \quad Norm\ (digits\ r \mathbin{+\!\!+} [d])
\end{aligned}
$$

The function *splus1* is similar to the function *splus* used in the definition of multiplication except for the change in type. In the algorithm for *step* we will need to distinguish three cases, depending on the number of digits in *x* and *y*, so we define

$$
\begin{aligned}
m \quad &= \quad length\ (digits\ x)\ (= length(digits\ r) + 1) \\
n \quad &= \quad length\ (digits\ y)
\end{aligned}
$$

Note that $m \le n + 1$ since *r*, being the remainder from the previous step, is less than *y* and so cannot have more digits than *y*. The definition of *step* is

$$
\begin{aligned}
step\ y\ (q, r)\ &d \\
\big| \quad m < n \qquad &= \quad astep\ x\ y \\
m == n \qquad &= \quad bstep\ x\ y \\
otherwise \qquad &= \quad cstep\ x\ y \\
\textbf{where}\ m \quad &= \quad length\ (digits\ r) + 1 \\
n \quad &= \quad length\ (digits\ y) \\
x \quad &= \quad splus1\ r\ d
\end{aligned}
$$

The three cases, *astep*, *bstep*, and *cstep*, are in increasing order of difficulty. The definition of *astep* is easy: if $m < n$, then the new quotient is 0 and the new remainder is *x*. Hence

$$
\begin{aligned}
astep \quad &:: \quad ArbInt \to ArbInt \to (Digit, ArbInt) \\
astep\ x\ y \quad &= \quad (0, x)
\end{aligned}
$$

Next, consider *bstep*. If $m = n$, then the new quotient *q* might be any value in the range $0 \le q < base$. However, we will see that in the final version of the algorithm, it will be a condition on the divisor *y* that $y \ge base/2$. Hence there can be a quotient of at most 1 and we can define

$$
\begin{aligned}
bstep \quad &:: \quad ArbInt \to ArbInt \to (Digit, ArbInt) \\
bstep\ x\ y \quad &= \quad \textbf{if}\ negative\ z\ \textbf{then}\ (0, x)\ \textbf{else}\ (1, z) \\
&\qquad \textbf{where}\ z = x - y
\end{aligned}
$$

The most complicated case is *cstep* when $m = n + 1$. Suppose $x = x_0 x_1 \ldots x_n$ and $y = y_1 y_2 \ldots y_n$ are nonnegative numerals with $x/y < base$. We would like a quick way of estimating $\lfloor x/y \rfloor$ and we can do this by looking at the first two digits of x and the first digit of y. For example, with $base = 10$ and $x = 37???$ and $y = 4???$, we would guess a quotient of 9 because $\lfloor 37/4 \rfloor = 9$. Similarly, with $x = 27???$ and the same y, we would guess a quotient of 6. On the other hand, with $x = 41???$ and the same y we would guess a quotient of 9, not 10, because 9 is the maximum quotient possible. Accordingly, define the guess $\hat{q}$ by

$$\hat{q} \;=\; \lfloor (x_0 \times base + x_1)/y_1 \rfloor \,\mathbf{min}\, (base - 1)$$

How much can $\hat{q}$ differ from the true quotient $q = \lfloor x/y \rfloor$? The answer, proved in Exercise 5.3.5, is that provided $y_1 \geq base/2$ we have $\hat{q} - 2 \leq q \leq \hat{q}$. In words, provided y_1 is sufficiently large, the guess $\hat{q}$ can only overestimate q, and then by at most 2.

We will take care of the assumption $y_1 \geq base/2$ in a moment; let us first see how to determine whether $\hat{q}$ is too large. First of all, by definition of floors, $\lfloor x/y \rfloor = \hat{q}$ if and only if

$$\hat{q} \times y \leq x < \hat{q} \times y + y$$

Next, since $\hat{q}$ is never an underestimate, we have

$$x < \lfloor x/y \rfloor \times y + y \leq \hat{q} \times y + y$$

Hence we obtain that $\lfloor x/y \rfloor = \hat{q}$ if and only if $\hat{q} \times y \leq x$. This leads to the following implementation of *cstep*:

```
cstep :: ArbInt → ArbInt → (Digit, ArbInt)
cstep x y
    |  not (negative r0)    =   (q, r0)
    |  not (negative r1)    =   (q − 1, r1)
    |  otherwise            =   (q − 2, r2)
    where q   =   guess x y
          r0  =   x − mult1 y q
          r1  =   r0 + y
          r2  =   r1 + y
```

The function *guess* is defined by

$$guess \quad :: \quad ArbInt \rightarrow ArbInt \rightarrow Digit$$
$$guess \, x \, y \quad = \quad \textbf{if } x0 \geq y1 \textbf{ then } base - 1 \textbf{ else } (x0 \times base + x1) \textbf{ div } y1$$
$$\textbf{where } x0 \quad = \quad xs \, !! \, 0$$
$$x1 \quad = \quad xs \, !! \, 1$$
$$xs \quad = \quad digits \, x$$
$$y1 \quad = \quad (digits \, y) \, !! \, 0$$

That leaves us with the problem of ensuring that the first digit of the divisor *y* is at least *base*/2. We can do this by multiplying both the dividend *x* and the divisor *y* by $d = \lfloor base/(y_1 + 1) \rfloor$. For a proof of this assertion see Exercise 5.3.6. The result of this scaling will leave the final remainder too large, and we will have to divide it by *d* at the end of the algorithm. Accordingly, we revise the earlier definition of *quotrem* to read

$$quotrem \quad :: \quad ArbInt \rightarrow ArbInt \rightarrow (ArbInt, ArbInt)$$
$$quotrem \, x \, y \quad = \quad finish \, d \, (scanl \, (step \, y') \, (0, Norm \, [\,]) \, (digits \, x'))$$
$$\textbf{where } x' \quad = \quad mult1 \, x \, d$$
$$y' \quad = \quad mult1 \, y \, d$$
$$d \quad = \quad base \, \textbf{div} \, (head \, (digits \, y) + 1)$$

$$finish \quad :: \quad Digit \rightarrow [(Digit, ArbInt)] \rightarrow (ArbInt, ArbInt)$$
$$finish \, d \, qrs \quad = \quad (norm \, (map \, fst \, qrs), div1 \, (snd \, (last \, qrs)) \, d)$$

$$div1 \quad :: \quad ArbInt \rightarrow Digit \rightarrow ArbInt$$
$$div1 \, x \, d \quad = \quad fst \, (quotrem1 \, x \, d)$$

As we said at the beginning, division is a complicated process; now the reader can appreciate why.

5.3.5 Showing numerals

The declaration of *ArbInt* as an instance of *Num* is not legitimate in Haskell unless we also declare *ArbInt* to be an instance of the type class *Show*. In the discussion of the *Show* class in Section 2.7 we said that this involved defining a function

$$showsPrec \quad :: \quad Int \rightarrow \alpha \rightarrow String \rightarrow String$$

The function *showsPrec* takes an integer as argument to enable the user to control whether the printed string is enclosed in brackets. It then takes the value to be converted and returns, not a string, but a function from strings to strings. The function *showsPrec* should satisfy the law

$$showsPrec \; d \; x \; xs \mathbin{+\!\!+} ys \;\; = \;\; showsPrec \; d \; x \; (xs \mathbin{+\!\!+} ys)$$

The extra argument *ys* is called an *accumulating* parameter and is there for efficiency. The reason is explained in Chapter 7. The auxiliary function *show* is defined by

$$show \; x \;\; = \;\; showsPrec \; 0 \; x \; [\,]$$

The argument 0 means that the result is never surrounded with brackets.

For completeness, we give the following instance declaration of *Show*. The undefined functions are part of the standard Haskell prelude (in fact, *showChar* is a synonym for (:) and *showString* is a synonym for (++)).

```
instance Show ArbInt where
  showsPrec k x
    │ isZero x      =   showChar '0'
    │ negative x    =   showChar '−' · showDigits (digits (negate x))
    │ otherwise     =   showDigits (digits x)

  showDigits :: [Digit] → String → String
  showDigits (d : ds)
    =   showString (show d) · showString(concat(map showDigit ds))

  showDigit    ::   Digit → String
  showDigit d  =   zeros ++ ds
                   where zeros  =   replicate (baseSize − length ds) '0'
                         ds     =   show d
```

All digits except the leading digit have to be padded with the correct number of 0 characters.

Exercises

5.3.1 The program for *addCarry* terminates if repeatedly replacing c by c **div** *base* eventually leads to a value c in the range $-1 \leq c < base$. Prove that this is the case.

5.3.2 Prove that $convert \cdot digits \cdot norm = convert$.

5.3.3 There is another way to define *norm* by using the function *scanr*. Recall that

$$scanr \ (\oplus) \ e \ [x_0, x_1, x_2] \ = \ [x_0 \oplus (x_1 \oplus (x_2 \oplus e)), x_1 \oplus (x_2 \oplus e), x_2 \oplus e, e]$$

Define $\oplus$ by $x \oplus (c, y) = ((x + c) \ \textbf{div} \ base, (x + c) \ \textbf{mod} \ base)$. Hence define *norm* using *scanr*.

5.3.4 Prove that the comparison operations work correctly when the arguments are possibly negative decimals.

5.3.5 Let $x = x_0 x_1 \ldots x_n$ and $y = y_1 y_2 \ldots y_n$. Set $\hat{q} = \lfloor (x_0 b + x_1)/y_1 \rfloor$, so that

$$\hat{q} y_1 \leq x_0 b + x_1 < \hat{q} y_1 + y_1$$

Using only these inequalities, together with two similar ones,

$$y_1 b^{n-1} \leq y < y_1 b^{n-1} + b^{n-1}$$
$$x_0 b^n + x_1 b^{n-1} \leq x < x_0 b^n + x_1 b^{n-1} + b^{n-1}$$

prove that $\hat{q} - 2 \leq \lfloor x/y \rfloor < \hat{q} + 1$ provided that $y_1 \geq b/2$.

5.3.6 Suppose y and b are integers with $1 \leq y < b$. Prove that

$$\lfloor b/2 \rfloor \leq y \lfloor b/(y + 1) \rfloor < b$$

5.3.7 Construct a function *toArb* :: *String* → *ArbInt* that converts a string of decimal digits into an element of *ArbInt*.

5.3.8 The definition of *quotrem* given in the text can be tuned in a number of ways. In particular, it is possible to improve the guess for q – see Knuth (1981) – and a number of length calculations can be avoided by using versions of addition and subtraction that produce $(n + 1)$-digit results from n-digit arguments. Show how to make *quotrem* more efficient.

5.4 Printing a calendar

In this section we will construct a program for printing a calendar. The aim is to design two functions *year* and *month* so that, for example, *year* 2000 will produce a complete calendar for the year 2000, and *month* $(1, 2000)$ will produce

```
          January 2000
     Su Mo Tu We Th Fr Sa
                        1
      2  3  4  5  6  7  8
      9 10 11 12 13 14 15
     16 17 18 19 20 21 22
     23 24 25 26 27 28 29
     30 31
```

The right way to tackle problems of this kind is to separate the construction phase from the printing phase. As logically independent tasks, we can consider how to provide the necessary information to build an abstract calendar and how to print it in the required format. If we succeed in this separation of concerns, modifications to the program, such as printing the calendar in a different format or printing only part of the calendar, will be easier to carry out.

5.4.1 Building a calendar

The primary purpose of a calendar is to provide a suitable presentation of the relationship between day names and dates. Each date is associated with a unique day name, so the abstract problem is to determine a function *day* that takes a date and returns the correct day name. Since we will need to do arithmetic on day names, we will code them as numbers, with Sunday as day 0, Monday as day 1, and so on. Accordingly, we introduce the type synonyms

$$
\begin{array}{lll}
\textbf{type } Date & = & (Day, Month, Year) \\
\textbf{type } Day & = & Int \\
\textbf{type } Month & = & Int \\
\textbf{type } Year & = & Int \\
\textbf{type } Dayname & = & Int
\end{array}
$$

Given a function $fstday :: (Month, Year) \to Dayname$ that returns the name of the first day in a month, we can define *day* by

$$
\begin{array}{lll}
day & :: & Date \to Dayname \\
day\,(d, m, y) & = & (fstday\,(m, y) + d - 1)\ \textbf{mod}\ 7
\end{array}
$$

In particular, $day\,(1, m, y) = fstday\,(m, y)$.

To determine *fstday* we need to know the lengths of the months and the day on which January 1 falls for the given year. The value of *fstday* is then obtained by indexing into a list of all first days for the year:

$$
\begin{array}{lll}
\textit{fstday} & :: & (\textit{Month}, \textit{Year}) \rightarrow \textit{Dayname} \\
\textit{fstday}\,(m, y) & = & (\textit{fstdays}\,y)\,!!\,(m - 1) \\[4pt]
\textit{fstdays} & :: & \textit{Year} \rightarrow [\textit{Dayname}] \\
\textit{fstdays} & = & \textit{take}\,12 \cdot \textit{map}\,(\textbf{mod}\,7) \cdot \textit{mtotals} \\[4pt]
\textit{mtotals} & :: & \textit{Year} \rightarrow [\textit{Int}] \\
\textit{mtotals}\,y & = & \textit{scanl}\,(+)\,(\textit{jan1}\,y)\,(\textit{mlengths}\,y) \\[4pt]
\textit{mlengths} & :: & \textit{Year} \rightarrow [\textit{Int}] \\
\textit{mlengths}\,y & = & [31, \textit{feb}, 31, 30, 31, 30, 31, 31, 30, 31, 30, 31] \\
& & \textbf{where } \textit{feb} = \textbf{if } \textit{leap}\,y \textbf{ then } 29 \textbf{ else } 28
\end{array}
$$

$$
\begin{array}{lll}
\textit{leap} & :: & \textit{Year} \rightarrow \textit{Bool} \\
\textit{leap}\,y & = & \textbf{if } y\,\textbf{mod}\,100 = 0 \textbf{ then } (y\,\textbf{mod}\,400 = 0) \textbf{ else } (y\,\textbf{mod}\,4 = 0)
\end{array}
$$

The list of first days is obtained by computing the accumulated totals of the month lengths, starting at the day on which January 1 falls, reducing these totals modulo 7 to find the day names for the first days of each month, and finally taking the first 12 values. Note that *scanl* applied to a list of length 12 produces a list of length 13; the last value on this list will be the day on which January 1 falls in the following year.

It remains to define *jan1*. In the Gregorian calendar, January 1 in the year 1 was a Monday. Hence, in order to discover *jan1 y*, we have to count all the days in the previous $(y - 1)$ years, add 1 and take the result modulo 7:

$$
\begin{array}{lll}
\textit{jan1}\,y & :: & \textit{Year} \rightarrow \textit{Dayname} \\
\textit{jan1}\,y & = & (365 \times x + x\,\textbf{div}\,4 - x\,\textbf{div}\,100 + x\,\textbf{div}\,400 + 1)\,\textbf{mod}\,7 \\
& & \textbf{where } x = y - 1
\end{array}
$$

The extra terms account for leap years.

5.4.2 Pictures

Let us now consider how to picture a calendar. The calendar for a year is built out of the calendar for individual months, so the idea is to build pictures out of smaller pictures. For the moment it is best to think of a picture simply as an element of some type *Picture*. Each picture is a rectangular entity with a positive height and width, so there are two primitive functions defined on pictures, *height* and *width*. We introduce two synonyms

> **type** *Height* = *Int*
> **type** *Width*   = *Int*

and write the types of *height* and *width* in the form

> *height* :: *Picture* → *Height*
> *width*   :: *Picture* → *Width*

To start with we will need some atomic pictures. Since our pictures are pictures of text, and the smallest piece of text is a single character, we could get away with a single function

> *pixel* :: *Char* → *Picture*

for converting a single character into a (1 × 1) picture.

We can build new pictures out of other ones in a number of ways. Two fairly obvious methods are to place one picture above another, or one picture beside another. So we introduce two combinators

> (**above**), (**beside**) :: *Picture* → *Picture* → *Picture*

It is clear what should happen if the widths of two pictures p and q are the same: the width of (p **above** q) will be the common width, and its height will be the sum of the heights of p and q. If the widths of p and q are not equal, then we have a decision to make: we can decide to align the thinner picture with the wider one in some way, or simply not define the value (p **above** q). Dual remarks apply to the operation (p **beside** q). Rather than make this decision now, we will wait to see whether a logical choice arises during the course of the development. Whatever we decide, both operators are associative; it doesn't matter whether we put p above q and then the result above r, or put p above the result of putting q above r.

Given **above** and **beside**, we can stack a nonempty list of pictures above one another, or spread a nonempty list of pictures beside one another:

> *stack*, *spread* :: [*Picture*] → *Picture*
> *stack*   = *foldr1* (**above**)
> *spread*   = *foldr1* (**beside**)

We choose to stack and spread only nonempty lists in order to avoid introducing empty pictures.

Using *spread* we can define a function for turning a nonempty string into a picture:

$$
\begin{aligned}
row \quad &:: \quad String \rightarrow Picture \\
row \quad &= \quad spread \cdot map\ pixel
\end{aligned}
$$

The function *row* turns a string into a $(1 \times n)$ picture, where $n > 0$ is the length of the string. Using *row* we can define a blank picture of given height and width:

$$
\begin{aligned}
blank \quad &:: \quad (Height, Width) \rightarrow Picture \\
blank \quad &= \quad stack \cdot map\ row \cdot blanks \\
&\qquad \textbf{where } blanks\ (h, w) = replicate\ h\ (replicate\ w\ `\sqcup\text{'})
\end{aligned}
$$

Two useful variants of *stack* and *spread* insert blank pictures between two pictures before combining them:

$$
\begin{aligned}
stackWith \quad &:: \quad Height \rightarrow [[Picture]] \rightarrow Picture \\
stackWith\ h \quad &= \quad foldr1\ (\oplus) \\
&\qquad \textbf{where } p \oplus q = p\ \textbf{above}\ (blank\ (h, width\ q)\ \textbf{above}\ q)
\end{aligned}
$$

$$
\begin{aligned}
spreadWith \quad &:: \quad Width \rightarrow [[Picture]] \rightarrow Picture \\
spreadWith\ w \quad &= \quad foldr1\ (\oplus) \\
&\qquad \textbf{where } p \oplus q = p\ \textbf{beside}\ (blank\ (height\ q, w)\ \textbf{beside}\ q)
\end{aligned}
$$

The function *stackWith h* stacks a list of pictures vertically with an inter-picture gap of height h; similarly with *spreadWith w*.

Given a list of lists of pictures we can build one large picture by tiling them, that is, arranging them as a rectangular array. There are two variants:

$$
\begin{aligned}
tile \quad &:: \quad [[Picture]] \rightarrow Picture \\
tile \quad &= \quad stack \cdot map\ spread \\[1ex]
tileWith \quad &:: \quad (Height, Width) \rightarrow [[Picture]] \rightarrow Picture \\
tileWith\ (h, w) \quad &= \quad stackWith\ h \cdot map\ (spreadWith\ w)
\end{aligned}
$$

Finally, we will need a function to display a picture on a terminal screen:

$$
showpic \quad :: \quad Picture \rightarrow String
$$

We will return to pictures and their representations after having seen how to make use of the combinators for picturing calendars.

5.4.3 Picturing a calendar

Recall that our objective is to define a function *year* for displaying a calendar for a year, and a function *month* for displaying the calendar for a single month. One way of defining *year* is to write

$$year \quad :: \quad Year \to String$$
$$year \quad = \quad showpic \cdot tileWith\,(1,4) \cdot group\,3 \cdot map\ picture \cdot months$$

The function *year* is defined as the composition of five simpler functions: *months* takes a year and turns it into a list of length 12 of information for each month; *picture* turns this information into a picture of the month; *group* 3 groups these pictures into a (4×3) array of pictures; *tileWith* $(1,4)$ combines these pictures, putting in one blank row between vertical components and four blank columns between horizontal components; finally, *showpic* converts the picture to printable form. The function *month* can be defined using a similar scheme, and is left as an exercise. The function *group n* is defined by

$$group \qquad :: \quad Int \to [\alpha] \to [[\alpha]]$$
$$group\ n\ xs \quad = \quad \textbf{if}\ null\ ys\ \textbf{then}\ [\,]\ \textbf{else}\ ys : group\ n\ zs$$
$$\textbf{where}\ (ys, zs) = splitAt\ n\ xs$$

The function *splitAt* was defined in Section 4.2.

It remains to define *picture* and *months*. For each month we will need its name, the year to which the month applies, the day name of the first of the month, and the number of days in the month. So we define

$$months \quad :: \quad Year \to [(String, Year, Dayname, Int)]$$
$$months\ y \quad = \quad zipp4\,(mnames, replicate\,12\ y, fstdays\ y, mlengths\ y)$$

The function *zipp4* is similar to *zipp* except that it produces a list of quadruples from a quadruple of lists.

The month names are given by a list:

$$mnames \quad :: \quad [String]$$
$$mnames \quad = \quad [\text{“January”, “February”, “March”,}$$
$$\text{“April”, “May”, “June”,}$$
$$\text{“July”, “August”, “September”,}$$
$$\text{“October”, “November”, “December”}]$$

The functions *fstdays* and *mlengths* were defined earlier.

Now we need to deal with *picture*. The picture of a month will consist of a heading and some entries, so we define

$$picture \quad :: \quad (String, Year, Dayname, Int) \rightarrow Picture$$
$$picture\,(m, y, d, s) \quad = \quad heading\,(m, y)\textbf{ above } entries\,(d, s)$$

Let us deal with *entries* first. Suppose we set up an array of consecutive numbers arranged so that the first day of the month occupies its rightful place. For example, with $d = 6$ (Saturday) we get the array

-5	-4	-3	-2	-1	0	1
2	3	4	5	6	7	8
9	10	11	12	13	14	15
16	17	18	19	20	21	22
23	24	25	26	27	28	29
30	31	32	33	34	35	36

Each of these numbers can be converted into a little picture of height 1 and width 3 and then combined with *tile*:

$$entries\,(d, s) \quad = \quad tile \cdot group\,7 \cdot pix$$
$$pix\,(d, s) \quad = \quad map\,(row \cdot rjustify\,3 \cdot pic)\,[1 - d\,..\,42 - d]$$
$$\textbf{where } pic\,n = \textbf{if } 1 \leq n \wedge n \leq s \textbf{ then } show\,n \textbf{ else } \text{""}$$

The result is a picture of width $7 \times 3 = 21$. Using this information, we can define *heading* by

$$heading\,(m, y) \quad = \quad banner\,(m, y)\textbf{ above } dnames$$
$$banner\,(m, y) \quad = \quad row\,(rjustify\,21\,(m + \text{"}_\sqcup\text{"} + show\,y))$$
$$dnames \quad = \quad \text{"}_\sqcup Su_\sqcup Mo_\sqcup Tu_\sqcup We_\sqcup Th_\sqcup Fr_\sqcup Sa\text{"}$$

This completes the definition of *year*.

5.4.4 Representing pictures

The final task is to settle on a representation of pictures. One possibility is to take

$$\textbf{type } Picture \quad = \quad (Height, Width, [[Char]])$$

However, not every triple (h, w, xss) represents a valid picture; we need $h = length\,xss$ and $h > 0$, and w should be the common (positive) length of the components of *xss*. With this representation we have

$$height\ (h, w, xss)\quad =\quad h$$
$$width\ (h, w, xss)\quad =\quad w$$
$$pixel\ c\qquad\qquad\quad =\quad (1, 1, [[c]])$$

The combinators (**above**) and (**beside**) can be implemented as

$$(h, w, xss)\ \mathbf{above}\ (j, v, yss)$$

$$
\begin{array}{ll}
(w == v) & =\quad (h + j, w, xss \mathbin{+\!\!+} yss)\\
otherwise & =\quad error\ \text{``above: different widths''}
\end{array}
$$

$$(h, w, xss)\ \mathbf{beside}\ (j, v, yss)$$

$$
\begin{array}{ll}
(h == j) & =\quad (h, w + v, zipWith\ (\mathbin{+\!\!+})\ xss\ yss)\\
otherwise & =\quad error\ \text{``beside: different heights''}
\end{array}
$$

Since we did not exploit the idea of putting two pictures with different widths above one another, or two pictures with different heights beside one another, we have decided to make both operations partial.

It remains to define *showpic*:

$$
\begin{array}{ll}
showpic & ::\quad Picture \rightarrow String\\
showpic\ (h, w, xss) & =\quad unlines\ xss
\end{array}
$$

The function *unlines* was defined in Section 5.2 and will be discussed again in the following section. All the other picture functions are defined in terms of the functions above, so we are finished.

Exercises

5.4.1 Simplify the expression for *jan*1 *y* using $(365 \bmod 7) = 1$.

5.4.2 Define *month* :: (*Month, Year*) $\rightarrow$ *String*.

5.4.3 Define a version of the calendar problem that prints a month with the days of the week running from Monday to Sunday.

5.4.4 Define a version of the calendar problem that has the days down the left-hand side rather than across the top.

5.4.5 Under what conditions does the interchange law

$$(p\ \mathbf{above}\ q)\ \mathbf{beside}\ (r\ \mathbf{above}\ s)\quad =\quad (p\ \mathbf{beside}\ r)\ \mathbf{above}\ (q\ \mathbf{beside}\ s)$$

hold?

5.4.6 Develop a modified algebra of pictures that contains a null picture *null* of zero height and width and is such that *null* is the unit of (**above**) and (**beside**).

5.5 Text processing

Our aim in this section is to construct a number of functions for processing text in various ways. Most of these functions come in pairs, one function doing the opposite of the other one.

A text can be viewed in many different ways. The basic view is that a text is just a list of characters, including both visible and invisible characters. For the moment, we suppose that there are just two invisible characters, a space character '␣' and a newline character '↓'. Later on, we will also allow a tab character, which we will denote by '⊣'. Depending on the problem, it may be more convenient to view a text as a list of words, or as a list of lines, or even as a list of paragraphs. Our primary objective is to develop functions for converting from one view of texts to another.

Let us start by introducing some type synonyms:

> **type** *Text* = [*Char*]
> **type** *Line* = [*Char*]
> **type** *Word* = [*Char*]

By definition, a *Line* is a list of characters not containing newlines, and a *Word* is a nonempty list of characters not containing spaces or newlines. These restrictions are not captured by the type synonyms but have to be enforced by the programs that create lines and words.

5.5.1 Texts as lines

Consider first the problem of converting a text into a list of lines. We are interested in constructing a function *lines* with type

> *lines* :: *Text* → [*Line*]

For example, we want to have

? *lines* "This is a ↓text ↓"
["This is a", "text", ""]

? *lines* "This is a ↓↓␣␣␣ ↓text ↓"
["This is a", "", "␣␣␣", "text", ""]

? *lines* "This is a text"
["This is a text"]

As these examples illustrate, any sequence of characters between two successive newline characters constitutes a line, as does the sequence of characters
from the beginning of the text up to the first newline (if any), and the sequence
of characters from the last newline to the end of the text. Note that the sequence
of characters after the last newline may be empty. The decision to break a text
up in this way reflects the view that a newline is a *separator* character between
lines rather than a *terminator* character to signal the end of a line. In particular,
it implies that the number of lines in a text is always one more than the number
of newline characters. An empty text therefore has one empty line in it.

The function *lines* can be specified as the inverse of a second function,
unlines, defined by

$$unlines \quad :: \quad [Line] \rightarrow Text$$
$$unlines \quad = \quad foldr1 \, (\oplus)$$
$$\text{where } xs \oplus ys = xs + \text{``}\bar{\text{\textdagger}}\text{''} + ys$$

The operator $\oplus$ is associative but does not have a unit, so the value of *unlines* [ ]
is not defined. Hence a definition by *foldr1* is appropriate. We have already used
unlines in Sections 5.2 and 5.4.

The relationship between *lines* and *unlines* is that

$$unlines \, (lines \, xs) \quad = \quad xs$$

for all sequences *xs* of characters. We also have

$$lines \, (unlines \, xss) \quad = \quad xss$$

for all lists *xss* of lists of characters that do not contain newlines. Using the
first equation, one can synthesise the following implementation of *lines*:

$$lines \quad :: \quad Text \rightarrow [Line]$$
$$lines \, xs \quad = \quad \textbf{if } null \, zs \textbf{ then } [ys] \textbf{ else } ys : lines \, (tail \, zs)$$
$$\textbf{where } (ys, zs) = span \, (\neq \text{`}\bar{\text{\textdagger}}\text{'}) \, xs$$

This breaks a text *xs* into *ys* (the longest initial segment of *xs* that does not
contain newlines), followed by *zs* (the rest of *xs*, if any). If *zs* is not empty, then
its first character is a newline, so the process of constructing additional lines
is performed on *tail zs*. Details of the synthesis are left as an exercise. We will
see other instances of similar definitions, so the pattern of computation above
deserves to be generalised.

Consider the two functions *breakOn* and *joinWith*, defined as follows:

$$breakOn \quad :: \quad (Eq\ \alpha) \Rightarrow \alpha \to [\alpha] \to [[\alpha]]$$
$$breakOn\ x\ xs \quad = \quad \textbf{if}\ null\ zs\ \textbf{then}\ [xs]\ \textbf{else}\ ys : breakOn\ x\ (tail\ zs)$$
$$\textbf{where}\ (ys, zs) = span\ (\neq x)\ xs$$

$$joinWith \quad :: \quad \alpha \to [[\alpha]] \to [\alpha]$$
$$joinWith\ x \quad = \quad foldr1\ (\oplus)$$
$$\textbf{where}\ xs \oplus ys = xs \mathbin{+\!\!+} [x] \mathbin{+\!\!+} ys$$

The relationship between these two functions is that

$$joinWith\ x\ (breakOn\ x\ xs) \quad = \quad xs$$

for all lists *xs*. In particular,

$$lines \quad = \quad breakOn\ `\!\!\updownarrow\!\!`$$
$$unlines \quad = \quad joinWith\ `\!\!\updownarrow\!\!`$$

5.5.2 Lines as words

By definition, a *word* is a nonempty sequence of visible characters. In a similar spirit to before, we can seek a definition of a function *words* :: *Line* → [*Word*] that breaks a line into a list of its words. The companion function *unwords* is defined by

$$unwords \quad :: \quad [Word] \to Line$$
$$unwords \quad = \quad joinWith\ `\sqcup`$$

This takes a nonempty list of words, puts in a single space between each word, and concatenates the result. It is tempting now to define *words* = *breakOn* `⊔`, but this idea is not quite correct: unlike a line, a word is a *nonempty* sequence of characters. Putting it another way, if two newline characters are adjacent, then there is an empty line between them; but if two space characters are adjacent, then there is no word between them. Instead, we define

$$words \quad :: \quad Line \to [Word]$$
$$words \quad = \quad filter\ (not \cdot null) \cdot breakOn\ `\sqcup`$$

This definition filters out empty words.

As one application of the functions *lines* and *words*, we can count the number of words in a text by

$$wordcount \quad :: \quad Text \to Int$$
$$wordcount \quad = \quad length \cdot concat \cdot map\ words \cdot lines$$

This breaks a text into lines, breaks each line into words, concatenates the result to obtain all the words in the text, and finally counts how many there are.

As another application, we can reformat a text by

$$format1 \quad :: \quad Text \to Text$$
$$format1 \quad = \quad unlines \cdot map\ formatLine \cdot lines$$

$$formatLine \quad :: \quad Line \to Line$$
$$formatLine \quad = \quad rebuild \cdot words$$
$$\textbf{where}\ rebuild\ ws = \textbf{if}\ null\ ws\ \textbf{then}\ [\,]\ \textbf{else}\ unwords\ ws$$

The function *formatLine* breaks a line into a list of its words. If this list is empty, then an empty line is returned; otherwise, the line is reformatted by removing redundant extra spaces between words. The function *format1* applies this operation to every line in the text. It therefore replaces lines containing only space characters by empty lines. Below, we will see a more sophisticated version, *format2*, of this function.

5.5.3 Tab characters

Some texts make use of tab characters. In order to display a text containing tabs, it is necessary to replace them by the right number of space characters to reach the next tab stop. For simplicity, we will suppose that tab stops are fixed at every t columns for some given constant t.

The function *detab*, for removing tabs, works line by line, so we can at once define

$$detab \quad :: \quad Text \to Text$$
$$detab \quad = \quad unlines \cdot map\ detabLine \cdot lines$$

The function *detabLine* removes tabs from a single line. One way to implement it is to break the line up into *fields*, that is, lists of characters that do not contain tabs. Introducing the type synonym

$$\textbf{type}\ Field \quad = \quad [Char]$$

we have

$$fields \quad :: \quad Line \to [Field]$$
$$fields \quad = \quad breakOn\ \text{`⊣'}$$

Now we can define

$$detabLine \quad :: \quad Line \to Line$$
$$detabLine \quad = \quad unfields \cdot fields$$

Unlike the functions *unlines* and *unwords*, the function *unfields* is not defined as *joinWith* '⊣' because we want to replace tabs by spaces. Since the number of spaces to which a tab expands depends on the number of characters to the left, we have to rebuild the line from left to right. So we define

$$unfields \quad :: \quad [Field] \to Line$$
$$unfields \quad = \quad foldl1\ (\oplus)$$
$$\textbf{where } xs \oplus ys = xs \mathbin{+\!\!+} spaces\ (t - (length\ xs)\ \textbf{mod}\ t) \mathbin{+\!\!+} ys$$

The term $xs \oplus ys$ puts in enough spaces after xs to reach the next tab stop, that is, the next multiple of t.

The problem with the program for *unfields* is that it is fairly inefficient: the length of the line up to the next tab is recomputed for each field. A better implementation is to use a *tupling* strategy, specifying a function *expand* by

$$expand \quad :: \quad [Field] \to (Line, Int)$$
$$expand\ fs \quad = \quad (unfields\ fs, length\ (unfields\ fs))$$

The tupling strategy for improving the performance of programs will be considered in Chapter 7. However, the following program for *expand* is quite easy to synthesise and we leave details as an exercise:

$$expand$$
$$= \quad foldl1\ (\oplus) \cdot map\ addLength$$
$$\textbf{where } addLength\ xs \quad = \quad (xs, length\ xs)$$
$$(xs, m) \oplus (ys, n) \quad = \quad (xs \mathbin{+\!\!+} spaces\ k \mathbin{+\!\!+} ys, m + k + n)$$
$$\textbf{where } k = t - m\ \textbf{mod}\ t$$

Now we can define $unfields = fst \cdot expand$.

5.5.4 Paragraphs

Some texts can also be viewed as a list of paragraphs. Such texts consist of continuous prose, without bits of mathematics, tables, poetry, programs, and so on. Logically, a paragraph is simply a nonempty list of words, so we declare

$$\textbf{type } Para \quad = \quad [Word]$$

The function *paras* converts a text into a list of its paragraphs:

$$paras \quad :: \quad Text \to [Para]$$
$$paras \quad = \quad map\ concat \cdot filter\ (not \cdot null) \cdot$$
$$breakOn\ [\,] \cdot map\ words \cdot lines$$

This takes a text, converts it to a list of lines, and converts each line to a list of words. Paragraph breaks are signalled by the presence of a line containing no words. The empty paragraphs are then filtered out, and the remaining ones are flattened into lists of words, discarding information about what words are on what lines.

The reverse process, that of rebuilding the line structure of a paragraph, is known as *filling*. To fill a paragraph is to arrange the words of the paragraph into a sequence of nonempty lines in such a way that, firstly, the length of each line does not exceed a fixed maximum and, secondly, the sequence as a whole gives an aesthetically pleasing appearance. Note carefully the essential difference between filling and formatting: filling says what words go on what lines, formatting says how they should be displayed.

One way of formalising the notion of a pleasing paragraph is to ask that some measure of *waste* be minimised. For instance, we might want the number of lines in the filled paragraph to be as small as possible. One simple algorithm for filling a paragraph is greedy in nature: at each stage select the longest initial segment of the remaining words that will fit within the maximum limit. For this algorithm to work, indeed for the filling problem to have any solution at all, it is necessary to assume that the maximum line limit is large enough to accommodate any single word. It can be shown that the greedy algorithm returns a shortest possible list of lines.

Suppose we are given a function *fillPara* with type

$$fillPara \quad :: \quad Int \rightarrow Para \rightarrow [[Word]]$$

The function *fillPara n* takes a nonempty list of words and structures it into a nonempty list of nonempty lists of words. Each component list of words will constitute a line in the reformatted text. We will give one implementation of *fillPara* below. We can now reformat a text by a function *format2*, defined by

$$format2 \quad :: \quad Int \rightarrow Text \rightarrow Text$$
$$format2\ n \quad = \quad unparas \cdot map\ (fillPara\ n) \cdot paras$$

This breaks a text into paragraphs, fills each paragraph, and then reconstitutes the text as a string. The function *unparas* can be defined by

$$unparas \quad :: \quad [[[Word]]] \rightarrow Text$$
$$unparas \quad = \quad unlines \cdot joinWith\ [\ ] \cdot map\ (map\ unwords)$$

This converts the words in each line of each paragraph back into a line, joins the lines together with empty lines, and converts the result back into a text by inserting newline characters.

We are left with the function *fillPara*, so let us conclude by implementing the greedy algorithm for filling a paragraph. The program is

$$fillPara \quad :: \quad Int \to Para \to [[Word]]$$
$$fillPara\ n\ ws \quad = \quad \textbf{if}\ null\ xs\ \textbf{then}\ [\,]\ \textbf{else}\ xs : fillPara\ n\ ys$$
$$\textbf{where}\ (xs, ys) = splitAt\ (greedy\ n)\ ws$$

This splits a list *ws* of words into the longest initial segment that will fit on a line of maximum width *n*, and the remaining words, if any. The process is continued recursively on the remaining words.

The function *greedy* is defined by

$$greedy \quad :: \quad Int \to [Word] \to Int$$
$$greedy\ n \quad = \quad length \cdot last \cdot filter\ ((\leq n) \cdot length \cdot unwords) \cdot inits1$$

The value of *greedy n ws* reads: the length of the longest nonempty initial segment *xs* of *ws* satisfying $length\,(unwords\,xs) \leq n$. The function *inits1* returns the list of nonempty initial segments of a list in increasing order of length; hence the last element in any subsequence of *inits1 ws* is the longest element of the subsequence. Recall that *unwords* is not defined on empty lists, which is why we generate only nonempty initial segments. Recall also our assumption that the line limit *n* is large enough to accommodate any single word, so filtering the initial segments of a nonempty sequence of words produces a nonempty subsequence.

Although this solves the problem, the program for *greedy* is inefficient because the value of *unwords* is recomputed for every nonempty initial segment of the given list of words. In fact, *greedy n* takes quadratic time in the size of the result. Let us finish by deriving a more efficient version.

As a first step, we can replace *filter* by *takeWhile* in the definition of *greedy*. The reason is that if initial segment *xs* fails the test, so $length\,(unwords\,xs) > n$, then so does any longer initial segment. We can combine this substitution with the property

$$length \cdot last \cdot takeWhile\ p \cdot inits1 \quad = \quad length \cdot takeWhile\ p \cdot inits1$$

It is easy to see why this law is valid: if *takeWhile p* (*inits1 xs*) returns the list

$$[[x_1], [x_1, x_2], \ldots, [x_1, x_2, \ldots, x_n]]$$

then the length of the last element, namely *n*, is the length of the whole list. Applying this rule gives the following expression for *greedy n*:

$$length \cdot takeWhile\ ((\leq n) \cdot length \cdot unwords) \cdot inits1$$

The next law we want to use is

$$map\ f \cdot takeWhile\ (p \cdot f)\quad =\quad takeWhile\ p \cdot map\ f$$

The aim is to apply this law to the expression for *greedy n* with $p = (\leq n)$ and $f = length \cdot unwords$. To do this, we will need the fact that

$$length\quad =\quad length \cdot map\ f$$

for any f. Applying first this law and then the one above, we obtain a new expression for *greedy n*:

$$length \cdot takeWhile\ (\leq n) \cdot map\ (length \cdot unwords) \cdot inits1$$

For the next step, recall that $unwords = foldr1\ (\oplus)$, where $xs \oplus ys = xs \mathbin{+\!\!+} \text{``}\sqcup\text{''} \mathbin{+\!\!+} ys$. An application of the fusion law for *foldr1* yields

$$length \cdot unwords\quad =\quad foldr1\ (\otimes) \cdot map\ length$$
$$\textbf{where}\ m \otimes n = m + 1 + n$$

Applying this result, we now obtain the following expression for *greedy n*:

$$length \cdot takeWhile\ (\leq n) \cdot map\ (foldr1\ (\otimes) \cdot map\ length) \cdot inits1$$

The next step is to use the functor property of *map*, to obtain the new expression

$$length \cdot takeWhile\ (\leq n) \cdot map\ (foldr1\ (\otimes)) \cdot map\ (map\ length) \cdot inits1$$

Next we make use of the naturality condition

$$map\ (map\ f) \cdot inits1\quad =\quad inits1 \cdot map\ f$$

to obtain a further simplification:

$$length \cdot takeWhile\ (\leq n) \cdot map\ (foldr1\ (\otimes)) \cdot inits1 \cdot map\ length$$

For the final step we would like to apply the following property of *scanl1*:

$$scanl1\ (\otimes)\quad =\quad map\ (foldl1\ (\otimes)) \cdot inits1$$

But, at the last hurdle, it seems that we have come unstuck: the above expression for *greedy n* contains $foldr1\ (\otimes)$ not $foldl1\ (\otimes)$. Fortunately, the first duality theorem comes riding over the hill to our rescue: $\otimes$ is an associative operator, as one can easily check. Moreover, the initial segments of a list are all finite. Hence we can replace $foldr1\ (\otimes)$ in the expression by $foldl1\ (\otimes)$.

The end result is that we can compute *greedy n* by the program

$$greedy\ n\ =\ length \cdot takeWhile\ (\leq n) \cdot scanl1\ (\otimes) \cdot map\ length$$

This version takes linear time in the length of the result.

Exercises

5.5.1 Prove that *unlines · lines = id*. Why is it not the case that *lines · unlines = id*?

5.5.2 Describe the lines for which *unwords · words* returns ⊥.

5.5.3 Suppose we adopt the convention that a newline character is a terminator for lines, rather than a separator. In this case the number of lines in the text is exactly the number of newline characters. We can then define *unlines* by

$$unlines\ =\ concat \cdot map\ (+\!\!+ ``\overline{}")$$

Use fold-map fusion to rewrite the definition of *unlines* as an instance of *foldr*. What is the corresponding definition of *lines*?

5.5.4 Synthesise the efficient program for *expand*.

5.5.5 Define a version of *detabLine* that does not first split a line into fields.

5.5.6 One way of compressing texts is to reduce the number of spaces and tabs to the minimum required to achieve the same spacing. Trailing spaces and tabs can be removed from the end of a line without affecting its visible appearance. Define a function *entab* for inserting tabs.

5.5.7 Why can't a text containing a mixture of prose and poetry be regarded as a list of paragraphs?

5.5.8 In the text, paragraphs are formatted by *left-justifying* lines. Devise an algorithm for formatting lines so that, except for the last line in a paragraph, they extend from the left to the right margin when displayed.

Chapter 6

Trees

Any recursive datatype that exhibits a nonlinear structure is generically called a *tree*. Trees serve as natural representations for any form of hierarchically organised data. The syntactic structure of arithmetic or functional expressions can also be modelled by a tree. Perhaps most useful of all, trees provide a generalisation of lists as a means for organising information and retrieving it efficiently.

There are numerous species and subspecies of tree. Trees can be classified according to the precise form of the branching structure, the location of information within the tree, and the relationship between the information stored in different parts of the tree. In the present chapter we will introduce one or two of the more common species, describe a little of the basic terminology associated with trees, and give one or two simple applications. Further applications are given in Chapter 8.

6.1 Binary trees

As its name implies, a binary tree is a tree with a simple two-way branching structure. There are two or three different subspecies of binary tree, but we will start by discussing the datatype

> **data** *Btree* α = *Leaf* α | *Fork* (*Btree* α) (*Btree* α)

A value of *Btree* α is either a *leaf node*, which contains a value of type α, or a *fork node*, which consists of two further trees, called the *left* and *right* subtrees of the node. A leaf is sometimes called an *external node*, or *tip*, and a fork node is sometimes called an *internal node*.

For example, the tree

$$Fork\ (Leaf\ 1)\ (Fork\ (Leaf\ 2)\ (Leaf\ 3))$$

consists of a node with a left subtree *Leaf* 1 and a right subtree which, in turn, consists of a left subtree *Leaf* 2 and a right subtree *Leaf* 3. Compare this tree with a second tree

$$Fork\ (Fork\ (Leaf\ 1)\ (Leaf\ 2))\ (Leaf\ 3)$$

Although the second tree contains the same sequence of numbers in its leaves as the first, the way the information is organised is quite different and the two expressions denote different values. In essence, different elements of *Btree α* express different ways of bracketing a sequence of values. For example, 1 (2 3) and (1 2) 3 are the two ways of bracketing 1 2 3. There are five ways of bracketing four values, namely

$$1\ (2\ (3\ 4))\quad 1\ ((2\ 3)\ 4)\quad (1\ 2)\ (3\ 4)\quad (1\ (2\ 3))\ 4\quad ((1\ 2)\ 3)\ 4$$

Hence there are five distinct binary trees with this sequence of leaf values.

Since we have used the names $xs, ys, \ldots$ to denote variables that range over sequences, we will use $xt, yt, \ldots$ to denote variables that range over trees.

6.1.1 Induction on trees

The principle of structural induction that we have seen for natural numbers and lists is easily extended to binary trees: in order to show that a proposition $P(xt)$ holds for all binary trees xt, it is sufficient to show:

Case ($\bot$). That $P(\bot)$ holds;

Case (*Leaf x*). That $P(Leaf\ x)$ holds for all x;

Case (*Fork xt yt*). That if both $P(xt)$ and $P(yt)$ hold, then $P(Fork\ xt\ yt)$ holds as well.

If we want $P(xt)$ to hold only for all finite trees, then it is sufficient to prove only the last two cases. By definition, a finite tree is one with a finite number of leaves. An example induction proof is given below.

6.1.2 Size and height

There are two important numerical measures on binary trees, size and height.
The *size* of a tree is the number of its leaf nodes:

$$\begin{cases} size & :: & Btree\ \alpha \rightarrow Int \\ size\ (Leaf\ x) & = & 1 \\ size\ (Fork\ xt\ yt) & = & size\ xt + size\ yt \end{cases}$$

The function *size* plays the same role for trees as *length* does for lists. In fact,
size = *length* · *flatten*, where

$$\begin{cases} flatten & :: & Btree\ \alpha \rightarrow [\alpha] \\ flatten\ (Leaf\ x) & = & [x] \\ flatten\ (Fork\ xt\ yt) & = & flatten\ xt \mathbin{+\!\!+} flatten\ yt \end{cases}$$

The function *flatten* produces the sequence of leaf values in left-to-right order.
A tree is finite if and only if it has a well-defined size.

There is a simple but important relationship between the number of external
and internal nodes in a finite binary tree: the former is always one more than
the latter. Suppose we count the number of internal nodes by the function
nodes, where

$$\begin{array}{lcl} nodes & :: & Btree\ \alpha \rightarrow Int \\ nodes\ (Leaf\ x) & = & 0 \\ nodes\ (Fork\ xt\ yt) & = & 1 + nodes\ xt + nodes\ yt \end{array}$$

prove

Then *size xt* = 1 + *nodes xt* for all finite trees *xt*. This result is proved by
structural induction over trees, and details are left as an exercise.

The second useful measure on trees is the notion of the *height* of a tree.
The height of a tree measures how far away the furthest leaf is:

$$\begin{array}{lcl} height & :: & Btree\ \alpha \rightarrow Int \\ height\ (Leaf\ x) & = & 0 \\ height\ (Fork\ xt\ yt) & = & 1 + (height\ xt\ \mathbf{max}\ height\ yt) \end{array}$$

For example, the tree

$$Fork\ (Leaf\ 1)\ (Fork\ (Leaf\ 2)\ (Leaf\ 3))$$

has height 2. The height of a tree *xt* is the maximum of the *depths* of the leaves
in *xt*. In the tree above, (*Leaf* 1) has depth 1, while (*Leaf* 2) and (*Leaf* 3) both

have depth 2. The function *depths* takes a tree and replaces the value at each leaf by the depth of the leaf in the tree:

$$
\begin{array}{lll}
depths & :: & Btree\ \alpha \to Btree\ Int \\
depths & = & down\ 0
\end{array}
$$

$$
\begin{array}{lll}
down & :: & Int \to Btree\ \alpha \to Btree\ Int \\
down\ n\ (Leaf\ x) & = & Leaf\ n \\
down\ n\ (Fork\ xt\ yt) & = & Fork\ (down\ (n+1)\ xt)\ (down\ (n+1)\ yt)
\end{array}
$$

If we define *maxBtree* by

$$
\begin{array}{lll}
maxBtree & :: & (Ord\ \alpha) \Rightarrow Btree\ \alpha \to \alpha \\
maxBtree\ (Leaf\ x) & = & x \\
maxBtree\ (Fork\ xt\ yt) & = & (maxBtree\ xt)\ \mathbf{max}\ (maxBtree\ yt)
\end{array}
$$

then *height* =, *maxBtree* · *depths*. For a proof, see Exercise 6.1.6.

A binary tree is said to be *perfect* if all its leaves have the same depth. For example, the tree

$$Fork\ (Fork\ (Leaf\ 1)\ (Leaf\ 2))\ (Fork\ (Leaf\ 3)\ (Leaf\ 4))$$

is a perfect binary tree. The size of a perfect binary tree is always a power of two and, disregarding the values in the leaves, there is exactly one perfect tree for each power of two.

Although two trees of the same size need not have the same height, the two measures are not independent. The following result is one of the most important facts about binary trees. It says that

$$height\ xt < size\ xt \le 2 \uparrow height\ xt$$

for all finite trees *xt*. Equivalently, taking logarithms to base two, we have

$$\lceil \log\ (size\ xt) \rceil \le height\ xt < size\ xt$$

where $\lceil x \rceil$ (the *ceiling* of x) denotes the smallest integer at least x. The proof of this fundamental relationship is by structural induction. We will prove one inequality and leave the other as an exercise.

Proof. We prove *size* $xt \le 2 \uparrow$ *height* xt by induction on *xt*.

Case (*Leaf x*). In a line, we have

$$size\ (Leaf\ x) = 1 = 2 \uparrow 0 = 2 \uparrow height\ (Leaf\ x)$$

Case (*Fork xt yt*). We reason:

$$size\,(Fork\ xt\ yt)$$

$=$ {definition of *size*}

$$size\ xt + size\ yt$$

$\leq$ {induction hypothesis}

$$2 \uparrow (height\ xt) + 2 \uparrow (height\ yt)$$

$\leq$ {arithmetic, writing $h = (height\ xt\ \textbf{max}\ height\ yt)$}

$$2 \uparrow h + 2 \uparrow h$$

$=$ {arithmetic}

$$2 \uparrow (1 + h)$$

$=$ {definition of h and *height*}

$$2 \uparrow (height\,(Fork\ xt\ yt))$$

$\square$

Given any list *xs* of positive length n, it is possible to construct a tree *xt* with

$$flatten\ xt = xs \quad \text{and} \quad height\ xt = \lceil \log n \rceil$$

Such a tree has minimum possible height. In general there will be more than one tree of minimum height with a given sequence of leaf values. Minimum height trees are useful because they ensure that the cost of retrieving a leaf value is as small as possible in the worst possible case.

One minimum height tree can be obtained by dividing up the (nonempty) input into two equal halves and recursively building a minimum height tree for each half:

```
mkBtree :: [α] → Btree α
mkBtree xs
    | (m == 0)     =  Leaf (unwrap xs)
    | otherwise    =  Fork (mkBtree ys) (mkBtree zs)
      where m       =  (length xs) div 2
            (ys, zs) =  splitAt m xs
```

Recall from Section 4.2 that $splitAt\ n\ xs = (take\ n\ xs, drop\ n\ xs)$. The function *unwrap* is defined by $unwrap\ [x] = x$. We will analyse the running time of this program in the following chapter, showing that *mkBtree* takes time proportional to $n \log n$ steps on a list of length n. As we will also see in the following chapter, it is possible to give an implementation of *mkBtree* that works in linear time.

6.1.3 Map and fold

The functions *map* and *fold* for lists have analogues *mapBtree* and *foldBtree* for trees. The function *mapBtree* is defined by

$$
\begin{aligned}
&mapBtree && :: && (\alpha \to \beta) \to Btree\ \alpha \to Btree\ \beta \\
&mapBtree\ f\ (Leaf\ x) && = && Leaf\ (f\ x) \\
&mapBtree\ f\ (Fork\ xt\ yt) && = && Fork\ (mapBtree\ f\ xt)\ (mapBtree\ f\ yt)
\end{aligned}
$$

The function *mapBtree* satisfies laws similar to that of *map*. In particular,

$$
\begin{aligned}
mapBtree\ id &= id \\
mapBtree\ (f \cdot g) &= mapBtree\ f \cdot mapBtree\ g
\end{aligned}
$$

Thus *mapBtree*, like *map*, is a functor. We also have

$$
map\ f \cdot flatten = flatten \cdot mapBtree\ f
$$

The function *foldBtree* has to provide a replacement for each of the constructors of *Btree* α. The two constructors have types

$$
\begin{aligned}
Leaf &:: \alpha \to Btree\ \alpha \\
Fork &:: Btree\ \alpha \to Btree\ \alpha \to Btree\ \alpha
\end{aligned}
$$

Hence *foldBtree* has to provide two replacement functions, f and g, with types

$$
\begin{aligned}
f &:: \alpha \to \beta \\
g &:: \beta \to \beta \to \beta
\end{aligned}
$$

The definition of *foldBtree* is

$$
\begin{aligned}
&foldBtree && :: && (\alpha \to \beta) \to (\beta \to \beta \to \beta) \to Btree\ \alpha \to \beta \\
&foldBtree\ f\ g\ (Leaf\ x) && = && f\ x \\
&foldBtree\ f\ g\ (Fork\ xt\ yt) && = && g\ (foldBtree\ f\ g\ xt)\ (foldBtree\ f\ g\ yt)
\end{aligned}
$$

Many operations on trees can be defined in terms of *foldBtree*. As examples, we have

$$
size = foldBtree\ (const\ 1)\ (+)
$$

$$
\begin{aligned}
height &= foldBtree\ (const\ 0)\ (\oplus) \\
&\textbf{where } m \oplus n = 1 + (m\ \textbf{max}\ n)
\end{aligned}
$$

$$flatten \quad = \quad foldBtree\ wrap\ (+\!\!+)$$

$$maxBtree \quad = \quad foldBtree\ id\ (\mathbf{max})$$

$$mapBtree\ f \quad = \quad foldBtree\ (Leaf \cdot f)\ Fork$$

In the first two examples, the standard function *const* is defined by

$$const \qquad :: \quad \alpha \rightarrow \beta \rightarrow \alpha$$
$$const\ x\ y \quad = \quad x$$

The function *wrap* is defined by $wrap\ x = [x]$.

6.1.4 Augmented binary trees

The binary trees introduced above have information only in the tips of the tree. A slight but important variation on the basic idea is to allow information to be stored in the nodes as well. The technique of labelling the internal nodes of a binary tree has many important applications in the design of efficient algorithms on trees. We will give one illustration now; others are given in the remainder of this chapter and in Chapter 8.

Suppose we augment binary trees with size information. More precisely, consider the datatype

$$\mathbf{data}\ Atree\ \alpha \quad = \quad Leaf\ \alpha \ \mid\ Fork\ Int\ (Atree\ \alpha)\ (Atree\ \alpha)$$

For simplicity we use the same constructor names as for *Btree*, though different names would have to be chosen in any script making use of both datatypes. In the datatype *Atree* α, the internal nodes are labelled with an integer. The idea is that in the element *Fork n xt yt*, the integer n satisfies the condition $n = size\ xt$, where *size* is defined in the same way as for *Btree* α. Of course, we have to ensure that this condition is satisfied when we construct the tree. We will do this by building fork nodes only through the use of a function *fork* defined by

$$fork \qquad :: \quad Atree\ \alpha \rightarrow Atree\ \alpha \rightarrow Atree\ \alpha$$
$$fork\ xt\ yt \quad = \quad Fork\ n\ xt\ yt$$
$$\qquad\qquad\qquad \mathbf{where}\ n = lsize\ xt + lsize\ yt$$

$$lsize \qquad\qquad\qquad :: \quad Atree\ \alpha \rightarrow Int$$
$$lsize\ (Leaf\ x) \qquad = \quad 1$$
$$lsize\ (Fork\ n\ xt\ yt) \quad = \quad n$$

For example, we can modify the function *mkBtree* to give a function *mkAtree* for erecting a minimum height augmented tree on a given sequence of values:

$$mkAtree :: [\alpha] \rightarrow Atree\ \alpha$$

$$
\begin{aligned}
mkAtree\ xs & \\
\quad (m == 0) &= Leaf\ (unwrap\ xs) \\
\quad otherwise &= fork\ (mkBtree\ ys)\ (mkBtree\ zs) \\
\textbf{where}\ m &= (length\ xs)\ \textbf{div}\ 2 \\
(ys, zs) &= splitAt\ m\ xs
\end{aligned}
$$

Now, suppose we want to implement a function *retrieve*, specified by

$$
\begin{aligned}
retrieve & :: Atree\ \alpha \rightarrow Int \rightarrow \alpha \\
retrieve\ xt\ k &= (flatten\ xt)\ !!\ k
\end{aligned}
$$

In words, *retrieve* indexes a tree in the same way that (!!) indexes a list. We can use the fact that

$$
\begin{aligned}
(xs \mathbin{+\!\!+} ys)\ !!\ k &= \textbf{if}\ k < m\ \textbf{then}\ xs\ !!\ k\ \textbf{else}\ ys\ !!\ (k - m) \\
&\quad \textbf{where}\ m = length\ xs
\end{aligned}
$$

to synthesise the following more efficient program for *retrieve*:

$$
\begin{aligned}
retrieve\ (Leaf\ x)\ 0 &= x \\
retrieve\ (Fork\ m\ xt\ yt)\ k & \\
&= \textbf{if}\ k < m\ \textbf{then}\ retrieve\ xt\ k\ \textbf{else}\ retrieve\ yt\ (k - m)
\end{aligned}
$$

This implementation of *retrieve* uses the size information stored in binary nodes to control the search for an element in a given position. What we have gained by this move is a potentially more efficient alternative to indexing a list. Instead of storing information in a list and using (!!) to retrieve values, we can turn the list into a minimum height binary tree via *mkAtree*, and then use *retrieve*. It is clear that *retrieve* takes a number of steps proportional to log n, where n is the length of the list, while (!!) may take a number of steps proportional to n. The former is much more efficient whenever the number of retrievals is large enough to outweigh the cost of computing *mkAtree*.

Exercises

6.1.1 How many binary trees are there of size five? Write a program to calculate the number of binary trees of size n for a given n.

6.1.2 Prove that the number of tips in a binary tree is always one more than the number of internal nodes.

6.1.3 The subtrees of a binary tree can be defined by

$$
\begin{array}{lcl}
subtrees & :: & Btree\ \alpha \rightarrow [Btree\ \alpha] \\
subtrees\ (Tip\ x) & = & [Tip\ x] \\
subtrees\ (Bin\ xt\ yt) & = & [Bin\ xt\ yt] \mathbin{+\!\!+} subtrees\ xt \mathbin{+\!\!+} subtrees\ yt
\end{array}
$$

State and prove a relationship between *length* (*subtrees xt*) and *size xt*.

6.1.4 Prove that *height xt* < *size xt*.

6.1.5 Prove that a list *xs* of length 2^n can be made into a minimum height tree *xt* satisfying *flatten xt* = *xs* in exactly one way.

6.1.6 Prove that *height* = *maxBtree · depths* by first proving the more general result

$$
(n+) \cdot height \quad = \quad maxBtree \cdot down\ n
$$

6.2 Binary search trees

Subject to an extra condition described below, a binary search tree is an element of the datatype

data $(Ord\ \alpha) \Rightarrow Stree\ \alpha \quad = \quad Null\ \mid\ Fork\ (Stree\ \alpha)\ \alpha\ (Stree\ \alpha)$

This is the first example of a datatype declaration that makes use of a *context*: the type *Stree α* is introduced only for types that are instances of the type class *Ord*. Elements of *Stree α* no longer have *Leaf* nodes, and the information stored in the labels has been moved to come between the two subtrees for a reason explained below. The new constructor *Null* denotes the empty tree. The datatype introduces a kind of tree that is either empty or consists of a node with a left subtree, a label, and a right subtree. This species of tree is also called a *labelled binary tree*. The function *flatten*, defined by

$$
\begin{array}{lcl}
flatten & :: & (Ord\ \alpha) \Rightarrow Stree\ \alpha \rightarrow [\alpha] \\
flatten\ Null & = & [\,] \\
flatten\ (Fork\ xt\ x\ yt) & = & flatten\ xt \mathbin{+\!\!+} [x] \mathbin{+\!\!+} flatten\ yt
\end{array}
$$

returns the list of labels in a tree in left-to-right order. The second equation for *flatten* shows why we have placed the label of each tree between the two subtrees.

There is an extra condition on elements of *Stree α* that make them binary search trees. The condition is that *flatten* should return a list in ascending order. This is where the type class *Ord* comes in. In symbols, *xt* is a binary search tree if *inordered xt* holds, where

$$
\begin{aligned}
inordered \quad &:: \quad (Ord\ \alpha) \Rightarrow Stree\ \alpha \rightarrow Bool \\
inordered \quad &= \quad ordered \cdot flatten
\end{aligned}
$$

Here, *ordered xs* is the condition that *xs* is in ascending order.

As its name suggests, binary search trees are devised for efficient searching. The function *member*, which determines whether a given value appears as the label of some node in a binary search tree, can be defined by

$$
\begin{aligned}
&member :: \alpha \rightarrow Stree\ \alpha \rightarrow Bool \\
&member\ x\ Null = False \\
&member\ x\ (Fork\ xt\ y\ yt) \\
&\qquad \left|
\begin{aligned}
(x < y) \quad &= \quad member\ x\ xt \\
(x == y) \quad &= \quad True \\
(x > y) \quad &= \quad member\ x\ yt
\end{aligned}
\right.
\end{aligned}
$$

In the worst case, the cost of evaluating *member x xt* is proportional to the height of *xt*, where the definition of height is a modification of the earlier definition:

$$
\begin{aligned}
height \qquad\qquad\qquad &:: \quad Stree\ \alpha \rightarrow Integer \\
height\ Null \qquad\quad &= \quad 0 \\
height\ (Fork\ xt\ x\ yt) \quad &= \quad 1 + (height\ xt\ \mathbf{max}\ height\ yt)
\end{aligned}
$$

The size of a binary search tree is the number of labels in the tree, and the fundamental relationship between size and height takes the modified form

$$ height\ t \le size\ t < 2 \uparrow (height\ t) $$

for all trees *t*. Equivalently, a binary search tree of size *n* has a height *h* satisfying

$$ \lceil \log(n + 1) \rceil \le h < n + 1 $$

One can build a binary search tree from a given sequence of values by modifying the definition of *mkBtree* given in the previous section:

$$
\begin{aligned}
mkStree \qquad\qquad &:: \quad (Ord\ \alpha) \Rightarrow [\alpha] \rightarrow Stree\ \alpha \\
mkStree\ [\ ] \qquad\quad &= \quad Null \\
mkStree\ (x : xs) \quad &= \quad Fork\ (mkStree\ ys)\ x\ (mkStree\ zs) \\
&\qquad\quad \mathbf{where}\ (ys, zs) = partition\ (\le x)\ xs
\end{aligned}
$$

The function *partition* is specified by

$$partition \quad :: \quad (\alpha \rightarrow Bool) \rightarrow [\alpha] \rightarrow ([\alpha], [\alpha])$$
$$partition \; p \; xs \quad = \quad (filter \; p \; xs, filter \; (not \cdot p) \; xs)$$

The implementation of *partition* as an instance of *foldr* is left as an exercise.

The difference between *mkStree* and *mkBtree* is that *mkStree* does not guarantee that the result has minimum possible height. For example, the value *x* in the second equation may be smaller than any element in *xs*, so *mkStree* may build a tree in which the left subtree of every node is *Null*. Whereas the function *mkBtree* can be implemented to run in linear time, the most efficient implementation of *mkStree* requires at least $n \log n$ steps on a list of length *n*.

The new version of *mkStree* can be used to implement the function *sort* for sorting a list:

$$sort \quad :: \quad (Ord \; \alpha) \Rightarrow [\alpha] \rightarrow [\alpha]$$
$$sort \quad = \quad flatten \cdot mkStree$$

This algorithm will be studied in the following chapter, and we will see that, by eliminating the intermediate tree, one can arrive at a version of a famous sorting algorithm called *quicksort*.

6.2.1 Insertion and deletion

Binary search trees are useful for representing sets efficiently, a topic that will be considered at greater length in Chapter 8. We will give the general flavour of the more advanced algorithms here by implementing functions that add and remove labels from a tree.

The function *insert* is easy to define:

$$insert :: (Ord\alpha) \Rightarrow \alpha \rightarrow Stree \; \alpha \rightarrow Stree \; \alpha$$
$$insert \; x \; Null = Fork \; Null \; x \; Null$$
$$insert \; x \; (Fork \; xt \; y \; yt)$$

$$
\begin{array}{lll}
(x < y) & = & Fork \; (insert \; x \; xt) \; y \; yt \\
(x = y) & = & Fork \; xt \; y \; yt \\
(x > y) & = & Fork \; xt \; y \; (insert \; x \; yt)
\end{array}
$$

Note that if a label is already present in the tree, then additional copies are not added.

The function *delete* is slightly more complicated:

delete :: (*Ord* α) ⇒ α → *Stree* α → *Stree* α
delete x *Null* = *Null*
delete x (*Fork* xt y yt)

(x < y)	=	*Fork* (*delete* x xt) y yt
(x == y)	=	*join* xt yt
(x > y)	=	*Fork* xt y (*delete* x yt)

The subsidiary function *join* has to join two trees while satisfying the equation

$$\textit{flatten} \, (\textit{join} \, xt \, yt) \quad = \quad \textit{flatten} \, xt \, \mathbin{++} \, \textit{flatten} \, yt$$

One possible implementation is to replace the rightmost empty subtree of the first tree by the second tree:

join   :: *Stree* α → *Stree* α → *Stree* α
join Null yt   = yt
join (*Fork* ut x vt) yt   = *Fork* ut x (*join* vt yt)

This definition is unsatisfactory since it results in a tree of greater height than necessary. The efficiency of tree membership and insertion depends on the height of the tree being traversed, and we would like to ensure that when joining trees we keep the height as small as is reasonably possible.

A second implementation is to promote the leftmost label of the second tree (if there is one) to be the new label of the joined tree. In other words, we can exploit the identity

$$xs \mathbin{++} ys \quad = \quad xs \mathbin{++} [\textit{head} \, y] \mathbin{++} \textit{tail} \, ys$$

This equation is valid provided *ys* is not the empty list. Suppose we specify the functions *headTree* and *tailTree* by

headTree   ::   *Stree* α → α
headTree   =   *head* · *flatten*

tailTree   ::   *Stree* α → *Stree* α
flatten · *tailTree*   =   *tail* · *flatten*

Then we can define

join xt yt
   = **if** *empty* yt **then** xt **else** *Fork* xt (*headTree* yt) (*tailTree* yt)

where

$$
\begin{array}{lll}
empty & :: & Stree\ \alpha \rightarrow Bool \\
empty\ Null & = & True \\
empty\ (Fork\ xt\ x\ yt) & = & False
\end{array}
$$

To check this definition of *join*, we reason

$flatten\ (join\ xt\ yt)$

=   {definition of *join*, assuming *not (empty yt)*}

$flatten\ (Fork\ xt\ (headTree\ yt)\ (tailTree\ yt))$

=   {definition of *flatten*}

$flatten\ xt \mathbin{+\!\!+} [headTree\ yt] \mathbin{+\!\!+} flatten\ (tailTree\ yt)$

=   {specification of *headTree* and *tailTree*}

$flatten\ xt \mathbin{+\!\!+} [head\ (flatten\ yt)] \mathbin{+\!\!+} tail\ (flatten\ yt)$

=   {identity on sequences}

$flatten\ xt \mathbin{+\!\!+} flatten\ yt$

It remains to implement *headTree* and *tailTree*. We can combine the two functions in a function *splitTree* satisfying

$$
\begin{array}{lll}
splitTree & :: & Stree\ \alpha \rightarrow (\alpha, Stree\ \alpha) \\
splitTree & = & pair\ (headTree, tailTree)
\end{array}
$$

An efficient definition of *splitTree* is easily synthesised, and turns out to be

$splitTree\ (Fork\ xt\ y\ yt)$
= **if** *empty xt* **then** (y, yt) **else** $(x, Fork\ wt\ y\ yt)$
   where $(x, wt) = splitTree\ xt$

Exercises

6.2.1 State the principle of structural induction for the type *Stree* α declared in this section, and use it to prove the fundamental relationship between size and height.

6.2.2 Define *mapStree* for the datatype *Stree* α.

6.2.3 Define *foldStree* for the datatype *Stree* α.

6.2.4 Prove that *ordered (insert x xt)* = *True* for all finite trees *xt*.

6.2.5 Let *hx* = *height xt* and *hy* = *height yt*. Give bounds on *height* (*join xt yt*) in terms of *hx* and *hy* for the two implementations of *join* considered in the text.

6.2.6 Synthesise the efficient program for *splitTree*.

6.3 Binary heap trees

Subject to a certain condition described below, a binary heap tree is an element of the datatype

$$\textbf{data}\ (Ord\ \alpha) \Rightarrow Htree\ \alpha\ =\ Null\ \mid\ Fork\ \alpha\ (Htree\ \alpha)\ (Htree\ \alpha)$$

The type *Htree* α is virtually identical to the type *Stree* α in the previous section, except that the label has been placed before the two subtrees rather than between them. Binary search trees and binary heap trees differ only in the relationship between the labels in different parts of the tree. The condition to be satisfied by a heap tree is that the label at each node has to be no greater than the labels in any subtree of the node. In other words, the labels along any path in the tree from the top downwards are always in ascending order.

We can formalise this condition in the following way. Consider first the function *flatten* defined by

$$
\begin{array}{lll}
flatten & :: & (Ord\ \alpha) \Rightarrow Htree\ \alpha \to [\alpha] \\
flatten\ Null & = & [\,] \\
flatten\ (Fork\ x\ xt\ yt) & = & x : merge\ (flatten\ xt)\ (flatten\ yt)
\end{array}
$$

$$
\begin{array}{lll}
merge & :: & (Ord\ \alpha) \Rightarrow [\alpha] \to [\alpha] \to [\alpha] \\
merge\ [\,]\ ys & = & ys \\
merge\ (x : xs)\ [\,] & = & x : xs
\end{array}
$$

$$
\begin{array}{l}
merge\ (x : xs)\ (y : ys) \\
\quad =\ \textbf{if}\ x \le y\ \textbf{then}\ x : merge\ xs\ (y : ys)\ \textbf{else}\ y : merge\ (x : xs)\ ys
\end{array}
$$

We met the idea of merging two ordered lists in Section 5.2. Now we can define

$$
\begin{array}{lll}
heapOrdered & :: & (Ord\ \alpha) \Rightarrow Htree\ \alpha \to Bool \\
heapOrdered & = & ordered \cdot flatten
\end{array}
$$

This definition is structurally identical to that of *inordered* in the previous section.

Binary heap trees are used for different purposes than binary search trees. While search trees are useful for general membership, insertion, and deletion operations, heap trees are better suited to a different set of operations. In particular, finding the smallest label in a heap can be done in constant time, but requires time proportional to the distance to the leftmost node with binary search trees. Two heaps can be merged together quickly, but combining two search trees is an expensive operation. These matters are dealt with in Chapter 8.

6.3.1 Building a heap

One way of building a binary heap tree is to define yet another version of *mkBtree*. However, although the program is quite short, it doesn't lead to the most efficient way of building a heap. It is possible to build a heap in linear time, as we will now show.

The idea is to compute *mkHeap* as the composition of two subsidiary functions:

$$mkHeap \quad :: \quad (Ord \; \alpha) \Rightarrow [\alpha] \to Htree \; \alpha$$
$$mkHeap \quad = \quad heapify \cdot mkHtree$$

The function *mkHtree* builds a tree of minimum height, not necessarily a tree satisfying *heapOrdered*, and *heapify* reorganises the labels to ensure that the result does satisfy this condition. We will show how to build a tree efficiently in the following chapter, so let us concentrate on *heapify*. We define

$$\begin{array}{lll} heapify & :: & Htree \; \alpha \to Htree \; \alpha \\ heapify \; Null & = & Null \\ heapify \; (Fork \; x \; xt \; yt) & = & sift \; x \; (heapify \; xt) \; (heapify \; yt) \end{array}$$

The function *sift* takes a label and two binary heap trees and rebuilds a tree in which the label is sifted downwards until the heap property is established:

$$\begin{array}{lll} sift & :: & \alpha \to Htree \; \alpha \to Htree \; \alpha \to Htree \; \alpha \\ sift \; x \; Null \; Null & = & Fork \; x \; Null \; Null \end{array}$$

sift x (Fork y a b) Null
$$= \quad \textbf{if } x \le y \textbf{ then } Fork \; x \; (Fork \; y \; a \; b) \; Null \textbf{ else } Fork \; y \; (sift \; x \; a \; b) \; Null$$
sift x Null (Fork z c d)
$$= \quad \textbf{if } x \le z \textbf{ then } Fork \; x \; Null \; (Fork \; z \; c \; d) \textbf{ else } Fork \; z \; Null \; (sift \; x \; c \; d)$$

$$sift\ x\ (Fork\ y\ a\ b)\ (Fork\ z\ c\ d)$$

$$
\begin{array}{llll}
\quad x \le (y \min z) & = & Fork\ x\ (Fork\ y\ a\ b)\ (Fork\ z\ c\ d) \\
\quad y \le (x \min z) & = & Fork\ y\ (sift\ x\ a\ b)\ (Fork\ z\ c\ d) \\
\quad z \le (x \min y) & = & Fork\ z\ (Fork\ y\ a\ b)\ (sift\ x\ c\ d)
\end{array}
$$

For brevity, we have used the single letters a, b, c, d to denote trees in this program. The code is straightforward and we omit a formal proof that the result satisfies *heapOrdered*.

Let us now show that *heapify* takes linear time when applied to a tree t of size n and minimum height $h = \lceil \log(n + 1) \rceil$. Observe that the operation *sift* is applied at every node of the tree and can take time proportional to the height of the node. Now, t has one tree of height h, namely t itself, up to two subtrees of height $h - 1$, up to four subtrees of height $h - 2$, and so on. Hence the total time required to perform *heapify* is proportional to at most

$$h + 2(h - 1) + 4(h - 2) + \cdots + 2^{h-1} = \sum_{k=1}^{h} 2^{h-k} k$$

steps. But

$$\sum_{k=1}^{h} k 2^{h-k} = 2^h \sum_{k=1}^{h} k/2^k < 2^{h+1} < 4(n + 1)$$

since $h = \lceil \log(n + 1) \rceil < \log(n + 1) + 1$.

Finally, we can use binary heap trees to obtain another algorithm for sorting:

$$
\begin{array}{lll}
sort & :: & (Ord\ \alpha) \Rightarrow [\alpha] \to [\alpha] \\
sort & = & flatten \cdot mkHeap
\end{array}
$$

This algorithm is known as *heapsort*.

Exercises

6.3.1 One way of building a tree is to take a list $[x_0, x_1, \ldots]$ and build a tree with x_0 as the label of the tree, x_1, x_2 as the labels of the two immediate subtrees, x_3, x_4, x_5, x_6 as the labels of the four granddaughter trees, and so on. This way of dividing a list into sublists of lengths that are successive powers of two can be implemented by a function *levels*, defined by

$$
\begin{array}{lll}
levels & :: & [\alpha] \to [[\alpha]] \\
levels & = & levelsWith\ 1
\end{array}
$$

Give the definition of *levelsWith*.

6.3.2 Next, the function *mkHtrees* takes the list of lists returned by *levels* and builds a list of trees:

$$mkHtrees \quad :: \quad (Ord\ \alpha) \Rightarrow [[\alpha]] \rightarrow [Htree\ \alpha]$$
$$mkHtrees \quad = \quad foldr\ addLayer\ [Null]$$

Applied to a list of labels $[x_0, x_1, \ldots]$ and a list of trees $[xt_0, xt_1, \ldots]$ the function *addLayer* produces the new list of trees

$$[Fork\ x_0\ xt_0\ xt_1, Fork\ x_1\ xt_2\ xt_3, \ldots]$$

If the list of trees is not long enough, it is filled with a sufficient number of empty trees. Give a definition of *addLayer*.

6.3.3 Using the previous exercises, give a definition of *mkHtree*. Give an informal argument to show that *mkHtree* takes linear time.

6.4 Rose trees

The name 'rose tree', a translation of rhododendron, has been coined by Lambert Meertens (see Section 6.6) to describe trees with a multi-way branching structure. The datatype *Rose* α is defined by

$$\textbf{data}\ Rose\ \alpha \quad = \quad Node\ \alpha\ [Rose\ \alpha]$$

An element of *Rose* α consists of a labelled node together with a list of subtrees. By definition, *external* nodes have no subtrees, while *internal* nodes have at least one. For example, *Node* 0 [ ] is a rose tree, and so is

$$Node\ 0\ [Node\ 1\ [\ ], Node\ 2\ [\ ], Node\ 3\ [\ ]]$$

It is even possible to have trees with an infinite number of immediate subtrees; for example,

$$Node\ 0\ [Node\ n\ [\ ]\ |\ n \leftarrow [1\ ..\ ]]$$

A tree t is *finitary* if every node of t has a finite number of immediate subtrees. The tree above is therefore not finitary. Note that a finitary tree need not have finite size. A rose tree t has *width* w if all nodes of t have at most w immediate subtrees. All finite rose trees have finite width. A rose tree is called k-ary if every internal node has exactly k immediate subtrees. Binary trees are structurally equivalent to 2-ary rose trees.

   The principle of induction for finitary rose trees says that, in order to show that a property $P(xt)$ holds for all finitary rose trees xt, it is sufficient to prove:

Case ($\perp$). That $P(\perp)$ holds.

Case (*Node x xts*). That $P(Node\ x\ xts)$ holds if $P(xt)$ holds for all trees *xt* in the (finite) list *xts*.

If we omit the first case, then we can conclude only that $P(xt)$ holds for all finite rose trees. Note the restriction to finitary trees in the statement of the induction principle. It is possible to formulate a more careful statement of what has to be shown in the second case when *xts* is a possibly partial list, but we will not do so.

The notions of size and height extend to rose trees. We have

$$
\begin{array}{lll}
size & :: & Rose\ \alpha \rightarrow Int \\
size\ (Node\ x\ xts) & = & 1 + sum\ (map\ size\ xts)
\end{array}
$$

$$
\begin{array}{lll}
height & :: & Rose\ \alpha \rightarrow Int \\
height\ (Node\ x\ xts) & = & 1 + maxlist\ (map\ height\ xts) \\
& & \textbf{where}\ maxlist = foldl\ (\textbf{max})\ 0
\end{array}
$$

According to this definition, the height of a rose tree is always greater than zero. It is left as an exercise to show that

$$
height \quad = \quad maxRose \cdot depths
$$

where

$$
\begin{array}{lll}
depths & :: & Rose\ \alpha \rightarrow Rose\ Int \\
depths & = & down\ 1
\end{array}
$$

$$
\begin{array}{lll}
down & :: & Int \rightarrow Rose\ \alpha \rightarrow Rose\ Int \\
down\ n\ (Node\ x\ xts) & = & Node\ n\ (map\ (down\ (n+1))\ xts)
\end{array}
$$

and

$$
\begin{array}{lll}
maxRose & :: & (Ord\ \alpha) \Rightarrow Rose\ \alpha \rightarrow \alpha \\
maxRose\ (Node\ x\ xts) & = & x\ \textbf{max}\ maxlist\ (map\ maxRose\ xts)
\end{array}
$$

A rose tree is said to be *perfect* if all its external nodes have the same depth. The basic relationship between *size* and *height* says that

$$
height\ xt \le size\ xt \le (k \uparrow (height\ xt) - 1)/(k - 1)
$$

for all finite *k*-ary rose trees. The proof is left as an exercise in induction. A perfect *k*-ary rose tree with height *h* has size $(k^h - 1)/(k - 1)$.

The fold function *foldRose* can also be defined for the datatype *Rose α*. Since

$$Node \quad :: \quad \alpha \rightarrow [Rose\ \alpha] \rightarrow Rose\ \alpha$$

the function *foldRose* takes a single argument *f* with type

$$f \quad :: \quad \alpha \rightarrow [\beta] \rightarrow \beta$$

for some type *β*. The definition of *foldRose* is

$$
\begin{array}{lll}
foldRose & :: & (\alpha \rightarrow [\beta] \rightarrow \beta) \rightarrow Rose\ \alpha \rightarrow \beta \\
foldRose\ f\ (Node\ x\ xts) & = & f\ x\ (map\ (foldRose\ f)\ xts)
\end{array}
$$

As examples, we have

$$
\begin{array}{lll}
size & = & foldRose\ f \quad \textbf{where}\ f\ x\ ns = 1 + sum\ ns \\
maxRose & = & foldRose\ f \quad \textbf{where}\ f\ x\ ns = x\ \textbf{max}\ maxlist\ ns
\end{array}
$$

The map function *mapRose* for rose trees is defined by

$$
\begin{array}{lll}
mapRose & :: & (\alpha \rightarrow \beta) \rightarrow Rose\ \alpha \rightarrow Rose\ \beta \\
mapRose\ f & = & foldRose\ (Node \cdot f)
\end{array}
$$

6.4.1 Representation by binary trees

Finite rose trees, with their multi-way branching structure, seem capable of modelling more general structures than binary trees, so it may come as a surprise that they are in one-to-one correspondence: every finite rose tree can be represented by a unique finite binary tree and conversely. The correspondence itself is not unique, but one method of associating rose trees with binary trees is exactly the same as that between expressions written in curried or noncurried form. For example, consider the two expressions

$$f\ (g\ (x, y)\ z, h\ (t)) \quad \text{and} \quad f\ (g\ x\ y)\ z\ (h\ t)$$

The expression on the left can be represented by the rose tree

$$Node\ f\ [Node\ g\ [Node\ x\ [\ ], Node\ y\ [\ ]], Node\ z\ [\ ], Node\ h\ [Node\ t\ [\ ]]]$$

The expression on the right in fully parenthesised form is

$$(f\ ((g\ x)\ y)\ z)\ (h\ t)$$

and can be represented by the binary tree

$$Fork\ (Fork\ (Fork\ (Leaf\ f)$$
$$(Fork\ (Fork\ (Leaf\ g)\ (Leaf\ x))\ (Leaf\ y)))$$
$$(Leaf\ z))$$
$$(Fork\ (Leaf\ h)\ (Leaf\ t))$$

We can convert a finite element of $Rose\,\alpha$ into an element of $Btree\,\alpha$ by a function *toB*, defined by

$$toB \quad\quad\quad :: \quad Rose\ \alpha \rightarrow Btree\ \alpha$$
$$toB\ (Node\ x\ xts) \quad = \quad foldl\ Fork\ (Leaf\ x)\ (map\ toB\ xts)$$

In words, to convert a rose tree to a binary tree we first convert all its subtrees (via *map toB*) and then combine the results into a single binary tree by folding from the left, following the left association order of application.

It is more difficult to implement the inverse correspondence *toR*. This function is specified by

$$toR \quad\quad\quad :: \quad Btree\ \alpha \rightarrow Rose\ \alpha$$
$$toR\ (toB\ xt) \quad = \quad xt$$

where *xt* ranges over finitary rose trees. In order to synthesise a program from this specification, we will need the following two properties of *toB*:

$$toB\ (Node\ x\ [\,]) \quad\quad\quad = \quad Leaf\ x$$
$$toB\ (Node\ x\ (xts + [xt])) \quad = \quad Fork\ (toB\ (Node\ x\ xts))\ (toB\ xt)$$

The first equation is immediate from the definition of *toB*, and the second can be proved by first applying the third duality theorem to rewrite the definition of *toB* in the form

$$toB\ (Node\ x\ xts) \quad = \quad foldr\ (flip\ Fork)\ (Leaf\ x)\ (reverse\ (map\ toB\ xts))$$

Further details are left as an exercise.

The synthesis of a program for *toR* is by cases.

Case $(Node\ x\ [\,])$. We reason:

$$toR\ (toB\ (Node\ x\ [\,])) = Node\ x\ [\,]$$
$$\Leftarrow \quad \{\text{first property of } toB\}$$
$$toR\ (Leaf\ x) = Node\ x\ [\,]$$

Case (*Node x* (*xts* ++ [*xt*])). We reason:

$$toR\,(toB\,(Node\,x\,(xts \mathbin{+\!\!+} [xt]))) = Node\,x\,(xts \mathbin{+\!\!+} [xt])$$

$\Leftarrow$ {second property of *toB*}

$$toR\,(Fork\,(toB\,(Node\,x\,xts)))\,(toB\,xt) = Node\,x\,(xts \mathbin{+\!\!+} [xt])$$

$\equiv$ {introducing *xb* = *toB* (*Node x xts*) and *yb* = *toB xt*}

$$toR\,(Fork\,xb\,yb) = Node\,x\,(xts \mathbin{+\!\!+} [xt])$$
where *Node x xts* = *toR xb*
$\quad\quad\quad\quad\;\; xt \quad\quad\quad = toR\,yb$

In the last step we used the specification of *toR* twice. In summary, we have derived

$$
\begin{array}{ll}
toR\,(Leaf\,x) & = \quad Node\,x\,[\,] \\
toR\,(Fork\,xb\,yb) & = \quad Node\,x\,(xts \mathbin{+\!\!+} [xt]) \\
& \quad\quad \textbf{where }\; Node\,x\,xts \;=\; toR\,xb \\
& \quad\quad\quad\quad\quad\;\; xt \;\;=\; toR\,yb
\end{array}
$$

This program is not very efficient since appending *xt* to *xts* takes time proportional to the length of *xts*. For a more efficient version, define

$$
\begin{array}{ll}
collect & :: \quad Btree\,\alpha \to [Rose\,\alpha] \to Rose\,\alpha \\
collect\,xb\,yts & = \quad Node\,x\,(xts \mathbin{+\!\!+} yts) \quad \textbf{where } Node\,x\,xts = toR\,xb
\end{array}
$$

In particular, *toR xb* = *collect xb* [ ]. It is now easy to derive that

$$
\begin{array}{ll}
collect\,(Leaf\,x)\,yts & = \quad Node\,x\,yts \\
collect\,(Fork\,xb\,yb)\,yts & = \quad collect\,xb\,(toR\,yb : yts)
\end{array}
$$

The idea here is to use an *accumulating parameter* to eliminate the expensive ++ operations. The accumulating parameter technique will be studied in the following chapter, but exactly the same idea is behind the transformation of the naive definition of *reverse* to the more efficient one.

6.4.2 Depth-first and breadth-first order

The function *flatten* lists the labels of a rose tree:

$$
\begin{array}{ll}
flatten & :: \quad Rose\,\alpha \to [\alpha] \\
flatten\,(Node\,x\,xts) & = \quad x : concat\,(map\,flatten\,xts)
\end{array}
$$

This function produces, in order, the label of the tree, the labels of the leftmost subtree, the labels of the second leftmost subtree, and so on. Labels are produced in what is known as *depth-first* order. As we will show in the following chapter, *flatten* takes time proportional to at most $n \log n$, where n is the size of of the tree, but it is possible to implement depth-first order in time proportional to n. Equally important, the amount of space required to carry out depth-first order is proportional to at most the height of the tree multiplied by the maximum number of subtrees of any node. The conclusion is that depth-first order is efficient both in time and space.

There is another way of flattening a rose tree, one that works level by level. The idea is to produce the label of the tree, then the labels of its immediate subtrees, then the labels at the next level, and so on. This way of producing the labels is known as *breadth-first* order. An example of a problem in which breadth-first order is required is given in Section 6.6. Breadth-first order has the advantage that it can be applied to an infinite tree, producing an infinite list of all label values. On the other hand, a depth-first ordering of an infinite tree will not in general produce an infinite list containing all the label values: in particular, if the leftmost path is infinite, then *flatten* will produce only those label values along this path.

Unlike depth-first order, the breadth-first ordering of a tree cannot be produced from a breadth-first ordering of its subtrees. We can, however, define a function *levels* by

$$\text{levels} \qquad \text{::} \quad Rose\ \alpha \rightarrow [[\alpha]]$$
$$\text{levels}\ (Node\ x\ xts) \quad = \quad [x] : combine\ (map\ levels\ xts)$$

for a suitable function *combine*, and then define

$$\text{level} \quad \text{::} \quad Rose\ \alpha \rightarrow [\alpha]$$
$$\text{level} \quad = \quad concat \cdot levels$$

The function *level* produces labels in breadth-first order.

The problem now is to specify *combine* :: $[[\alpha]] \rightarrow [\alpha]$. This function has to concatenate corresponding levels in the argument list. For example, given the list

$$[[[x1, x2], [x3, x4, x5], [x6]],\ [[y1]],\ [[z1, z2, z3], [z4]]]$$

the result returned by *combine* will be the list

$$[[x1, x2, y1, z1, z2, z3], [x3, x4, x5, z4], [x6]]$$

Suppose we define *index* by

$$index \quad :: \quad Int \rightarrow [[\alpha]] \rightarrow [\alpha]$$
$$index \; i \; xss \quad = \quad \textbf{if} \; i < length \; xss \; \textbf{then} \; xss \; !! \; i \; \textbf{else} \; [\,]$$

Then we can specify *combine* by the condition

$$index \; i \cdot combine \quad = \quad concat \cdot map \; (index \; i)$$

for all *i*. Since *concat* = *foldr* (++) [ ], it seems reasonable to look for a definition of *combine* of the form

$$combine \quad :: \quad [[\alpha]] \rightarrow [\alpha]$$
$$combine \quad = \quad foldr \; (\oplus) \; [\,]$$

for some suitable operator ⊕. Appeal to the fusion law for *foldr* gives us the specification of ⊕:

$$index \; i \; (xss \oplus yss) \quad = \quad index \; i \; xss \; ++ \; index \; i \; yss$$

It is now a straightforward exercise in synthesis to derive the following program for ⊕:

$$(\oplus) \qquad\qquad\qquad :: \quad [[\alpha]] \rightarrow [[\alpha]] \rightarrow [[\alpha]]$$
$$[\,] \oplus yss \qquad\qquad = \quad yss$$
$$(xs : xss) \oplus [\,] \qquad = \quad xs : xss$$
$$(xs : xss) \oplus (ys : yss) \quad = \quad (xs ++ ys) : (xss \oplus yss)$$

The operation (⊕) is similar to *zipWith* (++), except that the lists are not truncated to the length of the shorter one.

Although the two procedures, *flatten* and *level*, have the same time complexity, they have quite different space costs. The space required to carry out evaluation of *level t* is proportional to the size of *t*. To appreciate what this second statistic means, imagine a tree of height h with k subtrees at each node. Then *level* requires space proportional to h^k, whereas *flatten* requires space proportional to $h \times k$. It is simply not possible to flatten a large tree using breadth-first order without running out of available space. This point is taken up in Section 6.6, which deals with a problem requiring just such a tree.

Exercises

6.4.1 What relationship, if any, holds between the size and height of a rose tree?

6.4.2 Suppose t is a finitary but infinite rose tree. Does $toB\,t$ produce an infinite binary tree?

6.4.3 The efficient definition of toR was obtained in two stages, but if we also make use of the property $toB\,(toR\,xb) = xb$ for all finite binary trees xb, then we can do it in one stage. Define *collect* by

$$
\begin{aligned}
collect &\quad::\quad Btree\,\alpha \rightarrow [Rose\,\alpha] \rightarrow Btree\,\alpha \\
collect\,xb\,yts &\quad=\quad toR\,(foldl\,Fork\,xb\,(map\,toB\,yts))
\end{aligned}
$$

Use this definition of *collect* to derive the one given in the text.

6.4.4 Define the function *dfo* (for depth-first order) by

$$
\begin{aligned}
dfo &\quad::\quad [Rose\,\alpha] \rightarrow [\alpha] \\
dfo &\quad=\quad concat \cdot map\,flatten
\end{aligned}
$$

Synthesise the following program for *dfo*:

$$
\begin{aligned}
dfo\,[\,] &\quad=\quad [\,] \\
dfo\,(Node\,x\,xts : yts) &\quad=\quad [x] \,\text{+}\!\text{+}\, dfo\,(xts \,\text{+}\!\text{+}\, yts)
\end{aligned}
$$

How is *flatten* defined in terms of *dfo*?

6.4.5 Define the function *bfo* (for breadth-first order) by

$$
\begin{aligned}
bfo &\quad::\quad [Rose\,\alpha] \rightarrow [\alpha] \\
bfo &\quad=\quad concat \cdot combine \cdot map\,levels
\end{aligned}
$$

As a difficult exercise in synthesis, derive the following program for *bfo*:

$$
\begin{aligned}
bfo &\quad::\quad [Rose\,\alpha] \rightarrow [\alpha] \\
bfo\,[\,] &\quad=\quad [\,] \\
bfo\,(Node\,x\,xts : yts) &\quad=\quad [x] \,\text{+}\!\text{+}\, bfo\,(yts \,\text{+}\!\text{+}\, xts)
\end{aligned}
$$

6.5 Example: Huffman trees

A good illustration of the use of binary trees is in the problem of data compression. As many computer users know only too well, it is often necessary to store files of information as compactly as possible in order to free precious space for other, more urgent, purposes. Suppose the information to be stored is a text consisting of a sequence of characters. The ISO standard code used in Haskell uses eight bits to represent each of $2^8 = 256$ different characters, so a text of n characters contains $8n$ bits of information. The ISO standard is a fixed-length code, so the characters of the text can be recovered by decoding each successive group of eight bits.

One idea for reducing the total number of bits required to code a text is to abandon the notion of fixed-length codes, and seek instead a coding scheme based on the relative frequency of occurrence of the characters in the text. The basic idea is to take a sample piece of text, estimate the number of times each character appears, and choose short codes for the more frequent characters and longer codes for the rarer ones. For example, if we take the codes

$$t \longrightarrow 0$$
$$e \longrightarrow 10$$
$$x \longrightarrow 11$$

then "text" can be coded as the bit sequence 010110 of length 6.

It is important to realise that codes must be chosen in such a way as to ensure that the coded text can be deciphered uniquely. To illustrate, suppose the codes had been

$$t \longrightarrow 0$$
$$e \longrightarrow 10$$
$$x \longrightarrow 1$$

Under this scheme, "text" would be coded as the sequence 01010 of length 5. However, the string "tee" would be coded by exactly the same sequence, and obviously this is not what is wanted. The simplest way to prevent the problem arising is to choose codes so that no code is a proper initial segment (or *prefix*) of any other.

As well as requiring unique decipherability, we also want the coding to be *optimal.* An optimal coding scheme is one that minimises the expected length of the coded text. More precisely, if characters c_j, for $1 \leq j \leq n$, have probabilities of occurrence p_j, then we want to choose codes with lengths l_j such that

$$\sum_{j=1}^{n} p_j l_j$$

is as small as possible.

One method for constructing an optimal code satisfying the prefix property is called Huffman coding (after its inventor, David Huffman). Each character is stored as a tip of a binary tree, the structure of which is determined by the computed frequencies. The code for a character c is a sequence of binary values describing the path in the tree to the tip containing *c*. To illustrate the idea, consider the tree

$$Fork\ (Fork\ (Leaf\ 'x')\ (Leaf\ 'e'))\ (Leaf\ 't')$$

In this tree the character 'x' is coded by 00, the character 'e' by 01, and the character 't' by 1.

There are four aspects to the problem of implementing Huffman coding: (i) collecting information from a sample; (ii) building a binary tree; (iii) coding a text; and (iv) decoding a bit sequence. We will deal with coding and decoding first, then collection, and finally building a tree.

6.5.1   Coding and decoding

The function *decode* for decoding a bit sequence with respect to a given Huffman tree is fairly straightforward. We use a prefix of the bit sequence to traverse the tree until a tip is reached. The associated character is then produced and, if the remainder of the bit sequence is not empty, the tree is traversed again to find the next character. It is assumed that the bit sequence corresponds to a correct encoding; if it does not, then decoding will fail. The program is

$$
\begin{aligned}
&decode :: Btree\ Char \rightarrow [Bit] \rightarrow [Char] \\
&decode\ t\ cs \\
&\quad =\ \textbf{if}\ null\ cs\ \textbf{then}\ [\ ]\ \textbf{else}\ decode1\ t\ cs \\
&\qquad \textbf{where}\ decode1\ (Leaf\ x)\ cs \qquad\quad =\quad x : decode\ t\ cs \\
&\qquad\qquad\quad decode1\ (Fork\ xt\ yt)\ (0 : cs) \quad =\quad decode1\ xt\ cs \\
&\qquad\qquad\quad decode1\ (Fork\ xt\ yt)\ (1 : cs) \quad =\quad decode1\ yt\ cs
\end{aligned}
$$

The time for decoding is clearly linear in the length of the bit sequence, which is the best one can achieve.

The function *encode* for coding a sequence of characters with respect to a given Huffman tree is not so easy to define if one wants an efficient program. Huffman trees are good for finding the character associated with a given bit sequence, but poor at finding the bit sequence associated with a given character. What we would like to do is first transform the tree into something for which the second task can be made more efficient. One possibility is to define a function

$$transform \quad :: \quad Btree\ Char \rightarrow CodeTable$$

where

$$\textbf{type}\ CodeTable \quad = \quad [(Char, [Bit])]$$

The function *transform* produces a table consisting of a list of pairs of characters and bit sequences. Now we can define

$$
\begin{aligned}
&encode &&:: &&Btree\ Char \rightarrow [Char] \rightarrow [Bit] \\
&encode\ t &&= &&concat \cdot map\ (lookup\ codetable) \\
& && &&\textbf{where}\ codetable = transform\ t
\end{aligned}
$$

$$
\begin{aligned}
&lookup &&:: &&CodeTable \rightarrow Char \rightarrow [Bit] \\
&lookup\ ((x, bs) : xbs)\ y &&= &&\textbf{if}\ x == y\ \textbf{then}\ bs\ \textbf{else}\ lookup\ xbs\ y
\end{aligned}
$$

The time required to perform a *lookup* operation depends precisely on where in the table the character is found. It seems sensible to place characters that are likely to appear in the input before characters that are less likely. Since the frequency of occurrence corresponds inversely with the length of the associated bit sequence (after all, that is the whole point of Huffman coding), the conclusion is that the code table should be sorted in ascending order of length of second component. We hence define

$$
\begin{aligned}
&transform\ (Leaf\ x) &&= &&[(x, [\,])] \\
&transform\ (Fork\ xt\ yt) &&= &&hufmerge\ (transform\ xt)\ (transform\ yt)
\end{aligned}
$$

The function *hufmerge* merges two tables, adding a zero bit to all codes coming from the first table, and a one bit to codes coming from the second table:

$$
\begin{aligned}
&hufmerge &&:: &&CodeTable \rightarrow CodeTable \rightarrow CodeTable \\
&hufmerge\ [\,]\ ycs &&= &&[(y, 1 : cs) \mid (y, cs) \leftarrow ycs] \\
&hufmerge\ xbs\ [\,] &&= &&[(x, 0 : bs) \mid (x, bs) \leftarrow xbs]
\end{aligned}
$$

$$
\begin{aligned}
&hufmerge\ ((x, bs) : xbs)\ ((y, cs) : ycs) \\
&\quad \left|\
\begin{aligned}
&length\ bs \leq length\ cs &&= &&(x, 0 : bs) : hufmerge\ xbs\ ((y, cs) : ycs) \\
&otherwise &&= &&(y, 1 : cs) : hufmerge\ ((x, bs) : xbs)\ ycs
\end{aligned}
\right.
\end{aligned}
$$

The efficiency of the program can be improved substantially by avoiding the recomputation of the lengths of bit sequences. Code tables should therefore really have been lists of triples:

$$
\textbf{type}\ CodeTable\ =\ (Char, [Bit], Int)
$$

The third component describes the length of the second. We will leave this optimisation as an exercise.

6.5.2 Analysing the sample

We will assume that the sample contains all the characters in the text to be coded. The relative frequencies of the characters in the sample can be computed by first sorting to bring occurrences of the same character together, and then replacing runs of a single character by a pair consisting of the character and the number of times it is repeated. Finally, we can sort the result in ascending order of frequency. The program is

$$\begin{aligned} sample \quad &:: \quad [Char] \to [(Char, Int)] \\ sample \quad &= \quad sortby\ freq \cdot collate \cdot sortby\ id \end{aligned}$$

Recall from Section 5.2 that the function *sortby* has type

$$sortby \quad :: \quad (Ord\ \beta) \Rightarrow (\alpha \to \beta) \to [\alpha] \to [\alpha]$$

In particular, *sortby id* :: $[Char] \to [Char]$ sorts a list of characters into alphabetical order.

The function *collate* replaces runs of a single character by the character and the length of the run:

$$\begin{aligned} collate \quad &:: \quad [Char] \to [(Char, Int)] \\ collate\ [\,] \quad &= \quad [\,] \\ collate\ (x : xs) \quad &= \quad (x, 1 + length\ ys) : collate\ zs \\ & \quad\quad \textbf{where}\ (ys, zs) = span\ (== x)\ (x : xs) \end{aligned}$$

Recall that *span p xs* = (*takeWhile p xs, dropWhile p xs*).
Finally, the function *sortby freq*, where

$$\begin{aligned} freq \quad &:: \quad (Char, Int) \to Int \\ freq\ (x, m) \quad &= \quad m \end{aligned}$$

sorts a list of pairs into ascending order of frequency.

6.5.3 Building a Huffman tree

Now we turn to the most interesting part, which is building a Huffman tree. Having analysed the sample, we are given a list of pairs:

$$[(c_0, w_0), (c_1, w_1), \ldots, (c_n, w_n)]$$

where c_j ($0 \le j \le n$) are the characters and w_j ($0 \le j \le n$) are numbers, called *weights*, indicating the frequencies. The probability of character c_j occurring is therefore w_j/W, where $W = \sum w_j$. We are also given that $w_0 \le w_1 \le \cdots \le w_n$.

In outline, the procedure for building a Huffman tree is first to convert the above list of pairs into a list of trees, and then repeatedly to combine two trees with lightest weights until just one tree remains. The weight of a tree consisting of a single tip is the weight of the character contained in the tip, and the weight of a tree consisting of a binary node is the sum of the weights of its two subtrees. To avoid recomputing weights, it is convenient to label trees with their weights. Hence we introduce the type

> **data** *Huff* = *Tip Int Char* | *Node Int Huff Huff*

When the tree has been built, we can strip off the weight information by a function *unlabel* defined by

$$
\begin{array}{lll}
unlabel & :: & Huff \rightarrow Btree\ Char \\
unlabel\ (Tip\ w\ x) & = & Leaf\ x \\
unlabel\ (Node\ w\ xt\ yt) & = & Fork\ (unlabel\ xt)\ (unlabel\ yt)
\end{array}
$$

The function *mkHuff* for building a Huffman tree takes the form

$$
\begin{array}{lll}
mkHuff & :: & [(Char, Int)] \rightarrow Huff \\
mkHuff & = & unwrap \cdot until\ singleton\ combine \cdot map\ mktip
\end{array}
$$

where

$$
\begin{array}{lll}
mktip & :: & (Char, Int) \rightarrow Huff \\
mktip\ (c, w) & = & Tip\ w\ c
\end{array}
$$

The standard function *until p f* repeatedly applies *f* until *p* becomes true, and *singleton* is the test for a singleton list. The effect of *combine* on a list *ts* of trees is to combine two trees in *ts* with the lightest weights.

In order to determine at each stage which are the lightest trees, we simply keep the trees in increasing order of weight. Hence

$$
\begin{array}{lll}
combine & :: & [Huff] \rightarrow [Huff] \\
combine\ (xt : yt : xts) & = & insert\ (Node\ w\ xt\ yt)\ xts \\
& & \textbf{where}\ w = weight\ xt + weight\ yt
\end{array}
$$

$$
\begin{array}{lll}
weight & :: & Huff \rightarrow Int \\
weight\ (Tip\ w\ c) & = & w \\
weight\ (Node\ w\ x\ y) & = & w
\end{array}
$$

The function *insert* inserts a tree in the correct place to maintain the property that the list of trees is in ascending order of weight:

$$
\begin{aligned}
insert & :: & Huff &\rightarrow [Huff] \rightarrow [Huff] \\
insert\ xt\ yts & = & uts & +\!\!+\ [xt] +\!\!+\ vts \\
& & \textbf{where}\ (uts, vts) & =\ span\ p\ yts \\
& & p\ yt & =\ (weight\ yt \leq weight\ xt)
\end{aligned}
$$

Let us see this algorithm at work on an example. Consider the sequence

$$[(\text{'G'}, 8), (\text{'R'}, 9), (\text{'A'}, 11), (\text{'T'}, 13), (\text{'E'}, 17)]$$

of characters and their weights. The first step is to convert this into the list

$$[\textit{Tip}\ 8\ \text{'G'},\ \textit{Tip}\ 9\ \text{'R'},\ \textit{Tip}\ 11\ \text{'A'},\ \textit{Tip}\ 13\ \text{'T'},\ \textit{Tip}\ 17\ \text{'E'}]$$

The next step is to combine the first two trees and insert the result in the correct place:

$$
\begin{aligned}
&[\textit{Tip}\ 11\ \text{'A'}, \\
&\ \textit{Tip}\ 13\ \text{'T'}, \\
&\ \textit{Node}\ 17\ (\textit{Tip}\ 8\ \text{'G'})\ (\textit{Tip}\ 9\ \text{'R'}), \\
&\ \textit{Tip}\ 17\ \text{'E'}]
\end{aligned}
$$

The result of the second step is the list

$$
\begin{aligned}
&[\textit{Node}\ 17\ (\textit{Tip}\ 8\ G)\ (\textit{Tip}\ 9\ \text{'R'}), \\
&\ \textit{Tip}\ 17\ \text{'E'}, \\
&\ \textit{Node}\ 24\ (\textit{Tip}\ 11\ \text{'A'})\ (\textit{Tip}\ 13\ \text{'T'})]
\end{aligned}
$$

The third step gives

$$
\begin{aligned}
&[\textit{Node}\ 24\ (\textit{Tip}\ 11\ \text{'A'})\ (\textit{Tip}\ 13\ \text{'T'}), \\
&\ \textit{Node}\ 34\ (\textit{Node}\ 17\ (\textit{Tip}\ 8\ \text{'G'})\ (\textit{Tip}\ 9\ \text{'R'})) \\
&\qquad (\textit{Tip}\ 17\ \text{'E'})]
\end{aligned}
$$

The final tree is

$$
\begin{aligned}
&\textit{Node}\ 58\ (\textit{Node}\ 24\ (\textit{Tip}\ 11\ \text{'A'})\ (\textit{Tip}\ 13\ \text{'T'})) \\
&\qquad (\textit{Node}\ 34\ (\textit{Node}\ 17\ (\textit{Tip}\ 8\ \text{'G'})\ (\textit{Tip}\ 9\ \text{'R'})) \\
&\qquad\qquad (\textit{Tip}\ 17\ \text{'E'}))
\end{aligned}
$$

In this tree the characters 'A', 'T' and 'E' are coded by two-bit sequences and 'G' and 'R' by three-bit sequences.

The average, or *expected*, length of a character code is

$$\sum w_j l_j / \sum w_j$$

where l_j is the number of bits assigned to character c_j. In the above example this value is

$$((11 + 13 + 17) \times 2 + (8 + 9) \times 3)/(8 + 9 + 11 + 13 + 17) \quad = \quad 2.29\ldots$$

The crucial property of a Huffman code is that it minimises expected length. Putting it another way, a Huffman tree has the property that it is a binary tree, over tip values $w_1, w_2, \ldots, w_n$, which minimises the sum of the 'weighted' path lengths $w_j l_j$ for $1 \le j \le n$. For a proof of this fact, the reader should consult the references given at the end of the chapter

Exercises

6.5.1 Explain why a Huffman code has the prefix property.

6.5.2 Construct a code which does not satisfy the prefix property, but which nevertheless is such that every text can be uniquely decoded.

6.5.3 Optimise the definition of *transform* by including length information in code tables.

6.6   Example: Meertens' number

The aim of this section is to illustrate the use of rose trees in organising the search for a number with a peculiar property. The problem concerns the prime factorisation of numbers. For example, $400 = 2^4 3^0 5^2$ and $432 = 2^4 3^3 5^0$. Suppose we define $g(n)$ by taking the decimal representation $d_1 d_2 \ldots d_k$ of n and setting $g(n) = 2^{d_1} 3^{d_2} \ldots p_k^{d_k}$, where p_k is the kth prime. Thus, $g(402) = 400$ and $g(430) = 432$. The numbers n and $g(n)$ are not always so close together as these two instances suggest; in fact, most of the time they are wildly different. The question is: do they ever coincide?

The function g is named after Kurt Gödel who exploited the idea of coding a sequence of characters as a single number in his famous paper on the incompleteness of arithmetic. Here we are using the same device, coding a number by coding its decimal representation. If $n = g(n)$, then n is called a *Meertens' number*. The first Meertens' number was named in honour of a colleague of ours, Lambert Meertens, on the occasion of his twenty-five years at the CWI, Amsterdam.

The existence of a Meertens' number is not at all obvious. The number has to be even, and a little mental calculation shows that it cannot have one, two, or three digits. For example, any three-digit number would have to end with a zero and so be both divisible and not divisible by five. On the other hand, there are some near misses; the examples above show that there are numbers n for which n and $g(n)$ differ by at most two. Furthermore, as n increases the value $g(n)$ jumps about quite a lot, so there is no obvious reason why they should never coincide.

The problem is not specific to decimals of course. In base two each of the numbers 2, 6, and 10 is a Meertens' number. For example, 6 in binary is 110 and $6 = 2^1 3^1 5^0$. The number 10 is also a Meertens' number in base three: 10 in ternary is 101 and $10 = 2^1 3^0 5^1$. Such results are encouraging, but finding the Meertens' number for mere bits and bytes is not enough. Mere tens, on the other hand, would be quite appropriate.

Our aim now is to construct a program for finding Meertens' numbers. The most obvious method is to define

$$meertens \quad :: \quad [Integer]$$
$$meertens \quad = \quad [n \mid n \leftarrow [1 ..], n == godel\ n]$$

$$godel \quad :: \quad Integer \rightarrow Integer$$
$$godel\ n \quad = \quad product\ (zipWith\ (\uparrow)\ primes\ (digits\ n))$$

The function *digits* returns the digits of a natural number. The list of primes can be defined in a number of ways, including

$$primes \quad :: \quad [Int]$$
$$primes \quad = \quad [p \mid p \leftarrow [2 ..], prime\ p]$$

We will leave the definitions of *prime*, *product*, and *digits* as an exercise.

The value of *meertens* is either an infinite list (if there are an infinite number of Meertens' numbers) or a partial list. In either case, evaluation will not terminate. Even if we ask for *head meertens*, the computation turns out to be painfully slow. The Gödel number of each candidate is computed afresh and this takes a significant number of steps.

As preparation for a change in representation, we can rewrite the definition of *meertens* in the form

$$meertens \quad = \quad [n \mid (n, g) \leftarrow map\ gn\ [1 ..], n == g]$$
$$\textbf{where } gn\ n = (n, godel\ n)$$

The idea now is to define a rose tree *gtree* so that

$$level\ gtree \quad = \quad map\ gn\ [1 ..]$$

Recall from Section 6.4 that *level* produces the labels of a rose tree in breadth-first order. Each node in the tree *gtree*, apart from the very first, has 10 subtrees, one for each digit. The first tree has 9 subtrees since decimals begin with a nonzero digit. Each node in the tree is labelled with two integers, *n* and *g*, where *g* = *godel n* and the decimal representation of *n* defines the path in the tree to the given node. The tree therefore has type *Tree*, where

> **data** *Tree* = *Node Label* [*Tree*]
> **type** *Label* = (*Integer, Integer*)

The following program builds an infinite tree with a starting label of $(0,1)$, which is correct since $g(0) = 2^0 = 1$:

> *gtree* :: *Tree*
> *gtree* = *snip* (*mktree prps* $(0, 1)$)

The function *snip* snips off the leftmost branch to remove decimals beginning with zero:

> *snip*   :: *Tree* → *Tree*
> *snip* (*Node x ts*) = *Node x* (*tail ts*)

The work of building the tree is relegated to the function *mktree*. This function takes an infinite list *prps* of the powers of each prime and a label. The list *prps* is defined by

> *prps* :: [[*Integer*]]
> *prps* = *map powers primes*

The value of *powers p* is an infinite list $[1, p, p^2, \ldots]$ of powers of *p*:

> *powers*   :: *Integer* → [*Integer*]
> *powers p* = *iterate* (*p*×) 1

The standard function *iterate* is defined by

> *iterate*   :: $(\alpha \to \alpha) \to \alpha \to [\alpha]$
> *iterate f x* = *x* : *iterate f* (*f x*)

Now we define

> *mktree*   :: [[*Integer*]] → *Label* → *Tree*
> *mktree* (*ps* : *pps*) *x* = *Node x* (*map* (*mktree pps*) (*labels ps x*))

where

$$
\begin{array}{lll}
labels & :: & [Integer] \to Label \to [Label] \\
labels\ ps\ (n, g) & = & zip\ (map\ (m+)\ ds)\ (map\ (g\times)\ ps) \\
& & \textbf{where}\ m = 10 \times n;\quad ds = [0\,..\,9]
\end{array}
$$

The list *meertens* of Meertens' numbers can now be computed, in theory at least, by

$$
meertens\ =\ [n \mid (n, g) \leftarrow level\ gtree, n \mathbin{=\!\!=} g]
$$

There is no theoretical difficulty in printing out the labels of an infinite tree in breadth-first order because the ordering proceeds level by level. However, there is a substantial practical difficulty: the computation rapidly runs out of space and grinds to a halt. Searching a tree in breadth-first order requires space proportional to the size of the tree, and the size of Meertens' tree grows exponentially. No evaluator, real or imagined, has sufficient resources to proceed very far with the computation.

   The obvious solution is to restrict the height of the tree and to switch to depth-first search. We have to make the tree finite if we want to use depth-first search, because one cannot traverse an infinite Meertens' tree in depth-first order. If we build a tree of height k, then we can search for Meertens' numbers n in the range $1 \le n < 10^k$. The revised definition is

$$
\begin{array}{lll}
meertens & :: & Int \to [Integer] \\
meertens\ k & = & [n \mid (n, g) \leftarrow flatten\ (gtree\ k), n \mathbin{=\!\!=} g]
\end{array}
$$

The function *gtree* returns trees of given height:

$$
\begin{array}{lll}
gtree & :: & Int \to Tree \\
gtree\ k & = & snip\ (mktree\ prps\ (0, 1)) \\
& & \textbf{where}\ prps = map\ powers\ (take\ k\ primes)
\end{array}
$$

$$
\begin{array}{lll}
mktree & :: & [[Integer]] \to Label \to Tree \\
mktree\ [\,]\ x & = & Node\ x\ [\,] \\
mktree\ (ps : pps)\ x & = & Node\ x\ (map\ (mktree\ pps)\ (labels\ ps\ x))
\end{array}
$$

Notice that we have replaced *level* by *flatten* in the definition of *meertens*. It follows that *meertens* is no longer guaranteed to produce numbers in increasing order.

   The revised definition is faster, but it is still very slow. There is another optimisation that can usefully be applied. There is no point in generating any subtree with a label (n, g) in which $g \ge 10^k$ since, by construction, all labels

(n, g) in the tree have $n < 10^k$. To incorporate this test without carrying around an extra parameter, we will make the functions *mktree* and *labels* local to the definition of *gtree*:

$$
\begin{aligned}
&\textit{gtree } k = \\
&\quad \textit{snip } (\textit{mktree prps } (0, 1)) \\
&\quad \textbf{where} \\
&\quad \textit{prps} &&= &&\textit{map powers } (\textit{take k primes}) \\
&\quad \textit{mktree } [\,] \, x &&= &&\textit{Node x } [\,] \\
&\quad \textit{mktree } (ps : pps) \, x &&= &&\textit{Node x } (\textit{map } (\textit{mktree pps}) \, (\textit{labels ps x})) \\
&\quad \textit{labels ps } (n, g) &&= &&\textit{zip } (\textit{map } (m+) \, ds) \, (\textit{chop } (\textit{map } (g\times) \, ps)) \\
&\quad &&&&\textbf{where } m = 10 \times n \\
&\quad \textit{chop} &&= &&\textit{takeWhile } (< 10^k) \\
&\quad \textit{ds} &&= &&[0 \mathinner{.\,.} 9]
\end{aligned}
$$

Even with these optimisations the search is still fairly slow. Apart from studying the problem carefully to see what number theory can be applied, there is one general technique for improving matters, and we consider this next.

6.6.1   Deforestation

Deforestation is the general name for a programming technique that removes intermediate datatypes from a program. The idea will be considered in a general setting in the following chapter, but we will employ it now to get rid of the tree we have so carefully constructed. The saving will not be huge but it will be significant. If the resulting program can be sped up by, say, a factor of two, then the optimisation is worthwhile. (Surely by now the reader will have suspected, correctly, that the first Meertens' number is not a small one.)

Like all sound techniques for optimisation, deforestation can be carried out by program calculation. The theme of the calculation is to combine functions that produce and consume elements of an intermediate datatype. We begin by calculating, for $k > 0$, that

$$
\begin{aligned}
&\quad (\textit{flatten} \cdot \textit{gtree}) \, k \\
&= \quad \{\text{definition of } \textit{gtree}, \text{ with } \textit{prps} = \textit{map powers } (\textit{take k primes})\} \\
&\quad (\textit{flatten} \cdot \textit{snip} \cdot \textit{mktree prps}) \, (0, 1) \\
&= \quad \{\text{definition of } \textit{mktree}, \text{ with } \textit{ps} : \textit{pps} = \textit{prps} \text{ (since } k > 0)\} \\
&\quad (\textit{flatten} \cdot \textit{snip} \cdot \textit{Node } (0, 1) \cdot \textit{map } (\textit{mktree pps}) \cdot \textit{labels ps}) \, (0, 1)
\end{aligned}
$$

We continue by simplifying

$$flatten \cdot snip \cdot Node\, x \cdot map\, (mktree\, pps)$$

=   {since $snip \cdot Node\, x = Node\, x \cdot tail$}

$$flatten \cdot Node\, x \cdot tail \cdot map\, (mktree\, pps)$$

=   {since $tail \cdot map\, f = map\, f \cdot tail$}

$$flatten \cdot Node\, x \cdot map\, (mktree\, pps) \cdot tail$$

=   {since $flatten \cdot Node\, x = (x:) \cdot concat \cdot map\, flatten$}

$$(x:) \cdot concat \cdot map\, flatten \cdot map\, (mktree\, pps) \cdot tail$$

=   {since map is a functor}

$$(x:) \cdot concat \cdot map\, (flatten \cdot mktree\, pps) \cdot tail$$

The final expression suggests introducing the function *search*, defined by

$$search\, pps \;=\; flatten \cdot mktree\, pps$$

It is this function that captures the idea of deforestation. The building and flattening of a tree is combined in a single function.

The aim now is to get a recursive definition of *search*. The simplification of *search* [ ] is straightforward, and that of *search* (*ps* : *pps*) *x* is similar to that of *flatten* · *gtree*. The result is

$$search\, [\,]\, x \qquad = \quad [x]$$
$$search\, (ps : pps)\, x \;=\; x : concat\, (map\, (search\, ps)\, (labels\, ps\, x))$$

Here is the final program, in which we suppose $k > 0$:

$$meertens\; k = [n \mid (n, g) \leftarrow candidates\, (0, 1), n \mathbin{{=}{=}} g]$$

    where

candidates	=	$concat \cdot map\, (search\, pps) \cdot tail \cdot labels\, ps$
ps : *pps*	=	$map\, powers\, (take\, k\, primes)$
search [ ] *x*	=	$[x]$
search (*ps* : *pps*) *x*	=	$x : concat\, (map\, (search\, pps)\, (labels\, ps\, x))$
labels *ps* (*n*, *g*)	=	$zip\, (map\, (m+)\, ds)\, (chop\, (map\, (g\times)\, ps))$
		where $m = 10 \times n$
chop	=	$takeWhile\, (< 10^k)$
ds	=	$[0 .. 9]$

This program was run on a small, and rather ancient, machine with a limited amount of space:

```
? meertens 8
[81312000]
(2227857 reductions, 5423538 cells, 57 garbage collections)
```

As far as we are aware, 81312000 is the only known Meertens' number. To reiterate, it has the peculiar property that

$$2^8 3^1 5^3 7^1 11^2 13^0 17^0 19^0 \;=\; 81312000$$

Exercises

6.6.1 What is the first Meertens' number in base five?

6.6.2 In the definition of $g(n)$ the most significant digit of n is associated with the smallest prime. There is a variant in which the most significant digit is associated with the largest prime. Define h by taking $h(n) = 2^{d_k} 3^{d_{k-1}} \ldots p_k^{d_1}$, where $d_1 d_2 \ldots d_k$ is the decimal representation of n. What is the smallest number n for which $n = h(n)$?

6.6.3 Are there any *amicable* Meertens' numbers, that is, pairs of distinct integers m and n such that $m = g(n)$ and $n = g(m)$? More generally, are there any cycles?

6.6.4 Find another Meertens' number or prove that none exists!

6.7 Chapter notes

Good source books on trees include Cormen, Leiserson, and Rivest (1990) and Knuth (1973b). Rose trees, which also go under the name *general* trees, were so named in Meertens (1987). Gibbons' thesis (1991) contains a systematic treatment of a number of algorithms on trees.

Huffman coding was described in Huffman (1952); see also Hu (1982) and Knuth (1973a). Thompson (1996) also gives a functional program for Huffman coding.

The problem of computing Meertens' number was first considered in Bird (1991). Gödel numbering was used by Gödel in his 1931 proof of his famous theorem on the incompleteness of arithmetic; see the collected works: Gödel (1990). Popular accounts of the importance of this result on twentieth-century thought are given in Hofstadter (1979) and Penrose (1994).

Chapter 7

Efficiency

References to efficiency have increased during the previous chapter, and the time has come to focus on this important issue. In this chapter we will take a closer look at the underlying model of reduction and the time and space resources required to evaluate expressions. We will also describe a simple calculus for estimating the running time of programs, and present a number of programming techniques, some of which have already been exploited, for improving performance.

7.1 Lazy evaluation

Let us start by revisiting the evaluation of *square*(3+4) considered in Chapter 1. Recall that one reduction sequence is

$$\quad\quad square\ (3+4)$$

$$=\quad \{\text{definition of } +\}$$

$$\quad\quad square\ 7$$

$$=\quad \{\text{definition of } square\}$$

$$\quad\quad 7 \times 7$$

$$=\quad \{\text{definition of } \times\}$$

$$\quad\quad 49$$

Another reduction sequence is

$$\quad\quad square\ (3+4)$$

$$=\quad \{\text{definition of } square\}$$

$$(3 + 4) \times (3 + 4)$$

$$= \quad \{\text{definition of } +\}$$

$$7 \times (3 + 4)$$

$$= \quad \{\text{definition of } +\}$$

$$7 \times 7$$

$$= \quad \{\text{definition of } \times\}$$

$$49$$

These two reduction sequences illustrate two reduction policies, called *innermost* and *outermost* reduction, respectively. In the first sequence, each step reduces an *innermost redex*. The word 'redex' is short for 'reducible expression', and an innermost redex is one that contains no other redex. In the second sequence, each step reduces an *outermost* redex. An outermost redex is one that is contained in no other redex.

Here is another example. First, innermost reduction:

$$\mathit{fst}\,(\mathit{square}\,4, \mathit{square}\,2)$$

$$= \quad \{\text{definition of } \mathit{square}\}$$

$$\mathit{fst}\,(4 \times 4, \mathit{square}\,2)$$

$$= \quad \{\text{definition of } \times\}$$

$$\mathit{fst}\,(16, \mathit{square}\,2)$$

$$= \quad \{\text{definition of } \mathit{square}\}$$

$$\mathit{fst}\,(16, 2 \times 2)$$

$$= \quad \{\text{definition of } \times\}$$

$$\mathit{fst}\,(16, 4)$$

$$= \quad \{\text{definition of } \mathit{fst}\}$$

$$16$$

This reduction takes five steps. In the first two steps there was a choice of innermost redexes and the *leftmost* redex is chosen. The outermost reduction policy for the same expression yields

$$\mathit{fst}\,(\mathit{square}\,4, \mathit{square}\,2)$$

$$= \quad \{\text{definition of } \mathit{fst}\}$$

$$\mathit{square}\,4$$

$$= \quad \{\text{definition of } square\}$$

$$4 \times 4$$

$$= \quad \{\text{definition of } \times\}$$

$$16$$

This reduction sequence takes three steps. By using outermost reduction, evaluation of *square* 2 was avoided.

The two reduction policies have different characteristics. Sometimes outermost reduction will give an answer when innermost reduction fails to terminate (consider replacing *square* 2 by *undefined* in the expression above). However, if both methods terminate, then they give the same result.

Outermost reduction has the important property that if an expression has a normal form, then outermost reduction will compute it. Outermost reduction is also called *normal-order* on account of this property. It would seem therefore that outermost reduction is a better choice than innermost reduction, but there is a catch. As the first example shows, outermost reduction can sometimes require more steps than innermost reduction. The problem arises with any function whose definition contains repeated occurrences of an argument. By binding such an argument to a suitably large expression, the difference between innermost and outermost reduction can be made arbitrarily large.

This problem can be solved by representing expressions as *graphs* rather than trees. Unlike trees, graphs can share subexpressions. For example, the graph

$$(\bullet \times \bullet) \quad \quad (3 + 4)$$

represents the expression $(3 + 4) \times (3 + 4)$. Each occurrence of $3 + 4$ is represented by an arrow, called a *pointer*, to a single instance of $(3 + 4)$. Now, using outermost *graph reduction* we have

$$square \ (3 + 4)$$

$$= \quad \{\text{definition of } square\}$$

$$(\bullet \times \bullet) \quad \quad (3 + 4)$$

$$= \quad \{\text{definition of } +\}$$

$$(\bullet \times \bullet) \quad \quad 7$$

$$= \quad \{\text{definition of } \times\}$$

$$49$$

The reduction sequence has only three steps. The representation of expressions as graphs means that duplicated subexpressions can be shared and reduced at most once. With graph reduction, outermost reduction never takes more steps than innermost reduction. Henceforth we will refer to outermost graph reduction by its common name, *lazy evaluation*, and to innermost graph reduction as *eager evaluation*.

Shared subexpressions in a graph may also be introduced by local definitions. For instance, given the definition

$$roots\ a\ b\ c\ =\ ((-b-d)/e, (-b+d)/e)$$
$$\textbf{where}\ d\ =\ sqrt\ (square\ b - 4 \times a \times c)$$
$$e\ =\ 2 \times a$$

the first reduction step of *roots* 1 5 3 produces the graph

$$((-5 - \bullet)/\bullet, (-5 + \bullet)/\bullet) \qquad sqrt\ (square\ 5 - 4 \times 1 \times 3) \qquad (2 \times 1)$$

Actually, there are three additional pointers not shown on this graph, one pointer for each of the variables *a*, *b*, and *c*. These pointers point to single occurrences of the expressions 1, 5, and 3.

Arrows have no meaning except to indicate binding and sharing. Both

$$(square\ \bullet) \qquad (3 + 4)$$

and *square* (3 + 4) are equivalent ways of writing the same expression. The size of an expression or graph can be measured by counting the total number of arguments involved. For example, the expression above has size three because *square* has one argument and + has two. Similarly, the expression *square* 3 + *square* 4 has size four since each occurrence of *square* has one argument and + has two. The graph

$$(\bullet \times \bullet) \qquad (3 + 4)$$

also has size four (× and + each have two arguments).

We will adopt lazy evaluation as our model of computation because it has two desirable properties: (i) it terminates whenever any reduction order terminates, and (ii) it requires no more (and possibly fewer) steps than eager evaluation. To be precise, the time and space required to evaluate an expression e_0 is defined as follows. Suppose

$$e_0 \Rightarrow e_1 \Rightarrow e_2 \Rightarrow \cdots \Rightarrow e_n$$

is a sequence of outermost graph reduction steps yielding the normal form e_n. Then the time required to reduce e_0 to normal form is defined to be n and the space required is defined to be the size of the largest graph in the reduction sequence, that is, the maximum of the sizes of $e_0, \ldots, e_n$. It is reasonable to choose maximum expression size rather than total expression size because the space used for one reduction step can always be reused at the next step. To put it another way, the critical limitation is the width of the piece of paper on which the calculation is done, not its length. With the help of an eraser (in programming terms, a *garbage collector*) space can be reclaimed for subsequent steps.

Defining time and space in this fashion has its limitations. In particular, the number of reduction steps does not correspond exactly to the elapsed time between submitting an expression for evaluation and getting the result. No account has been taken of the time required to find an outermost redex in a possibly complicated expression. Since expressions can get arbitrarily large, this search time cannot be regarded as constant.

The space measure also has its limitations. One problem is that it takes no account of the process of *printing*. To illustrate, printing [1 .. 1000] does not require 1000 units of space, even though reduction of the expression [1 .. 1000] to the normal form $1 : 2 : \ldots : 1000 : [\,]$ does require this amount. Printing a list involves printing the head of the list, throwing the head away, and printing the rest. The situation is, however, complicated by another aspect. Suppose we defined

$$numbers \quad = \quad [1 .. 1000]$$

in a script. This time, evaluating *numbers* does use up 1000 units of space. The space cannot be thrown away after printing because there is a pointer to *numbers* in the program. It is a consequence of lazy evaluation that no expression at the end of an arrow is evaluated more than once. Hence the first evaluation of *numbers* leaves *numbers* bound to an evaluated list of length 1000. As a result, the space occupied by a script can grow with repeated evaluations of the functions contained in it.

For such reasons, we will concentrate almost exclusively on time efficiency in the analysis of programs. However, one technique for the limited control of space is given in Section 7.5.

Exercises

7.1.1 Describe the innermost, outermost, and outermost graph reduction sequences for each of the following expressions:

> *head* $[1 .. 1000]$
> *map f* $[1 .. 3]$ **where** $f\, n = 10 \times 10 + n$

7.1.2 One definition of *sort* is to take *sort* = *foldr insert* [ ], where

> $insert\, x\, [\,]$ = $[x]$
> $insert\, x\, (y : ys)$ =   **if** $x \le y$ **then** $x : y : ys$ **else** $y : insert\, x\, ys$

Give, in detail, the eager and lazy evaluation reduction sequences for the expression *sort* $[3, 4, 2, 1]$, explaining where they differ.

7.1.3 Suppose we define *minlist* = *head* · *sort*, where *sort* is defined in the previous question. How many reduction steps (approximately) are required to evaluate *minlist* on a list of n numbers, with both lazy and eager evaluation?

7.1.4 Same question, but for *maxlist* = *last* · *sort*.

7.2 Asymptotic analysis

In general, one is less interested in estimating the cost of evaluating a particular expression than in comparing the performance of one definition of a function with another. For example, consider the following two programs for reversing a list:

> $reverse\, [\,]$ = $[\,]$
> $reverse\, (x : xs)$ = $reverse\, xs \mathbin{+\!\!+} [x]$
>
> $reverse'$ = $foldl\, prefix\, [\,]$ **where** $prefix\, xs\, x = x : xs$

It was claimed in Section 4.5 that the second program is more efficient than the former, taking at most a number of steps proportional to n on a list of length n, while the first program takes n^2 steps. The aim of this section is to show how to make such claims more precise and to justify them.

7.2.1 Order notation

To avoid explaining some special mathematical notation, the awkward phrase 'taking at most a number of steps proportional to' has appeared up to now whenever efficiency is discussed. It is time to replace it by something shorter.

Order notation is described in many books on the mathematics of computing science, so we will content ourselves with recalling the basic definitions, and giving some simple examples.

Given two functions f and g on the natural numbers, we say that f is order *at most* g, and write $f = O(g)$ if there is a positive constant C and a natural number n_0 such that $f(n) \leq Cg(n)$ for all $n \geq n_0$. In other words, f is bounded above by some constant times g for all sufficiently large arguments. The notation is abused to the extent that one conventionally writes, for example, $f(n) = O(n^2)$ rather than the more correct $f = O(square)$. Similarly, one writes $f(n) = O(n)$ rather than $f = O(id)$.

The main use of O-notation is to hide constants; for example, we can write

$$\sum_{j=1}^{n} j = O(n^2) \quad \text{and} \quad \sum_{j=1}^{n} j^2 = O(n^3)$$

without bothering about the exact constants involved. However, O-notation must be used with care. Although we write $f = O(g)$, we don't actually mean that f is equal to $O(g)$. It is better to think of $O(g)$ standing by itself on the right of an equation as denoting the *set* of functions f satisfying the property described above, and to interpret the equals sign in $f = O(g)$ as set membership. Then one is never tempted to write $O(g) = f$, or to conclude that $f = g$ from the assertions $f = O(h)$ and $g = O(h)$.

However, we will write expressions such as the following:

$$O(n) + O(n), \quad \sum_{n=1}^{N} O(n^2), \quad T(n) = 2T(n/2) + O(n)$$

When $O(g)$ appears in a formula it stands for some unnamed function f satisfying $f = O(g)$. In particular, $O(n) + O(n)$ denotes the sum of two anonymous functions f_1 and f_2, where $f_1(n) = O(n)$ and $f_2 = O(n)$. Since it follows that $f_1(n) + f_2(n) = O(n)$, it is legitimate to conclude that $O(n) + O(n) = O(n)$.

On the other hand, the expression $\sum_{n=1}^{N} O(n^2)$ does *not* mean

$$O(1^2) + O(2^2) + \cdots + O(N^2)$$

Instead, it denotes the sum $\sum_{n=1}^{N} f(n)$, where f is a *single* function satisfying $f(n) = O(n^2)$. In this case we have $\sum_{n=1}^{N} O(n^2) = O(N^3)$.

What O-notation brings out is an upper bound on the *asymptotic* growth of functions. For this reason, estimating the performance of a program using O-notation is called *asymptotic upper-bound analysis*. For example, the time complexity of *reverse* on a list of length n is $O(n^2)$, and the complexity of *reverse'* is $O(n)$. However, saying that *reverse* takes $O(n^2)$ steps on a list of length n does not mean that it does not take, say, $O(n)$ steps. For more precision we need additional notation.

We say that f is order *at least* g, and write $f = \Omega(g)$ if there exists a positive constant C and natural number n_0 such that $f(n) \geq Cg(n)$ for all $n \geq n_0$. Since C is not required to be a whole number, we have $f = O(g)$ if and only if $g = \Omega(f)$. Now, to say that *reverse* takes $\Omega(n^2)$ steps on a list of length n is to put a lower bound on the number of steps required to evaluate *reverse* on any list of length n.

Putting the two kinds of bound together, we say f is order *exactly* g, and write $f = \Theta(g)$ if $f = O(g)$ and $f = \Omega(g)$. In other words, $f = \Theta(g)$ if there are two positive constants C_1 and C_2 such that

$$C_1 g(n) \leq f(n) \leq C_2 g(n)$$

for all sufficiently large n. Then we can assert that the time of *reverse* is $\Theta(n^2)$ and the time of *reverse'* is $\Theta(n)$. These two functions are atypical in that lower and upper bounds on running times do not normally coincide. In general, the time required to evaluate a function f on a list of length n will depend not only on n but on the actual elements in the list. For some lists the evaluation may be quick, while on others the evaluation may be slow. In general we can only make statements such as 'the running time of f is $\Omega(g)$ and $O(h)$'. If we want more information, then we have to consider the best-case and worst-case performance (and, perhaps, average-case performance) separately. Then one can make statements such as 'in the worst case, the running time of f is $\Theta(n^2)$'.

7.2.2 Timing analysis

Given a function f we will write $T(f)(n)$ to denote an asymptotic estimate of the number of reduction steps required to evaluate f on an argument of 'size' n in the worst case. Moreover, for reasons explained in a moment, we will assume eager, not lazy, evaluation as the reduction strategy. In particular, we can write

$$T(reverse)(n) \quad = \quad \Theta(n^2)$$
$$T(reverse')(n) \quad = \quad \Theta(n)$$

The definition of T requires some amplification. Firstly, $T(f)$ does not refer to the time complexity of a function f but to the complexity of a given *definition* of f. Time complexity is a property of an expression, not of the value of that expression.

Secondly, we do not formalise the notion of size, since different measures are appropriate in different situations. For example, the cost of evaluating

$xs + ys$ is best measured in terms of m and n, where $m = length\ xs$ and $n = length\ ys$. In fact, we have

$$T(\mathbin{+\!\!+})(m, n)\quad =\quad \Theta(m)$$

The proof is left as an exercise. Next, consider *concat xss*. Here the measure of *xss* is more difficult. In the simple case that *xss* is a list of length m, consisting of lists all of length n, we have

$$T(concat)(m, n)\quad =\quad \Theta(mn)$$

We will prove this result below. The estimate for $T(concat)$ therefore refers only to lists of lists with a common length; though limited, such restrictions make timing analyses more tractable.

The third remark is to emphasise that $T(f)(n)$ is an estimate of worst-case running time only. This will be sufficient for our purposes, although best-case and average-case analyses are also important in practice.

The fourth and crucial remark is that $T(f)(n)$ is determined under an eager evaluation model of reduction. The reason is simply that estimating the number of reduction steps under lazy evaluation is difficult, and is still the subject of ongoing research. To illustrate, consider the definition

$$minlist\quad =\quad head \cdot sort$$

Under eager evaluation, the time to evaluate *minlist* on a list of length n is given by

$$T(minlist)(n)\quad =\quad T(sort)(n) + T(head)(n)$$

In other words, to compute *minlist* on a list of length n, we first sort the list, taking $T(sort)(n)$ reduction steps, and then compute the head of the result (which is also a list of length n), taking $T(head)(n)$ steps. This equation does not hold under lazy evaluation, since the number of reduction steps required to find the head of *sort xs* does not necessarily mean that *sort xs* has to be reduced to normal form. It all depends on the precise algorithm used for *sort*. Timing analysis under eager reduction is simpler because it is compositional. Since lazy evaluation never requires more reduction steps than eager evaluation, any upper bound for $T(f)(n)$ will also be an upper bound under lazy evaluation. Furthermore, in many cases of interest, a lower bound for $T(f)(n)$ will also be a lower bound under lazy evaluation.

7.2.3 Reverse and concat

Let us now analyse the program for *reverse*. We have

$$T(reverse)(0) \quad = \quad O(1)$$
$$T(reverse)(n+1) \quad = \quad T(reverse)(n) + T(+\!\!+)(n, 1)$$

The expression $O(1)$ denotes some constant, the precise value of which is not of interest. Since $\Theta(1) = O(1)$, we could have used $\Theta(1)$ in the first equation. The second equation says that to reverse a list of length $n+1$ we have to reverse a list of length n and then concatenate it with a list of length one. The equation exploits the property that *reverse* does not change the length of the list. Program analysis depends on such facts, which is why it is not simply a mechanical exercise that can be delegated to a computer.

The recursive equation for $T(reverse)$ is simple to solve. Using the estimate $T(+\!\!+)(n, m) = \Theta(n)$, we obtain

$$T(reverse)(n) = \sum_{k=0}^{n} \Theta(k) \quad = \quad \Theta(n^2)$$

For the analysis of the second function *reverse'* we can proceed in two different ways. The first is to eliminate *foldl* in favour of a direct recursive definition:

$$reverse'\ xs \qquad = \quad accum\ [\ ]xs$$
$$accum\ ws\ [\ ] \qquad = \quad ws$$
$$accum\ ws\ (x : xs) \quad = \quad accum\ (x : ws)\ xs$$

The function *accum* has two arguments. If we denote the lengths of the two arguments by m and n, then

$$T(accum)(m, 0) \qquad = \quad O(1)$$
$$T(accum)(m, n+1) \quad = \quad O(1) + T(accum)(m, n)$$

The term $O(1)$ in the second equation accounts for the cons operation. The solution is $T(accum)(m, n) = \Theta(n)$ and so $T(reverse')(n) = \Theta(n)$.

The second method is less formal. Evaluating *foldl f e* on a list of length n involves n computations of f. When f is a constant time operation, such as *prefix*, we get at once that the total time is $\Theta(n)$ steps.

As another example, the function *concat* can be defined directly by

$$concat\ [\ ] \qquad = \quad [\ ]$$
$$concat\ (xs : xss) \quad = \quad xs + \!\!+\ concat\ xss$$

For the timing analysis, let the argument to *concat* be a list of length m consisting of lists each of length n. The resulting list then has length mn. Then we have

$$\begin{aligned} T(concat)(0, n) &= O(1) \\ T(concat)(m + 1, n) &= T(concat)(m, n) + T(+\!\!+)(n, mn) \end{aligned}$$

Since $T(+\!\!+)(n, mn) = \Theta(n)$, we get

$$T(concat)(m, n) = \sum_{k=0}^{m} \Theta(n) = \Theta(mn)$$

The above definition of *concat* is exactly what we would get from the definition *concat* = *foldr* $(+\!\!+)$ [ ] by eliminating the *foldr*. Since $+\!\!+$ is associative with unit [ ], we could also have defined *concat* by *concat* = *foldl* $(+\!\!+)$ [ ]. Eliminating *foldl* as in the definition of *reverse'* leads to the program

$$\begin{aligned} concat\ xss &= accum\ [\,]\ xss \\ accum\ ws\ [\,] &= wss \\ accum\ ws\ (xs : xss) &= accum\ (ws +\!\!+ xs)\ xss \end{aligned}$$

For the analysis of *accum* let the first list have length k, and the second list be a list of length m of lists each of length n. Then we have

$$\begin{aligned} T(accum)(k, 0, n) &= O(1) \\ T(accum)(k, m + 1, n) &= T(accum)(k + n, m, n) + T(+\!\!+)(k, n) \end{aligned}$$

Since $T(+\!\!+)(k, n) = \Theta(k)$, we obtain

$$T(accum)(k, m, n) = \sum_{j=0}^{m-1} \Theta(k + jn) = \Theta(k + m^2 n)$$

Hence for this definition of *concat* we have $T(concat)(m, n) = \Theta(m^2 n)$. The conclusion is that using *foldr* rather than *foldl* in the definition of *concat* leads to an asymptotically faster program.

Exercises

7.2.1 Prove that $f = O(g)$ if and only if $g = \Omega(f)$.

7.2.2 What, precisely, does $O(1)$ mean? Prove that $f = O(1)$ if and only if $f = \Theta(1)$.

7.2.3 Prove that $n^{100} = O(2^n)$.

7.2.4 Using O-notation, estimate $\sum_{k=0}^{n} k2^k$.

7.2.5 Prove that $T(+\!\!+)(m, n) = \Theta(m)$.

7.2.6 Use induction to prove that if $k \geq 2$ and

$$
\begin{aligned}
T(0) &= O(1) \\
T(n + 1) &= kT(n) + \Theta(k^{n+1})
\end{aligned}
$$

then $T(n) = \Theta(nk^n)$. What is the solution if $k = 1$?

7.3 Accumulating parameters

By adding an extra parameter to a function we can sometimes improve the running time. The most important use of the idea is to eliminate possibly expensive $+\!\!+$ operations from a program. To take a basic example, consider the function *revcat* defined by

$$
\begin{aligned}
revcat &\quad :: \quad [\alpha] \rightarrow [\alpha] \rightarrow [\alpha] \\
revcat\ xs\ ys &\quad = \quad reverse\ xs +\!\!+ ys
\end{aligned}
$$

It is clear that *reverse xs* = *revcat xs* [ ], so *reverse* can be defined in terms of *revcat*. It is a simple matter to derive a direct recursive program for *revcat*, and the result is

$$
\begin{aligned}
revcat\ [\,]\ ys &\quad = \quad ys \\
revcat\ (x : xs)\ ys &\quad = \quad revcat\ xs\ (x : ys)
\end{aligned}
$$

Since *revcat xs ys* = *accum ys xs*, where *accum* was defined in the previous section, it is clear from the timing analysis of *accum* that the new program for *reverse* takes linear time.

To appreciate what is really going on, it is instructive to write down the program for *revcat* in terms of function composition:

$$
\begin{aligned}
revcat\ [\,] &\quad = \quad id \\
revcat\ (x : xs) &\quad \dot{=} \quad revcat\ xs \cdot (x :)
\end{aligned}
$$

Equivalently, *revcat* = *foldr f id*, where $f\ x\ g = g \cdot (x :)$. By exactly the same means we obtain

$$
(+\!\!+) \quad = \quad foldr\ consdot\ id, \quad \textbf{where}\ consdot\ x\ g = (x :) \cdot g
$$

It is this expression for $+\!\!+$ that underlies most uses of the accumulating parameter technique: concatenation is replaced by the composition of cons operations. For instance, we can argue

> *reverse xs*
>
> =   {since [ ] is the unit of ++}
>
>   (++) (*reverse xs*) [ ]
>
> =   {above expression for ++}
>
>   (*foldr consdot id* (*reverse xs*) [ ]
>
> =   {third duality theorem}
>
>   *foldl* (*flip consdot*) *id xs* [ ]

This gives another linear-time program for *reverse*, essentially the same as before except that *revcat* is expressed using *foldl* rather than *foldr*.

7.3.1 Flattening a binary tree

Here is another example: the function *flatten* for flattening a binary tree was defined in Section 6.1 by

> *flatten*   ::   *Btree* $\alpha \to [\alpha]$
>
> *flatten* (*Leaf x*)   =   [*x*]
>
> *flatten* (*Fork xt yt*)   =   *flatten xt* ++ *flatten yt*

Now define

> *flatcat*   ::   *Btree* $\alpha \to [\alpha] \to [\alpha]$
>
> *flatcat xt xs*   =   *flatten xt* ++ *xs*

We have *flatten xt* = *flatcat xt* [ ]. Synthesis of a recursive program for *flatcat* gives

> *flatcat* (*Leaf x*) *xs*   =   *x* : *xs*
>
> *flatcat* (*Fork xt yt*) *xs*   =   *flatcat xt* (*flatcat yt xs*)

Let us now compare the running times of *flatten* and *flatcat*. Let $T(flatten)(h)$ estimate the time required to flatten a perfect binary tree of height h. Recall from the previous chapter that such a tree has 2^h leaves. We have

> $T(flatten)(0)$ = $O(1)$
>
> $T(flatten)(h+1)$ = $2T(flatten)(h) + T(++)(2^h, 2^h)$

The second equation follows because the two subtrees of a perfect binary tree of height $h + 1$ both have size 2^h.

Since $T(+)(m, n) = \Theta(m)$, we obtain

$$T(\textit{flatten})(h + 1) \quad = \quad 2T(\textit{flatten})(h) + \Theta(2^h)$$

An induction argument now gives that $T(\textit{flatten})(h) = \Theta(h2^h)$, so *flatten* takes $O(s\log s)$ steps on a perfect binary tree of size s.

Now let $T(\textit{flatcat})(h, n)$ estimate the time required to compute the expression *flatcat xt xs*, where *xt* is a perfect binary tree of height h, and *xs* is a list of length n. Then we have

$$
\begin{aligned}
T(\textit{flatcat})(0, n) \quad &= \quad O(1) \\
T(\textit{flatcat})(h + 1, n) \quad &= \quad O(1) + T(\textit{flatcat})(h, 2^h + n) + T(\textit{flatcat})(h, n)
\end{aligned}
$$

It is easy to show by induction that $T(\textit{flatcat})(h, n) = \Theta(2^h)$, so the new program for *flatten* takes linear time in the size of the tree.

7.3.2 Depth-first order

Exactly the same technique can be applied to the function *flatten* for rose trees. Here the definition of *flatten* is

$$
\begin{aligned}
\textit{flatten} \quad &:: \quad \textit{Rose } \alpha \rightarrow [\alpha] \\
\textit{flatten } (\textit{Node x xts}) \quad &= \quad x : \textit{concat } (\textit{map flatten xts})
\end{aligned}
$$

This time, let us analyse the program for *flatten* before trying to improve it. Let $T(\textit{flatten})(h, k)$ estimate the time to flatten a perfect k-ary tree of height $(h + 1)$. Recall that such a tree has size

$$s(h, k) = (k^{h+1} - 1)/(k - 1) = \Theta(k^h)$$

Now we have

$$
\begin{aligned}
T(\textit{flatten})(0, k) \quad &= \quad O(1) \\
T(\textit{flatten})(h + 1, k) \quad &= \quad O(1) + T(\textit{concat})(k, s) + T(\textit{map flatten})(h, k)
\end{aligned}
$$

where $s = s(h, k)$. The term $T(\textit{map flatten})(h, k)$ estimates the running time of *map flatten* on a list of length k consisting of trees all of height h. In general, given a list of length k, consisting of elements each of size n, we have

$$T(\textit{map } f)(k, n) \quad = \quad kT(f)(n) + \Theta(k)$$

Hence, since $O(1) + \Theta(k) = \Theta(k)$, we obtain

$$T(\textit{flatten})(h + 1, k) \quad = \quad T(\textit{concat})(k, s) + kT(\textit{flatten})(h, k) + \Theta(k)$$

Since $T(concat)(k, s) = \Theta(ks) = \Theta(k^{h+1})$, we obtain

$$T(\text{flatten})(h + 1, k) \;=\; \Theta(k^{h+1}) + kT(\text{flatten})(h, k)$$

One can now show by induction that $T(\text{flatten})(h, k) = \Theta(hk^h) = \Theta(s \log s)$. Hence flattening a tree by *flatten* takes a time that is asymptotically greater than the size of the tree.

Having established that the above method of flattening a tree is not the best possible, let us see what an accumulating parameter can do. Define *dfcat* by

$$
\begin{aligned}
&dfcat && :: && Rose\ \alpha \rightarrow [\alpha] \rightarrow [\alpha] \\
&dfcat\ xts\ xs && = && concat\ (map\ flatten\ xts) \mathbin{+\!\!+} xs
\end{aligned}
$$

We have *flatten xt* = *dfcat* [*xt*] [ ]. The aim now is to synthesise a recursive program for *dfcat*. Here is the inductive case:

> $dfcat\ (Node\ x\ xts : yts)\ xs$
>
> = {definition}
>
> $concat\ (map\ flatten\ (Node\ x\ xts : yts)) \mathbin{+\!\!+} xs$
>
> = {definition of *map* and *concat*}
>
> $flatten\ (Node\ x\ xts) \mathbin{+\!\!+} concat\ (map\ flatten\ yts) \mathbin{+\!\!+} xs$
>
> = {definition of *flatten*}
>
> $x : concat\ (map\ flatten\ xts) \mathbin{+\!\!+} concat\ (map\ flatten\ yts) \mathbin{+\!\!+} xs$
>
> = {definition of *dfcat*}
>
> $x : concat\ (map\ flatten\ xts) \mathbin{+\!\!+} dfcat\ yts\ xs$
>
> = {definition of *dfcat*}
>
> $x : dfcat\ xts\ (dfcat\ yts\ xs)$

The result is the following program for *dfcat*:

$$
\begin{aligned}
&dfcat\ [\,]\ xs && = && xs \\
&dfcat\ (Node\ x\ xts : yts)\ xs && = && x : dfcat\ xts\ (dfcat\ yts\ xs)
\end{aligned}
$$

For the timing analysis, let $T(dfcat)(h, n)$ estimate the time required to compute *dfcat xts xs*, where *xts* is a list of length n, each member of which is a perfect k-ary tree of height $(h + 1)$. We will ignore the size of *xs* since it does not affect the estimate.

We have

$$
\begin{aligned}
T(dfcat)(h, 0) &= O(1) \\
T(dfcat)(0, n+1) &= O(1) + T(dfcat)(0, n) \\
T(dfcat)(h+1, n+1) &= O(1) + T(dfcat)(h, k) + T(dfcat)(h+1, n)
\end{aligned}
$$

The first estimate counts the cost of evaluating the first equation for *dfcat*, the second counts the cost of evaluating the second equation for *dfcat* when the first element of the first list is a tree of height 1 (and so has no subtrees), and the third estimate counts the remaining costs.

The first two equations give $T(dfcat)(0, n) = \Theta(n)$. An induction argument gives that $T(dfcat)(h, n) = \Theta(k^h n)$, so $T(dfcat)(h, 1) = \Theta(k^h) = \Theta(s)$. Flattening a tree using an accumulating parameter can be done in time proportional to the size of the tree.

7.3.3   Show

As a final example of the use of an accumulating parameter, consider the type class *Show*. Recall from Sections 2.7 and 5.3 that the class declaration for *Show* contains the method

$$
showsPrec \quad :: \quad Int \rightarrow \alpha \rightarrow String \rightarrow String
$$

We can now say what the third argument of *showsPrec* is: it is an accumulating parameter. Use of an accumulating parameter is necessary if we want to print nonlinear datatypes in linear time.

Exercises

7.3.1 The function *digits* :: $Int \rightarrow [Digit]$ can be defined by

$$
digits\ n \quad = \quad \textbf{if } n < 10 \textbf{ then } [n] \textbf{ else } digits\ (n \textbf{ div } 10) \mathbin{+\!+} [n \textbf{ mod } 10]
$$

How long does computation of *digits n* take? Improve the running time by using an accumulating parameter.

7.3.2 Consider the function *unfoldl* defined by

$$
\begin{aligned}
unfoldl \quad &:: \quad (\alpha \rightarrow Bool) \rightarrow (\alpha \rightarrow (\alpha, \beta)) \rightarrow \alpha \rightarrow [\beta] \\
unfoldl\ p\ f\ x \quad &= \quad \textbf{if } p\ x \textbf{ then } [\,] \textbf{ else } unfoldl\ p\ f\ y \mathbin{+\!+} [z] \\
&\qquad \textbf{where } (y, z) = f\ x
\end{aligned}
$$

Use an accumulating parameter to give a more efficient definition.

7.4 Tupling

The technique of program optimisation known as *tupling* is dual to that of accumulating parameters: a function is generalised, not by including an extra argument, but by including an extra result. Our aim in this section is to illustrate this important technique through a number of instructive examples.

7.4.1 Building a tree

Consider the function *mkBtree*, defined in Section 6.1, for building a minimum height tree with a given (nonempty) sequence as tips:

$$mkBtree :: [\alpha] \rightarrow Btree\ \alpha$$

$$mkBtree\ xs$$

$$\quad = \quad \textbf{if } m == 0 \textbf{ then } Leaf\ (head\ xs) \textbf{ else } Fork\ (mkBtree\ ys)\ (mkBtree\ zs)$$

$$\qquad \textbf{where } ys \quad = \quad take\ m\ xs$$

$$\qquad\qquad\quad zs \quad = \quad drop\ m\ xs$$

$$\qquad\qquad\quad m \quad = \quad (length\ xs)\ \textbf{div}\ 2$$

To analyse this program, suppose *xs* is a list of length 2^k. The time to compute *length xs*, *take m xs*, and *drop m xs*, where $m = 2^{k-1}$, is therefore $\Theta(2^k)$, so

$$T(mkBtree)(0) \qquad = \quad O(1)$$

$$T(mkBtree)(k+1) \quad = \quad 2T(mkBtree)(k) + \Theta(2^k)$$

The solution is $T(mkBtree)(k) = \Theta(k2^k)$. Hence, to build a minimum height tree from a given list of length n takes $\Theta(n\log n)$ steps.

Now consider the function *mktwo* defined by

$$mktwo \qquad\quad :: \quad Int \rightarrow [\alpha] \rightarrow (Btree\ \alpha, [\alpha])$$

$$mktwo\ n\ xs \quad = \quad (mkBtree\ (take\ n\ xs), drop\ n\ xs)$$

It is clear that *mkBtree xs = fst (mktwo (length xs) xs)*, so *mkBtree* can be computed by computing *mktwo*. The aim now is to give a recursive program for *mktwo*. It is easy to calculate

$$mktwo\ 1\ xs \quad = \quad (Leaf\ (head\ xs), tail\ xs)$$

For the recursive case, we will need the laws

$$take\ m \cdot take\ n \quad = \quad take\ m$$

$$drop\ m \cdot take\ n \quad = \quad take\ (n - m) \cdot drop\ m$$

$$drop\ n \qquad\qquad = \quad drop\ m \cdot drop\ (n - m)$$

which hold provided $m \le n$. Now, we argue for $n > 1$ that

$$mktwo\ n\ xs$$

=   {definition of *mktwo*}

$(mkBtree\ (take\ n\ xs),\ drop\ n\ xs)$

=   {definition of *mkBtree*, using laws above with $m = n\ \textbf{div}\ 2$}

$(Fork\ (mkBtree\ (take\ m\ xs))\ (mkBtree\ (take\ (n - m)\ (drop\ m\ xs))),$
$drop\ n\ xs)$

=   {setting $(xt, ys) = mktwo\ m\ xs$ and using third law above}

$(Fork\ xt\ (mkBtree\ (take\ (n - m)\ ys)),\ drop\ (n - m)\ ys)$

=   {setting $(yt, zs) = mktwo\ (n - m)\ ys$}

$(Fork\ xt\ yt,\ zs)$

In summary:

$$mktwo\ n\ xs$$
$$=\ \textbf{if}\ n == 1\ \textbf{then}\ (Leaf\ (head\ xs),\ tail\ xs)\ \textbf{else}\ (Fork\ xt\ yt,\ zs)$$
$$\textbf{where}\ (xt, ys)\ \ =\ \ mktwo\ m\ xs$$
$$(yt, zs)\ \ =\ \ mktwo\ (n - m)\ ys$$
$$m\ \ \ \ \ \ \ \ \ =\ \ n\ \textbf{div}\ 2$$

The timing analysis for *mktwo* gives in the recursive case that

$$T(mktwo)(n)\ \ =\ \ T(mktwo)(m) + T(mktwo)(n - m) + O(1)$$
$$\textbf{where}\ m = n\ \textbf{div}\ 2$$

The solution is $T(mktwo)(n) = \Theta(n)$. Using *mktwo* as a subsidiary function, we have improved the asymptotic complexity of *mkBtree* by a logarithmic factor.

7.4.2 Fibonacci function

Another example where tupling can improve the order of growth of the time complexity of a program is provided by the Fibonacci function:

$$fib\ 0\ \ \ \ \ \ =\ \ 0$$
$$fib\ 1\ \ \ \ \ \ =\ \ 1$$
$$fib\ (n + 2)\ \ =\ \ fib\ n + fib\ (n + 1)$$

The time to evaluate *fib n* by these equations is given by $T(fib)(n)$, where

$$T(fib)(0) \quad = \quad O(1)$$
$$T(fib)(1) \quad = \quad O(1)$$
$$T(fib)(n+2) \quad = \quad T(fib)(n) + T(fib)(n+1) + O(1)$$

The timing function $T(fib)$ therefore satisfies equations very like that of *fib* itself. It is easy to check by induction that $T(fib)(n) = \Theta(fib\ n)$, so the time to compute *fib* is proportional to the size of the result. Since *fib n* $= \Theta(\phi^n)$, where ϕ is the golden ratio $\phi = (1 + \sqrt{5})/2$, the time is therefore exponential in *n*.

Now consider the function *fibtwo* defined by

$$fibtwo\ n \quad = \quad (fib\ n, fib\ (n+1))$$

Clearly, *fib n* = *fst (fibtwo n)*. Synthesis of a recursive program for *fibtwo* yields

$$fibtwo\ 0 \quad = \quad (0, 1)$$
$$fibtwo\ (n+1) \quad = \quad (b, a+b), \quad \textbf{where}\ (a, b) = fibtwo\ n$$

It is clear that this program takes linear time. In this example, the tupling strategy leads to a dramatic increase in efficiency, from exponential to linear.

7.4.3   Filling paragraphs

The examples above involved tupling two functions, but the same idea can be used to good effect by tupling a *list* of functions. In this form, tupling is usually referred to as *tabulation*. A simple example is provided by the problem of filling paragraphs, a problem we considered in Section 5.5. We are given a list *ws* of words and we want to find a list of lines *wss* such that *ws* = *concat wss*, with the additional constraints that each line in *wss* should be short enough to fit within some given width, and that *wss* should minimise some notion of waste. For simplicity, we will assume that waste is determined by some given numerical function *waste* that takes the value ∞ if the paragraph contains a line that will not fit in the given width. The algorithm in Section 5.5 was greedy in nature: if at some stage the remaining list of words is *ws*, then the next line consists of the longest initial segment of *ws* that will fit within the given width. Here, we tackle the general problem of selecting a best possible next line, not necessarily the longest legal initial segment of the remaining input.

The definition of *fill* takes the form

$$fill \quad :: \quad [Word] \rightarrow [Line]$$
$$fill \quad = \quad best \cdot fills$$

$$best :: [[Line]] \rightarrow [Line]$$
$$best =$$
   $foldl1$ $better$
   where $better$ uss vss = **if** $waste$ $uss \leq waste$ vss **then** uss **else** vss

The function *fills* gives all possible ways of filling the paragraph:

$$fills \qquad\qquad :: \quad [Word] \rightarrow [[Line]]$$
$$fills\ [\ ] \qquad\quad = \quad [[\ ]]$$
$$fills\ (w : ws) \quad = \quad [us : vss \mid (us, vs) \leftarrow splits\ (w : ws), vs \leftarrow fills\ vs]$$

The function *splits* is specified by the condition that if xs is a nonempty list, then *splits* xs returns a list of all pairs (us, vs) such that $us \mathbin{+\!\!+} vs = xs$ and us is not empty. The function *splits* can be defined in a number of ways, including

$$splits \qquad\qquad :: \quad [\alpha] \rightarrow [([\alpha], [\alpha])]$$
$$splits\ (w : ws) \quad = \quad zip\ (map\ (w :)\ (inits\ ws))\ (tails\ ws)$$

Here, *inits* ws returns the list of initial segments of ws in increasing order of length, and *tails* ws returns the tail segments in decreasing order of length. The function *splits* therefore returns a list of pairs of possible splits in which the first component of each pair is a nonempty list.

How long does this program for *fill* take? There are $\Theta(2^n)$ ways of partitioning a sequence of length n into a list of nonempty lists, so *fills* returns $\Theta(2^n)$ results and the time complexity of *fill* is at least $\Omega(2^n)$.

To improve the program, we need the assumption that

$$best \cdot map\ (us :) \quad = \quad (us :) \cdot best$$

In words, given a fixed first line, a best paragraph is obtained by taking a best paragraph for the remaining lines. This condition is an instance of what is known as the *principle of optimality* in texts on algorithm design.

Given the assumption, it is easy to calculate that *fill* can be defined by

$$fill\ [\ ] \qquad\quad = \quad [\ ]$$
$$fill\ (w : ws) \quad = \quad best\ [us : fill\ vs \mid (us, vs) \leftarrow splits\ (w : ws)]$$

Assuming that *best* and *splits* each takes linear time, we have

$$T(fill)(0) \qquad\ = \quad O(1)$$
$$T(fill)(n + 1) \quad = \quad \Theta(n) + \sum_{k=0}^{n} T(fill)(k)$$

The solution of this recurrence relation is $T(fill)(n) = \Theta(2^n)$, so *fill* still takes exponential time. The reason is that *fill vs* is recomputed for every tail sequence of *ws*. The situation is very similar to that of the Fibonacci function, except that instead of having two recursive terms, there is a list of them.

The solution is similar: define *filltails* by

$$filltails \quad = \quad map\ fill \cdot tails$$

We have *fill* = *head* · *filltails*, so *fill* can be computed by computing *filltails*. It remains to give a recursive program for *filltails*. The base case

$$filltails\ [\ ] \quad = \quad [[\ ]]$$

is easy, and for the inductive case we argue first that

> *fill* (*w* : *ws*)
>
> =   {definition of *fill*}
>
> *best* [*us* : *fill vs* | (*us*, *vs*) ← *splits* (*w* : *ws*)]
>
> =   {definition of *splits*}
>
> *best* [*us* : *fill vs* | (*us*, *vs*) ← *zip* (*map* (*w* :) (*inits ws*)) (*tails ws*)]
>
> =   {claim}
>
> *best* [(*w* : *us*) : *vss* | (*us*, *vss*) ← *zip* (*inits ws*) (*map fill* (*tails ws*))]
>
> =   {definition of *filltails*}
>
> *best* [(*w* : *us*) : *vss* | (*us*, *vss*) ← *zip* (*inits ws*) (*filltails ws*)]

Proof of the claim is left as an exercise. Now we can argue

> *filltails* (*w* : *ws*)
>
> =   {definition of *filltails*, plus routine simplification}
>
> *fill* (*w* : *ws*) : *filltails ws*
>
> =   {above calculation of *fill*, setting *fts* = *filltails ws*}
>
> *best* [(*w* : *us*) : *vss* | (*us*, *vss*) ← *zip* (*inits ws*) *fts*)] : *fts*

In summary,

> *filltails* [ ] = [[ ]]
>
> *filltails* (*w* : *ws*) =
>
>   *best* [(*w* : *us*) : *vss* | (*us*, *vss*) ← *zip* (*inits ws*, *fts*)] : *fts*
>   **where** *fts* = *filltails ws*

For the timing analysis, we have

$$T(\textit{filltails})(0) \quad = \quad O(1)$$
$$T(\textit{filltails})(n+1) \quad = \quad \Theta(n) + T(\textit{filltails})(n)$$

The solution is $T(\textit{filltails})(n) = \Theta(n^2)$. The revised program for *fill* therefore takes quadratic time.

It is possible to improve the program for *fill* still further. Once a line is too long to fit in the given width there is no point in generating any longer lines for they will not fit either. This obvious but important fact is not explicit in the program above, but is hidden in the definition of *waste*. By bringing it to the surface and exploiting it, one can arrange to truncate *filltails* to a list of length at most *m*, for some *m* depending on the given width. The program for *filltails* will therefore take $O(mn)$ steps, which is linear for fixed *m*.

7.4.4 Average

The final illustration of tupling achieves a more modest increase in efficiency. Compared to the asymptotic improvements recorded above, the example leads to at best a constant factor improvement in running time.

The function *average* is defined on nonempty lists of numbers by

$$average \quad :: \quad [Float] \rightarrow Float$$
$$average \, xs \quad = \quad (sum \, xs)/(length \, xs)$$

Evaluation of *average* requires two traversals of the argument, but by tupling we can bring it down to one. Define *sumlen* by

$$sumlen \, xs \quad = \quad (sum \, xs, length \, xs)$$

We have $average' = uncurry \, (/) \cdot sumlen$. The direct recursive definition of *sumlen* is

$$sumlen \, [x] \quad = \quad (x, 1)$$
$$sumlen \, (x:y:xs) \quad = \quad (x+z, n+1), \quad \textbf{where} \, (z, n) = sumlen \, (y:xs)$$

The function *average'* involves a single traversal of its argument. The two versions both take $\Theta(n)$ steps on a list of length n, and from the point of view of timing there may be little to choose between them. The time saved by not traversing a list a second time may be lost again by having to form a pair at each step. Exactly the same situation arises with *splitAt* (see Section 4.2) and *span* (see Section 5.2). So, why bother with a program that traverses its argument only once?

The answer has to do with space. There is a very great advantage of *average'* over *average* when it comes to space. Consider the evaluation of

$$average\,[1 .. 1000]$$

Since *average xs* contains two occurrences of *xs* on the right-hand side of its definition, the list created by evaluation of [1 .. 1000] as a result of the first traversal is retained for the second traversal. In other words, computing the average of a very long list according to the first definition may result in the evaluator running out of available space. With the second definition of *average* we can arrange it so that the computation proceeds in constant space. This is the subject of the following section.

Exercises

7.4.1 Suppose $T(k + 1) = 2T(k) + \Theta(2^k)$. Prove that $T(k) = \Theta(2^k)$.

7.4.2 Suppose $T(n) = T(m) + T(n - m) + O(1)$, where $m = n\,\textbf{div}\,2$. Prove that $T(n) = \Theta(n)$.

7.4.3 Prove by induction that *fib* $n = (\phi^n - \hat{\phi}^n)/\sqrt{5}$, where $\phi = (1 + \sqrt{5})/2$ and $\hat{\phi} = (1 - \sqrt{5})/2$ are the two roots of $x^2 = x + 1$.

7.4.4 Assuming that *better* $(us : uss)\,(us : vss) = us : better\,uss\,vss$, prove that *best* $\cdot$ *map* $(us :) = (us :) \cdot best$.

7.5 Controlling space

Consider reduction of the term *sum* [1 .. 1000], where *sum* = *foldl* (+) 0:

$$
\begin{aligned}
&\quad sum\,[1 .. 1000] \\
&= foldl\,(+)\,0\,[1 .. 1000] \\
&= foldl\,(+)\,(0 + 1)\,[2 .. 1000] \\
&= foldl\,(+)\,((0 + 1) + 2)\,[3 .. 1000] \\
&\quad \vdots \\
&= foldl\,(+)\,(\cdots ((0 + 1) + 2) + \cdots + 1000)\,[\,] \\
&= (\cdots ((0 + 1) + 2) + \cdots + 1000) \\
&= 500500
\end{aligned}
$$

The point to notice is that in computing *sum* [1 .. *n*] by outermost reduction the expressions grow in size proportional to *n*. On the other hand, if we use a judicious mixture of outermost and innermost reduction steps, then we can obtain the following reduction sequence:

$$sum \, [1 .. 1000]$$

$$= \quad foldl \, (+) \, 0 \, [1 .. 1000]$$
$$= \quad foldl \, (+) \, (0 + 1) \, [2 .. 1000]$$
$$= \quad foldl \, (+) \, 1 \, [2 .. 1000]$$
$$= \quad foldl \, (+) \, (1 + 2) \, [3 .. 1000]$$
$$= \quad foldl \, (+) \, 3 \, [3 .. 1000]$$

$$\vdots$$

$$= \quad foldl \, (+) \, 500500 \, [\,]$$
$$= \quad 500500$$

The maximum size of any expression in this sequence is bounded by a constant. In short, reducing $sum[1 .. n]$ to normal form by purely outermost reduction requires $\Omega(n)$ space, while a combination of innermost and outermost reduction requires only $O(1)$ space.

This suggests that it would be useful to have a way of controlling reduction order, and we now introduce a special function, *strict*, that allows us to do so.

7.5.1   Head-normal form and the function strict

Reduction order may be controlled by use of the special function *strict*. A term of the form *strict f e* is reduced by first reducing *e* to *head-normal form*, and then applying *f*. An expression *e* is in head-normal form if *e* is a function or if *e* takes the form of a datatype constructor applied to zero or more arguments. Every expression in normal form is in head-normal form, but not vice versa. For example, $e_1 : e_2$ is in head-normal form but is in normal form only when e_1 and e_2 are both in normal form. Similarly, *Fork* $e_1 \, e_2$ and (e_1, e_2) are in head-normal form but are not in normal form unless e_1 and e_2 are in normal form. In the expression *strict f e*, the term *e* will itself be reduced by outermost reduction, except, of course, if further calls of *strict* appear while reducing *e*.

As a simple example, let $succ \, x = x + 1$. Then

$$succ \, (succ \, (8 \times 5))$$
$$= \quad succ \, (8 \times 5) + 1$$
$$= \quad ((8 \times 5) + 1) + 1$$

$$= \quad (40 + 1) + 1$$
$$= \quad 41 + 1$$
$$= \quad 42$$

On the other hand,

$$strict\ succ\ (strict\ succ\ (8 \times 5))$$
$$= \quad strict\ succ\ (strict\ succ\ 40)$$
$$= \quad strict\ succ\ (succ\ 40)$$
$$= \quad strict\ succ\ (40 + 1)$$
$$= \quad strict\ succ\ 41$$
$$= \quad succ\ 41$$
$$= \quad 41 + 1$$
$$= \quad 42$$

Both cases perform the same reduction steps, but in a different order.

Currying applies to *strict* as to anything else. From this it follows that if f is a function of three arguments, writing $strict\ (f\ e_1)\ e_2\ e_3$ causes the second argument e_2 to be reduced early, but not the first or third.

Given this, we can define a function *sfoldl*, a strict version of *foldl*, as follows:

$$sfoldl\ (\oplus)\ a\ [\ ] \qquad = \quad a$$
$$sfoldl\ (\oplus)\ a\ (x:xs) \quad = \quad strict\ (sfoldl\ (\oplus))\ (a \oplus x)\ xs$$

With $sum = sfoldl\ (+)\ 0$ we now have

$$sum\ [1 .. 1000]$$
$$= \quad sfoldl\ (+)\ 0\ [1 .. 1000]$$
$$= \quad strict\ (sfoldl\ (+))\ (0 + 1)\ [2 .. 1000]$$
$$= \quad sfoldl\ (+)\ 1\ [2 .. 1000]$$
$$= \quad strict\ (sfoldl\ (+))\ (1 + 2)\ [3 .. 1000]$$
$$= \quad sfoldl\ (+)\ 3\ [3 .. 1000]$$
$$\vdots$$
$$= \quad sfoldl\ (+)\ 500500\ [\ ]$$
$$= \quad 500500$$

This reduction sequence evaluates *sum* in constant space.

Let us now consider the function *average'* of the previous section; this function can be defined by

$$
\begin{aligned}
average' &= uncurry\ (/) \cdot sumlen \\
sumlen &= foldl\ f\ (0,0) \\
&\quad \textbf{where } f\ (s,n)\ x = (s + x, n + 1)
\end{aligned}
$$

Suppose we replace *foldl* in the definition of *sumlen* by *sfoldl*; do we then obtain a constant space program for *average'*? To appreciate why the answer is no, consider the reduction sequence

$$
\begin{aligned}
&\quad sumlen\ [1\mathinner{\ldotp\ldotp}1000] \\
&= sfoldl\ f\ (0,0)\ [1\mathinner{\ldotp\ldotp}1000] \\
&= strict\ (sfoldl\ f)\ (0 + 1, 0 + 1)\ [2\mathinner{\ldotp\ldotp}1000] \\
&= sfoldl\ f\ (0 + 1, 0 + 1)\ [2\mathinner{\ldotp\ldotp}1000] \\
&= strict\ (sfoldl\ f)\ ((0 + 1) + 2, (0 + 1) + 1)\ [3\mathinner{\ldotp\ldotp}1000] \\
&= sfoldl\ f\ ((0 + 1) + 2, (0 + 1) + 1)\ [3\mathinner{\ldotp\ldotp}1000]
\end{aligned}
$$

and so on. The problem is that an expression such as $((0+1)+2, (0+1)+1)$ is in head-normal form so no further evaluation is required by *strict*. The resulting evaluation of *sumlen* $[1\mathinner{\ldotp\ldotp}n]$ will use $\Theta(n)$ units of space. The solution is to make not only *foldl f* strict, but also to make *f* strict by defining

$$
\begin{aligned}
f'\ (s,n)\ x &= strict\ (strict\ tuple\ (s + x))\ (n + 1) \\
&\quad \textbf{where } tuple\ a\ b = (a, b)
\end{aligned}
$$

The revised reduction sequence now reads

$$
\begin{aligned}
&\quad sumlen\ [1\mathinner{\ldotp\ldotp}1000] \\
&= sfoldl\ f'\ (0,0)\ [1\mathinner{\ldotp\ldotp}1000] \\
&= strict\ (sfoldl\ f')\ (strict\ (strict\ tuple\ (0 + 1))\ (0 + 1))\ [2\mathinner{\ldotp\ldotp}1000] \\
&= strict\ (sfoldl\ f')\ (strict\ (strict\ tuple\ (0 + 1))\ 1)\ [2\mathinner{\ldotp\ldotp}1000] \\
&= strict\ (sfoldl\ f')\ (strict\ (strict\ tuple\ 1)\ 1)\ [2\mathinner{\ldotp\ldotp}1000] \\
&= strict\ (sfoldl\ f')\ (1, 1)\ [2\mathinner{\ldotp\ldotp}1000] \\
&= sfoldl\ f'\ (1, 1)\ [2\mathinner{\ldotp\ldotp}1000]
\end{aligned}
$$

and so on. It is clear that this sequence has the desired behaviour.

The operational definition of *strict* can be re-expressed in the following way:

$$
strict\ f\ x = \textbf{if } x = \perp \textbf{ then } \perp \textbf{ else } f\ x
$$

Recall that a function f is said to be strict if $f \perp = \perp$. It follows from the above equation that $f = strict\ f$ if and only if f is a strict function. To see this, just consider the values of $f\ x$ and *strict f x* in the two cases $x = \perp$ and $x \neq \perp$. This explains the name *strict*.

Furthermore, if f is strict, but not everywhere $\perp$, and $e \neq \perp$, then reduction of $f\ e$ eventually entails reduction of e. Thus, if f is a strict function, evaluation of $f\ e$ and *strict f e* perform the same reduction steps, though possibly in a different order. In other words, when f is strict, replacing it by *strict f* does not change the meaning or the asymptotic time required to apply it, although it may change the space required by the computation.

It is easy to show that if $\perp \oplus x = \perp$ for every x, then $fold (\oplus) \perp xs = \perp$ for every finite list *xs*. In other words, if $(\oplus)$ is strict in its left argument, then *foldl* $(\oplus)$ is strict, and so is equivalent to *strict* $(foldl\ (\oplus))$, and hence also equivalent to *sfoldl* $(\oplus)$. It follows that replacing *foldl* by *sfoldl* in the definition of *sum* is valid, and the same replacement is valid whenever *foldl* is applied to a binary operation that is strict in its first argument.

7.5.2 Fold revisited

The first duality theorem, given in Section 4.5, states that if $(\oplus)$ is associative with identity e, then

$$foldr\ (\oplus)\ e\ xs\quad =\quad foldl\ (\oplus)\ e\ xs$$

for all finite lists *xs*. On the other hand, the two expressions may have different time and space complexities. Which one to use depends on the properties of $\oplus$.

First, suppose that $\oplus$ is strict in both arguments, and can be computed in $O(1)$ time and $O(1)$ space. Examples that fall into this category are $(+)$ and $(\times)$. In this case it is not hard to verify that *foldr* $(\oplus)$ e and *foldl* $(\oplus)$ e both require $O(n)$ time and $O(n)$ space to compute on a list of length n. However, the same argument used above for *sum* generalises to show that, in this case, *foldl* may safely be replaced by *sfoldl*. While *sfoldl* $(\oplus)$ a still requires $O(n)$ time to evaluate on a list of length n, it only requires $O(1)$ space. So, in this case, *sfoldl* is the clear winner.

If $\oplus$ does not satisfy the above properties, then choosing a winner may not be so easy. A good rule of thumb, though, is that if $\oplus$ is nonstrict in either argument, then *foldr* is usually more efficient than *foldl*. We saw one example in Section 7.2: the function *concat* is more efficiently computed using *foldr* than using *foldl*. Observe that while ++ is strict in its first argument, it is not strict in its second.

Another example is provided by the function *and* = *foldr* $(\wedge)$ *True*. Like ++, the operator $\wedge$ is strict in its first argument, but nonstrict in its second. In particular, *False* ∧ *x* returns *False* without evaluating *x*. Assume we are given a list *xs* of *n* boolean values and *k* is the first value for which *xs* !! *k* = *False*. Then evaluation of *foldr* (∧) *True xs* takes $O(k)$ steps, whereas *foldl* (∧) *True xs* requires $\Omega(n)$ steps. Again, *foldr* is a better choice.

To summarise: for functions, such as + or ×, that are strict in both arguments and can be computed in constant time and space, *sfoldl* is more efficient. But for functions, such as ∧ and ++, that are nonstrict in some argument, *foldr* is often more efficient.

Exercises

7.5.1 Write down a definition of the function *sum* that does not use *strict* but nevertheless does evaluate in constant space.

7.5.2 How should *minlist* be defined?

7.6   Fusion, finite differencing, and deforestation

The final group of techniques have a common theme and are best treated together. The theme is that, having expressed the solution to a problem in terms of the composition $f_1 \cdot f_2 \cdot \cdots \cdot f_n$ of a number of functions, efficiency may be increased by combining, or *fusing*, two or more of the subsidiary functions f_k into a single function.

We have already met fusion in the context of fold operations on lists. Recall from Section 4.5 that

$$f \cdot foldr\ g\ a\ =\ foldr\ h\ (f\ a)$$

provided *f* is a strict function and $f \cdot (g\ x) = (h\ x) \cdot f$. Operationally, the left-hand side says that a value is assembled out of the elements of a list, and then is consumed by a function to produce a second value. The right-hand side says that, provided a certain condition holds, the second value can be produced directly from the elements of the list. The condition $f \cdot (g\ x) = (h\ x) \cdot f$ asserts that the value returned by *f* can be computed *incrementally*. The terms *finite differencing* and *formal differentiation* have also been used to describe this situation.   We have seen a paradigm application of finite differencing in the problem of the maximum segment sum, considered in Section 4.5. Recall that this reduced a $\Theta(n^3)$ running time to $\Theta(n)$.

One particular use of fusion is to eliminate intermediate datatypes from a program. This particular device is called *deforestation*. We saw one example in Section 6.6, and in the rest of this section we consider one more.

7.6.1 Quicksort

Recall the function *sort* of Section 6.2:

$$sort \;=\; flatten \cdot mkStree$$

The function *mkStree* builds a binary search tree, and *flatten* lists its labels in ascending order. The definitions were

$$\textbf{data } (Ord\ \alpha) \Rightarrow Stree\ \alpha \;=\; Null \mid Fork\ (Stree\ \alpha)\ \alpha\ (Stree\ \alpha)$$

$$
\begin{array}{lll}
mkStree & :: & (Ord\ \alpha) \Rightarrow [\alpha] \rightarrow Stree\ \alpha \\
mkStree\ [\,] & = & Null \\
mkStree\ (x : xs) & = & Fork\ (mkStree\ ys)\ x\ (mkStree\ zs) \\
& & \textbf{where } (ys, zs) = partition\ (\leq x)\ xs
\end{array}
$$

$$
\begin{array}{lll}
partition & :: & (\alpha \rightarrow Bool) \rightarrow [\alpha] \rightarrow ([\alpha], [\alpha]) \\
partition\ p\ xs & = & (filter\ p\ xs, filter\ (not \cdot p)\ xs)
\end{array}
$$

$$
\begin{array}{lll}
flatten & :: & Stree\ \alpha \rightarrow [\alpha] \\
flatten\ Null & = & [\,] \\
flatten\ (Fork\ xt\ x\ yt) & = & flatten\ xt + [x] + flatten\ yt
\end{array}
$$

The aim now is to fuse the computation of *flatten* and *mkStree*, thereby eliminating values of type *Stree* α from the program. The result is a function *qsort* defined by

$$
\begin{array}{lll}
qsort & :: & (Ord\ \alpha) \Rightarrow [\alpha] \rightarrow [\alpha] \\
qsort\ [\,] & = & [\,] \\
qsort\ (x : xs) & = & qsort\ ys + [x] + qsort\ zs \\
& & \textbf{where } (ys, zs) = partition\ (\leq x)\ xs
\end{array}
$$

This is a version of a famous algorithm, called *quicksort*.

   To time *qsort xs*, suppose *xs* is a list of length $n > 0$. The list *filter* $(\leq x)$ *xs* can have any length k in the range $0 \leq k < n$, in which case *filter* $(> x)$ *xs* has length $n - k - 1$. Since T estimates the worst-case running time, we have to choose the maximum timing estimate taken over all possible splits. Hence

$$T(qsort)(n) \;=\; \mathbf{max}_{0 \leq k < n}(T(qsort)(k) + T(qsort)(n - k - 1) + \Theta(n))$$

The $\Theta(n)$ term accounts both for the time to evaluate *ys* and *zs* on a list of length n, and for the concatenation of the sorted results. Since the worst case occurs when $k = 0$ or $k = n - 1$, we obtain

$$T(qsort)(n + 1) \;=\; T(qsort)(n) + \Theta(n)$$

The solution is $T(qsort)(n) = \Theta(n^2)$. Hence quicksort is a quadratic-time algorithm in the worst case. On the other hand, quicksort is efficient on average, taking $O(n \log n)$ steps.

Can we improve the performance of *qsort*? The presence of the ++ operations signal that the accumulating parameter technique is likely to prove beneficial. Suppose we define *qcat* by

$$qcat \qquad :: \quad (Ord\ \alpha) \Rightarrow [\alpha] \rightarrow [\alpha] \rightarrow [\alpha]$$
$$qcat\ xs\ ys \quad = \quad qsort\ xs ++ ys$$

Routine synthesis now yields

$$qsort\ xs \qquad\qquad = \quad qcat\ xs\ [\ ]$$
$$qcat\ [\ ]\ ws \qquad\quad = \quad ws$$
$$qcat\ (x:xs)\ ws \quad = \quad qcat\ ys\ (x : qcat\ zs\ ws)$$
$$\textbf{where}\ (ys, zs) = partition\ (\leq x)\ xs$$

The result is a program that is faster than before, but which is still of quadratic-time complexity.

There is another optimisation of *qsort*, one that involves space rather than time. In the computation of *partition* $(\leq x)\ xs$, the list xs is traversed twice. A similar situation arose with the function *average* in Section 7.4, so we should combine the two traversals into one with an appeal to the tupling technique.

It is easy to rewrite the definition of *partition* in the form

$$partition\ p$$
$$= \quad foldr\ f\ ([\ ], [\ ])$$
$$\textbf{where}\ f\ y\ (ys, zs) = \textbf{if}\ p\ y\ \textbf{then}\ (y : ys, zs)\ \textbf{else}\ (ys, y : zs)$$

In this version the argument list is traversed once.

Having rewritten the definition of *partition*, it may be thought that the program for *qsort* is now as space efficient as possible, but unfortunately it is not. For some inputs of length n the space required by the program is $\Omega(n^2)$. This situation is referred to as a *space leak*. A space leak is a hidden loss of space efficiency. The space leak in the above program for quicksort occurs with an input which is already sorted, but in decreasing order. To explain why it arises, let us rewrite the recursive case for *qsort* in the equivalent form

$$qsort\ (x:xs) \quad = \quad qsort\ (fst\ p) ++ [x] ++ qsort\ (snd\ p)$$
$$\textbf{where}\ p = partition\ (\leq x)\ xs$$

If $(x:xs)$ has length $(n+1)$ and is in decreasing order, then $p = partition(\leq x)xs$ is a pair of lists in which the first component has length n and the second component length zero. Evaluation of p is triggered by evaluating the term $qsort\ (fst\ p)$. However, the n units of space occupied by p cannot be reclaimed until the corresponding term $qsort\ (snd\,p)$ is evaluated when the pointer to p can be thrown away. Between these two evaluations further triples are generated. The first occupies $n - 1$ units of space, the second $n - 2$ units, and so on. The total space required to carry out the computation is therefore $\Omega(n^2)$.

In practice, this means that evaluation of $qsort$ on some large inputs will abort due to insufficient available space. The solution is somehow to force evaluation of $partition$ and, equally important, to bind ys and zs to the respective components of the resulting pair, not to the pair itself.

One way of bringing about this situation is to fuse the computation of $partition$ into the main program. Define the function $qhelp$ by

$$qhelp\ x\ xs\ us\ vs\ =\ qsort\ (us \mathbin{+\!\!+} ys) \mathbin{+\!\!+} [x] \mathbin{+\!\!+} qsort\ (vs \mathbin{+\!\!+} zs)$$
$$\textbf{where}\ (ys, zs) = partition\ (\leq x)\ xs$$

In particular, we have

> $qsort\ (x : xs)$
>
> $=$ {definition of $qsort$, writing $(ys, zs) = partition\ (\leq x)\ xs$}
>
> $qsort\ ys \mathbin{+\!\!+} [x] \mathbin{+\!\!+} qsort\ zs$
>
> $=$ {definition of $qhelp$}
>
> $qhelp\ x\ xs\ [\ ]\ [\ ]$

It follows that $qsort$ can be defined in terms of $qhelp$ by

$$qsort\ [\ ]\quad\ =\ [\ ]$$
$$qsort\ (x : xs)\ =\ qhelp\ x\ xs\ [\ ]\ [\ ]$$

The final step is to synthesise a recursive definition of $qhelp$. The base case is

$$qhelp\ x\ [\ ]\ us\ vs\ =\ qsort\ us \mathbin{+\!\!+} [x] \mathbin{+\!\!+} qsort\ vs$$

For the recursive case $qhelp\ x\ (y : xs)\ us\ vs$, observe that

$$partition\ (\leq x)\ (y : xs)\ =\ \textbf{if}\ y \leq x\ \textbf{then}\ (y : ys, zs)\ \textbf{else}\ (ys, y : zs)$$
$$\textbf{where}\ (ys, zs) = partition\ (\leq x)\ xs$$

For brevity, we will calculate the recursive case assuming $y \leq x$:

> $qhelp\ x\ (y : xs)\ us\ vs$
>
> $=$ {definition of $qhelp$, writing $(ys, zs) = partition\ (\leq x)\ xs$}

$$qsort\ (us + y : ys) + [x] + qsort\ (vs + zs)$$

=   {claim: (see below)}

$$qsort\ (y : us + ys) + [x] + qsort\ (vs + zs)$$

=   {definition of $qhelp$}

$$qhelp\ x\ xs\ (y : us)\ vs$$

The claim is that if ys is any permutation of xs, then $qsort\ xs = qsort\ ys$. The claim is intuitively obvious: sorting a list depends only on the elements in the list, not on their order. A formal proof is omitted. This property of sorting is crucial to the development of a space efficient implementation of quicksort.

The result is the following program for $qsort$:

```
qsort [ ]              =   [ ]
qsort (x : xs)         =   qhelp x xs [ ] [ ]
qhelp x [ ] us vs      =   qsort us + [x] + qsort vs
qhelp x (y : xs) us vs =   if  y ≤ x
                           then  qhelp x xs (y : us) vs
                           else  qhelp x xs us (y : vs)
```

The result is a fairly unappealing program that, nevertheless, now has an $O(n)$ space complexity. Furthermore, the accumulating parameter technique can again be invoked to bring the running time down by a small constant factor.

In functional programming there are better ways to sort than by using quicksort. On the other hand, it is fascinating to study a single problem in which the techniques of deforestation, accumulating parameters, tupling, and fusion, all play a role.

Exercises

7.6.1 The value $select\ k\ xs$, where $select\ k = (!!k) \cdot sort$, selects the kth largest element of a nonempty list. In particular, $minlist = select\ 0$. Taking $sort = qsort$, use fusion to produce a more efficient algorithm for $select$.

7.6.2 If one assumes that each possible split in the recursive case of quicksort is equally likely, and the same is true of all subsequent splits, then the average case estimate $A(qsort)$ of $qsort$ satisfies

$$A(qsort)(n+1) = \frac{1}{n} \sum_{k=0}^{n} (A(qsort)(k) + A(qsort)(n-k) + \Theta(n))$$

Prove that $A(qsort)(n) = \Theta(n \log n)$.

7.7 Chapter notes

For more information on lazy evaluation and graph reduction, consult the books Peyton Jones (1987) and Peyton Jones and Lester (1991). Asymptotic notation and the solution of recurrence relations using O-notation is covered in Cormen et al. (1990). The subject of asymptotic timing analyses of lazy functional programs is still a research area; for various approaches to the problem, see Bjerner and Holmström (1989), Sands (1995), and Wadler (1987).

The idea of fusing two computations is as old as the subject of program transformation itself; for an early reference on the technique in a functional setting, see Burstall and Darlington (1977). The accumulating parameter technique is studied in Bird (1984).

For more on the tupling strategy of program optimisation, see Bird (1980) and Pettorossi (1984). The principle of optimality, and its importance to dynamic programming algorithms (of which the paragraph problem is an example), is discussed in most books on algorithm design; see Bellman (1957) where the technique was first discussed, and also de Moor (1994) which presents the ideas in a categorical setting. Bird and de Moor (1997) contains a systematic account of the use of dynamic programming in solving optimisation problems. The problem of filling a paragraph is treated in Bird (1986) and in Knuth and Plass (1981).

The idea of eliminating intermediate datatypes from a computation is studied in Wadler (1984, 1990b); see also Bird and de Moor (1997) for other examples.

Quicksort is due to Hoare (1962). Hughes (1984) was the first to notice the space leak in quicksort when expressed as a functional program. See Runciman and Röjemo (1996) for techniques for identifying space leaks.

Chapter 8

Abstract datatypes

The aim of this chapter is to introduce the idea of an *abstract datatype* and the mechanisms provided by Haskell for defining them. Broadly speaking, abstract datatypes differ from those introduced by a **data** declaration in that one can choose how to represent their values. Each choice of representation leads to a different implementation of the datatype. The main ideas are worked out in the study of four abstract datatypes: sets, bags, arrays, and queues. In each example, the datatype is specified formally, possible representations are suggested, and the efficiency of different implementations is compared.

8.1 Basic concepts

The effect of a **data** declaration is to introduce a new datatype by describing how its elements are constructed. Each element is named by an expression built only from the constructors of the datatype. Moreover, different names denote different elements. By using pattern matching on the constructors, we can define operations that generate and process elements of the datatype in any fashion we choose. Accordingly, there is no need to postulate the existence of any additional primitive operations. Types in which the values are described, but the operations are not, are called *concrete* types.

The situation is just the reverse with *abstract* datatypes. An abstract datatype is defined not by naming its values, but by naming its operations. For example, *Float* is an abstract datatype in Haskell. We are given the primitive comparison and arithmetic operations, and also a means for displaying floating-point numbers, but it is not stated how such numbers are represented by the Haskell evaluator, and we cannot do pattern matching with them. In general, the programmer who uses an abstract datatype may not know, and may even be prevented from knowing, how the elements of the datatype are represented. Such *abstraction barriers* are useful when more than one programmer is working on a project, and even when a single programmer is working on a non-trivial task. In particular, a representation can be changed without affecting the validity of scripts that make use of the datatype.

8.1.1   An example

Let us now give an example of an abstract datatype. Suppose a programmer wants to make use of a datatype *Queueα* of queues over an arbitrary type α. The basic idea of a queue is that one can add elements to the rear of a queue and take elements off the front of a (nonempty) queue. A queue is therefore a species of finite list with a restricted set of operations. The programmer wants an efficient implementation of *Queue α* but is not interested in providing it. Instead, he or she may ask another programmer to provide a suitable implementation, or may use an off-the-shelf solution supplied by the system environment. How can this situation be realised?

Firstly, the programmer wants to know what primitive operations are given. Suppose that the queue operations are

$$
\begin{array}{lll}
empty & :: & Queue\ \alpha \\
join & :: & \alpha \rightarrow Queue\ \alpha \rightarrow Queue\ \alpha \\
front & :: & Queue\ \alpha \rightarrow \alpha \\
back & :: & Queue\ \alpha \rightarrow Queue\ \alpha \\
isEmpty & :: & Queue\ \alpha \rightarrow Bool
\end{array}
$$

The list of operations, together with their types, is called the *signature* of the datatype *Queue α*.

Secondly, the programmer needs to know what these operations mean. The names and types give some clues, as does an informal description, but more precise information is needed. Users of the datatype need to know what they can rely on, and the implementor of the datatype needs to know what has to be provided.

8.1.2   Algebraic specifications

One way of supplying the information is to give what is called an *algebraic* or *axiomatic* specification of *Queue α*. This consists of a list of *axioms* that the operations should satisfy. One possible list is as follows:

$$
\begin{array}{lll}
isEmpty\ empty & = & True \\
isEmpty\ (join\ x\ xq) & = & False
\end{array}
$$

$$front\ (join\ x\ empty) \quad = \quad x$$
$$front\ (join\ x\ (join\ y\ xq)) \quad = \quad front\ (join\ y\ xq)$$

$$back\ (join\ x\ empty) \quad = \quad empty$$
$$back\ (join\ x\ (join\ y\ xq)) \quad = \quad join\ x\ (back\ (join\ y\ xq))$$

The first thing to notice is that these equations look very much like formal definitions of *isEmpty*, *front*, and *back*, based on a datatype with constructors *empty* and *join*. Indeed, they were designed precisely with this idea in mind. However, they should be properly understood only as expressing certain relationships between the five functions. The implementor is not forced to implement queues by a datatype with *empty* and *join* as constructors.

The axiomatic specification of *Queue α*, together with what can be derived from it, is the only thing that users of the datatype can rely on. In particular, no value for *back empty* is prescribed by the specification. From the user's point of view, *back empty* = ⊥, the undefined queue. Depending on how we interpret the axioms, it may be possible to distinguish between ⊥ and *join x* ⊥. For example, the axioms for *isEmpty* do not prescribe a value for *isEmpty* ⊥ but, depending on the interpretation of the second axiom for *isEmpty*, we might be able to deduce that *isEmpty* (*join x* ⊥) = *False*. To resolve this ambiguity, we add another axiom to the specification, namely that *join x* is a *strict* function for all *x*. Then we have

$$isEmpty\ (join\ x\ \bot) = isEmpty\ \bot = \bot$$

The major consequence of *join x* being strict is that there are no partial queues (apart from ⊥) or infinite queues. It is left as an exercise to prove by induction that if *join x* is strict, then *foldr join empty xs* = ⊥ for all infinite lists *xs*. The implementor of *Queue α* therefore does not have to provide for infinite queues.

It follows that every queue, apart from ⊥, can be expressed as a finite number of *join* and *back* applications to the queue *empty*. Furthermore, by using the axioms for *back*, we can eliminate occurrences of *back* from such an expression. It is also clear that different expressions in terms of *join* and *empty* describe different queues. Hence each queue can be named by a unique expression in terms of *join* and *empty*. It will not, however, be the case that elements of every abstract datatype can be named by unique expressions.

8.1.3 Representations

In order to implement an abstract type, a programmer has to provide a representation of its values, define the operations of the type in terms of this

representation, and show that the implemented operations satisfy the prescribed specification. Apart from these obligations, the implementor is free
to choose between different representations on the grounds of efficiency, simplicity, or taste. In the following section we will describe mechanisms provided
by Haskell for hiding the implementation of an abstract type so that reference
to the chosen representation is not permitted elsewhere in the script.

Let us now continue the example by providing two implementations of the
abstract type *Queue* α.

First implementation.   The first implementation makes use of finite lists to
represent queues. The implementations of the operations are as follows:

$$joinc \quad :: \quad \alpha \rightarrow [\alpha] \rightarrow [\alpha]$$
$$joinc\ x\ xs \quad = \quad xs \mathbin{+\!\!\!+} [x]$$

$$emptyc \quad :: \quad [\alpha]$$
$$emptyc \quad = \quad [\ ]$$

$$isEmptyc \quad :: \quad [\alpha] \rightarrow Bool$$
$$isEmptyc\ xs \quad = \quad null\ xs$$

$$frontc \quad :: \quad [\alpha] \rightarrow \alpha$$
$$frontc\ (x:xs) \quad = \quad x$$

$$backc \quad :: \quad [\alpha] \rightarrow [\alpha]$$
$$backc\ (x:xs) \quad = \quad xs$$

The implemented operations are given different names to distinguish them
from the abstract ones. All operations take constant time, except for *joinc*
which takes $\Theta(n)$ steps, where n is the number of elements in the queue. (Actually, this apparently obvious statement requires qualification, but we will postpone discussion to the end of the section.)

The next task is to show that the implemented operations satisfy the axioms
of the specification. In the present case this is easy because there is a one-to-
one correspondence between queues and finite lists (plus $\perp$), and so each of the
axioms holds when the implemented operations are substituted for the abstract
ones. We can formalise this correspondence with the help of two functions,
abstr and *reprn*, defined by

$$abstr \quad :: \quad [\alpha] \rightarrow Queue\ \alpha$$
$$abstr \quad = \quad foldr\ join\ empty \cdot reverse$$

$$
\begin{array}{lll}
reprn & :: & Queue\ \alpha \rightarrow [\alpha] \\
reprn\ empty & = & [\ ] \\
reprn\ (join\ x\ xq) & = & reprn\ xq \mathbin{+\mkern-8mu+} [x]
\end{array}
$$

For example, $abstr\,[1,2] = join\,2\,(join\,1\,empty)$. It is left as an exercise to show that $reprn \cdot abstr$ is the identity function on finite lists, and $abstr \cdot reprn$ is the identity function on queues.

Second implementation.   In the second implementation, the idea is to represent a queue xq by a pair of lists (xs, ys) such that the elements of xq are, in order, the elements of the list $xs \mathbin{+\mkern-8mu+} reverse\ ys$. By breaking the list into two pieces and reversing the second piece, we hope to make the queue operations more efficient. We will also impose an additional constraint on the representation: queues will be represented by pairs (xs, ys) in which if xs is empty, then ys is empty too. Thus not every pair of lists represents a queue; in particular, $([\ ], [x])$ does not represent a valid queue. This constraint has to be maintained by the programs that create queues. Note also that two distinct pairs of lists may represent the same queue. For example, both $([1,2], [\ ])$ and $([1], [2])$ represent the queue $join\,2\,(join\,1\,empty)$.

For this implementation we can define the function $abstr$ by

$$
\begin{array}{lll}
abstr & :: & ([\alpha], [\alpha]) \rightarrow Queue\ \alpha \\
abstr\ (xs, ys) & = & (foldr\ join\ empty \cdot reverse)\ (xs \mathbin{+\mkern-8mu+} reverse\ ys)
\end{array}
$$

The function $abstr$ is not injective, so there is no function $reprn$ that is left-inverse to $abstr$, and so no one-to-one correspondence between queues and pairs of finite lists.

We also need to formalise the fact that not all representations are valid. We do this with a function $valid$ defined by

$$
\begin{array}{lll}
valid & :: & ([\alpha], [\alpha]) \rightarrow Bool \\
valid\ (xs, ys) & = & not\ (null\ xs) \lor null\ ys
\end{array}
$$

The function $valid$ formalises what is known as a *datatype invariant*, an idea that we have already met in a number of places. For example, in the discussion of rational numbers in Section 3.5 we represented rational numbers only by pairs of integers in what was called canonical form. Similarly, binary search trees were trees constrained by a certain datatype invariant. The pair $(abstr, valid)$ formalises the representation of queues by pairs of lists.

Here are the implemented operations:

$$
\begin{array}{lll}
emptyc & = & ([\,],[\,]) \\
isEmptyc\ (xs, ys) & = & null\ xs \\
joinc\ x\ (ys, zs) & = & mkValid\ (ys, x : zs) \\
frontc\ (x : xs, ys) & = & x \\
backc\ (x : xs, ys) & = & mkValid\ (xs, ys) \\
\\
mkValid & :: & ([\alpha], [\alpha]) \to ([\alpha], [\alpha]) \\
mkValid\ (xs, ys) & = & \textbf{if}\ null\ xs\ \textbf{then}\ (reverse\ ys, [\,])\ \textbf{else}\ (xs, ys)
\end{array}
$$

The function *mkValid* maintains the datatype invariant, using the fact that

$$
[\,] + reverse\ ys\ =\ reverse\ ys + [\,]
$$

All operations now take constant time except for *backc*. In particular, computation of *join x (ys, zs)* takes constant time because if *ys* is empty, then *zs* is empty and reversing [*x*] takes constant time. The function *back* will take constant time except when the first list is a singleton. (Again, at the end of the section we will qualify these remarks on timing estimates.) The second implementation therefore has a different efficiency than the first, and at the end of the section we will show that the efficiency is superior.

The proof that the second implementation satisfies the specification is also different from the previous one in that the axioms, as stated, do *not* hold for the implemented operations. Consider the two axioms for *back*:

$$
\begin{array}{lll}
back\ (join\ x\ empty) & = & empty \\
back\ (join\ x\ (join\ y\ xq)) & = & join\ x\ (back\ (joinc\ y\ xq))
\end{array}
$$

If these axioms hold for the implemented operations, then the following equation should be true:

$$
\begin{aligned}
&backc\ (joinc\ x\ (joinc\ y\ (joinc\ z\ emptyc)))\ = \\
&backc\ (joinc\ x\ (backc\ (joinc\ y\ (joinc\ z\ (joinc\ w\ emptyc)))))
\end{aligned}
$$

However, as one can easily check, the left-hand side simplifies to $([y, x], [\,])$ and the right-hand side to $([y], [x])$. What we have not taken into account is that, although the two pairs of lists are different, they represent the same queue.

The problem is resolved by realising that an equational axiom is intended to mean that both sides should deliver the same queue, not the same representation. Thus, we should require only that the equation

$$
abstr \cdot backc \cdot joinc\ x \cdot joinc\ y\ =\ abstr \cdot joinc\ x \cdot backc \cdot joinc\ y
$$

holds. More generally, for every axiom of the form $f = g$, where f and g return queues, we require only that

$$abstr \cdot fc \quad = \quad abstr \cdot gc$$

where fc and gc are the results when the implemented operations are substituted for the abstract ones. If f and g return other values, then the function *abstr* is omitted in the equation above.

There is another potential problem, though it is not exhibited in the way we have written the definitions of the operations. We could have written the definition of *join* in the equivalent form

$$join \, x \, ([\,], [\,]) \quad = \quad ([x], [\,])$$
$$join \, x \, (y : ys, zs) \quad = \quad (y : ys, x : zs)$$

This definition is correct because of the datatype invariant on valid representations. Now, assuming that we had defined *join* by the two cases above, consider the axiom

$$isEmpty \, (join \, x \, xq) \quad = \quad False$$

Replacing *isEmpty* and *join* by *isEmptyc* and *joinc*, and xq by the pair (ys, zs), the axiom translates to

$$isEmptyc \, (joinc \, x \, (ys, zs)) \quad = \quad False$$

This equation does not hold for all ys and zs. If $ys = [\,]$ and zs is a nonempty list, the left-hand side reduces to $\perp$ by case exhaustion in the definition of *joinc*. The resolution of the problem is clear: queues should be replaced in the axioms only by *valid* representations, so the equation above needs to be verified only when (ys, zs) is a valid representation.

We can summarise the situation using the following notation: if $f = g$ is an axiom, where f and g return queues, then it is sufficient to prove

$$abstr \cdot fc \quad = \quad abstr \cdot gc \quad (\text{modulo } valid)$$

where fc and gc are the results when the implemented operations are substituted for the abstract ones.

There is another, more modular way to proceed. It is sufficient to show that the following equations hold (all modulo *valid*):

$$abstr \, emptyc \quad = \quad empty$$
$$abstr \cdot joinc \, x \quad = \quad join \, x \cdot abstr$$

$$abstr \cdot frontc \; = \; front \cdot abstr$$
$$abstr \cdot backc \; = \; back \cdot abstr$$
$$isEmptyc \quad = \; isEmpty \cdot abstr$$

Using the fact that, by assumption, the abstract operations satisfy the axioms, we can now prove that the implemented ones do (modulo $abstr$ and $valid$). For example,

$$abstr \cdot backc \cdot joinc \, x \cdot joinc \, y \; = \; back \cdot join \, x \cdot join \, y \cdot abstr$$
$$abstr \cdot joinc \, x \cdot backc \cdot joinc \, y \; = \; join \, x \cdot back \cdot join \, y \cdot abstr$$

and the two right-hand sides are equal by the second equation for $back$.

8.1.4 Interaction and amortised costs

Other things being equal, the best implementation of an abstract datatype is one that makes the operations as efficient as possible. In practice, though, there is usually a trade-off: one operation can be made more efficient only at the expense of another operation. The crafting of an implementation requires judgement as to where best to put one's effort in obtaining efficiency. There may also be requirements attached to the specification of the datatype, in that one operation or another may be required to possess a certain efficiency.

There is a complicating factor when using an abstract datatype with a lazy functional language: evaluation of a particular operation may take place in stages throughout the total computation. For example, consider the first implementation of queues. We said before that all operations take constant time except for *join*, which takes linear time in the length of the queue. In fact, this statement is correct only under a policy of eager evaluation; under lazy evaluation the situation is more complicated. To see why, consider evaluation of

$$(front \cdot join \, n \cdot join \, (n-1) \cdots join \, 1) \; empty$$

To compute *front* the queue has to be reduced to the form $x : xs$. Hence the queue is first reduced in $\Theta(n)$ steps to

$$((([1] + [2]) + [3]) + \cdots) + [n]$$

and the first element is returned in a further $\Theta(n)$ steps. Subsequently, a demand for the front of the back of the queue takes another $\Theta(n)$ steps. In other words, the total cost of $\Theta(n^2)$ steps required to build the queue is paid for in instalments when we demand information about the elements.

This might seem a small point – after all, costs are paid in full by the end of the computation – but we can imagine a scenario in which the difference can be important. Suppose we set up an *interactive* program to simulate queues. The subject of how to write such programs will be covered in Chapter 10, but the following session should give the general idea:

? *interact queue*

Welcome to Queue. Type "quit" to quit.
> *join* 1
ok
> *join* 2
ok
> *front*
1
> *quit*
bye

The interactive program sets up an empty queue. We then give a sequence of *commands* to add elements to the queue, display the front element, and so on. Each command is acknowledged, either by displaying the requested result, or by saying "ok".

The point about this scenario is that the programmer who implements the interaction (for a chosen representation of queues) can exercise total control over the point at which evaluation takes place. The interaction can be made to run eagerly, in which case the evaluation of the result of a *join* command takes place before its acknowledgement, or it can be made to run lazily, in which case evaluation takes place when a *front* or *isEmpty* command is given, or something between the two. Depending on the policy, the user will perceive different delays between giving a command and receiving an acknowledgement.

Given this scenario, we can talk about *amortised* costs as well as *worst-case* costs. There are a number of ways of defining amortised costs, but a simple approach is the following. Suppose we can show that, for all n, a sequence of n queue commands takes worst-case time $T(n)$ steps in total. Then the average or *amortised* cost per operation is $T(n)/n$ steps. Under this scheme, each operation receives the same amortised cost, so amortised cost is a measure of the efficiency of the chosen representation as a whole. It does not depend on the speed at which the interaction is driven, which only controls when the actual costs are paid.

In contrast, the worst-case cost of an individual operation, that is, the maximum delay that may be experienced between giving a command and receiving an acknowledgement, depends on both the representation and the eagerness of the interaction. By definition, the worst-case cost $T(n)$ of an operation is the maximum number of reduction steps required to process the operation when it appears in any sequence of n commands. The timing estimates stated previously for the first implementation of queues are worst-case estimates under an eagerly-driven interaction.

Let us look at amortised costs in the two implementations of queues. In the first implementation, the worst-case time for n queue operations is $\Theta(n^2)$ steps in total. For example, this is the time required to execute $n/2$ joins followed by $(n/2) - 1$ backs, and then to ask whether the result is empty. The amortised cost per operation is therefore $\Theta(n)$ steps. This is also the worst-case time of any individual operation.

Compare this to the second implementation of queues. Here, a list of length k is reversed only when there have been k joining operations since the previous list reversal, or the start of the interaction. It follows that a sequence of n queue operations takes $O(n)$ steps in total, so the amortised cost per operation is $O(1)$ steps. On the other hand, the worst-case performance for any individual operation in the sequence is $\Theta(n)$ steps. The second implementation of queues is therefore superior. In Section 8.6 we will describe two even better implementations of queues.

Exercises

8.1.1 Finite lists can also be considered as an abstract datatype. For example, consider the operations

$$
\begin{array}{lll}
nil & :: & List\ \alpha \\
null & :: & List\ \alpha \rightarrow Bool \\
cons & :: & \alpha \rightarrow List\ \alpha \rightarrow List\ \alpha \\
head & :: & List\ \alpha \rightarrow \alpha \\
tail & :: & List\ \alpha \rightarrow List\ \alpha
\end{array}
$$

Give an algebraic specification of lists.

8.1.2 Following on from the previous question, an element of *List* α can be represented by a pair (f, n) where $f :: Nat \rightarrow \alpha$ and $n :: Nat$. The value n is the length of the list and $f\ k$ is the element at position k. Formalise this representation by providing a suitable abstraction function, and implement the list operations.

8.1.3 Check that the first implementation of queues satisfies the algebraic specification.

8.1.4 Using the fusion law for *foldr*, show that $reprn \cdot foldr\,join\,empty = reverse$. Hence conclude that $reprn \cdot abstr$ is the identity function on finite lists. Using the characterisation that every queue is either *empty* or of the form *join x xq* for some *x* and some queue *xq*, prove that $abstr \cdot reprn$ is the identity function on queues.

8.1.5 Simplify the representation of queues by pairs of lists by not imposing the datatype invariant mentioned in the text. Thus it is not required that the second component be empty if the first one is. How does the implementation of the operations change?

8.1.6 Consider the problem of describing a simple line editor. Suppose a *Line* is a sequence of characters $c_1 c_2 \ldots c_n$ together with a position p, where $0 \le p \le n$, called the *cursor*. The following operations on lines are required:

$$
\begin{array}{rcl}
newline & :: & Line \\
moveStart & :: & Line \rightarrow Line \\
moveEnd & :: & Line \rightarrow Line \\
moveLeft & :: & Line \rightarrow Line \\
moveRight & :: & Line \rightarrow Line \\
insert & :: & Char \rightarrow Line \rightarrow Line \\
delete & :: & Line \rightarrow Line
\end{array}
$$

The informal description of these operations is as follows: (i) the constant *newline* denotes an empty line; (ii) *moveLeft* moves the cursor one position to the left (if possible); similarly for *moveRight*; (iii) *moveStart* places the cursor at the beginning of the line; similarly, *moveEnd* places the cursor at the end of the line; (iv) *delete* deletes the character at the cursor position; and finally (v) *insert x* inserts a new character *x* at the cursor position. Give an algebraic specification for *Line*. Suggest a suitable representation for *Line*, implement the given operations, and show that they meet their specifications.

8.2 Modules

Haskell provides a mechanism, called a *module*, for defining abstract datatypes. In fact the module mechanism of Haskell can be used for more general purposes, but we will confine ourselves to explaining how it works for abstract datatypes. Here is an example module:

```
module Queue (Queue, empty, isEmpty, join, front, back) where
newtype Queue α = MkQ ([α], [α])
empty   ::   Queue α
empty   =    MkQ ([ ], [ ])

isEmpty                      ::   Queue α → Bool
isEmpty (MkQ (xs, ys))       =    null xs

join                         ::   α → Queue α → Queue α
join x (MkQ (ys, zs))        =    mkValid (ys, x : zs)

front                        ::   Queue α → α
front (MkQ (x : xs, ys))     =    x

back                         ::   Queue α → Queue α
back (MkQ (x : xs, ys))      =    mkValid (xs, ys)

mkValid :: ([α], [α]) → Queue α
mkValid (xs, ys)
   =   if null xs then MkQ (reverse ys, [ ]) else MkQ (xs, ys)
```

This module contains the second implementation of queues described in the previous section. Note that *Queue* α is implemented by a **newtype** declaration rather than as a type synonym for pairs of lists. The reason for this is explained below.

The first line of the declaration introduces a module called *Queue*. Module names begin with upper-case letters. The declaration also contains an *export* list consisting of the name of the abstract datatype (also called *Queue*), together with its operations. No other types and values declared in the module may be used elsewhere. In particular, the constructor *MkQ* is not exported, so values of type *Queue* α cannot be created in scripts that make use of the datatype, except with the help of the five named operations. In other words, the implementation of *Queue* α described in the module is hidden in any script that makes use of the module.

To use the module in a script we have to *import* it with a declaration

> **import** *Queue*

Such a declaration is made at the beginning of a script. For example, here is a script that imports the datatype *Queue* and defines two function for converting between lists and queues:

> **import** *Queue*

toQ	::	$[\alpha] \rightarrow$ *Queue* α
toQ	=	*foldr join empty · reverse*
fromQ	::	*Queue* $\alpha \rightarrow [\alpha]$
fromQ q	=	**if** *isEmpty q* **then** [ ] **else** *front q* : *fromQ* (*back q*)

It is left as an exercise to show *fromQ · toQ* is the identity function on finite lists.

The remaining point requiring explanation is why we have chosen to implement *Queue* α as a new type rather than a type synonym. The reason has to do with the desire to keep the implementation hidden. Type synonyms are simply devices for giving alternative names to existing types. A synonym and its definition are completely interchangeable. In particular, a type synonym inherits the class methods defined for the underlying type. So, if *Queue* α was declared as a type synonym, we could break the abstraction barrier. For example,

? *join* 1 (*join* 2 *empty*)
([2], [1])

? *join* 1 (*join* 2 *empty*) == *join* 2 (*join* 1 *empty*)
False

It was not our intention to provide an equality test on queues, but since (==) is defined on ($[\alpha], [\alpha]$) whenever it is defined on α, we nevertheless have one. Similarly, since ($[\alpha], [\alpha]$) is an instance of *Show* whenever α is, we can reveal how queues are represented. Introducing *Queue* α by a **newtype** declaration means that new class instances can be declared for *Queue* α, and that old class instances defined for the underlying type no longer apply. In this way, the abstraction barriers can be maintained without sacrificing efficiency.

Exercises

8.2.1 Prove that *fromQueue · toQueue* is the identity function on finite lists.

8.3 Sets

The primary example of an abstract datatype is the datatype of sets. Sets are ubiquitous in mathematics and are also useful in many programming tasks. Sets can be represented by lists, lists with no duplicates, ordered lists, trees, boolean functions, and so on. Different representations are appropriate in different circumstances, depending on the precise repertoire of operations to be provided and their required efficiency.

There are numerous operations on sets, including the following:

$$
\begin{array}{lcl}
empty & :: & Set\ \alpha \\
isEmpty & :: & Set\ \alpha \rightarrow Bool \\
member & :: & Set\ \alpha \rightarrow \alpha \rightarrow Bool \\
insert & :: & \alpha \rightarrow Set\ \alpha \rightarrow Set\ \alpha \\
delete & :: & \alpha \rightarrow Set\ \alpha \rightarrow Set\ \alpha \\
\\
union & :: & Set\ \alpha \rightarrow Set\ \alpha \rightarrow Set\ \alpha \\
meet & :: & Set\ \alpha \rightarrow Set\ \alpha \rightarrow Set\ \alpha \\
minus & :: & Set\ \alpha \rightarrow Set\ \alpha \rightarrow Set\ \alpha
\end{array}
$$

These eight operations may not all be wanted in a particular application. A type based on the first five operations is often called a *dictionary*. Dictionaries are useful as a general device for maintaining a list of tasks to be performed. Tasks can be done in any order and have to be done only once. New tasks are created one by one and added to the list; tasks are ticked off when they have been completed.

The algebraic specification of *Set* α can be formulated as the following list of axioms:

$$
\begin{array}{lcl}
insert\ x\ (insert\ x\ xs) & = & insert\ x\ xs \\
insert\ x\ (insert\ y\ xs) & = & insert\ y\ (insert\ x\ xs) \\
\\
isEmpty\ empty & = & True \\
isEmpty\ (insert\ x\ xs) & = & False \\
\\
member\ empty\ y & = & False \\
member\ (insert\ x\ xs)\ y & = & (x = y) \vee member\ xs\ y
\end{array}
$$

$delete\ x\ empty = empty$
$delete\ x\ (insert\ y\ xs)$
$\quad = \ \textbf{if}\ x = y\ \textbf{then}\ delete\ x\ xs\ \textbf{else}\ insert\ y\ (delete\ x\ xs)$

$$union \; xs \; empty \qquad = \quad xs$$
$$union \; xs \; (insert \; y \; ys) \quad = \quad insert \; y \; (union \; xs \; ys)$$

$$meet \; xs \; empty = empty$$
$$meet \; xs \; (insert \; y \; ys)$$
$$\qquad = \quad \textbf{if} \; member \; xs \; y \; \textbf{then} \; insert \; y \; (meet \; xs \; ys) \; \textbf{else} \; meet \; xs \; ys$$

$$minus \; xs \; empty \qquad = \quad xs$$
$$minus \; xs \; (insert \; y \; ys) \quad = \quad minus \; (delete \; y \; xs) \; ys$$

We will also assume, as for queues, that all operations are strict, so only finite sets can be constructed.

The first two axioms are different in nature from the others. The first one states that inserting an element twice in a set is the same as inserting it once. The second equation states that it doesn't matter in which order two elements are inserted into a set. Although every set can be expressed in terms of *empty* and *insert* alone, such expressions are not unique. In other words, there are no canonical forms for sets.

Two crucial operations are *isEmpty* and *member*; without them there would be no way to tell two sets apart. Unlike queues, there is no operation for extracting an element from a set. It is simply not possible, without further assumptions on the type of the elements of a set, to specify a function that returns an element of a set. The element cannot be chosen arbitrarily, because functions return the same result given the same argument. For example, the definition

$$choose \qquad\qquad :: \quad Set \; \alpha \to \alpha$$
$$choose \; (insert \; x \; xs) \quad = \quad x$$

does not work because it leads to an inconsistency:

$$choose \; (insert \; x \; (insert \; y \; xs)) = x$$
$$choose \; (insert \; x \; (insert \; y \; xs)) = choose \; (insert \; y \; (insert \; x \; xs)) = y$$

On the other hand, if α is restricted to instances of the type class *Ord*, we could always extract the minimum (or maximum) element of a finite nonempty set.

For a different reason, it is not possible to implement *member* unless *Set* α is restricted to those types α that are instances of the type class *Eq*. In order to determine whether a value is in a set, we have to be able to compare it with the elements of the set. In particular, it is not possible to implement sets of functions and be able to tell two nonempty sets apart.

8.3.1 Representation by lists

Assuming α is an instance of *Eq*, we can represent sets by lists. The abstraction function in this case is

$$
\begin{aligned}
abstr &:: \quad [\alpha] \to Set\ \alpha \\
abstr &= \quad foldr\ insert\ empty
\end{aligned}
$$

There are two reasonable definitions of valid representations:

$$
\begin{aligned}
valid\ xs &= \quad True \\
valid\ xs &= \quad nonduplicated\ xs
\end{aligned}
$$

With the first definition, all lists are allowed as valid representations of sets. In such a case, we can implement the set operations quite simply. For example,

$$
\begin{aligned}
member\ xs\ x &= \quad some\ (== x)\ xs \\
insert\ x\ xs &= \quad x : xs \\
delete\ x\ xs &= \quad filter\ (\neq x)\ xs \\
union\ xs\ ys &= \quad xs \mathbin{+\!\!+} ys \\
minus\ xs\ ys &= \quad filter\ (not \cdot member\ ys)\ xs
\end{aligned}
$$

The function *some* is defined by

$$
\begin{aligned}
some &:: \quad (\alpha \to Bool) \to [\alpha] \to Bool \\
some\ p &= \quad or \cdot map\ p
\end{aligned}
$$

Like the companion function $all\ p = and \cdot map\ p$, the function $some\ p$ is a useful programming idiom. Notice, in passing, how the type assigned to *member* is exploited in the definition of *minus*. In the definition of the curried function *member* there is a choice as to which argument should come first, the set or the element. It is more convenient to put the set first. In fact, the type signature

$$
member \quad :: \quad Set\ \alpha \to (\alpha \to Bool)
$$

expresses one half of a correspondence between sets and boolean-valued functions.

There are some advantages of this simple representation, but the disadvantages are greater. The major advantage is that *insert* is a constant-time operation. The problem, though, is that the length of the representing list can be much larger than the size of the represented set, so the implementations of the other operations are inefficient. To be more precise, suppose that *xs* and *ys* both have length n and both represent sets of size N. Then, in the worst case, evaluation of *delete x xs* takes $\Omega(n)$ steps and evaluation of *minus xs ys* takes

$\Omega(n^2)$ steps. Since n can be arbitrarily larger than N, the operations cannot be guaranteed to be executable within any prescribed time bound.

To be more precise still, we should consider amortised costs. It is not too difficult to show that the worst-case cost of demanding information, say by a *member* test, from a set built by n dictionary operations is $\Theta(n^2)$ steps, so the amortised cost of the dictionary operations is $\Theta(n)$.

A better representation is to adopt the second definition of *valid* and restrict the lists to have distinct elements. Under this representation, the operations *insert* and *union* are implemented as follows:

$$
\begin{aligned}
insert\ x\ xs &= x : filter\ (\neq x)\ xs \\
union\ xs\ ys &= xs \mathbin{+\!\!+} filter\ (not \cdot member\ xs)\ ys
\end{aligned}
$$

Under this representation the length of the representing list and the size of the represented set are the same. However, the time for *insert* increases to $\Theta(N)$, where N is the size of the set, and the time for *union* is $\Omega(N^2)$ in the worst case. The amortised cost of the dictionary operations is $\Theta(N)$ steps.

To improve on the above representations we need to assume that α is an instance of the type class *Ord*. Recall that *Ord* is a subclass of *Eq*. Then we can represent sets by lists in increasing order. The datatype invariant *valid* in this case is that *valid* holds for a list only if the elements of the list are in strictly increasing order. Under this representation, we can improve the implementation of *member* to read

$$
\begin{aligned}
member\ xs\ x\ &=\ \textbf{if}\ null\ ys\ \textbf{then}\ False\ \textbf{else}\ (x == head\ ys) \\
&\quad\ \textbf{where}\ ys = dropWhile\ (< x)\ xs
\end{aligned}
$$

Though still $\Omega(N)$ in the worst case, the search for x in xs is made more efficient by not looking past the first y for which $y \geq x$.

Here is the implementation of *union* under this new representation:

$$
\begin{aligned}
union\ [\ ]\ ys &= ys \\
union\ (x : xs)\ [\ ] &= x : xs
\end{aligned}
$$

$$
\begin{aligned}
&union\ (x : xs)\ (y : ys) \\
&\quad \left|
\begin{array}{lll}
(x < y) &= x : union\ xs\ (y : ys) \\
(x == y) &= x : union\ xs\ ys \\
(x > y) &= y : union\ (x : xs)\ ys
\end{array}
\right.
\end{aligned}
$$

The function *union* is like *merge* except that duplicated elements are removed. The implementation of *minus* and *meet* are similar and are left as exercises.

The advantage of the new representation is that the running times for *union*, *meet*, and *minus* drop to $\Theta(N)$ steps. On the other hand, the running times of the dictionary operations *member*, *insert*, and *delete* are $\Omega(N)$ in the worst case. In the remainder of the section we will show how the dictionary operations can be implemented more efficiently by moving to trees.

8.3.2 Representation by trees

We have already suggested in Section 6.2 how binary search trees can be used to represent sets. Here are the relevant definitions again, this time organised as a module:

> **module** *Set* (*Set, empty, isEmpty, member, insert, delete*) **where**
> **data** *Stree α* = *Null* | *Fork* (*Stree α*) *α* (*Stree α*)
>
> *empty* :: *Set α*
> *empty* = *Null*
>
> *isEmpty*   :: *Set α → Bool*
> *isEmpty Null*   = *True*
> *isEmpty* (*Fork xt y zt*) = *False*
>
> *member* :: (*Ord α*) ⇒ *Stree α → α → Bool*
> *member Null x = False*
> *member* (*Fork xt y zt*) *x*
> | (*x < y*)   =   *member xt x*
> | (*x == y*)   =   *True*
> | (*x > y*)   =   *member zt x*
>
> *insert* :: (*Ord α*) ⇒ *α → Stree α → Stree α*
> *insert x Null = Fork Null x Null*
> *insert x* (*Fork xt y zt*)
> | (*x < y*)   =   *Fork* (*insert x xt*) *y zt*
> | (*x == y*)   =   *Fork xt y zt*
> | (*x > y*)   =   *Fork xt y* (*insert x zt*)

$delete :: (Ord \; \alpha) \Rightarrow \alpha \rightarrow Stree \; \alpha \rightarrow Stree \; \alpha$

$delete \; x \; Null = Null$

$delete \; x \; (Fork \; xt \; y \; zt)$

$$
\begin{array}{lll}
\quad (x < y) & = & Fork \; (delete \; x \; xt) \; y \; zt \\
\quad (x == y) & = & join \; xt \; zt \\
\quad (x > y) & = & Fork \; xt \; y \; (delete \; x \; zt)
\end{array}
$$

$$
\begin{array}{lll}
join & :: & Stree \; \alpha \rightarrow Stree \; \alpha \rightarrow Stree \; \alpha \\
join \; xt \; yt & = & \textbf{if } isEmpty \; yt \; \textbf{then } xt \; \textbf{else } Fork \; xt \; y \; zt \\
& & \textbf{where } (y, zt) = splitTree \; yt
\end{array}
$$

$splitTree :: Stree \; \alpha \rightarrow (\alpha, Stree \; \alpha)$

$splitTree \; (Fork \; xt \; y \; zt)$

$\quad = \quad \textbf{if } isEmpty \; xt \; \textbf{then } (y, zt) \; \textbf{else } (u, Fork \; vt \; y \; zt)$

$\quad\quad \textbf{where } (u, vt) = splitTree \; xt$

It is left as an exercise to provide the functions *abstr* and *valid*, and so formalise the representation of sets by binary search trees.

Two extra functions, *join* and *splitTree*, are defined in this module but they are not listed among the exports in the module header, so they cannot be used in scripts that import the module *Set*. Note carefully that *join* will not serve as an implementation of the function *union* on sets. The value of *join* $xt \; yt$ is defined under the assumption that every element in xt is smaller than every element in yt. In fact, this representation of sets by trees is not particularly useful if one wants to implement nondictionary operations efficiently.

The execution time of the operations *member*, *insert*, and *delete* depends on the height of the tree representing the set. In the worst case, each operation takes $\Theta(height \; t)$ steps, where

$$
\begin{array}{lll}
height & :: & Stree \; \alpha \rightarrow Int \\
height \; Null & = & 0 \\
height \; (Fork \; xt \; y \; zt) & = & 1 + (height \; xt \; \textbf{max} \; height \; zt)
\end{array}
$$

Recall that a tree of size n has a height h satisfying

$$\lceil \log(n + 1) \rceil \leq h < n + 1$$

Since a set of size n may be represented by a tree of height n, the dictionary operations take $\Omega(n)$ steps in the worst case. On the other hand, a set of size n may be represented by a tree of height $\log(n + 1)$, so the dictionary operations take $O(\log n)$ in the best case. The way to bring these two bounds together is to build only trees with a height h satisfying $h = O(\log n)$, and we consider this next.

8.3.3 Balanced trees

There are various schemes for building search trees with reasonably small height. The one we will adopt is called a *height-balanced* binary search tree, and also an *AVL tree* after the names of its Russian inventors, G. Adelson-Velski and Y. Landis. The insertion and deletion algorithms on AVL trees are very similar to those for ordinary binary search trees. We begin by defining balanced trees formally.

A binary search tree is *height-balanced* if the heights of the left and right subtrees of each node differ by at most one. This property is formalised with a function *balanced* defined by

$$
\begin{array}{lll}
balanced & :: & Stree\ \alpha \rightarrow Bool \\
balanced\ Null & = & True \\
balanced\ (Fork\ xt\ x\ zt) & = & abs\ (height\ xt - height\ zt) \le 1 \land \\
& & balanced\ xt \land balanced\ zt
\end{array}
$$

The tree xt is balanced if $balanced\ xt = True$. In particular, a perfect binary search tree is balanced since every node has two subtrees with equal heights. A balanced tree representing a set may not have the minimum possible height of all trees that represent the set, but its height is always reasonably small. More precisely, if xt is a balanced binary search tree of size n and height h, then

$$h\ \le\ 1.4404 \log(n + 1) + O(1)$$

The proof of this result uses induction in a rather indirect way.

Proof. Suppose $H(n)$ is the maximum possible height of a balanced tree of size n. Our objective is to put an upper bound on $H(n)$. We will do this by turning the problem around. Suppose $S(h)$ is the minimum possible size of a balanced tree of height h. Taking a tree of size n and height $H(n)$, we therefore have $S(H(n)) \le n$, so we can estimate H by estimating S.

Since *Null* is the only tree with height 0, it is clear that $S(0) = 0$. Similarly, there is only one kind of tree with height 1, namely a tree of the form *Fork Null x Null*, so $S(1) = 1$. The smallest possible balanced tree with height $h + 2$ has two balanced subtrees, one with height $h + 1$ and the other with height h. Hence

$$S(h + 2)\ =\ S(h + 1) + S(h) + 1$$

It is at this point that induction comes in. A simple induction argument shows that $S(h) = \mathit{fib}\,(h + 2) - 1$, where fib is the Fibonacci function. To complete the proof we will need the following fact about the Fibonacci function, which can also be proved by induction. Let ϕ and ψ be the two roots of the quadratic equation $x^2 - x - 1 = 0$, that is, $\phi = (1 + \sqrt{5})/2$ and $\psi = (1 - \sqrt{5})/2$. Then $\mathit{fib}\,n = (\phi^n - \psi^n)/\sqrt{5}$. Furthermore, since $\psi^n < 1$, we obtain that $\mathit{fib}\,n > (\phi^n - 1)/\sqrt{5}$. Hence

$$(\phi^{H(n)+2} - 1)/\sqrt{5} - 1 < \mathit{fib}\,(H(n) + 2) - 1 = S(H(n)) \leq n$$

Taking logarithms, we obtain

$$(H(n) + 2)\log\phi < \log(n + 1) + O(1)$$

Since $\log\phi = 1/1.4404\ldots$, the result now follows. □

By representing sets by balanced binary search trees, we can guarantee that each of the dictionary operations take $O(\log n)$ steps, where n is the size of the set. The implementations of the operations basically follow the same scheme as above, except that at various points rebalancing is required to maintain the invariant *balanced*. In the remainder of the section we will present the details of the insertion and deletion operations.

8.3.4 Representation by balanced trees

We will want to maintain information about the heights of subtrees, so we first augment the type *Stree* α with height information:

```
data AStree α  =  Null | Fork Int (AStree α) α (AStree α)

fork         ::  AStree α → α → AStree α → AStree α
fork xt y zt  =  Fork h xt y zt
                 where h = 1 + (ht xt max ht zt)

ht           ::  AStree α → Int
ht Null       =  0
ht (Fork h xt y zt)  =  h
```

By building trees with *fork* we maintain the invariant that the integer label of a tree is its height. Furthermore, if *xt* and *zt* are binary search trees, and *y* lies between the largest value in *xt* and the smallest value in *zt*, then *fork xt y zt* builds a binary search tree. However, the result will only be a balanced tree if *xt* and *zt* are both balanced and differ in height by at most 1.

In order to ensure that only balanced trees are built, we will need a variant of *fork* which, for the sake of a name, we will call *spoon*. Its type is the same as that of *fork*:

$$spoon \quad :: \quad AStree \; \alpha \to \alpha \to AStree \; \alpha \to AStree \; \alpha$$

Apart from using *spoon* instead of *Fork*, the new definitions of *insert* and *delete* are exactly the same as before:

$$insert :: (Ord \; \alpha) \Rightarrow \alpha \to AStree \; \alpha \to AStree \; \alpha$$
$$insert \; x \; Null = fork \; Null \; x \; Null$$
$$insert \; x \; (Fork \; h \; xt \; y \; zt)$$

$$
\begin{array}{lll}
(x < y) & = & spoon \; (insert \; x \; xt) \; y \; zt \\
(x == y) & = & Fork \; h \; xt \; y \; zt \\
(x > y) & = & spoon \; xt \; y \; (insert \; x \; zt))
\end{array}
$$

$$delete :: (Ord \; \alpha) \Rightarrow \alpha \to AStree \; \alpha \to AStree \; \alpha$$
$$delete \; x \; Null = Null$$
$$delete \; x \; (Fork \; h \; xt \; y \; zt)$$

$$
\begin{array}{lll}
(x < y) & = & spoon \; (delete \; x \; xt) \; y \; zt \\
(x == y) & = & join \; xt \; zt \\
(x > y) & = & spoon \; xt \; y \; (delete \; x \; zt))
\end{array}
$$

$$
\begin{array}{lll}
join & :: & AStree \; \alpha \to AStree \; \alpha \to AStree \; \alpha \\
join \; xt \; yt & = & \textbf{if} \; isEmpty \; yt \; \textbf{then} \; xt \; \textbf{else} \; spoon \; xt \; y \; zt \\
& & \textbf{where} \; (y, zt) = splitTree \; yt
\end{array}
$$

$$
\begin{array}{lll}
splitTree & :: & AStree \; \alpha \to (\alpha, AStree \; \alpha) \\
splitTree \; (Fork \; h \; xt \; y \; zt) \\
& = & \textbf{if} \; isEmpty \; xt \; \textbf{then} \; (y, zt) \; \textbf{else} \; (u, spoon \; vt \; y \; zt) \\
& & \textbf{where} \; (u, vt) = splitTree \; xt
\end{array}
$$

It remains to implement *spoon*. Since a single insertion or deletion can alter the height of any subtree of a tree by at most 1, it is sufficient to implement *spoon xt y zt* under the assumption that *xt* and *zt* are both balanced binary search trees whose heights can differ by at most 2. We will discuss only the case $ht \; xt = ht \; zt + 2$; the other interesting case, $ht \; zt = ht \; xt + 2$, is dual. And of course, if *xt* and *zt* differ in height by at most 1, then we can implement *spoon* as a *fork*.

Since *xt* has positive height, it is not the empty tree, so suppose that

$$xt = Fork\ n\ ut\ v\ wt$$

The value of *spoon* depends on the relative heights of *ut* and *wt*. There are two cases. Firstly, suppose *ht wt ≤ ht ut*, so all of the following relationships hold:

$$ht\ zt = ht\ xt - 2 = ht\ ut - 1 \le ht\ wt \le ht\ ut$$

In this case we can define

$$spoon\ xt\ y\ zt = rotr\ (fork\ xt\ y\ zt)$$

where *rotr* rotates a tree to the right:

rotr	::	*AStree α → AStree α*
rotr (*Fork m* (*Fork n ut v wt*) *y zt*)	=	*fork ut v* (*fork wt y zt*)

To check that this is correct, we reason

$$abs\ (ht\ ut - ht\ (fork\ wt\ y\ zt))$$

=   {definition of height}

$$abs\ (ht\ ut - 1 - (ht\ wt\ \textbf{max}\ ht\ zt))$$

=   {since *ht zt ≤ ht wt*}

$$abs\ (ht\ ut - 1 - ht\ wt)$$

≤   {since *ht ut − 1 ≤ ht wt ≤ ht ut*}

    1

In the second case, suppose *ht wt = 1 + ht ut*. In this case, *wt* cannot be the empty tree, so suppose *wt = Fork p rt s tt*. In this case, *xt* takes the form

$$xt = Fork\ n\ ut\ v\ wt \quad \textbf{where}\ wt = Fork\ p\ rt\ s\ tt$$

Furthermore, all of the following relationships hold:

$$ht\ zt = ht\ xt - 2 = ht\ ut = ht\ wt - 1 = (ht\ rt\ \textbf{max}\ ht\ tt)$$

In this case we can define

$$spoon\ xt\ y\ zt = rotr\ (fork\ (rotl\ xt)\ y\ zt)$$

where *rotl* rotates a tree to the left:

$$rotl \qquad\qquad\qquad\qquad\qquad\quad :: \quad AStree\ \alpha \rightarrow AStree\ \alpha$$
$$rotl\ (Fork\ n\ ut\ v\ (Fork\ p\ rt\ s\ tt)) \quad = \quad fork\ (fork\ ut\ v\ rt)\ s\ tt$$

To check that this is correct, note that

$$spoon\ xt\ y\ zt \quad = \quad fork\ (fork\ ut\ v\ rt)\ s\ (fork\ tt\ y\ zt)$$

so we can argue

$$abs\ (ht\ (fork\ ut\ v\ rt) - ht\ (fork\ tt\ y\ zt))$$

= \{definition of height\}

$$abs\ ((ht\ ut\ \mathbf{max}\ ht\ rt) - (ht\ tt\ \mathbf{max}\ ht\ zt))$$

= \{since *ht tt* ≤ *ht zt*\}

$$abs\ ((ht\ ut\ \mathbf{max}\ ht\ rt) - ht\ zt)$$

= \{since *ht rt* ≤ *ht ut*\}

$$abs\ (ht\ ut - ht\ zt)$$

= \{since *ht ut* = *ht zt*\}

   0

The complete definition of *spoon* is as follows:

$$spoon\ xt\ y\ zt$$

$(hz + 1 < hx) \wedge (bias\ xt < 0)$	=	$rotr\ (fork\ (rotl\ xt)\ y\ zt)$
$(hz + 1 < hx)$	=	$rotr\ (fork\ xt\ y\ zt)$
$(hx + 1 < hz) \wedge (0 < bias\ zt)$	=	$rotl\ (fork\ xt\ y\ (rotr\ zt))$
$(hx + 1 < hz)$	=	$rotl\ (fork\ xt\ y\ zt)$
otherwise	=	$fork\ xt\ y\ zt$

$$\mathbf{where}\ hx = ht\ xt;\ \ hz = ht\ zt$$

$$bias :: AStree\ \alpha \rightarrow Int$$
$$bias\ (Fork\ h\ xt\ y\ zt) \quad = \quad ht\ xt - ht\ zt$$

$$rotr :: AStree\ \alpha \rightarrow AStree\ \alpha$$
$$rotr\ (Fork\ m\ (Fork\ n\ ut\ v\ wt)\ y\ zt) \quad = \quad fork\ ut\ v\ (fork\ wt\ y\ zt)$$

$$rotl :: AStree\ \alpha \rightarrow AStree\ \alpha$$
$$rotl\ (Fork\ m\ ut\ v\ (Fork\ n\ rt\ s\ tt)) \quad = \quad fork\ (fork\ ut\ v\ rt)\ s\ tt$$

Evaluation of *spoon* takes constant time, as one can easily check by inspection.

To summarise: using a balanced binary search tree one can implement the dictionary operations so that *member*, *insert*, and *delete* each take $O(\log n)$ steps, where n is the size of the set.

Exercises

8.3.1 Implement *meet* and *minus*, assuming sets are represented by lists in strictly increasing order.

8.3.2 Sets can be represented by boolean-valued functions. What is the abstraction function in this case? All of the set operations described in the text, except one, can be implemented quite easily under this representation. Give details, and isolate the difficult one.

A set can also be represented by a pair of values, a boolean-valued function, and an integer that represents the size of the set. Show that the troublesome operation is easy to implement under the new representation. Does this cause difficulties with any of the other operations?

8.3.3 Formalise the representation of sets by binary search trees by providing definitions of *abstr* and *valid*.

8.3.4 Insert the letters of EQUATION into an initially empty tree and draw the result. Do this for binary search trees and balanced binary search trees.

8.3.5 Suppose we want to represent sets by binary search trees, but also want to implement *union xs ys* with a time complexity $O(m + n)$, where m and n are the sizes of *xs* and *ys*. Show how this can be done.

8.3.6 Recall that $S(h)$ denotes the size of the smallest balanced tree with height h, and $H(n)$ denotes the height of the tallest tree with size n. Both S and H are monotonic functions with $h \leq H(S(h))$ and $S(H(n)) \leq n$. Use these facts to prove $S(h) \leq n \equiv h \leq H(n)$. [The functions S and H exemplify what is known as a *Galois correspondence*.]

8.3.7 Why does at most one tree require rebalancing after an insert operation into a balanced binary search tree?

8.3.8 How many binary trees of size 3 are there and what is the average height? Now suppose a binary search tree is built by inserting some permutation of *ABC* into an initially empty tree. How many different trees are possible and what is the average height? What if the insertions are balanced tree insertions?

8.3.9 Draw up a table, labelling the rows with the various set operations, and the columns with the various set representations. Using O-notation, fill in the table with times taken by each operation under each representation.

8.4 Bags

Bags, unlike sets, are more commonly found in computing than in mathematics, where they are usually called *multisets*. A bag is like a set in that the order of its elements is immaterial, and like a list in that duplicate elements matter. For example,

$$\{\![1, 2, 2, 3]\!\} = \{\![3, 2, 1, 2]\!\} \quad \text{and} \quad \{\![1, 2, 2, 3]\!\} \neq \{\![1, 2, 3]\!\}$$

Suppose we want an abstract datatype *Bag* α, restricted to those α that are instances of *Ord*, on which the following operations are defined:

$$
\begin{array}{lll}
mkBag & :: & [\alpha] \rightarrow Bag\ \alpha \\
isEmpty & :: & Bag\ \alpha \rightarrow Bool \\
union & :: & Bag\ \alpha \rightarrow Bag\ \alpha \rightarrow Bag\ \alpha \\
minBag & :: & Bag\ \alpha \rightarrow \alpha \\
delMin & :: & Bag\ \alpha \rightarrow Bag\ \alpha
\end{array}
$$

The function *mkBag* converts a finite list into a bag of its elements, *isEmpty* determines whether a bag is empty, and *union* takes the bag union of two bags. For example,

$$union\ \{\![1, 2, 2, 3]\!\}\ \{\![2, 4]\!\} \quad = \quad \{\![1, 2, 2, 2, 3, 4]\!\}$$

The function *minBag* returns the smallest element in a nonempty bag, and *delMin* deletes one occurrence of the smallest element. These last two operations are meaningful only if bags are restricted to types that are instances of *Ord*.

Let us now give an algebraic specification of *Bag* α. One possibility is the following list of axioms:

$$
\begin{array}{lcl}
isEmpty\ (mkBag\ xs) & = & null\ xs \\
union\ (mkBag\ xs)\ (mkBag\ ys) & = & mkBag\ (xs + \!\!+\ ys) \\
minBag\ (mkBag\ xs) & = & minlist\ xs \\
delMin\ (mkBag\ xs) & = & mkBag\ (deleteMin\ xs)
\end{array}
$$

The function *deleteMin* deletes one occurrence of the smallest element of a nonempty list; its definition is left as an exercise.

Another way to specify *Bag* α is to introduce two *hidden* constructors, *empty* and *insert*, and define the other operations in terms of them. In this case, the axioms are

$$
\begin{aligned}
insert\ x\ (insert\ y\ xb) &= insert\ y\ (insert\ x\ xb) \\
mkBag &= foldr\ insert\ empty \\
union\ xb\ empty &= xb \\
union\ xb\ (insert\ y\ yb) &= insert\ y\ (union\ xb\ yb) \\
minBag\ (insert\ x\ empty) &= x \\
minBag\ (insert\ x\ (insert\ y\ xb)) &= x\ \mathbf{min}\ minBag\ (insert\ y\ xb)
\end{aligned}
$$

The axioms for *delMin* are left as an exercise. The hidden functions are not provided as operations on bags, but serve only to aid the specification. The first equation for *insert* says that it does not matter in which order two elements are added to a bag; unlike the corresponding operation for sets, adding the same element twice to a bag is different from adding it once.

The two operations *empty* and *insert* might well have been provided as primitive operations on bags. In fact, together with *minBag* and *delMin*, they constitute a useful datatype known as a *priority queue*. Elements joining a priority queue possess a certain priority rating. Queue elements are processed in order of priority. Thus, *minBag* replaces *front* and *delMin* replaces *back*.

It is easy to implement bags by nondecreasing lists, rather like we did for sets in the previous section. This time, the union operation is exactly like *merge* since duplicates are not removed. The *mkBag* operation is implemented by *sort*. Under this representation, the running times for the various operations in the worst case are as follows:

$$
\begin{aligned}
mkBag\ xs \quad &takes \quad \Theta(n\log n)\ steps \\
isEmpty\ xb \quad &takes \quad \Theta(1)\ steps \\
union\ xb\ yb \quad &takes \quad \Theta(m+n)\ steps \\
minBag\ xb \quad &takes \quad \Theta(1)\ steps \\
delMin\ xb \quad &takes \quad \Theta(1)\ steps
\end{aligned}
$$

In the first line, $n = length\ xs$, and in the third line, m and n are the sizes of the two bags xb and yb.

In the remainder of the section we are going to implement the bag operations so that they will have the following time complexities in the worst case:

$$
\begin{aligned}
mkBag\ xs \quad &takes \quad \Theta(n)\ steps \\
isEmpty\ xb \quad &takes \quad \Theta(1)\ steps \\
union\ xb\ yb \quad &takes \quad \Theta(\log m + \log n)\ steps \\
minBag\ xb \quad &takes \quad \Theta(1)\ steps \\
delMin\ xb \quad &takes \quad \Theta(\log n)\ steps
\end{aligned}
$$

The time for *mkBag* drops by a logarithmic factor, while the time for *delMin* increases by a logarithmic factor. The big payoff, though, is with *union* whose running time is decreased from linear to logarithmic.

8.4.1 Implementation by heaps

The implementation of bags is by leftist size-augmented binary heap trees. Binary heap trees were defined in Section 6.3, and the size-augmented version is declared by

> **data** *Htree* α = *Null* | *Fork Int* α (*Htree* α) (*Htree* α)

A *leftist* tree has the property that the size of each left subtree is at least as large as the size of the corresponding right subtree. We will construct such trees with the help of a function *fork*, defined by

> *fork*   :: $\alpha \rightarrow$ *Htree* $\alpha \rightarrow$ *Htree* α
> *fork x yt zt* = **if** $m < n$ **then** *Fork p x zt yt* **else** *Fork p x yt zt*
> $\qquad\qquad\qquad$ **where** m = *size yt*
> $\qquad\qquad\qquad\qquad\quad$ n = *size zt*
> $\qquad\qquad\qquad\qquad\quad$ p = $m + n + 1$

> *size*   :: *Htree* $\alpha \rightarrow$ *Int*
> *size Null*   = 0
> *size* (*Fork n x yt zt*) = n

The function *fork* takes a label and two heaps and builds a *Fork* by installing the necessary size information and swapping the order of the two heaps if necessary to ensure that the left one is the larger of the two. It is left as an exercise to define the functions *abstr* and *valid* that formalise the representation of bags by leftist heaps.

Leaving aside *mkBag* for the moment, the other heap operations are implemented as follows:

> *isEmpty*   :: *Htree* $\alpha \rightarrow$ *Bool*
> *isEmpty Null*   = *True*
> *isEmpty* (*Fork n x yt zt*) = *False*

> *minBag*   :: *Htree* $\alpha \rightarrow \alpha$
> *minBag* (*Fork n x yt zt*)   = x

$$delMin \qquad\qquad\qquad :: \quad Htree\ \alpha \rightarrow Htree\ \alpha$$
$$delMin\ (Fork\ n\ x\ yt\ zt) \quad = \quad union\ yt\ zt$$

$$union \qquad\qquad\qquad\qquad :: \quad Htree\ \alpha \rightarrow Htree\ \alpha \rightarrow Htree\ \alpha$$
$$union\ Null\ yt \qquad\qquad\quad = \quad yt$$
$$union\ (Fork\ m\ u\ vt\ wt)\ Null \quad = \quad Fork\ m\ u\ vt\ wt$$

$$union\ (Fork\ m\ u\ vt\ wt)\ (Fork\ n\ x\ yt\ zt)$$
$$\left|\begin{array}{lll} u \le x & = & fork\ u\ vt\ (union\ wt\ (Fork\ n\ x\ yt\ zt)) \\ x < u & = & fork\ x\ yt\ (union\ (Fork\ m\ u\ vt\ wt)\ zt) \end{array}\right.$$

The *union* operation is implemented by merging two heaps along their *right spines*; this is the path in the heap from the topmost node to the rightmost *Null*. The cost of evaluating *union* is clearly proportional to the sum of the lengths of the right spines of the two heaps, so the next task is to estimate this quantity. Define *lrs* (length of right spine) by

$$lrs \qquad\qquad\qquad\quad :: \quad Htree\ \alpha \rightarrow Int$$
$$lrs\ Null \qquad\qquad\quad = \quad 0$$
$$lrs\ (Fork\ n\ x\ yt\ zt) \quad = \quad 1 + lrs\ zt$$

The claim is that if xt is a leftist tree of size n, then $lrs\ xt \le \lfloor \log(n+1) \rfloor$.

Proof. The proof is by induction on xt. The base case is immediate. For the induction step, suppose $xt = Fork\ n\ x\ yt\ zt$, where $size\ yt = p$ and $size\ zt = q$ and $p \ge q$. We can now argue:

$$lrs\ (Fork\ n\ x\ yt\ zt)$$
$$= \quad \{\text{definition of } lrs\}$$
$$1 + lrs\ zt$$
$$= \quad \{\text{induction hypothesis}\}$$
$$1 + \lfloor \log(q+1) \rfloor$$
$$= \quad \{\text{arithmetic}\}$$
$$\lfloor \log(2q+2) \rfloor$$
$$\le \quad \{\text{since } n = p + q + 1 \ge 2q + 1\}$$
$$\lfloor \log(n+1) \rfloor$$

$\square$

It follows from this result that the function *union* has the required time complexity. Since *delMin* involves a single call of *union*, this function too has the required time complexity.

It remains to implement *mkBag*. We use the tupling technique from Section 7.4:

$$
\begin{array}{lcl}
mkBag & :: & [\alpha] \rightarrow Htree\ \alpha \\
mkBag\ xs & = & fst\ (mkTwo\ (length\ xs)\ xs)
\end{array}
$$

$$
\begin{array}{l}
mkTwo :: Int \rightarrow [\alpha] \rightarrow (Htree\ \alpha, [\alpha]) \\
mkTwo\ n\ xs
\end{array}
$$

$$
\begin{array}{lll}
\quad\left|\begin{array}{lll}
(n == 0) & = & (Null, xs) \\
(n == 1) & = & (fork\ (head\ xs)\ Null\ Null, tail\ xs) \\
otherwise & = & (union\ xt\ yt, zs)
\end{array}\right. \\
\quad\quad\textbf{where}\ (xt, ys) & = & mkTwo\ m\ xs \\
\quad\quad\quad\quad\ (yt, zs) & = & mkTwo\ (n - m)\ ys \\
\quad\quad\quad\quad\ m & = & n\ \textbf{div}\ 2
\end{array}
$$

As we have seen in Section 7.4, this implementation of *mkBag* takes linear time in the length of the list.

Exercises

8.4.1 Build heaps for the letters in HELLO and WORLD and draw the heap of their union.

8.4.2 Define *deleteMin* :: $(Ord\ \alpha) \rightarrow [\alpha] \rightarrow [\alpha]$.

8.4.3 Give the axioms for *delMin* in terms of *insert* and *empty*.

8.4.4 What is the advantage of providing an operation *mkBag* when it can easily be defined as *foldr insert empty*?

8.4.5 Install *Bag* α as an abstract type by giving an appropriate module declaration.

8.4.6 Why make $n == 1$ a special case in the definition of *mkBag*?

8.4.7 Write a function *sortBag* :: $(Ord\ \alpha) \Rightarrow Bag\ \alpha \rightarrow [\alpha]$. This function should use only the specified operations on bags.

8.5 Flexible arrays

We have seen how trees of various kinds can be used to implement sets and bags efficiently, now we will see how they can be used to implement a datatype called *flexible arrays*. The type *Flex α* has the following operations:

$$
\begin{array}{lcl}
empty & :: & Flex\ \alpha \\
isEmpty & :: & Flex\ \alpha \rightarrow Bool \\
access & :: & Flex\ \alpha \rightarrow Int \rightarrow \alpha \\
update & :: & Flex\ \alpha \rightarrow Int \rightarrow \alpha \rightarrow Flex\ \alpha \\
hiext & :: & \alpha \rightarrow Flex\ \alpha \rightarrow Flex\ \alpha \\
hirem & :: & Flex\ \alpha \rightarrow Flex\ \alpha \\
loext & :: & \alpha \rightarrow Flex\ \alpha \rightarrow Flex\ \alpha \\
lorem & :: & Flex\ \alpha \rightarrow Flex\ \alpha
\end{array}
$$

Flexible arrays are a species of finite list in which one can access and change elements identified by their position in the list, but one can add and remove elements only from the two ends of the list. The names *hiext* and *hirem* are short for *high-extend* and *high-remove*. Similarly, *loext* and *lorem* are short for *low-extend* and *low-remove*. Array indexing begins at 0, so adding an element at the low end means that the positions of the previous elements increase by 1. Exercise 8.5.6 deals with a variant datatype in which two additional quantities, the lower and upper bounds, are included for a more general indexing scheme.

A formal specification of *Flex α* can be based on the three constructor functions *empty*, *hiext*, and *loext*. The first axiom states that

$$hiext\ x \cdot loext\ y \ = \ loext\ y \cdot hiext\ x$$

Although each array can be expressed in terms of the constructors, such expressions are not unique. However, by applying the axiom above, every array can be named by a unique expression in which all occurrences of *loext* precede any occurrences of *hiext*. The remaining operations are characterised in terms of the constructors. For example,

$$
\begin{array}{lcl}
hirem\ empty & = & error \\
hirem\ (hiext\ x\ xf) & = & xf \\
hirem\ (loext\ x\ empty) & = & empty \\
hirem\ (loext\ x\ (hiext\ y\ xf)) & = & loext\ x\ xf \\
hirem\ (loext\ x\ (loext\ y\ xf)) & = & loext\ x\ (hirem\ (loext\ y\ xf))
\end{array}
$$

$$
\begin{aligned}
access\ empty\ k &= error\ \text{``subscript out of range''} \\
access\ (loext\ x\ xf)\ 0 &= x \\
access\ (loext\ x\ xf)\ (k+1) &= access\ xf\ k
\end{aligned}
$$

$$
access\ (hiext\ x\ xf)\ k
$$

$$
\begin{aligned}
\left|\ \begin{array}{ll}
k < n &= access\ xf\ k \\
k == n &= x \\
k > n &= error
\end{array}\right. \\
\textbf{where } n = length\ xf
\end{aligned}
$$

The last axiom for *access* depends on a hidden function *length*, defined by

$$
\begin{aligned}
length &:: Flex\ \alpha \rightarrow Int \\
length\ empty &= 0 \\
length\ (hiext\ x\ xf) &= length\ xf + 1 \\
length\ (loext\ x\ xf) &= length\ xf + 1
\end{aligned}
$$

The definition of *lorem* is dual to that of *hirem*, and *update* is similar to *access*. The specifications of these functions, together with *isEmpty*, are left as exercises.

If flexible arrays are implemented as lists, the operations *access*, *update*, *hirem*, and *lorem* will take $\Theta(n)$ steps in the worst case, where n is the size of the array. The other operations take constant time. The amortised cost of the array operations is also $\Theta(n)$ steps. In the remainder of the section we will describe a simple implementation, designed by V. Dielissen and A. Kaldewaij, which guarantees that all operations can be performed in $O(\log n)$ steps.

8.5.1 Implementation

The implementation is to use *quasi-perfect* size-augmented binary trees. We will postpone explaining what a quasi-perfect tree is until we have described some of the basic operations. The type *Flex* α is declared by

$$
\textbf{data } Flex\ \alpha\ =\ Null\ \mid\ Leaf\ \alpha\ \mid\ Fork\ Int\ (Flex\ \alpha)\ (Flex\ \alpha)
$$

The type *Flex* α is a variant of binary trees, with an added constructor *Null* and size information in the fork nodes.

The datatype invariant on elements of *Flex* α consists of three conditions. The first condition is that we will only build a tree *Fork n xt yt* in which n is the sum of the sizes of *xt* and *yt*. That means we can define *size* by

$$
\begin{array}{lll}
size & :: & Flex\ \alpha \to Int \\
size\ Null & = & 0 \\
size\ (Leaf\ x) & = & 1 \\
size\ (Fork\ n\ xt\ yt) & = & n
\end{array}
$$

The second constraint on *Flex α* is that we will only build *leaf* trees. A leaf tree is either the empty tree *Null* or a nonempty tree in which the empty tree does not occur as a subtree. This condition is formalised by

$$
\begin{array}{lll}
isLeafTree & :: & Flex\ \alpha \to Bool \\
isLeafTree\ xt & = & isEmpty\ xt \lor isLeafy\ xt
\end{array}
$$

where

$$
\begin{array}{lll}
isLeafy\ Null & = & False \\
isLeafy\ (Leaf\ x) & = & True \\
isLeafy\ (Fork\ n\ xt\ yt) & = & isLeafy\ xt \land isLeafy\ yt
\end{array}
$$

$$
\begin{array}{lll}
isEmpty & :: & Flex\ \alpha \to Bool \\
isEmpty\ Null & = & True \\
isEmpty\ (Leaf\ x) & = & False \\
isEmpty\ (Fork\ n\ xt\ yt) & = & False
\end{array}
$$

In conformity with Section 6.1 we will define the height of a leaf tree by

$$
\begin{array}{lll}
height & :: & Flex\ \alpha \to Int \\
height\ Null & = & 0 \\
height\ (Leaf\ x) & = & 0 \\
height\ (Fork\ n\ xt\ yt) & = & 1 + (height\ xt\ \mathbf{max}\ height\ yt)
\end{array}
$$

A leaf tree of size *n* has height at least $\lceil \log n \rceil$. The third constraint, considered below, is that we will only build quasi-perfect trees.

The static array operations – those that do not extend or contract the array – are implemented as in Section 6.1:

$$
\begin{array}{lll}
empty & :: & Flex\ \alpha \\
empty & = & Null
\end{array}
$$

$access :: Flex \; \alpha \rightarrow Int \rightarrow \alpha$
$access \; (Leaf \; x) \; 0 = x$
$access \; (Fork \; n \; xt \; yt) \; k$
$\quad = \quad$ if $k < m$ then $access \; xt \; k$ else $access \; yt \; (k - m)$
$\qquad$ where $m = size \; xt$

$update :: Flex \; \alpha \rightarrow Int \rightarrow \alpha \rightarrow Flex \; \alpha$
$update \; (Leaf \; y) \; 0 \; x = Leaf \; x$
$update \; (Fork \; n \; xt \; yt) \; k \; x$

$$\begin{array}{lll} k < m & = & Fork \; n \; (update \; xt \; k \; x) \; yt \\ otherwise & = & Fork \; n \; xt \; (update \; yt \; k \; x) \end{array}$$

$\qquad$ where $m = size \; xt$

The operations $access$ and $update$ take $O(h)$ steps, where h is the height of the binary tree.

8.5.2 Adding one-sided flexibility

Forget for a moment the operations $loext$ and $lorem$, and suppose that arrays can be extended and contracted only at the high end. The basic strategy is to implement $hiext$ and $hirem$ in such a way that the resulting tree has a height that is logarithmic in its size. For this reason, the following straightforward implementation of $hiext$ is rejected:

$$\begin{array}{lll} hiext & :: & \alpha \rightarrow Flex \; \alpha \rightarrow Flex \; \alpha \\ hiext \; x \; Null & = & Leaf \; x \\ hiext \; x \; (Leaf \; y) & = & Fork \; 2 \; (Leaf \; y) \; (Leaf \; x) \\ hiext \; x \; (Fork \; n \; xt \; yt) & = & Fork \; (n + 1) \; (Fork \; n \; xt \; yt) \; (Leaf \; x) \end{array}$$

This implementation of $hiext$ always increases the height of the tree by 1; consequently, building a tree of size n by starting with the empty tree and applying $hiext$ to n values will result in a tree of height n.

Instead, the aim is to increase the height of the tree only when it is absolutely necessary. In particular, adding an element to a perfect tree – a tree with 2^k leaves all at the same depth – will inevitably increase the height of the tree. For a perfect tree xt of size 2^k, we can define

$$hiext \; x \; xt \quad = \quad Fork \; (2^k + 1) \; xt \; (Leaf \; x)$$

The idea can be extended. Say a tree is *left-perfect* if the left subtree of every node is perfect. Also, recall from the previous section that a *leftist* tree is one in which the size of the left subtree of each node is at least as large as the size of the corresponding right subtree. There is exactly one leftist left-perfect tree (an *llp-tree* for short) of any given size; moreover, it has the minimum possible height. The proof is an induction argument. In the inductive case, suppose xt is a llp-tree of size n, where $n \geq 2$. The left subtree of xt is perfect and has size 2^k for some k, and the right subtree has size $m > 0$, where

$$m \leq 2^k \quad \text{and} \quad n = 2^k + m$$

Hence $2^k < n \leq 2^{k+1}$. The left subtree of xt therefore has a size that is the largest power of 2 strictly smaller than n. Since the left and right subtrees of xt are also llp-trees, the shape of xt is determined uniquely. Moreover, its height is $k + 1 = \lceil \log n \rceil$, which is the minimum possible.

Another immediate fact is that if xt is an llp-tree, then xt is perfect if and only if its left and right subtrees have the same size. Using this result, we can implement *hiext* on llp-trees by

$$
\begin{aligned}
hiext\ x\ Null \quad &= \quad Leaf\ x \\
hiext\ x\ (Leaf\ y) \quad &= \quad Fork\ 2\ (Leaf\ y)\ (Leaf\ x)
\end{aligned}
$$

$$
\begin{aligned}
&hiext\ x\ (Fork\ n\ xt\ yt) \\
&\quad \left|\
\begin{aligned}
size\ xt &\mathrel{==} size\ yt \quad &= \quad Fork\ (n + 1)\ (Fork\ n\ xt\ yt)\ (Leaf\ x) \\
otherwise\ & &= \quad Fork\ (n + 1)\ xt\ (hiext\ x\ yt)
\end{aligned}
\right.
\end{aligned}
$$

The function *hiext* returns a llp-tree whenever its second argument is a llp-tree. The operation *hirem* is implemented as follows:

$$
\begin{aligned}
hirem \qquad\qquad\qquad &:: \quad Flex\ \alpha \rightarrow Flex\ \alpha \\
hirem\ (Leaf\ x) \qquad &= \quad Null \\
hirem\ (Fork\ (n + 1)\ xt\ yt) \quad &= \quad fork\ n\ xt\ (hirem\ yt)
\end{aligned}
$$

$$
\begin{aligned}
&fork :: Int \rightarrow Flex\ \alpha \rightarrow Flex\ \alpha \rightarrow Flex\ \alpha \\
&fork\ n\ xt\ yt \\
&\quad \left|\
\begin{aligned}
isEmpty\ xt &\quad = \quad yt \\
isEmpty\ yt &\quad = \quad xt \\
otherwise &\quad = \quad Fork\ n\ xt\ yt
\end{aligned}
\right.
\end{aligned}
$$

8.5.3 Adding full flexibility

The operations *loext* and *lorem* are dual to *hiext* and *hirem* and can be implemented by *rightist right-perfect* trees (rrp-trees). The problem is how to combine the two kinds of tree. One solution is not to combine them, and to represent a flexible array by a pair of trees, the left component representing the lower half of the array, and the right component the upper. This is a perfectly adequate solution, except that it leads to a case analysis in *hirem* and *lorem* when one of the component trees is empty.

Dielissen and Kaldewaij's solution is more subtle and more beautiful: allow the four properties to co-exist in the one tree. By definition, a *quasi-perfect* tree is one in which all left subtrees are rightist and right-perfect, and all right subtrees are leftist and left-perfect. Perfect trees are quasi-perfect and the shape of a quasi-perfect tree *Fork n xt yt* is completely determined by the sizes of *xt* and *yt*. The maximum possible height *h* of a quasi-perfect tree of size $n > 0$ is given by

$$h \;=\; 1 + \mathbf{max}_{0 \le m < n} \left(\lceil \log m \rceil \; \mathbf{max} \; \lceil \log(n - m) \rceil \right)$$

More simply, $h = 1 + \lceil \log n \rceil$, one more than the minimum possible.

A quasi-perfect tree is neither an llp-tree nor an rrp-tree: the left subtree of any right subtree of the tree is perfect but the left subtree of the tree itself is not necessarily perfect. Accordingly, we have to modify the definition of *hiext* slightly. Dual remarks apply to *loext* and the resulting programs take the form

$$
\begin{aligned}
hiext\ x\ Null \quad &=\quad Leaf\ x \\
hiext\ x\ (Leaf\ y) \quad &=\quad Fork\ 2\ (Leaf\ y)\ (Leaf\ x) \\
hiext\ x\ (Fork\ n\ xt\ yt) \quad &=\quad Fork\ (n + 1)\ xt\ (hi\ x\ yt)
\end{aligned}
$$

$$
\begin{aligned}
hi &:: \alpha \rightarrow Flex\ \alpha \rightarrow Flex\ \alpha \\
hi\ x\ (Leaf\ y) &= Fork\ 2\ (Leaf\ y)\ (Leaf\ x) \\
hi\ x\ (Fork\ n\ xt\ yt) & \\
\end{aligned}
$$

$$
\begin{array}{ll}
\quad size\ xt \mathbin{==} size\ yt \quad &=\quad Fork\ (n + 1)\ (Fork\ n\ xt\ yt)\ (Leaf\ x) \\
\quad otherwise \quad &=\quad Fork\ (n + 1)\ xt\ (hiext\ x\ yt)
\end{array}
$$

The definition of *loext* is dual:

$$
\begin{aligned}
loext\ x\ Null \quad &=\quad Leaf\ x \\
loext\ x\ (Leaf\ y) \quad &=\quad Fork\ 2\ (Leaf\ x)\ (Leaf\ y) \\
loext\ x\ (Fork\ n\ xt\ yt) \quad &=\quad Fork\ (n + 1)\ (lo\ x\ xt)\ yt
\end{aligned}
$$

$$
\begin{aligned}
lo &:: \alpha \rightarrow Flex\ \alpha \rightarrow Flex\ \alpha \\
lo\ x\ (Leaf\ y) &= Fork\ 2\ (Leaf\ x)\ (Leaf\ y) \\
lo\ x\ (Fork\ n\ xt\ yt) & \\
\end{aligned}
$$

$$
\begin{array}{ll}
\quad size\ xt \mathbin{==} size\ yt \quad &=\quad Fork\ (n + 1)\ (Leaf\ x)\ (Fork\ n\ xt\ yt) \\
\quad otherwise \quad &=\quad Fork\ (n + 1)\ (lo\ x\ xt)\ yt
\end{array}
$$

The definition of *hirem* is the same as before, and the definition of *lorem* is left as an exercise.

Exercises

8.5.1 Write down the possible quasi-perfect trees of size 6.

8.5.2 Give the functions *abstr* and *valid* for the representation of flexible arrays by quasi-perfect binary trees.

8.5.3 Give the implementation of *lorem*.

8.5.4 Flexible arrays can be used to represent queues. Explain how, and give the time complexities of the various queue operations.

8.5.5 Suppose that flexible arrays are augmented with two additional operations

$$minFlex, maxFlex \quad :: \quad (Ord\ \alpha) \Rightarrow Flex\ \alpha \rightarrow \alpha$$

The operation *minFlex* returns the minimum element in a nonempty array. Show how, by augmenting binary trees with additional information, these operations can be implemented to run in constant time.

8.5.6 A bounded flexible array is a flexible array with two integer values, *lower* and *upper*, denoting the lower and upper bounds of the index positions. The lowest element of the array *xs* is *xs* !! *lower* and the highest element is *xs* !! (*upper* − 1). Show how bounded flexible arrays can be implemented with quasi-perfect trees.

8.6 Queues

To complete a quartet of abstract datatypes, let us revisit the type *Queue* α from Section 8.1. Recall that the implementation in terms of pairs of lists was

$$
\begin{array}{lcl}
empty & = & ([\,],[\,]) \\
isEmpty\ (xs,ys) & = & null\ xs \\
join\ x\ (ys,zs) & = & mkValid\ (ys,x:zs) \\
front\ (x:xs,ys) & = & x \\
back\ (x:xs,ys) & = & mkValid\ (xs,ys)
\end{array}
$$

$$mkValid\ (xs,ys) \quad = \quad \textbf{if } null\ xs \textbf{ then } (reverse\ ys,[\,]) \textbf{ else } (xs,ys)$$

The functions *abstr* and *valid*, which formalise the representation of queues by pairs of lists, were defined by

$$abstr\ (xs, ys) \quad = \quad (foldr\ join\ empty \cdot reverse)\ (xs \mathbin{+\!\!+} reverse\ ys)$$
$$valid\ (xs, ys) \quad = \quad not\ (null\ xs) \vee null\ ys$$

Recall also that the amortised cost of the queue operations is $O(1)$ steps, while the worst-case cost is $\Theta(n)$ steps on a queue of size n.

For this representation of queues, the worst-case cost applies under any interactive scenario. If the interaction is driven eagerly, then a *back* command can take $\Theta(n)$ steps because a list of length n has to be reversed. If the interaction is driven lazily, then executing a *front* command after a *back* can take $\Theta(n)$ steps because that is the time required to produce the first element of a reversed list.

The aim of this section is to show that we can do better. Firstly, there is an implementation of queues which ensures that the worst-case cost can be reduced to $\Theta(\log n)$ steps, provided the interaction is driven at a certain speed. Secondly, there is an even better implementation that brings the worst-case cost down to $O(1)$ steps. Both implementations are due to Chris Okasaki.

8.6.1 First implementation

The first implementation represents a queue by four quantities, a pair of lists as before, and their lengths. The function *abstr* is defined by

$$abstr \qquad\qquad :: \quad (Int, Int, [\alpha], [\alpha]) \rightarrow Queue\ \alpha$$
$$abstr\ (m, n, xs, ys) \quad = \quad foldr\ join\ empty\ (ys \mathbin{+\!\!+} reverse\ xs)$$

The function *valid* is defined by

$$valid \qquad\qquad :: \quad (Int, Int, [\alpha], [\alpha]) \rightarrow Bool$$
$$valid\ (m, n, xs, ys) \quad = \quad (m \geq n) \wedge m = length\ xs \wedge n = length\ ys$$

The datatype invariant is stronger than before: previously we required only that if *xs* is empty, then *ys* is empty too; now we require that the length of *xs* is at least as great as the length of *ys*.

Except for the definition of *mkValid*, the implementation is virtually the same as before:

$$
\begin{aligned}
empty &= (0, 0, [\,], [\,]) \\
isEmpty\ (m, n, xs, ys) &= (m == 0) \\
join\ x\ (m, n, xs, ys) &= mkValid\ (m, n + 1, xs, x : ys) \\
front\ (m, n, x : xs, ys) &= x \\
back\ (m + 1, n, x : xs, ys) &= mkValid\ (m, n, xs, ys)
\end{aligned}
$$

Here is part of the definition of *mkValid*:

> *mkValid* (*m, n, xs, ys*)
> | $m \geq n$ = (*m, n, xs, ys*)
> | $m + 1 == n$ = ...

To fill in the dots, we have to perform a *rotation*. This operation takes

$$(m, n, xs, ys) \quad \text{into} \quad (m + n, 0, xs \mathbin{+\!\!+} reverse\ ys, [\ ])$$

The trick behind the faster implementation is to parcel out the computation of $xs \mathbin{+\!\!+} reverse\ ys$ among the other operations, ensuring that each piece produces exactly one element of the result. To perform the trick, recall that one efficient implementation of *reverse* is to use an accumulating parameter:

> *reverse xs* = *revcat xs* [ ]
> *revcat* [ ] *ys* = *ys*
> *revcat* (*x : xs*) *ys* = *revcat xs* (*x : ys*)

The same idea is used in the computation of $xs \mathbin{+\!\!+} reverse\ ys$. Define the function *rot* (short for rotate) by

> *rot* :: $[\alpha] \to [\alpha] \to [\alpha] \to [\alpha]$
> *rot xs ys zs* = *xs* $\mathbin{+\!\!+}$ *revcat ys zs*

Clearly, $xs \mathbin{+\!\!+} reverse\ ys = rot\ xs\ ys\ [\ ]$. This expression will be computed only in the case *length xs* + 1 = *length ys*, so we can implement *rot* by

> *rot* [ ] [*y*] *zs* = *y : zs*
> *rot* (*x : xs*) (*y : ys*) *zs* = *x : rot xs ys* (*y : zs*)

Note that each step in the evaluation of *rot* produces one new element of the result. Note also that the invariant *length xs* + 1 = *length ys* is maintained in the subsequent call of *rot*.

The full definition of *mkValid* is

> *mkValid* (*m, n, xs, ys*)
> | $m \geq n$ = (*m, n, xs, ys*)
> | $m + 1 == n$ = (*m + n*, 0, *rot xs ys* [ ], [ ])

The interaction is driven at a speed between fully eager and fully lazy. In processing each join or back command, the function *mkValid* is reduced, but only to head-normal form, that is, a quadruple. This reduction takes one evaluation step. After processing any command, the queue is always in the form of a quadruple, so processing an *isEmpty* or *join* command takes $O(1)$ steps.

It remains to estimate the cost of *front* and *back*. Both *front* and *back* are defined by pattern matching and require that the third component of the quadruple be reduced to the form $x : xs$. In general, the third component xs_0 of the quadruple (m, n, xs_0, ys_0) takes the form

$$
\begin{aligned}
xs_0 &= rot\ xs_1\ ys_1\ zs_1 \\
xs_1 &= rot\ xs_2\ ys_2\ zs_2 \\
&\vdots \\
xs_{n-1} &= rot\ xs_n\ ys_n\ zs_n
\end{aligned}
$$

for some $n \geq 0$, where the lists xs_n and ys_k $(0 \leq k \leq n)$ and zs_k $(1 \leq k \leq n)$ are fully evaluated. Moreover, for $1 \leq k \leq n$, we have

$$length\ xs_k + 1 = length\ ys_k$$

by the invariant on *rot*. Also, from the definition of *rot* we have, for $0 \leq k < n$, that

$$length\ xs_{k+1} + length\ ys_{k+1} \leq length\ xs_k$$

Hence $length\ xs_{k+1} < (length\ xs_k)/2$ for $0 \leq k < n$.

It follows that reducing xs_0 to the form $x : xs$ involves at most a logarithmic number of reductions of *rot* to the same form. But each *rot* can be reduced to this form in one step. Evaluation of *front* and *back* therefore takes $O(\log n)$ steps on a queue of size n.

To understand what is going on, it may be helpful to consider evaluation of the commands

$$join\ 1;\ join\ 2;\ \ldots;\ join\ 14$$

Here are the states of the queue after processing these commands on an initially empty queue:

$$(0, 0, [\ ], [\ ])$$
$$\rightarrow \quad \{\text{after processing } join\ 1\}$$
$$(1, 0, rot\ [\ ]\ [1]\ [\ ], [\ ])$$
$$\rightarrow \quad \{\text{after processing } join\ 2\}$$
$$(1, 1, rot\ [\ ]\ [1]\ [\ ], [2])$$
$$\rightarrow \quad \{\text{after processing } join\ 3\}$$
$$(3, 0, rot\ (rot\ [\ ]\ [1]\ [\ ])\ [2, 3]\ [\ ], [\ ])$$

$\rightarrow$ {after processing *join* 4, *join* 5 and *join* 6}

$(3, 3, rot \ (rot \ [\ ] \ [1] \ [\ ]) \ [2, 3] \ [\ ], [4, 5, 6])$

$\rightarrow$ {after processing *join* 7}

$(7, 0, rot \ (rot \ (rot \ [\ ] \ [1] \ [\ ]) \ [2, 3] \ [\ ]) \ [4, 5, 6, 7] \ [\ ], [\ ])$

The pattern should now be clear: the next 7 joins result in

$(7, 7, rot \ (rot \ (rot \ [\ ] \ [1] \ [\ ]) \ [2, 3] \ [\ ]) \ [4, 5, 6, 7] \ [\ ], [8, \dots, 14])$

It is only when *join* 15 is applied that another rotation is invoked. Applying a *back* command to the queue above involves three reductions of *rot*.

8.6.2 Second implementation

The game now is to ensure that no queue operation takes more than $O(1)$ steps in the worst case. We can do this by ensuring that *rot xs ys zs* is applied only to evaluated lists *xs*; that is, *xs* is not itself of the form *rot* applied to some arguments. This is achieved by forcing one step of the evaluation of *xs* during each evaluation of the other operations. Evaluation is forced by maintaining an extra list in the representation; on the other hand, it is no longer necessary to maintain the lengths of the lists

The representation of *queues* is by triples of lists. The function *abstr* is defined by

$$
\begin{aligned}
abstr &\quad :: \quad ([\alpha], [\alpha], [\alpha]) \rightarrow Queue \ \alpha \\
abstr \ (xs, ys, zs) &\quad = \quad (foldr \ join \ empty \cdot reverse) \ (xs \ +\!\!+ \ reverse \ ys)
\end{aligned}
$$

The function *valid* is defined by

$$
\begin{aligned}
valid &\quad :: \quad ([\alpha], [\alpha], [\alpha]) \rightarrow Bool \\
valid \ (xs, ys, zs) &\quad = \quad length \ xs = length \ ys + length \ zs \ \wedge \ isTail \ xs \ zs
\end{aligned}
$$

The test *isTail xs zs* returns *True* if *zs* is a tail segment of *xs*. In fact, the definition of *valid* does not quite express the whole truth, because the representation of *xs* and *zs* is *shared* in the graph-reduction model of evaluation; *zs* is not a distinct list, but points to the unevaluated portion of *xs*. If this portion is not empty, then reducing *zs* to head-normal form results automatically in generating one additional element of *xs*.

Here are the implemented operations:

$$empty \qquad\qquad = \quad ([\,],[\,],[\,])$$
$$isEmpty\ (xs, ys, zs) \quad = \quad null\ xs$$
$$join\ x\ (xs, ys, zs) \quad = \quad mkValid\ (xs, x : ys, zs)$$
$$front\ (x : xs, ys, zs) \quad = \quad x$$
$$back\ (x : xs, ys, zs) \quad = \quad mkValid\ (xs, ys, zs)$$

$$mkValid\ (xs, ys, [\,]) \qquad = \quad (zs, [\,], zs)$$
$$\textbf{where}\ zs = rot\ xs\ ys\ [\,]$$
$$mkValid\ (xs, ys, z : zs) \quad = \quad (xs, ys, zs)$$

The sharing of the first and third components is introduced by the **where** clause in the first equation for *mkValid*. Evaluating the second equation for *mkValid* results in one more evaluation of the first component.

The interaction is driven at the same speed as before. Evaluating the test *isEmpty* (xs, ys, zs) involves reducing xs to head-normal form. This may involve a call of *rot*, but *rot* reduces to head-normal form in one reduction step, so *isEmpty* takes $O(1)$ steps. Evaluating *join* involves reducing *mkValid* $(xs, x : ys, zs)$ to head-normal form. Reducing zs to head-normal form takes $O(1)$ steps, so *join* takes $O(1)$ steps. As a side-effect, one more element of xs is computed whenever zs reduces to a nonempty list. Evaluating *front* $(x : xs, ys, zs)$ takes $O(1)$ steps because the first component is already evaluated. Finally, *back* takes $O(1)$ steps for the same reason that *join* does.

Exercises

8.6.1 Show the final state of the queue after executing

$$join\ 1;\ \ldots;\ join\ 14;\ back;\ front$$

8.6.2 What alternative representation of queues ensures a worst-case running time of $\Theta(\log n)$ for any operation on a queue of size n?

8.6.3 By definition a *deque* is a double-ended queue in which one can add and remove elements from either end. The representation of queues by pairs of lists can be extended to deal with deques. How can this be done to ensure an amortised cost of $O(1)$ steps per deque operation?

8.7 Chapter notes

The algebraic specification of abstract datatypes is described in Guttag and Horning (1978). Two useful source texts on datatypes and their specifications are Martin (1986) and Harrison (1989). Amortised complexity is described in Cormen et al. (1990) and, in a functional setting, in Schoenmakers (1992) and Okasaki (1996).

The original presentation of AVL trees can be found in Adelson-Velski and Landis (1962); see also Knuth (1973b). There are many other balanced tree schemes; for example, Cormen et al. (1990) discusses *red-black trees*, and Andersson (1993) a simple scheme based on two operations, *skew* and *split*.

The simple implementation of flexible arrays is described in Dielissen and Kaldewaij (1995); see also Hoogerwoord (1991). The fast queue implementations can be found in Okasaki (1995). Okasaki's thesis (1996) contains a wealth of additional material on purely functional data structures.

Chapter 9

Infinite lists

Although infinite lists and trees have been introduced alongside their finite
counterparts, the emphasis so far has mainly been on computing with finite
structures. The aim of this chapter is to explain in a little more detail than
before exactly what an infinite list is, and how an infinite list can be represented by a *cyclic* structure in a lazy functional language. We will describe a
new technique for proving properties of infinite lists, and discuss a number of
applications in which infinite and cyclic lists can be used to good effect. In particular, infinite lists can serve to model sequences of events ordered in time, so
they provide one suitable framework in which to study *interactive* processes.

9.1 Review

We begin by reviewing some material on infinite lists. Just as the finite list of
integers from m to n is denoted by $[m .. n]$, the infinite list of all integers from
m upwards is denoted by $[m ..]$. Thus, in a session one might have

? $[1 ..]$
$[1, 2, 3, 4, 5, 6, 7, 8, 9, 10, 11, 12, 13, 14, 15, 16, \{Interrupted!\}$

It would take forever to print this list in full, so we interrupt it.

Infinite lists can be used just like any other lists in a program. A function
can take an infinite list as an argument or return an infinite list as a result. For
example, the following statements about infinite lists are all true:

$$\textit{take}\, n\, [1 ..] \quad = \quad [1 .. n]$$
$$[m ..]\, !!\, n \quad = \quad m + n$$
$$\textit{map fact}\, [0 ..] \quad = \quad \textit{scanl}\, (\times)\, 1\, [1 ..]$$

It is also possible to use infinite lists in list comprehensions. For example, the expression

$$[square\ x \mid x \leftarrow [1..\ ],\ odd\ x]$$

denotes the list of all odd squares. It is even possible to have an infinite list of infinite lists. For example, in Section 6.6 we made use of the infinite list of infinite lists of powers of each prime:

$$prps \quad :: \quad [[Integer]]$$
$$prps \quad = \quad map\ powers\ primes$$

It is important *not* to assume that infinite lists in computing have the same kinds of properties as infinite sets do in conventional mathematics. For example, in set theory the expression

$$\{x^2 \mid x \in \{0, 1, 2, 3, \ldots\};\ x^2 < 10\}$$

denotes the finite set of all squares less than 10. However, if we type the corresponding list comprehension in a session then we get

? $[square\ x \mid x \leftarrow [0..\ ],\ square\ x < 10]$
$[0, 1, 4, 9$

What has happened here is that the computer determines the first three elements and then goes into an infinite loop searching for some element in the infinite list $[4, 5, 6, \ldots]$ whose square is less than 10. Although it is reasonable to expect a mathematician to recognise that there is no such value, it is not reasonable to expect the same degree of sophistication from a computer program. In other words, we do not suppose that a mechanical evaluator is capable of conducting proofs, however trivial they might be. This does not mean that the behaviour of the computer is unmathematical, only that set theory is not the right theory for describing computations. As we have seen, the value of the above expression is the *partial* list $0 : 1 : 4 : 9 : \bot$.

Incidentally, it is not difficult to rewrite the expression so that it does return a finite list of all squares less than 10. The list comprehension is equivalent to

$$filter\ (< 10)\ (map\ square\ [0..\ ])$$

and changing *filter* to *takeWhile* yields the desired result:

? $takeWhile\ (< 10)\ (map\ square\ [0..\ ])$
$[0, 1, 4, 9]$

The mathematician's knowledge that one can stop looking as soon as the first square greater than 10 is encountered is here encoded by the programmer's decision to use *takeWhile* to write the expression.

9.1.1 Induction

We saw in Chapter 4 how induction can be used to prove properties of infinite lists. Provided $P(xs)$ is an equation involving a list xs, we can show that $P(xs)$ holds for all infinite lists xs by establishing:

Case ($\bot$). That $P(\bot)$ holds.

Case ($x : xs$). That if $P(xs)$ holds, then $P(x : xs)$ also holds for every x.

Note carefully that there is a proviso in the statement of the induction principle, namely that $P(xs)$ should take the form of an equation. Without the proviso, the two cases above are sufficient only to prove that $P(xs)$ holds for all *partial* lists xs. With the proviso, we then get for free that $P(xs)$ holds for all infinite lists xs. In the following section we will explain the nature of the relationship between partial lists and infinite lists, and show why the proviso – or at least a generalisation of it – is necessary.

Exercises

9.1.1 Can every element of *prps* be printed by first flattening the list of lists with *concat*? If not, show how to define an infinite list that does return a list of all powers of all primes.

9.1.2 Does $map(\times 3)[0..] = iterate(+3)0$? What is the value of this expression when $(=)$ is replaced by $(==)$?

9.1.3 Give conditions under which *filter p xs* = *takeWhile p xs*.

9.1.4 The Sieve of Eratosthenes is a method for generating the list of all prime numbers. The idea is to start with the infinite list $2, 3, \ldots$ and then repeatedly apply the following process: (i) mark the first element p of the list as prime; and (ii) delete all multiples of p from the list. Step (ii) can be implemented by the function *sieve*, defined by

$$sieve\,(p : xs) \;\; = \;\; [x \mid x \leftarrow xs, x \bmod p \neq 0]$$

Using *iterate*, write down an expression for the list *primes* of all primes. Hence define expressions for returning the first 1000 primes, and all the primes less than 1000.

9.2 Infinite lists as limits

In mathematics, infinite objects are defined as *limits* of infinite sequences of approximations. For example, the irrational number

$$\pi \;=\; 3.14159265358979323846\cdots$$

can be defined as the limit of the infinite sequence of rational approximations

    3, 3.1, 3.14, 3.141, 3.1415, ...

The first element of the sequence, 3, is a fairly crude approximation to π. The next element, 3.1, is a little better; 3.14 is better still, and so on.

    Similarly, an infinite list can also be regarded as the limit of a sequence of approximations. For example, the infinite list [1 ..] is the limit of the infinite sequence of partial lists

    $\bot$, $1:\bot$, $1:2:\bot$, $1:2:3:\bot$, ...

Again, the sequence consists of better and better approximations to the intended limit. The first term, $\bot$, is the undefined element, and thus a very crude approximation: it tells us nothing about the limit. The next term, $1 : \bot$, is a slightly better approximation: it tells us that the limit is a list whose first element is 1, but says nothing about the rest of the list. The following term, $1 : 2 : \bot$, is a little better still, and so on. Each successively better approximation is derived by replacing $\bot$ with a more defined value, and thus gives more information about the limit.

    Here is another sequence of approximations whose limit is [1 ..]:

    $\bot$, $1:2:\bot$, $1:2:3:4:\bot$, $1:2:3:4:5:6:\bot$, ...

This sequence is a subsequence of the one above but it *converges* to the same limit.

    Here is a sequence of approximations that does *not* converge to a limit:

    $\bot$, $1:\bot$, $2:1:\bot$, $3:2:1:\bot$, ...

The problem with this sequence is that it gives conflicting information: the second term says that the limit begins with 1; however, the third term says the the limit begins with 2, and the fourth term says that it begins with 3, and so on. No approximation tells us anything about the intended limit and the sequence does not converge.

    It should not be thought that the limit of a sequence of lists is necessarily infinite. For example, the sequence

    $\bot$, $1:\bot$, [1], [1], ...

in which every element after the first two is [1], is a perfectly valid sequence with limit [1]. Similarly,

$$\bot, \quad 1:\bot, \quad 1:2:\bot, \quad 1:2:\bot, \quad \ldots$$

is a sequence with limit $1:2:\bot$. Finite and partial lists are limits of sequences possessing only a finite number of distinct elements.

9.2.1 Approximation ordering

The way to formalise the property that an infinite sequence of partial lists converges to a limit is to introduce the notion of an *approximation ordering* $\sqsubseteq$ on the elements of each type. The assertion $x \sqsubseteq y$ means that x is an approximation to y. The ordering $\sqsubseteq$ will be reflexive ($x \sqsubseteq x$), transitive ($x \sqsubseteq y$ and $y \sqsubseteq z$ implies $x \sqsubseteq z$), and anti-symmetric ($x \sqsubseteq y$ and $y \sqsubseteq x$ implies $x = y$). However, it is not the case that every pair of elements have to be comparable by $\sqsubseteq$. Thus $\sqsubseteq$ is what is known as a *partial* ordering. Note that $\sqsubseteq$ is a mathematical operator (like =), and not a Haskell operator returning boolean results.

We will now give a brief sketch of how $\sqsubseteq$ is defined for various types. The subject, called *Domain Theory*, is a large one and full details can be found in the references at the end of the chapter.

The approximation ordering for numbers, booleans, characters, and any other enumerated type, is defined by

$$x \sqsubseteq y \quad \equiv \quad (x = \bot) \lor (x = y)$$

The operator $\lor$ on the right should be read as a mathematical connective. The first clause says that $\bot$ is an approximation to everything. In other words, $\bot$ is the *bottom* element of the ordering. This explains why $\bot$ is pronounced 'bottom'. The value $\bot$ is the bottom element of $\sqsubseteq$ for every type. The above ordering is *flat*. With a flat ordering one either knows everything there is to know about a value, or one knows absolutely nothing.

The approximation ordering on the type (α, β) is defined by $\bot \sqsubseteq (x, y)$ and

$$(x, y) \sqsubseteq (x', y') \quad \equiv \quad (x \sqsubseteq x') \land (y \sqsubseteq y')$$

The occurrences of $\sqsubseteq$ on the right refer to the orderings on α and β, respectively. The ordering $\sqsubseteq$ on (α, β) is not flat, even when the component orderings on α and β are flat. For example, in $(Bool, Bool)$ we have the following chain of distinct elements:

$$\bot \sqsubseteq (\bot, \bot) \sqsubseteq (\bot, False) \sqsubseteq (True, False)$$

The ordering $\sqsubseteq$ on $[\alpha]$ is defined by $\bot \sqsubseteq xs$ and

$$[\,] \sqsubseteq xs \qquad\qquad \equiv \quad xs = [\,]$$
$$(x : xs) \sqsubseteq (y : ys) \quad\equiv\quad (x \sqsubseteq y) \wedge (xs \sqsubseteq ys)$$

These equations should be read as an inductive definition of a mathematical assertion, not as a Haskell definition. The second condition says that [ ] approximates only itself, and the third condition says that $(x : xs)$ is an approximation to $(y : ys)$ if and only if x is an approximation to y and xs is an approximation to ys. The first occurrence of $\sqsubseteq$ on the right-hand side refers to the approximation ordering on α.

As two examples, we have

$$[1, \bot, 3] \sqsubseteq [1, 2, 3] \quad \text{and} \quad 1 : 2 : \bot \sqsubseteq [1, 2, 3]$$

However, $1 : 2 : \bot$ and $[1, \bot, 3]$ are not related by $\sqsubseteq$.

The approximation ordering for each type α is assumed to have another property in addition to those described above: each *chain* of approximations $x_0 \sqsubseteq x_1 \sqsubseteq \ldots$ has to possess a limit which is also a member of α. The limit, which we denote by $\lim_{n \to \infty} x_n$, is defined by two conditions:

1. $x_n \sqsubseteq \lim_{n \to \infty} x_n$ for all n. This condition states that the limit is an *upper bound* on the sequence of approximations.

2. If $x_n \sqsubseteq y$ for all n, then $\lim_{n \to \infty} x_n \sqsubseteq y$. This condition states that the limit is the *least* upper bound.

The definition of the limit of a chain of approximations applies to every type. Partial orderings possessing this property are called *complete*. Domain theory is the study of complete partial orderings (CPOs for short).

For lists there is a useful function *approx* that produces approximations to a given list. The definition is

$$
\begin{array}{lll}
approx & :: & Integer \to [\alpha] \to [\alpha] \\
approx\ (n + 1)\ [\,] & = & [\,] \\
approx\ (n + 1)\ (x : xs) & = & x : approx\ n\ xs
\end{array}
$$

The definition of *approx* is very similar to that of *take* except that, by case exhaustion, we have *approx* $0\ xs = \bot$ for all xs. For example,

$$
\begin{array}{lll}
approx\ 0\ [1] & = & \bot \\
approx\ 1\ [1] & = & 1 : \bot \\
approx\ 2\ [1] & = & 1 : [\,]
\end{array}
$$

For $n \geq 2$ we have *approx* $n\,[1] = [1]$. The crucial property of *approx*, and one we will exploit in the following section, is that

$$\lim_{n \to \infty} approx\ n\ xs\ =\ xs$$

for all lists *xs*, finite, partial, or infinite. The proof, an induction on *xs*, is left as Exercise 9.2.6.

9.2.2 Computable functions

One can describe many functions but only some of them are computable. There are two properties of computable functions that are not shared by arbitrary functions. Firstly, a computable function *f* is *monotonic* with respect to the approximation ordering. In symbols,

$$x \sqsubseteq y\ \Rightarrow\ f\,x \sqsubseteq f\,y$$

for all *x* and *y*. Roughly speaking, monotonicity states that the more information you supply about the argument, the more information you get as a result. Secondly, a computable function *f* is *continuous*, which means that

$$f\,(\lim_{n \to \infty} x_n)\ =\ \lim_{n \to \infty} f\,x_n$$

for all chains of approximations $x_0 \sqsubseteq x_1 \sqsubseteq \ldots$. Roughly speaking, continuity states that there are no surprises on passage to the limit.

For example, since $[1 \mathrel{..}\,]$ is the limit of the sequence

$$\bot,\ 1 : \bot,\ 1 : 2 : \bot,\ 1 : 2 : 3 : \bot, \ldots$$

we can compute *map square* $[1 \mathrel{..}\,]$ as follows:

$$
\begin{aligned}
map\ square\ \bot &= \bot \\
map\ square\ (1 : \bot) &= 1 : \bot \\
map\ square\ (1 : 2 : \bot) &= 1 : 4 : \bot \\
map\ square\ (1 : 2 : 3 : \bot) &= 1 : 4 : 9 : \bot
\end{aligned}
$$

$\ldots$

The limit of this sequence is the infinite list $[1, 4, 9, \ldots]$ of squares. Similarly,

$$
\begin{aligned}
filter\ (< 10)\ \bot &= \bot \\
filter\ (< 10)\ (1 : \bot) &= 1 : \bot \\
filter\ (< 10)\ (1 : 4 : \bot) &= 1 : 4 : \bot \\
filter\ (< 10)\ (1 : 4 : 9 : \bot) &= 1 : 4 : 9 : \bot \\
filter\ (< 10)\ (1 : 4 : 9 : 16 : \bot) &= 1 : 4 : 9 : \bot
\end{aligned}
$$

$\ldots$

Every element of the sequence after the third is equal to $1 : 4 : 9 : \perp$, and so
that is also the limit of the sequence. On the other hand,

$$
\begin{array}{ll}
\textit{takeWhile} (< 10) \perp & = \quad \perp \\
\textit{takeWhile} (< 10) (1 : \perp) & = \quad 1 : \perp \\
\textit{takeWhile} (< 10) (1 : 4 : \perp) & = \quad 1 : 4 : \perp \\
\textit{takeWhile} (< 10) (1 : 4 : 9 : \perp) & = \quad 1 : 4 : 9 : \perp \\
\textit{takeWhile} (< 10) (1 : 4 : 9 : 16 : \perp) & = \quad 1 : 4 : 9 : [\,] \\
\textit{takeWhile} (< 10) (1 : 4 : 9 : 16 : 25 : \perp) & = \quad 1 : 4 : 9 : [\,] \\
\quad \ldots
\end{array}
$$

The limit of this sequence is $1 : 4 : 9 : [\,] = [1, 4, 9]$.

9.2.3   Chain completeness

Suppose we have established by induction that a mathematical property $P(xs)$
is true for all partial lists xs. Under what conditions can we assert that $P(xs)$ is
true for all infinite lists xs as well? Since an infinite list xs is the limit of a chain
of approximations $xs_0, xs_1, \ldots$, all of which are partial lists, we know that $P(xs_i)$
holds for all i. It is clear now that the property we are after is that P should hold
in the limit if it holds for each approximation. This property of P is called *chain
completeness*. Chain completeness appears similar to continuity but differs
in two respects. One is that the chain completeness of P does not imply the
converse property that if P is false for all approximations, then P is false for
the limit, that is, that $\neg P$ is chain complete. Secondly, P is a mathematical
assertion, not a function returning a boolean value, so it does not live in the
same universe as continuous functions.

Not all assertions are chain complete. For example, consider the assertion
that *drop n xs* $= \perp$ for some n. This assertion is clearly true for every partial
list, but true of no infinite list.

Fortunately, a wide range of assertions are chain complete. In particular, an
assertion $P(xs)$ of the form $e_1 \sqsubseteq e_2$, where e_1 and e_2 are expressions involving
xs, is chain complete. Any free variables in these expressions are assumed to
be *universally quantified*. Thus, if n and ys are variables occurring in e_1 and e_2,
then the assertion means that $e_1 \sqsubseteq e_2$ for *all* n and ys. Notice that the assertion
above is not of this form since the variable n is *existentially quantified*: the
equation *drop n xs* $= \perp$ is asserted for some n, not for all n.

If $P(xs)$ and $Q(xs)$ are chain complete, then so is $P(xs) \wedge Q(xs)$ (again, $\wedge$ is
used here as a propositional connective, not as an operation on boolean values).
In particular, an assertion of the form $e_1 = e_2$ is chain complete because it is

equivalent to $e_1 \sqsubseteq e_2 \wedge e_2 \sqsubseteq e_1$. Similarly, an assertion consisting of a list of equations is chain complete.

Exercises

9.2.1 Draw a directed graph depicting the approximation ordering on the type $(Bool, Bool)$, drawing an edge from x to y if $x \sqsubseteq y$.

9.2.2 Is the function $f : Int \rightarrow Int$, defined by $f \perp = 0$ and $f x = 1$ for $x \neq \perp$, computable?

9.2.3 Using the fact that all computable functions are monotonic and continuous, argue that one cannot define a computable function *sort* that correctly sorts an infinite list.

9.2.4 Is $[2, 4, 6, 8, \ldots]$ the limit of the following sequence of approximations?

$$\perp, \ 2 : \perp, \ 2 : \perp : 6 : \perp, \ 2 : \perp : 6 : \perp : 10 : \perp, \ldots$$

If not, what is?

9.2.5 Prove by induction that $approx\ n\ xs \sqsubseteq approx\ (n + 1)\ xs$ for all n and xs.

9.2.6 Prove by induction that $approx\ n\ xs \sqsubseteq xs$ for all n, and that if $approx\ n\ xs \sqsubseteq ys$ for all n, then $xs \sqsubseteq ys$.

9.3 Properties of infinite lists

Unfortunately, the principle of induction is not always sufficient to establish every property of infinite lists we would like. Consider, for instance, the function *iterate* defined by

$$
\begin{aligned}
iterate &\ ::\ (\alpha \rightarrow \alpha) \rightarrow \alpha \rightarrow [\alpha] \\
iterate\ f\ x &\ =\ x : iterate\ f\ (f\ x)
\end{aligned}
$$

The function *iterate* returns an infinite list. It satisfies the following equation:

$$iterate\ f\ x\ =\ x : map\ f\ (iterate\ f\ x)$$

This equation asserts that two infinite lists are equal. However, we cannot use induction to prove the result because there is no appropriate argument on which to do induction.

So, how do we prove such results? One tempting possibility is to prove that elements in corresponding positions are equal; in other words, to make use of the plausible assertion that two lists xs and ys are equal just in the case that $xs \,!!\, n = ys \,!!\, n$ for all natural numbers n. Unfortunately, this assertion is false.

As one counterexample, take $xs = \perp$ and $ys = [\perp]$. These lists are different but indexing with any natural number returns $\perp$ in all cases.

Another possibility is to make use of the function *approx* defined in the previous section. Recall that

$$\lim_{n \to \infty} approx\ n\ xs\ \ =\ \ xs$$

for all lists *xs*. It follows that if *approx n xs = approx n ys* for all *n*, then *xs = ys*. More generally, we can prove $xs \sqsubseteq ys$ by showing *approx n xs* $\sqsubseteq$ *approx n ys* for all *n*.

Let us now use this idea to prove the property of *iterate* given above. Using the definition of *iterate*, we can formulate the following equivalent statement of the desired result:

$$iterate\ f\ (f\ x)\ \ =\ \ map\ f\ (iterate\ f\ x)$$

Proof. We prove

$$approx\ n\ (iterate\ f\ (f\ x))\ \ =\ \ approx\ n\ (map\ f\ (iterate\ f\ x))$$

by induction on *n*.

Case (0). Obvious, since *approx* 0 *xs* = $\perp$ for any list *xs*.

Case (*n* + 1). For the left-hand side, we reason:

$$approx\ (n + 1)\ (iterate\ f\ (f\ x))$$
$=$ {definition of *iterate*}
$$approx\ (n + 1)\ (f\ x : iterate\ f\ (f\ (f\ x)))$$
$=$ {definition of *approx*}
$$f\ x : approx\ n\ (iterate\ f\ (f\ (f\ x)))$$
$=$ {induction hypothesis}
$$f\ x : approx\ n\ (map\ f\ (iterate\ f\ (f\ x)))$$

For the right-hand side, we reason:

$$approx\ (n + 1)\ (map\ f\ (iterate\ f\ x))$$
$=$ {definition of *iterate*}
$$approx\ (n + 1)\ (map\ f\ (x : iterate\ f\ (f\ x)))$$

=   {definition of *map*}

$\quad$ *approx* $(n + 1)$ $(f\, x : map\, f\ (iterate\, f\ (f\, x)))$

=   {definition of *approx*}

$\quad$ $f\, x : approx\, n\ (map\, f\ (iterate\, f\ (f\, x)))$

The two sides are the same, establishing the case and the proof.   □

We will give one more example. Consider the infinite list *nats* defined by

$$nats \quad :: \quad [Integer]$$
$$nats \quad = \quad 0 : map\ (+1)\ nats$$

We will prove *nats* = [0 ..] by showing that *approx n nats* = *approx n* [0 ..] for all natural numbers *n*. To do this, we will need the subsidiary result that

$$approx\ n \cdot map\ f \quad = \quad map\ f \cdot approx\ n$$

for all *f* and *n*. In other words, *approx n* commutes with *map f*. The proof is left as an exercise. The induction step for our assertion is

$\quad$ *approx* $(n + 1)$ *nats*

=   {definition of *nats*}

$\quad$ *approx* $(n + 1)$ $(0 : map\ (+1)\ nats)$

=   {definition of *approx*}

$\quad$ $0 : approx\ n\ (map\ (+1)\ nats)$

=   {since *approx* and *map* commute}

$\quad$ $0 : map\ (+1)\ (approx\ n\ nats)$

=   {induction hypothesis}

$\quad$ $0 : map\ (+1)\ approx\ n\ [0 ..]$

=   {since *approx* and *map* commute}

$\quad$ $0 : approx\ n\ (map\ (+1)\ [0 ..])$

=   {definition of *map*}

$\quad$ $0 : approx\ n\ [1 ..]$

=   {definition of *approx*}

$\quad$ *approx* $(n + 1)$ $[0 ..]$

Exercises

9.3.1 Prove that *iterate* $(+a)$ $b = [(i \times a) + b \mid i \leftarrow [0 ..]]$.

9.3.2 Suppose we define *fibs* $= 0 : 1 : [x + y \mid (x, y) \leftarrow zip\ fibs\ (tail\ fibs)]$. Prove that *fibs* $= map\ fib\ [0 ..]$, where *fib* is the Fibonacci function. State carefully any subsidiary results that you use in the proof.

9.3.3 Prove that $xs = ys$ if and only if *take n xs* $=$ *take n ys* for all n.

9.4 Cyclic structures

Data structures, like functions, may be defined recursively. As a simple example, consider the definition

$$
\begin{aligned}
one &\ ::\ [Int] \\
ones &\ =\ 1 : ones
\end{aligned}
$$

We have

$$
\begin{aligned}
ones &\ =\ 1 : ones \\
&\ =\ 1 : 1 : ones \\
&\ =\ 1 : 1 : 1 : ones \\
&\quad \vdots
\end{aligned}
$$

The name *ones* is bound to the infinite list $[1, 1, 1, \ldots]$.

Recall from Chapter 7 that expressions are represented by graphs in the evaluator. The representation of *ones* as a graph is particularly interesting, as it involves a cyclic structure:

The entire infinite list is therefore represented with a fixed amount of space. As a second example, consider the definition

$$
\begin{aligned}
more &\ ::\ String \\
more &\ =\ \text{“More ”} \mathbin{+\!\!+} andmore
\end{aligned}
$$
$$
\mathbf{where}\ andmore = \text{“and more ”} \mathbin{+\!\!+} andmore
$$

The value of *more* is also an infinite list:

? putStr more
More and more and more and more and more and m{*Interrupted!*}

After *more* has been evaluated, it will be represented by the graph

'M' : 'o' : 'r' : 'e' : ' ' : 'a' : 'n' : 'd' : ' ' : 'm' : 'o' : 'r' : 'e' : ' ' :

which again involves a cycle.

We now consider three further examples of the use of cyclic structures.

9.4.1 Repeat

The function *repeat* is such that *repeat* x is the infinite list $[x, x, x, \ldots]$, so the definition of *ones* above is equivalent to

$$ones \;=\; repeat\; 1$$

One way to define *repeat* is

$$repeat \quad :: \quad \alpha \to [\alpha]$$
$$repeat\; x \;=\; x : repeat\; x$$

This definition is correct, but does *not* create a cyclic structure. If *ones* and *repeat* are defined as above, then after displaying the first five elements, *ones* will be represented by the graph

$$1 : 1 : 1 : 1 : 1 : repeat\; 1$$

which is not cyclic. If the next element of the list is displayed, the subterm *repeat* 1 will be replaced by 1 : *repeat* 1. Consequently, the list *ones* grows longer with each evaluation. On the other hand, if the definition of *repeat* is changed to

$$repeat\; x \;=\; xs \quad \textbf{where}\; xs = x : xs$$

then the definition of *ones* in terms of *repeat* will produce the same cyclic structure as before.

9.4.2 Iterate

Here is a new definition of the function *iterate*, this time using a cyclic structure:

$$iterate\; f\; x \;=\; xs \quad \textbf{where}\; xs = x : map\; f\; xs$$

Consider the term *iterate* (2×) 1. The first few steps of evaluating this term are as follows:

$$iterate\,(2\times)\,1$$

$$\Rightarrow \quad 1 : map\,(2\times)$$

$$\Rightarrow \quad 1 : 2 : map\,(2\times)$$

$$\Rightarrow \quad 1 : 2 : 4 : map\,(2\times)$$

In particular, if $f\,x$ can be computed in $O(1)$ steps, then the first n elements of *iterate f x* can be computed in $O(n)$ steps.

If we eliminate the **where** clause from the above definition, we get yet another definition of *iterate*:

$$iterate\,f\,x \quad = \quad x : map\,f\,(iterate\,f\,x)$$

We showed earlier in the chapter that *iterate* satisfies this equation. The new definition does not use cyclic lists, and turns out to be much less efficient than the previous definition. Considering again the term *iterate* (2×) 1, the first few steps of evaluating this term are

$$iterate\,(2\times)\,1$$
$$\Rightarrow \quad 1 : map\,(2\times)\,(iterate\,(2\times)\,1)$$
$$\Rightarrow \quad 1 : 2 : map\,(2\times)\,(map\,(2\times)\,(iterate\,(2\times)\,1))$$
$$\Rightarrow \quad 1 : 2 : 4 : map\,(2\times)\,(map\,(2\times)\,(map\,(2\times)\,(iterate\,(2\times)\,1)))$$

It can be seen that evaluating the first n terms requires $\Omega(n^2)$ steps. In this example, the use of cyclic structures is essential in achieving efficiency.

9.4.3 The Hamming problem

A well-known problem, due to the mathematician W. R. Hamming, is to write a program that produces an infinite list of numbers with the following properties:

(i) The list is in strictly increasing order.
(ii) The list begins with the number 1.
(iii) If the list contains the number x, then it also contains the numbers $2 \times x$, $3 \times x$, and $5 \times x$.
(iv) The list contains no other numbers.

Thus, the required list begins with the numbers

$$1, 2, 3, 4, 5, 6, 8, 9, 10, 12, 15, 16, \ldots$$

The Hamming problem is important, as it is typical of a class of problems known as *closure problems*. In general, a closure problem specifies a collection of *initial elements* and a class of *generator functions*. In this case, we are asked to find the closure of the initial element 1 under the generating functions (2×), (3×), and (5×). The Hamming problem has a particularly efficient solution because the generating functions are *monotonic* under (<); for example, (2×) is monotonic because $x < y$ implies $2x < 2y$; similarly for the other generators.

The key to the solution is to make use of the function *merge* that takes two infinite lists of numbers in increasing order, and merges these into a single list of numbers in increasing order, removing duplicates:

$$merge \quad :: \quad [Integer] \to [Integer] \to [Integer]$$
$$merge\ (x : xs)\ (y : ys)$$
$$\begin{array}{lll}
\quad x < y & = & x : merge\ xs\ (y : ys) \\
\quad x == y & = & x : merge\ xs\ ys \\
\quad x > y & = & y : merge\ (x : xs)\ ys
\end{array}$$

Given *merge* it is easy to define *hamming*:

$$hamming \quad :: \quad [Integer]$$
$$hamming \quad = \quad 1 : merge\ (map\ (2\times)\ hamming)$$
$$(merge\ (map\ (3\times)\ hamming)$$
$$(map\ (5\times)\ hamming))$$

Initially, *hamming* will be represented by the following cyclic structure:

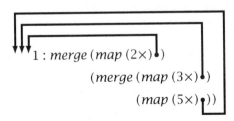

After the first seven elements of *hamming* have been printed, the above structure will have reduced to the following:

$$1 : 2 : 3 : 4 : 5 : 6 : 8 : merge\,(10 : map\,(2\times)\,)$$
$$(9 : merge\,(map\,(3\times)\,)$$
$$(10 : map\,(5\times)\,))$$

Note that first *n* elements of the list *hamming* can be computed in $O(n)$ steps.

An obvious generalisation of the Hamming problem is to replace the numbers 2, 3, and 5 by arbitrary positive numbers *a*, *b*, and *c*. We then have

$$hamming'\,a\,b\,c \;\; = \;\; 1 : merge\,(map\,(a\times)\,(hamming'\,a\,b\,c))$$
$$(merge\,(map\,(b\times)\,(hamming'\,a\,b\,c))$$
$$(map\,(c\times)\,(hamming'\,a\,b\,c)))$$

This solution produces the correct answer, but does not form a cyclic structure, and so requires $\Omega(n^2)$ steps to compute the first *n* elements of the result list. It is left as an exercise to modify *hamming'* so that it does form a cyclic structure.

Exercises

9.4.1 Define *dither* by

$$dither \;\; = \;\; yes$$
$$\textbf{where}\; yes \quad = \quad \text{``Yes.''} \mathbin{+\!\!+} no$$
$$no \quad = \quad \text{``No!''} \mathbin{+\!\!+} maybe$$
$$maybe \quad = \quad \text{``Maybe?''} \mathbin{+\!\!+} yes$$

What will be printed if *dither* is typed in a session? Draw the graph of the cyclic structure that represents this value.

9.4.2 Draw the four cyclic graphs that represent *hamming* after the first 1, 2, 3, and 4 elements have been printed.

9.4.3 Modify *hamming'* so that it forms a cyclic structure.

9.4.4 We can generalise the Hamming problem by replacing the multiples 2, 3, 5 with a list *as* of positive numbers. That is, we wish to find a list in increasing order that begins with 1 and such that if *x* is in the list and *a* is in *as*, then $a \times x$ is in the list. Write a program to solve the generalised Hamming problem.

9.4.5 We can also generalise the Hamming problem by replacing 1 with a list *bs* of positive numbers sorted in ascending order. That is, we now wish to find a list in ascending order such that every b in bs is in the list, and if x is in the list then $2x$, $3x$, and $5x$ are in the list. Write a program to solve this version of the Hamming problem.

9.5 Example: the paper-rock-scissors game

Our next example is instructive as well as entertaining. Not only does it introduce the idea of using infinite lists to model a sequence of interactions between processes, it also provides a concrete illustration of the necessity for formal analysis.

The paper-rock-scissors game is a familiar one to children, though it is known by different names in different places. The game is played by two people facing one another. Behind their backs, each player forms a hand in the shape of either a rock (a clenched fist), a piece of paper (a flat palm), or a pair of scissors (two fingers extended). At a given instant, both players bring their hidden hand forward. The winner is determined by the rule 'paper wraps rock, rock blunts scissors, and scissors cut paper'. Thus, if player 1 produces a rock and player 2 produces a pair of scissors, then player 1 wins because rock blunts scissors. If both players produce the same object, then the game is a tie and neither wins. The game continues in this fashion for a fixed number of rounds agreed in advance.

Our objective in this section is to write a program to play and score the game. We begin by introducing the types

$$\textbf{data } Move \;\; = \;\; Paper \mid Rock \mid Scissors$$
$$\textbf{type } Round \;\; = \;\; (Move, Move)$$

In order to score a round, we need the function

$$score :: Round \rightarrow (Int, Int)$$
$$score\,(x, y)$$

$$
\begin{array}{|lll}
x \textbf{ beats } y & = & (1, 0)\\
y \textbf{ beats } x & = & (0, 1)\\
otherwise & = & (0, 0)
\end{array}
$$

The comparison function **beats** can be defined by nine equations. Alternatively, we can define

$$(\textbf{beats}) \;\; :: \;\; Move \rightarrow Move \rightarrow Bool$$
$$x \textbf{ beats } y \;\; = \;\; (m + 1 == n) \lor (m == n + 2)$$
$$\textbf{where } m = code\,x; \;\; n = code\,y$$

$$
\begin{array}{lll}
code & :: & Move \rightarrow Int \\
code\ Paper & = & 0 \\
code\ Rock & = & 1 \\
code\ Scissors & = & 2
\end{array}
$$

Each player in the game will be represented by a certain strategy. For instance, one simple strategy is, after the first round, always to produce what the opposing player showed in the previous round. This strategy will be called *reciprocate*, or *recip* for short. Another strategy, which we will call *smart*, is to determine a move by analysing the number of times the opponent has produced each of the three possible objects, and calculating an appropriate response based on probabilities.

We will consider the details of particular strategies, and how they can be represented, later on. For the moment, suppose the type *Strategy* is given in some way. The function *rounds* will have type

$$
rounds \ :: \ (Strategy, Strategy) \rightarrow [Round]
$$

This function takes a pair of strategies and returns the infinite list of rounds that ensue when each player follows his or her assigned strategy. Given *rounds* we can define a function *match* that determines the result of playing a given number of rounds of the game. The definition is

$$
\begin{array}{lll}
match & :: & Int \rightarrow (Strategy, Strategy) \rightarrow (Int, Int) \\
match\ n & = & total \cdot map\ score \cdot take\ n \cdot rounds
\end{array}
$$

$$
\begin{array}{lll}
total & :: & [(Int, Int)] \rightarrow (Int, Int) \\
total & = & pair\ (sum \cdot map\ fst, sum \cdot map\ snd)
\end{array}
$$

9.5.1 Representing strategies

In order to complete the model of the game, we must decide on how strategies are to be represented, and so supply the necessary definition of *rounds*. There are at least two methods for representing strategies and it is instructive to compare them in some detail. In the first, we take

$$
\textbf{type}\ Strategy \ = \ [Move] \rightarrow Move
$$

Here, a strategy is a function which takes the (finite) list of moves made by the opponent so far and returns an appropriate move for the subsequent round.

For example, the *recip* strategy can be implemented by

$$
\begin{array}{lll}
recip & :: & Strategy \\
recip\ ms & = & \textbf{if}\ null\ ms\ \textbf{then}\ Rock\ \textbf{else}\ last\ ms
\end{array}
$$

The first move is arbitrary, and here we have chosen *Rock*. The second strategy *smart* can be implemented by

> *smart*   ::   *Strategy*
> *smart ms*   =   **if** *null ms* **then** *Rock* **else** *choose* (*count ms*)

> *count*   ::   [*Move*] → (*Int, Int, Int*)
> *count*   =   *foldl* (⊕) (0, 0, 0)

> (⊕)   ::   (*Int, Int, Int*) → *Move* → (*Int, Int, Int*)
> (*p, r, s*) ⊕ *Paper*   =   (*p* + 1, *r*, *s*)
> (*p, r, s*) ⊕ *Rock*   =   (*p*, *r* + 1, *s*)
> (*p, r, s*) ⊕ *Scissors*   =   (*p*, *r*, *s* + 1)

Again, *Rock* is some arbitrarily chosen first move. The function *count* counts the number of times each move has been made.

The function *choose* determines a move by analysing the three numbers *p*, *q*, and *r*. In order to define this function, suppose *random* :: *Int* → *Int* is a function that takes a positive integer *n* and returns some integer *m* in the range $0 \le m < n$. One way to implement this function is to generate an infinite list of pseudo-random integers, and then pick the *n*th element of this list, scaling appropriately. We will not go into further details, but see Exercise 9.5.1.

We can now define *choose* by

> *choose* :: (*Int, Int, Int*) → *Move*
> *choose* (*p, r, s*)
> | *m* < *p*   =   *Scissors*
> | *m* < *p* + *r*   =   *Paper*
> | *otherwise*   =   *Rock*
>   **where** *m* = *random* (*p* + *r* + *s*)

The function *choose* determines an appropriate move depending on whether *m* falls in one of the three ranges

$$0 \le m < p \quad \text{or} \quad p \le m < p + r \quad \text{or} \quad p + r \le m < p + r + s$$

For example, if *p* is large, then *smart* will choose *Scissors* with a large probability (because scissors cuts paper); and if *r* is large, then *smart* will choose *Paper* with high probability (because paper wraps rock); and so on.

We can now define the function *rounds*:

> *rounds*   ::   (*Strategy, Strategy*) → [*Round*]
> *rounds* (*f, g*)   =   (*map last* · *tail* · *iterate* (*extend* (*f, g*))) [ ]

$$extend \qquad :: \quad (Strategy, Strategy) \rightarrow [Round] \rightarrow [Round]$$
$$extend\,(f, g)\,rs \;\; = \;\; rs +\!\!+ [(f\,(map\,snd\,rs),\,g\,(map\,fst\,rs))]$$

The function *extend* appends a new pair of moves to the list of existing rounds, and *rounds* generates the infinite list of rounds by repeatedly applying *extend* to the initially empty list.

The definition of *rounds* is clumsy. More importantly, it is not very efficient. Suppose a strategy takes time proportional to the length of the input to compute its result. It follows that *extend* takes $\Omega(n)$ steps to update a game of n rounds by a new one. Therefore, to compute a game of N rounds requires $\Omega(N^2)$ steps.

A second representation. For comparison, let us now consider another way we might reasonably represent strategies. This time we take

$$\textbf{type}\;\; Strategy \;\; = \;\; [Move] \rightarrow [Move]$$

In the new representation, a strategy is a function that takes the infinite list of moves made by the opponent and returns the infinite list of replies. For example, the strategy *recip* is now implemented by the equation

$$recip\,ms \;\; = \;\; Rock : ms$$

This strategy returns *Rock* the first time, and thereafter returns just the move made by the opponent in the previous round. Observe that this version of *recip* produces each successive output with constant delay.

The strategy *smart* can be reprogrammed as follows:

$$smart\,xs \;\; = \;\; Rock : map\,choose\,(counts\,xs)$$
$$counts \qquad = \;\; tail \cdot scanl\,(\oplus)\,(0,0,0)$$

The function *counts* computes the running counts of the three possible moves. The *smart* strategy is also efficient in that it produces each successive output with constant delay.

With our new model of strategies we can redefine the function *rounds* to be

$$rounds\,(f, g) \;\; = \;\; zip\,xs\,ys$$
$$\textbf{where}\;\, xs = f\,ys; \;\;\; ys = g\,xs$$

Here, xs is the list of replies computed by f in response to the list ys which, in turn, is the list of replies made by g in response to xs. To ensure that $rounds(f, g)$ does generate an infinite list of well-defined (that is, non $\bot$) moves, we require that the pair of mutually recursive definitions, $xs = f\,ys$ and $ys = g\,xs$, generates infinite lists of well-defined elements. We will discuss this aspect below. If f and g satisfy the requirement, then the new definition of *rounds* computes the first n moves of the game in $O(n)$ steps, assuming that f and g compute each new move with constant delay. Thus, the second method for modelling strategies leads to a more efficient program than the earlier one.

9.5.2 Cheating

Unfortunately, however, there is a crucial flaw with the second representation: it offers no protection against a strategy that cheats! Consider the strategy

$$cheat\ xs \quad = \quad map\ trumps\ xs$$

where

$$
\begin{array}{lll}
trumps & :: & Move \rightarrow Move \\
trumps\ Paper & = & Scissors \\
trumps\ Rock & = & Paper \\
trumps\ Scissors & = & Rock
\end{array}
$$

The first reply of *cheat* is the move guaranteed to beat the opponent's first move; similarly for subsequent moves. To see that *cheat* cannot be prevented from subverting the game, consider a match in which it is played against *recip*. Suppose xs and ys are defined by $xs = cheat\ ys$ and $ys = recip\ xs$. The values xs and ys are the limits of the chain of approximations $xs_0, xs_1, \ldots$ and $ys_0, ys_1, \ldots$, respectively, where $xs_0 = ys_0 = \bot$ and

$$
\begin{array}{lll}
xs_{n+1} & = & cheat\ ys_n \\
ys_{n+1} & = & recip\ xs_n
\end{array}
$$

Now, we have

$$
\begin{array}{lll}
xs_1 = cheat\ \bot & = & \bot \\
ys_1 = recip\ \bot & = & Rock : \bot
\end{array}
$$

$$
\begin{array}{lll}
xs_2 = cheat\ (Rock : \bot) & = & Paper : \bot \\
ys_2 = recip\ \bot & = & Rock : \bot
\end{array}
$$

$$
\begin{array}{lll}
xs_3 = cheat\ (Rock : \bot) & = & Paper : \bot \\
ys_3 = recip\ (Paper : \bot) & = & Rock : Paper : \bot
\end{array}
$$

$$
\begin{array}{lll}
xs_4 = cheat\ (Rock : Paper : \bot) & = & Paper : Scissors : \bot \\
ys_4 = recip\ (Paper : \bot) & = & Rock : Paper : \bot
\end{array}
$$

Continuing in this way, we see that the limits of these sequences are indeed infinite lists of well-defined moves and, moreover, *cheat* always triumphs.

The strategy *cheat* is not the only one that can cheat. Here are three more:

$$cunning\ xs\ =\ trumps\ (head\ xs) : cunning\ (tail\ xs)$$
$$oneshot\ xs\ =\ trumps\ (head\ xs) : recip\ (tail\ xs)$$
$$devious\ xs\ =\ take\ 2\ (recip\ xs) + cheat\ (drop\ 2\ xs)$$

The *cunning* strategy is equal to *cheat* on infinite lists, but whereas *cheat* $\bot = \bot$, we have *cunning* $\bot = \bot : \bot : \bot : ....$ The strategy *oneshot* cheats on the first move, but thereafter acts like *recip*. The strategy *devious* plays fair for two moves, and then cheats.

Can we find a way to protect against such strategies? To answer this question, we need to take a closer look at what constitutes an honest strategy. Informally speaking, a strategy f is honest if the first move is computed in the absence of any information about the opponent's first move, the second move is computed without any information about the opponent's second move, and so on. Moreover, each of these moves should be well-defined, given that the opponent's moves are well-defined.

More precisely, define open(n, xs) to be the assertion that the first n moves in the list xs are well-defined. Then f is *honest* if

$$open(n, xs)\ \Rightarrow\ open(n + 1, f\ xs)$$

for all n and all lists xs.

It is easy to show that *recip* is honest. On the other hand, *cheat* is not honest because open($0, \bot$) holds but open($1, \bot$) does not, and

$$open(1, cheat\ \bot)\ \equiv\ open(1, \bot)$$

It is easy to check that the other cheating strategies are not honest. Nor, by the way, is the strategy *dozy*, where

$$dozy\ xs\ =\ repeat\ undefined$$

Although *dozy* doesn't actually cheat, it never returns a well-defined move.

Having identified the source of criminal, or lackadaisical, behaviour, can we ensure that only honest strategies are admitted to the game? The answer is a qualified yes: although it is not possible for a mechanical evaluator to recognise cheating (in the same way that it is not possible to recognise $\bot$, or strategies that do not return well-defined moves), it is possible to define a function *police* so that if f is an honest strategy and xs is an infinite sequence of well-defined moves, then *police* f $xs = f$ xs. On the other hand, if f is not honest at some point, then the game ends at that point in $\bot$. A more precise statement is given in Exercise 9.5.8. Operationally speaking, *police* works by forcing f to return the first (well-defined!) element of its output before it gives f the first element of its input. Similarly for the other elements. The definition is

$$police\ f\ xs \quad = \quad ys \ \textbf{where}\ ys = f\ (synch\ xs\ ys)$$

$$synch \quad :: \quad [Move] \rightarrow [Move] \rightarrow [Move]$$
$$synch\ (x : xs)\ (y : ys)$$
$$\qquad = \quad \textbf{if}\ defined\ y\ \textbf{then}\ x : synch\ xs\ ys\ \textbf{else}\ undefined$$

The test *defined y* returns *True* if y is a well-defined move, and $\perp$ otherwise; a suitable definition is left as an exercise. The proof, due to Berend Sijtsma, that this implementation meets its specification is rather involved, so we will relegate it to the exercises.

It follows from the above analysis that to prevent cheating we must rewrite the definition of *rounds* as follows:

$$rounds\ (f, g) \quad = \quad zip\ xs\ ys$$
$$\qquad\qquad \textbf{where}\ xs = police\ f\ ys; \quad ys = police\ g\ xs$$

Exercises

9.5.1 One way to generate an infinite list of pseudo-random numbers is by

$$randoms \quad :: \quad [Int]$$
$$randoms \quad = \quad iterate\ f\ seed$$
$$\qquad\qquad \textbf{where}\ f\ x = (a \times x + c)\ \textbf{mod}\ m$$

The four magic numbers here are: (i) the starting value *seed*; (ii) the multiplier a; (iii) the increment c; and (iv) the modulus m. The method is known as the *linear congruential method*. The four numbers should not be chosen randomly; see Knuth (1981) for the principles of choosing the numbers appropriately. Use this method to construct a suitable implementation of the function *random* of the text.

9.5.2 Give a suitable definition of *defined* :: *Move* → *Bool*.

9.5.3 Suppose in the definition of *police*, the definition of *synch* was replaced by the simpler

$$synch\ (x : xs)\ (y : ys) \quad = \quad x : synch\ xs\ ys$$

Show that the new version of *police* allows the *cunning* strategy to escape detection.

9.5.4 The assertion open(n, xs) can be defined inductively by taking open$(0, xs)$ to be true, and

$$\text{open}(n + 1, xs) \;=\; \text{defined}(\textit{head xs}) \wedge \text{open}(n, \textit{tail xs})$$

The assertion defined(x) is true if x is a well-defined move, and false otherwise. Prove the following facts:

$$\text{open}(n, xs) \;\equiv\; \text{open}(n, \textit{approx n xs})$$
$$\text{open}(n, xs) \wedge xs \sqsubseteq ys \;\Rightarrow\; \textit{approx n xs} = \textit{approx n ys}$$
$$\text{open}(n, xs) \wedge xs \sqsubseteq ys \;\Rightarrow\; \text{open}(n, ys)$$

9.5.5 Using the results of the previous exercise, show that if f is honest and open(n, xs), then $\textit{approx } (n + 1) (f \textit{ xs}) = \textit{approx } (n + 1) (f (\textit{approx n xs}))$.

9.5.6 Prove that

$$\text{open}(n, zs) \;\Rightarrow\; \textit{approx n } (\textit{synch xs ys}) = \textit{approx n xs}$$

for all lists zs and all partial (and hence infinite) lists xs.

9.5.7 Use the previous two exercises to show that if f is honest and open(n, xs), then

$$\textit{approx } (n + 1) (\textit{police f xs}) \;=\; \textit{approx } (n + 1) (f \textit{ xs})$$

Hence show that $(\textit{police f xs}) \mathbin{!!} k = (f \textit{ xs}) \mathbin{!!} k$ for all k $(0 \le k \le n)$.

9.5.8 Prove that

$$\text{open}(n, f \textit{ xs}) \wedge \neg\text{open}(n + 1, f \textit{ xs}) \;\Rightarrow\; (\textit{police f xs}) \mathbin{!!} n = \bot$$

Explain why this fact is too weak to detect cheating. (Hint: take xs to be an infinite list of well-defined moves, and $f = \textit{cheat}$.) The result we are after in the remaining exercises is

$$\text{open}(n, f (\textit{approx n xs})) \wedge \neg\text{open}(n + 1, f (\textit{approx n xs}))$$
$$\Rightarrow\; (\textit{police f xs}) \mathbin{!!} n = \bot$$

In words, if f cheats at some (first) move n by failing to give $(n+1)$ well-defined replies for n well-defined inputs, then $\textit{police f xs}$ returns $\bot$ at move number n.

9.5.9 Prove that

$$\neg\text{open}(n + 1, zs) \;\Rightarrow\; \textit{synch xs zs} \sqsubseteq \textit{approx n xs}$$

for all lists zs and all partial (and hence all infinite) lists xs.

9.5.10 Assuming $\neg open(n + 1, f\ (approx\ n\ xs))$, prove that

$$\neg open(n + 1, zs)$$
$$\Rightarrow\quad f\ (synch\ xs\ zs) \sqsubseteq f\ (approx\ n\ xs) \wedge \neg open(n + 1, f\ (synch\ xs\ zs))$$

9.5.11 If $ys = f\ (synch\ xs\ ys)$, then ys is the limit of the sequence of approximations ys_k, where $ys_0 = \bot$ and $ys_{k+1} = f\ (synch\ xs\ ys_k)$. Using the previous exercise, prove that

$$\neg open(n + 1, f\ (approx\ n\ xs))\quad \Rightarrow\quad police\ f\ xs \sqsubseteq f\ (approx\ n\ xs)$$

Hence complete the proof of the claim in Exercise 9.5.8.

9.6 Stream-based interaction

So far, all of our sessions with the computer have involved a uniform and simple pattern of interaction: the user types an expression to be evaluated at the keyboard, and then the value of this expression is printed on the screen. This style of interaction is suited for a wide range of purposes, but sometimes other forms of interaction are required. As a trivial example, we might want everything typed on the keyboard to be echoed on the screen, but with lower-case letters converted to upper-case. We might also want to play games interactively with the computer. More serious examples include a program to run a functional computer interactively, or even a complete operating system.

Our aim in this section is to give a highly simplified view of one way in which interactive programs can be written. The method, called *stream-based interaction*, is the one adopted in some functional languages, and was also used in early versions of Haskell. However, Haskell now provides an alternative, much more general approach for handling interaction, and we will be discussing this approach in the following chapter.

In the stream-based method, an interactive program is written as a function f with type

$$f\ ::\ String \rightarrow String$$

When f is run interactively, the input to f will be the sequence of characters typed at the keyboard. The output of f will printed in the normal way. As a simple example, the function

$$map\ capitalise\ ::\ String \rightarrow String$$

is an interactive program for converting lower-case characters to upper-case. The definition of *capitalise* was given in Section 2.2.

To run an interactive program, Haskell provides a command

$$interact \; :: \; (String \to String) \to IO \, ()$$

We will explain the type $IO \, ()$ in the following chapter. Now, if in a session, we type $interact \, (map \, capitalise)$, then the evaluator enters an interactive mode, waiting for input from the keyboard. If we type the string "Hello, world!", then we will see the output

? *interact* (*map capitalise*)
HELLO, WORLD!

The program is fully interactive: that is, as soon as 'H' is typed on the keyboard, an 'H' appears on the screen, and then when 'e' is typed an 'E' appears on the screen, and so on. The program will run until the interrupt key is typed or the computer is turned off.

One can also design an interactive program that terminates. For example,

$$
\begin{aligned}
capitalises \quad &:: \quad String \to String \\
capitalises \quad &= \quad takeWhile \, (\neq \text{'.'}) \cdot map \, capitalise
\end{aligned}
$$

behaves in the same way as *map capitalise*, but terminates execution when a full-stop character is typed. Note that the full-stop character will *not* be echoed on the screen.

Suppose we wanted a different style of interaction, exemplified by

? *interact echoCap*
Hello, world!
HELLO, WORLD!

Goodbye, cruel world!
GOODBYE, CRUEL WORLD!

This time, each line typed by the user is first echoed on the screen before being capitalised. Here we have to design *echoCap* so that it interleaves echoing and the result of capitalisation:

$$
\begin{aligned}
echoCap \, xs \quad = \quad & ys \,+\!\!+\, \text{"↓"} \,+\!\!+ \\
& map \, capitalise \, ys \,+\!\!+\, \text{"↓"} \,+\!\!+\, echoCap \, (tail \, zs) \\
& \textbf{where} \; (ys, zs) = span \, (\neq \text{'↓'}) \; xs
\end{aligned}
$$

The input *xs* is decomposed into the string *ys* of characters before the first newline, and the remaining string *zs*. The string *ys* is echoed to the screen, followed by a newline, and then capitalised. Another newline is printed, and the

remainder of the input is treated similarly. Note carefully that the responsibility for interleaving input and output correctly is entirely in the programmer's
hands.

The above form of interaction is called *stream-based* because it makes essential use of the fact that lists are evaluated lazily. The word 'stream' is often
used as a synonym for lazy lists. For example, the behaviour of the *capitalises*
program described above is modelled by the following sequence of partial lists:

$$
\begin{array}{lcl}
\textit{capitalise}\ \bot & = & \bot \\
\textit{capitalise}\ (\text{`H'} : \bot) & = & \text{`H'} : \bot \\
\textit{capitalise}\ (\text{`H'} : \text{`e'} : \bot) & = & \text{`H'} : \text{`E'} : \bot \\
\textit{capitalise}\ (\text{`H'} : \text{`e'} : \text{`l'} : \bot) & = & \text{`H'} : \text{`E'} : \text{`L'} : \bot \\
\textit{capitalise}\ (\text{`H'} : \text{`e'} : \text{`l'} : \text{`l'} : \bot) & = & \text{`H'} : \text{`E'} : \text{`L'} : \text{`L'} : \bot \\
\cdots
\end{array}
$$

The sequence can be viewed as a history of the interactive session. When nothing has been typed at the keyboard, nothing has appeared on the screen. When
an 'H' has been typed, an 'H' has appeared on the screen. When "He" has been
typed, "HE" has appeared on the screen. And so on. If we type a full-stop
character, then the history ends:

$$
\textit{capitalise}\ (\text{`H'} : \text{`e'} : \text{`l'} : \text{`l'} : \text{`.'} : \bot) = [\text{`H'}, \text{`E'}, \text{`L'}, \text{`L'}]
$$

Just as earlier $\bot$ was used to denote a computation that has not yet completed,
here $\bot$ is used to denote input that has not yet been typed at the keyboard, and
output that has not yet appeared on the screen. A special case of a computation
that has not yet completed is a computation that will never complete, that is, an
infinite loop. Similarly, two special cases of input and output are the input that
results when the keyboard is never touched again and the output that causes
the screen never to be printed on again. These, too, are all denoted by $\bot$.

9.6.1 Discussion

The model presented above is too simple for most practical purposes. In a
serious application one wants to do other things than reading and printing
characters to a screen. For example, one also wants to open and read files, to
write to or delete files, and in general to interact with all the mechanisms that
are available in the world outside the confines of a functional programming
language.

Interaction takes place in time, and the order in which events occur has
to be managed correctly by the programmer. In the stream-based approach,
this ordering of events is represented by the order of the elements in a list; in

other words, it is represented in the data and not reflected primarily in the way the program is composed. In the following chapter we will consider another approach to interaction, indeed, a general method for writing programs that have to control an orderly sequence of events. In this approach, the order is made explicit in the way the program is composed.

Exercises

9.6.1 Write an interactive program to interleave individual characters and their upper-case equivalents. For example, typing "Hello, world!" should produce

$$HHeElLlLoO,, wWoOrRlLdD!!$$

9.6.2 Write a utility program *read* with type

$$read \quad :: \quad String \rightarrow (String \rightarrow String \rightarrow String) \rightarrow String \rightarrow String$$

The function *read msg f* denotes an interactive program that first prints a message *msg* on the screen, then reads the next line *xs* from the keyboard and echoes it as it is read, and then evaluates the function *f xs* on the remainder of the input.

9.6.3 Write a similar utility program *write* with type

$$write \quad :: \quad String \rightarrow (String \rightarrow String) \rightarrow String \rightarrow String$$

The function *write msg f* first writes the message *msg* on the screen, and then evaluates *f* on the input.

9.6.4 Write an interactive program to model a queue, as illustrated in Section 8.1.

9.6.5 The backspace character '←' when typed at the keyboard indicates that the previously typed character should be deleted, and when printed on the screen causes the cursor to be moved back one position. Write a utility function *readEdit* that is similar to *read* except that '←' can be used to edit the input. For example, typing "goop←d" followed by a newline should cause the string "good" to be entered. (For echoing, note that a character already printed on the screen can be removed by printing "←␣←"; this backs over the character, writes a space in its place, and then moves the cursor back over the space.)

9.7 Chapter notes

Domain theory grew out of the work of Dana Scott in the late 1960s, see Scott (1976) and Scott (1982). An accessible account of the basic mathematics is given in Davey and Priestley (1990); see also Gunter (1992) for a modern treatment of domains and their importance in the semantics of programming languages.

Sijtsma's thesis (1988) studies various aspects of infinite-list programs, and gives a number of techniques for reasoning about infinite lists. One chapter is devoted to the proof of fairness in the paper–rock–scissors game.

Gordon's thesis (1993) contains a useful history of the various approaches to the treatment of interaction in a functional setting.

One of the most exciting recent developments in programming semantics has been the use of games and strategies to provide a model for interactive processes. See the chapters by S. Abramsky and M. Hyland in Pitts and Dyber (1997) for readable accounts of the basic ideas.

Chapter 10

Monads

This chapter introduces a new style of functional programming, called *monadic* programming. Monadic programs provide a simple and attractive way to cope with interaction in a functional setting. But, as we will see, a monadic style of programming is capable of much more: it provides a structuring mechanism for dealing with a range of problems, including exception handling, parsing, and state-based computations. In a sense, a monadic style enables one to write functional programs that mimic imperative programs, those programs constructed in imperative languages such as Pascal and C.

We begin by considering a particular monad, the input–output monad $IO\ \alpha$, for expressing programs that involve interaction, a topic that was introduced at the end of the previous chapter. We will use this example to motivate the definition of a monad, as well as give a number of examples of interactive programs. After that, we will explore other ways in which monads can be used to good effect, and introduce the fundamental laws for reasoning about monadic programs.

10.1 Monadic interaction

The type of commands in Haskell is denoted by $IO\ ()$. An expression of type $IO\ ()$ denotes an *action*; when evaluated, the action is *performed*. The type $IO\ ()$ is an abstract type in the sense of Chapter 8, so we are not told how values of the type are represented; what is important is the operations that the type provides. In fact, we will be interested in the operations of the more general type $IO\ \alpha$, but we start with the simple version first.

One fundamental operation is a function to print a character:

$$putChar\ ::\ Char \rightarrow IO\ ()$$

For instance, evaluating *putChar* '!' prints an exclamation mark:

? *putChar* '!'

!

Another command is *done* :: *IO* (); when performed *done* does nothing:

? *done*

?

Next, we need a way to combine commands. One such operator is

$$(\gg) \quad :: \quad IO\,() \rightarrow IO\,() \rightarrow IO\,()$$

If *p* and *q* are commands, then *p* ≫ *q* is a command that, when performed, first does *p* and then does *q*. Using (≫), we can implement the function *write*, which has the same effect as the Haskell predefined function *putStr*:

```
write          ::  String → IO ()
write [ ]       =   done
write (c : cs)  =   putChar c ≫ write cs
```

One can also express *write* in terms of *foldr*:

$$write \quad = \quad foldr\,(\gg)\ done \cdot map\ putChar$$

The function *writeln* is similar to *write*, except that it prints a newline character after printing the string:

```
writeln    ::  String → IO ()
writeln cs  =   write cs ≫ putChar '↲'
```

The type *IO* () is adequate for output, but needs to be generalised for input. The type *IO* α is the type of commands that yield a value of type α. Thus, the special case *IO* () is when α is instantiated to the nullary type () that contains just one proper member, also written (). This type was discussed briefly in Chapter 2.

A primitive operation on the more general type reads a character:

```
getChar  ::  IO Char
```

When the user types some characters at the keyboard, *getChar* returns the first character. In Haskell, the default convention is that *getChar* echoes the character to the screen. We will see how to use *getChar* in a moment.

The generalisation of *done* is the command that does nothing and returns a named value:

$$return \ :: \ \alpha \rightarrow IO \ \alpha$$

For instance, performing the command *return* 42 returns the value 42 without consuming any input. In particular,

$$done \ :: \ IO \ ()$$
$$done \ = \ return \ ()$$

The generalisation of ($\gg$) is an operator with type

$$(\gg) \ :: \ IO \ \alpha \rightarrow IO \ \beta \rightarrow IO \ \beta$$

If p and q are commands, then $p \gg q$ is a command that, when performed, first does p, ignores the value returned, and then does q. For example,

? *getChar* $\gg$ *done*
x

After entering the command (ended by typing a newline), the user typed the letter 'x'. The command *getChar* echoed it to the screen, and then the command *done* terminated the interaction.

The type of *getChar* $\gg$ *done* is *IO* () and, as we have said, expressions of this particular type can be evaluated in a session, causing commands to be performed. On the other hand, expressions of type *IO* α for $\alpha \neq$ () cannot be evaluated during a session; for example,

? *getChar*
ERROR: Cannot find *show* function for *IO Char*

Haskell provides no mechanism for printing values of type *IO Char*. We will see in a moment how the programmer can process the value returned by a command of type *IO* α.

It is clear that the command $p \gg q$ is useful only when the value returned by p is not interesting, since there is no way that q can depend on it. What is wanted is a more general operator

$$(\triangleright) \ :: \ IO \ \alpha \rightarrow (\alpha \rightarrow IO \ \beta) \rightarrow IO \ \beta$$

The combination $p \triangleright q$ is a command that, when performed, first does p, returning a value x of type α, then does $q \ x$, returning a final value y of type β. We will leave it as an exercise to show that ($\gg$) can be defined in terms of ($\triangleright$). The Haskell syntax for $\triangleright$ is >>=.

Here is an example using ($\triangleright$):

? *getChar* ▷ *putChar*
xx

After entering this command, which has type *IO* (), the user typed the letter 'x'; the command *getChar* echoed this character to the screen; the function *putChar* was then applied to the character, causing it to be printed once more.

Using (▷), we can define a function *readn* for reading a fixed number of characters from the keyboard:

$$
\begin{aligned}
readn & \quad :: \quad Int \rightarrow IO\ String \\
readn\ 0 & \quad = \quad return\ [\ ] \\
readn\ (n+1) & \quad = \quad getChar \triangleright q \\
& \qquad \textbf{where}\ q\ c \quad = \quad readn\ n \triangleright r \\
& \qquad\qquad\qquad \textbf{where}\ r\ cs = return\ (c:cs)
\end{aligned}
$$

This has a straightforward reading: to get a string of length $(n+1)$, first get a character c, then get a string cs of length n, and finally return the string $(c:cs)$. The use of nested **where** clauses is clumsy, and we will introduce a superior notation in a moment.

Probably more useful than *readn* is a function *readln* that reads a line of text from the keyboard, that is, the list of characters up to but not including the first newline character:

$$
\begin{aligned}
readln & \quad :: \quad IO\ String \\
readln & \quad = \quad getChar \triangleright q \\
& \qquad \textbf{where}\ q\ c \quad = \quad \textbf{if}\ c == \text{`}\!\!\downarrow\!\!\text{'} \\
& \qquad\qquad\qquad\qquad \textbf{then}\ \ return\ [\ ] \\
& \qquad\qquad\qquad\qquad \textbf{else}\ \ \ readln \triangleright r \\
& \qquad\qquad\qquad\qquad \textbf{where}\ r\ cs = return\ (c:cs)
\end{aligned}
$$

To summarise, the input–output monad *IO* α is an abstract type on which the following operations, at least, are available:

$$
\begin{aligned}
return & \quad :: \quad \alpha \rightarrow IO\ \alpha \\
(\triangleright) & \quad :: \quad IO\ \alpha \rightarrow (\alpha \rightarrow IO\ \beta) \rightarrow IO\ \beta
\end{aligned}
$$

$$
\begin{aligned}
putChar & \quad :: \quad Char \rightarrow IO\ () \\
getChar & \quad :: \quad IO\ Char
\end{aligned}
$$

The first two operations are combining forms that characterise the class of types called *monads*. Thus, by definition, M is a monad when the following operations are given:

$$
\begin{aligned}
return & \quad :: \quad \alpha \rightarrow M\ \alpha \\
(\triangleright) & \quad :: \quad M\ \alpha \rightarrow (\alpha \rightarrow M\ \beta) \rightarrow M\ \beta
\end{aligned}
$$

These two operations are required to satisfy certain laws, which we will come to in due course. The remaining primitive operations *putChar* and *getChar* of *IO α* are specific to input and output. Haskell provides a range of other primitive functions for input and output, some of which we will mention below.

10.1.1 Monads and do notation

We can declare monads as a type class in Haskell:

> **class** *Monad m* **where**
> *return* :: $\alpha \rightarrow m\,\alpha$
> (▷) :: $m\,\alpha \rightarrow (\alpha \rightarrow m\,\beta) \rightarrow m\,\beta$

The class *Monad* is our first example of a type class in which the restricted variable ranges over type constructors rather than over types. To emphasise this, we will use roman rather than greek letters (in fact, Haskell uses roman letters for both kinds). The type constructor *IO* is an example of a monad, the corresponding instance declaration being supplied as primitive.

For instances of the class *Monad*, Haskell provides a notation – called **do** notation – as an alternative to writing combinations of ▷ with nested **where** clauses. For example, the above program for *readn* can be written in the alternative form

> *readn* :: *Int* → *IO String*
> *readn* 0 = *return* [ ]
> *readn* (*n* + 1) = **do** *c* ← *getChar*
>   *cs* ← *readn n*
>   *return* (*c* : *cs*)

This reads: perform the command *getChar* and bind the result to *c*; then perform *readn n* and bind the result to *cs*; finally, return (*c* : *cs*).

Similarly, *readln* can be written using **do** notation as follows:

> *readln* :: *IO String*
> *readln* = **do** *c* ← *getChar*
>   **if** *c* == '↲'
>   **then** *return* [ ]
>   **else** **do** *cs* ← *readln*
>   *return* (*c* : *cs*)

Notice the layout of the conditional expression, with the indentation of the **then** and **else** clauses. These are made necessary by Haskell's rules of layout.

Alternatively, as with **where** clauses, a **do** clause can be written with braces and semi-colons to make the separation of clauses explicit. For example,

$$readn\,(n+1) \;\; = \;\; \textbf{do}\,\{c \leftarrow getChar;\;\; cs \leftarrow readn\,n;\;\; return\,(c:cs)\}$$

For a general monad M, a **do** expression has the form **do** $\{C;\, r\}$, where C is a list of one or more commands separated by semicolons, and r is an expression of type $M\,\beta$, which is also the type of the entire **do** expression. Each command takes the form '$x \leftarrow p$', where x is a variable, or possibly a tuple of variables; if p is an expression of type $M\,\alpha$, then the type of x is α. In the particular case $\alpha = ()$, the command $() \leftarrow p$ can be abbreviated to p.

The translation of a **do** expression into $\triangleright$ operations and **where** clauses is governed by two rules:

$$\textbf{do}\,\{r\} \;\; = \;\; r$$

$$\textbf{do}\,\{x \leftarrow p;\; C;\; r\} \;\; = \;\; p \triangleright q \quad \textbf{where } q\,x = \textbf{do}\,\{C;\; r\}$$

It is easy to check that the former definitions of *readn* and *readln* are equivalent to the new ones by applications of these rules, a task we leave as an exercise.

10.1.2 Examples

Let us now look at some simple examples of the use of $IO\,\alpha$. First, here is an interactive program for reading a character and revealing its numeric value:

$$
\begin{aligned}
&reveal \quad :: \quad IO\,() \\
&reveal \quad = \quad \textbf{do}\; c \leftarrow getChar \\
&\qquad\qquad\qquad putChar\,`\!\!\uparrow\!' \\
&\qquad\qquad\qquad write\,(show\,(ord\,c))
\end{aligned}
$$

When *reveal* is performed, the user types a character, and the computer prints its numeric value.

Next, here is an interactive program that prompts for a string, and then says whether the string is a palindrome:

$$
\begin{aligned}
&palindrome \quad :: \quad IO\,() \\
&palindrome \quad = \quad \textbf{do}\; write\;\text{``Enter a string:}\_\text{''} \\
&\qquad\qquad\qquad\qquad cs \leftarrow getLine \\
&\qquad\qquad\qquad\quad \textbf{if}\; palin\,cs \\
&\qquad\qquad\qquad\qquad \textbf{then}\quad writeln\;\text{``Yes''} \\
&\qquad\qquad\qquad\qquad \textbf{else}\quad writeln\;\text{``No''}
\end{aligned}
$$

$$
\begin{array}{lll}
palin & :: & String \rightarrow Bool \\
palin\ xs & = & (ys == reverse\ ys) \\
& & \textbf{where}\ ys = map\ toUpper\ (filter\ isLetter\ xs)
\end{array}
$$

The definition of *isLetter* is left as an exercise. An example session might be

? *palindrome*
Enter a string: Madam, I'm Adam!
Yes

? *palindrome*
Enter a string: A Man, a plan, a canal - Suez!
No

As a more complicated example, here is a program to play the game of "hang-man". In this game, one player thinks of a word, and the other player tries to deduce the word by making a sequence of guesses. For each guess, the computer (which acts as mediator between the players) prints the secret word with all those letters not guessed so far replaced by a '-'. The game ends when all letters have been guessed correctly. An example session might go

```
? hangman
Think of a word:
----
Now try to guess it!
guess: last
--al

guess: dial
--al
guess: opal
-oal
guess: foal
-oal
guess: goal
You got it!
```

The program takes the form

$$
\begin{array}{lll}
hangman & :: & IO\ () \\
hangman & = & \textbf{do}\ writeln\ \text{"Think of a word:"} \\
& & \qquad word \leftarrow silentReadln \\
& & \qquad writeln\ \text{"Now try to guess it!"} \\
& & \qquad guess\ word
\end{array}
$$

The command *silentReadln* reads a line from the keyboard, but does not echo the characters. Instead, it prints a '-' for each character read. To implement this, we need another Haskell primitive function, *getCh*, which is similar to *getChar* except that the character is not echoed. In fact

$$getChar = \textbf{do} \{c \leftarrow getCh;\ putChar\ c;\ return\ c\}$$

The command *silentReadln* is now implemented as follows:

```
silentReadln  ::  IO String
silentReadln  =  do c ← getCh
                    if c == '¬'
                    then  do putChar c
                             return [ ]
                    else  do putChar '-'
                             cs ← silentReadln
                             return (c : cs)
```

The command *guess word* accepts input from the keyboard until the guess matches *word*:

```
guess         ::  String → IO ()
guess word    =  do write "guess:␣"
                    cs ← readln
                    if cs == word
                    then  writeln "You got it!"
                    else  do writeln (compare word cs)
                             guess word

compare       ::  String → String → String
compare word cs  =  map check word
                    where check w = if member cs w then w else '-'
```

Finally, here is a suggestive example that makes use of two Haskell file-handling primitives:

```
readFile   ::  FilePath → IO String
writeFile  ::  FilePath → String → IO ()
```

The type *FilePath* is a synonym for *String*; files are named by strings using some implementation-specific convention. The example is to read a file, remove all non-ASCII characters, and write the result to a second file:

$$
\begin{array}{lll}
\textit{filterFile} & :: & IO\,() \\
\textit{filterFile} & = & \textbf{do}\ \textit{write}\ \text{“Enter input file:}_\sqcup\text{”} \\
& & \quad \textit{infile} \leftarrow \textit{getLine} \\
& & \quad \textit{write}\ \text{“Enter output file:}_\sqcup\text{”} \\
& & \quad \textit{outfile} \leftarrow \textit{getLine} \\
& & \quad \textit{xs} \leftarrow \textit{readFile infile} \\
& & \quad \textit{writeFile outfile}\ (\textit{filter isAscii xs}) \\
& & \quad \textit{writeln}\ \text{“Filtering successful”}
\end{array}
$$

The function *isAscii* is defined in a Haskell library.

As the foregoing examples show, writing monadic programs using **do** nota-tion is very similar to writing traditional imperative programs in a language such as Pascal or C. But there are differences; for example, the function *readFile* reads a file lazily on demand. Consequently, the two commands

$$
\begin{array}{l}
\textit{xs} \leftarrow \textit{readFile infile} \\
\textit{writeFile outfile}\ (\textit{filter isAscii xs})
\end{array}
$$

do not cause the entire contents of the file to be written into memory before being filtered and written out.

Another difference with imperative programming is that the monadic style is available in Haskell as an optional extra: for those portions of a program that are independent of interaction, all of the functional techniques we have seen in previous chapters still apply.

Exercises

10.1.1 Define $(\gg)$ in terms of $(\vartriangleright)$.

10.1.2 What is the effect of the command *foldl* $(\gg)$ *done* $\cdot$ *map putChar*?

10.1.3 When performed, *getChar* reads a character and returns the character. Describe the effect of performing *getChar* $\vartriangleright$ *return*. What relationship between $\vartriangleright$ and *return* does this suggest?

10.1.4 Describe the effect of performing *return* ‘!’ $\vartriangleright$ *putChar*. What relation-ship between $\vartriangleright$ and *return* does this suggest?

10.1.5 Using $\vartriangleright$, define an operator $\diamond$ with type

$$
(\diamond) \quad :: \quad (\alpha \to IO\,\beta) \to (\beta \to IO\,\gamma) \to (\alpha \to IO\,\gamma)
$$

Using $\diamond$, define $\vartriangleright$.

10.1.6 By expanding **do** notation, show that

$$\mathbf{do}\ \{C;\ \mathbf{do}\ \{D;\ r\}\}\ \ =\ \ \mathbf{do}\ \{C;\ D;\ r\}$$

10.1.7 Rewrite the *reveal* program so that it repeatedly prompts for a character, revealing its numeric value, until the user types a particular character, 'q' say, to terminate the interaction.

10.1.8 The hangman game is perhaps too easy. Modify the response to a guess so that letters are revealed only if they are present in the guess in the correct position.

10.2   Variations on an evaluator

In this section we are going to examine several variations on an evaluator for simple arithmetic expressions. The aim is to show how a monadic style can capture the essential similarities between the variations, and – more importantly – enable each variation to be installed without changing the basic structure of the program. We will begin with a simple evaluator, and then add certain features. Specifically, we will add:

- Error handling, which involves modifying each recursive call to check for and handle errors appropriately.

- An operation count, which involves modifying each recursive call to pass around such counts appropriately.

- An execution trace, which involves modifying each recursive call to pass around such traces appropriately.

In each case, the bookkeeping involved is straightforward, but tedious. Worse, it threatens to overwhelm the essential simplicity of the evaluator with a welter of detail. After giving these variations, we will revisit them, showing how a monadic approach can be used to install each variation with far less fuss.

10.2.1   The basic evaluator

The evaluator acts on terms, which for purposes of illustration are taken to be excessively simple:

data *Term*   =   *Con Int* | *Div Term Term*

A term is either a constant *Con x*, where *x* is an integer, or a quotient, *Div t u*, where *t* and *u* are terms.

The basic evaluation function is defined by

$$
\begin{array}{lll}
eval & :: & Term \rightarrow Int \\
eval\,(Con\,x) & = & x \\
eval\,(Div\,t\,u) & = & (eval\,t)\ \mathbf{div}\ (eval\,u)
\end{array}
$$

The function *eval* takes a term to an integer. If the term is a constant, the constant is returned. If the term is a quotient, its subterms are evaluated and the quotient is computed.

The following will be used as running examples:

$$
\begin{array}{lll}
answer, wrong & :: & Term \\
answer & = & Div\,(Div\,(Con\,1972)\,(Con\,2))\,(Con\,23) \\
wrong & = & Div\,(Con\,2)\,(Div\,(Con\,1)\,(Con\,0))
\end{array}
$$

Here's a simple trial of the evaluator:

? eval answer
42

?eval wrong
[*BOOM!*]

The problem with the second example is that division by zero yields an un-defined result. Undefined operations may be implemented in any way, and this particular computer implements division by zero with an explosion.

10.2.2   Exceptions

After we go out and buy a new computer, we may wish to modify our evaluator to check for division by zero and return a suitable error message. It is not appro-priate to use the primitive function *error* for this purpose, since the evaluator may be used interactively. The aim is not to abort the evaluator, but merely to handle the error and display a suitable message to the user. Such *exception handling* may be mimicked by introducing a type to represent computations that may raise an exception:

$$
\begin{array}{lll}
\mathbf{data}\ Exc\ \alpha & = & Raise\,Exception\ |\ Return\,\alpha \\
\mathbf{type}\ Exception & = & String
\end{array}
$$

A computation *Exc* α will either raise an exception or return a value of type α. Exceptions carry an error message, represented as a string.

It is straightforward, but tedious, to adapt the evaluator to this representation. We write the new evaluator in a particular way to emphasise the order in
which the computation is to be performed:

$$
\begin{array}{lll}
eval & :: & Term \rightarrow Exc\ Int \\
eval\ (Con\ x) & = & Return\ x
\end{array}
$$

$$
\begin{array}{l}
eval\ (Div\ t\ u) \\
\quad = \quad h\ (eval\ t) \\
\qquad \textbf{where} \\
\qquad h\ (Raise\ e) \quad = \quad Raise\ e \\
\qquad h\ (Return\ x) \quad = \quad h'\ (eval\ u) \\
\qquad\qquad \textbf{where} \\
\qquad\qquad h'\ (Raise\ e') = Raise\ e' \\
\qquad\qquad h'\ (Return\ y) \\
\qquad\qquad\quad = \quad \textbf{if}\ y == 0 \\
\qquad\qquad\qquad\qquad \textbf{then}\ \ Raise\ \text{“division by zero”} \\
\qquad\qquad\qquad\qquad \textbf{else}\ \ \ Return\ (x\ \textbf{div}\ y)
\end{array}
$$

At each call of the evaluator, the form of the result is checked by the auxiliary
handling functions h and h'. If an exception was raised it is re-raised, and if a
value was returned it is processed.

We can also specify how to display an exception, by installing $Exc\ \alpha$ as an
instance of *Show* (for simplicity, we define the function *show* only):

$$
\begin{array}{l}
\textbf{instance}\ Show\ \alpha \Rightarrow Show\ (Exc\ \alpha)\ \textbf{where} \\
\quad show\ (Raise\ e) \quad = \quad \text{“exception: ”} + e \\
\quad show\ (Return\ x) \quad = \quad \text{“value: ”} + show\ x
\end{array}
$$

Here is a session with the new evaluator:

? eval answer
value: 42

? eval wrong
exception: division by zero

10.2.3 State

As another variation, suppose we want to count the number of divisions performed during evaluation. One way is to introduce an additional component,
called the *state*. The state in this instance is an integer, initialised to zero at the
start of the computation, and incremented by one each time a division occurs.

Such a state may be mimicked by introducing a type to represent computations that act on state, called a *state transformer*:

> **newtype** *St α* = *MkSt* (*State* → (α, *State*))
> **type** *State*   = *Int*

A state transformer of type *St α* is a function that takes a state, and returns a value of type α paired with a new state. The state will be used to count division steps, and so is represented by an integer.

The constructor *MkSt* makes *St* a new type, distinct from the underlying function type. The auxiliary function *apply* applies a state transformer to a state, yielding a value paired with a new state:

> *apply*   ::   *St α* → *State* → (α, *State*)
> *apply* (*MkSt f*) *s* = *f s*

Here is the new evaluator:

> *eval*   ::   *Term* → *St Int*
> *eval* (*Con x*)   = *MkSt f*
>   **where** *f s* = (*x*, *s*)
>
> *eval* (*Div t u*)   = *MkSt f*
>   **where**
>   *f s*   = (*x* **div** *y*, *s″* + 1)
>   **where**
>   (*x*, *s′*)   =   *apply* (*eval t*) *s*
>   (*y*, *s″*) =   *apply* (*eval u*) *s′*

At each call of the evaluator, the resulting state transformer is applied to the old state, and the value and new state are returned. Care must be taken to pass on the state properly – it is all too easy accidentally to write *s* where we should write *s′*.

We can also specify how to display a state transformer:

> **instance** *Show α* ⇒ *Show* (*St α*) **where**
>   *show f*   =   "value: " ++ *show x* ++ ", count: " ++ *show s*
>   **where** (*x*, *s*) = *apply f* 0

A state transformer *f* is displayed by applying it to the initial state 0, and then displaying the final value and count. Here is a session with the new evaluator:

? *eval answer*
value: 42, count: 2

10.2.4 Output

Finally, say we want to display a trace of the execution steps. Output can be mimicked by introducing a type to represent computations that generate output:

$$\textbf{newtype } \textit{Out } \alpha \;\; = \;\; \textit{MkOut } (\textit{Output}, \alpha)$$
$$\textbf{type } \textit{Output} \;\;\;\; = \;\; \textit{String}$$

A value of type $\textit{Out } \alpha$ consists of the generated output paired with the computed value.

Here is the modified evaluator:

$$
\begin{array}{lll}
\textit{eval} & :: & \textit{Term} \to \textit{Out Int} \\
\textit{eval } (\textit{Con } x) & = & \textit{MkOut } (\textit{line } (\textit{Con } x)\, x, x) \\
\textit{eval } (\textit{Div } t\, u) & = & \textit{MkOut } (\textit{ox} \mathbin{+\!\!+} \textit{oy} \mathbin{+\!\!+} \textit{line } (\textit{Div } t\, u)\, z, z) \\
& & \textbf{where } \textit{MkOut } (\textit{ox}, x) \;\; = \;\; \textit{eval } t \\
& & \phantom{\textbf{where }} \textit{MkOut } (\textit{oy}, y) \;\; = \;\; \textit{eval } u \\
& & \phantom{\textbf{where }} z \phantom{\textit{MkOut } (\textit{oy}, y)} = \;\; x \textbf{ div } y
\end{array}
$$

$$
\begin{array}{lll}
\textit{line} & :: & \textit{Term} \to \textit{Int} \to \textit{Output} \\
\textit{line } t\, x & = & \text{``term: ''} \mathbin{+\!\!+} \textit{show } t \mathbin{+\!\!+} \text{``, yields ''} \mathbin{+\!\!+} \textit{show } x \mathbin{+\!\!+} \text{``\textasciitilde''}
\end{array}
$$

At each call of the evaluator the outputs are collected and assembled to form the output of the enclosing call. The function $\textit{line}$ generates one line of the output. We assume the usual definition of $\textit{show}$ on terms, and specify how to display a computation with output:

$$\textbf{instance } \textit{Show } \alpha \Rightarrow \textit{Show } (\textit{Out } \alpha) \textbf{ where}$$
$$\textit{show } (\textit{MkOut } (\textit{ox}, x)) \;\; = \;\; \textit{ox} \mathbin{+\!\!+} \text{``value: ''} \mathbin{+\!\!+} \textit{show } x$$

Here is a session with the new evaluator:

? eval answer
term: *Con* 1972, yields 1972
term: *Con* 2, yields 2
term: *Div* (*Con* 1972) (*Con* 2), yields 986
term: *Con* 23, yields 23
term: *Div* (*Div* (*Con* 1972) (*Con* 2)) (*Con* 23), yields 42
value: 42

In passing, it is worthwhile mentioning that it is easy to install the execution trace so that it prints in reverse order: just replace

$$\textit{ox} \mathbin{+\!\!+} \textit{oy} \mathbin{+\!\!+} \textit{line } (\textit{Div } t\, u)\, z \quad \textbf{by} \quad \textit{line } (\textit{Div } t\, u)\, z \mathbin{+\!\!+} \textit{oy} \mathbin{+\!\!+} \textit{ox}$$

10.2.5   A monadic evaluator

The basic evaluator is easily rewritten to make use of a monad *m*:

$$
\begin{array}{lll}
eval & :: & Monad\ m \Rightarrow Term \rightarrow m\ Int \\
eval\ (Con\ x) & = & return\ x \\
eval\ (Div\ t\ u) & = & \mathbf{do}\ x \leftarrow eval\ t \\
& & \quad y \leftarrow eval\ u \\
& & \quad return\ (x\ \mathbf{div}\ y)
\end{array}
$$

The type of *eval* indicates that it takes a term and performs a 'computation' *m* yielding an integer. To evaluate *Con x*, just return *x*. To evaluate *Div t u*, first evaluate *t*, bind *x* to the result, then evaluate *u*, bind *y* to the result, and then return *x* **div** *y*.

The new evaluator is a little more complex than the original one, but it is much more flexible. Each of the variations discussed above may be achieved simply by defining *m* to be an appropriate instance of the *Monad* class, and by making one or two local modifications.

First of all, in the basic evaluator a computation is simply the value returned. The *identity* monad is declared by first introducing a new type *Id α*, isomorphic to *α*:

$$
\mathbf{newtype}\ Id\ \alpha \quad = \quad MkId\ \alpha
$$

$$
\begin{array}{ll}
\mathbf{instance}\ Monad\ Id\ \mathbf{where} \\
\quad return\ x & = \quad MkId\ x \\
\quad (MkId\ x) \rhd q & = \quad q\ x
\end{array}
$$

In the identity monad, *Id* is isomorphic to the identity function on types, *return* is isomorphic to the identity function, and (▷) is isomorphic to functional application, except that the argument comes before the function.

We can also specify how to display elements of type *Id α*:

$$
\begin{array}{l}
\mathbf{instance}\ Show\ \alpha \Rightarrow Show\ (Id\ \alpha)\ \mathbf{where} \\
\quad show\ (MkId\ x) \quad = \quad \text{“value: ”} \mathbin{+\!\!+} show\ x
\end{array}
$$

The evaluator *evalId* is exactly *eval*, but specialised to *m = Id*:

$$
\begin{array}{lll}
evalId & :: & Term \rightarrow Id\ Int \\
evalId & = & eval
\end{array}
$$

For example:

? *evalId answer*
value: 42

In the exception monad, a computation may either raise an exception or return a value. Here we define

> **instance** *Monad Exc* **where**
>   *return x*   =   *Return x*
>   (*Raise e*) ▷ *q*   =   *Raise e*
>   (*Return x*) ▷ *q* =   *q x*

The call *return x* simply returns the value *x*. The call *p* ▷ *q* examines the result of the computation *p*; if it is an exception, it is re-raised; otherwise the function *q* is applied to the value returned. (It is a good exercise to check the types.)

We also define operations specific to the monad. In this case, there is an operation to raise an exception:

> *raise*   ::   *Exception* → *Exc* α
> *raise e* =   *Raise e*

To add error handling, we take the monadic evaluator as above, and just replace the term *return* (*x* **div** *y*) by a conditional expression:

> *evalEx*   ::   *Term* → *Exc Int*
> *evalEx* (*Con x*)   =   *return x*
> *evalEx* (*Div t u*) =   **do** *x* ← *eval t*
>   *y* ← *eval u*
>   **if** *y* == 0
>   **then** *raise* "division by zero"
>   **else**   *return* (*x* **div** *y*)

Rather than rewrite the program from scratch, we only had to make a small change to the code.

Next, in the state monad, a computation accepts an initial state and returns a value paired with the final state. The instance declaration for *St* α is

> **instance** *Monad St* **where**
>   *return x*   =   *MkSt f*   **where** *f s* = (*x*, *s*)
>
>   *p* ▷ *q*   =   *MkSt f*
>   **where**
>   *f s*   =   *apply* (*q x*) *s'*
>   **where** (*x*, *s'*) = *apply p s*

The call *return x* returns the state transformer that yields value *x* and leaves the state unchanged. The call *p* ▷ *q* applies the state transformer *p* to the initial state s, yielding value x and intermediate state s'; then it applies the state transformer $q\,x$ to state s'.

We also define operations specific to the monad. In this case, there is an operation to increment the state:

$$
\begin{aligned}
tick \quad &:: \quad St\ () \\
tick \quad &= \quad MkSt\ f \quad \textbf{where}\ f\ s = ((), s + 1)
\end{aligned}
$$

To add execution counts, we take the monadic evaluator as above, and just add a call to *tick* at the right point. Rather than rewrite the program from scratch, we only have to make a small, local change. Here is the result:

$$
\begin{aligned}
evalSt \quad &:: \quad Term \rightarrow St\ Int \\
evalSt\ (Con\ x) \quad &= \quad return\ x \\
evalSt\ (Div\ t\ u) \quad &= \quad \textbf{do}\ x \leftarrow evalSt\ u \\
&\qquad\quad y \leftarrow evalSt\ t \\
&\qquad\quad tick \\
&\qquad\quad return\ (x\ \textbf{div}\ y)
\end{aligned}
$$

Finally, in the output monad *Out* α, a computation consists of the generated output paired with the final value. The instance declaration for *Out* α is

$$
\begin{aligned}
\textbf{instance}\ &Monad\ Out\ \textbf{where} \\
return\ x \quad &= \quad MkOut\ (\text{``''}, x) \\
p \triangleright q \quad &= \quad MkOut\ (ox \mathbin{+\!\!+} oy, y) \\
&\qquad \textbf{where}\ MkOut\ (ox, x) \quad = \quad p \\
&\qquad\qquad\quad\ MkOut\ (oy, y) \quad = \quad q\,x
\end{aligned}
$$

The call *return x* returns empty output paired with x. The call $p \triangleright q$ extracts an output ox and value x from computation p, then extracts an output oy and value y from computation $q\,x$, and returns the output formed by concatenating ox and oy, paired with the value y.

We also define operations specific to the monad. In this case, there is an operation to generate output:

$$
\begin{aligned}
out \quad &:: \quad Output \rightarrow Out\ () \\
out\ ox \quad &= \quad MkOut\ (ox, ())
\end{aligned}
$$

To add execution traces to the monadic evaluator, we take the monadic evaluator as above, and just decorate it with calls to generate output:

$$
\begin{aligned}
evalOut \quad &:: \quad Term \rightarrow Out\ Int \\
evalOut\ (Con\ x) \quad &= \quad \textbf{do}\ out\ (line\ (Con\ x)\ x) \\
&\qquad\quad return\ x
\end{aligned}
$$

$$evalOut\ (Div\ t\ u)\ =\ \mathbf{do}\ x \leftarrow evalOut\ t$$
$$y \leftarrow evalOut\ u$$
$$out\ (line\ (Div\ t\ u)\ (x\ \mathbf{div}\ y))$$
$$return\ (x\ \mathbf{div}\ y)$$

To get the output in the reverse order, all that is required is to change the definition of ▷, replacing $ox \mathbin{+\!\!+} oy$ by $oy \mathbin{+\!\!+} ox$. This is even simpler than the change required in the previous version of the program.

The lesson to be learned from these examples is that a monadic style of programming is highly suitable when the program under construction may require modification due to changes in specification. Any changes are localised in the definition of the monad, and at one or two places in the program. There is no need for a major restructuring of the program with every added bell and whistle. In Section 10.4 we return to the evaluators, and tackle the question of how different features can be combined.

Exercises

10.2.1 Modify the evaluator with exceptions to specify an alternative term to evaluate in case of an exception. More specifically, extend the type *Term* to include a new term *Try Term Term*. To evaluate *Try t u*, first evaluate *t* and, if it succeeds, return its value; but if evaluation raises an exception, then evaluate *u*. Here's a transcript of how the program should behave:

? *eval* (*Try* (*Div* (*Con* 1) (*Con* 0)) (*Con* 42))
42

Define a corresponding *try* operation on the type *Exc* to facilitate the modification.

10.2.2 In the evaluator that counts the number of division, the use of state is somewhat heavy-handed. Instead of keeping track of a current state, each computation can simply return a value paired with the number of operations required to compute it:

$$\mathbf{data}\ Count\ \alpha\ =\ (\alpha, Counter)$$
$$\mathbf{type}\ Counter\ =\ Int$$

Modify the evaluator to use this new computation type.

10.2.3 Modify the evaluator with state to be able to access the state in a computation (so the shortcut of the previous exercise won't work). More specifically, extend the type *Term* to include a new term *Count*. The value of *Count* is the number of operations performed so far, a quantity that is retrieved by accessing the state. Here's a transcript of how the program should behave:

? *eval* (*Div* (*Div* (*Div* (*Con* 6) (*Con* 3)) *Count*) *Count*)
1

The answer here is 1 because the first instance of *Count* evaluates to 1 (since the division of 6 by 3 is performed earlier) and the second instance returns 2 (since the divisions of 6 by 3 and 2 by 1 are performed earlier). Define a corresponding *count* operation on the type *St* to facilitate the modification.

10.2.4 Modify the evaluator with output so that it only traces selected parts of the computation. More specifically, extend the type *Term* with two extra terms, *Trace Term* and *Untrace Term*. Tracing should be turned on for all subterms surrounded by *Trace* and turned off for all subterms surrounded by *Untrace*. To support this change, a computation should be represented by a function, the argument of which is a boolean that indicates whether tracing is on. Define suitable operations on computations to set and access the tracing status.

10.3 Monad laws

We have now seen a number of instances of the class *Monad*, including *IO*, *Id*, *Exc*, *St*, and *Out*. In each case, the operations *return* and $\triangleright$ have to satisfy a number of laws. In this section we will state the monad laws in a number of different but equivalent ways. First, recall the types of *return* and $\triangleright$:

$$\begin{aligned} return &:: \quad \alpha \to m\,\alpha \\ (\triangleright) &:: \quad m\,\alpha \to (\alpha \to m\,\beta) \to m\,\beta \end{aligned}$$

The first law states that *return* is a right unit of $\triangleright$:

$$p \triangleright return \;=\; p$$

The second law states that *return* is a 'left unit' of $\triangleright$ in the following sense:

$$(return\ e) \triangleright q \;=\; q\,e$$

The third law states that $\triangleright$ is 'associative' in the following sense:

$$(p \triangleright q) \triangleright r \;=\; p \triangleright s \quad \textbf{where } s\,x = (q\,x \triangleright r)$$

We have already encountered many examples of operations with type $\alpha \to \alpha \to \alpha$ that have a left and right unit and are associative; algebraists call these *monoids*. As we have introduced them, monads differ from monoids in that, instead of an operation with type $\alpha \to \alpha \to \alpha$ for appropriate α, we have a binding operation. However, as we will see below, $\triangleright$ can also be defined in terms of a monoid operation. Category theorists are infamous for stealing terms from philosophy, starting with the theft of *category* itself from Kant. The abduction of *monad* from Leibniz was aided and abetted by the pun on monoid.

For each of the monads we have considered, it is easy to prove that the monad laws hold. The left unit law for the exception monad is immediate from the definition of ▷. Here is a proof of the right unit law for the state monad. Recall that

> **instance** *Monad St* **where**
>   *return x* = *MkSt f*   **where** *f s* = (*x*, *s*)
>
>   *p* ▷ *q* = *MkSt f*
>   **where**
>   *f s* = *apply* (*q x*) *s'*
>   **where** (*x*, *s'*) = *apply p s*
>
>   *apply*   ::   *St* $\alpha \rightarrow$ *State* $\rightarrow$ (α, *State*)
>   *apply* (*MkSt f*) *s* = *f s*

In the proof, we use a form of extensionality: *p* = *q* if *apply p s* = *apply q s* for all states *s*:

>   *apply* (*p* ▷ *return*) *s*
> =   {definition of ▷ (in the state monad) and *apply*}
>   *apply* (*return x*) *s'* **where** (*x*, *s'*) = *apply p s*
> =   {definition of *return* and *apply*}
>   (*x*, *s'*) **where** (*x*, *s'*) = *apply p s*
> =   {simplification}
>   *apply p s*

Here is a proof of the associative law for the output monad. Recall that

> **instance** *Monad Out* **where**
>   *return x* = *MkOut* ("", *x*)
>   *p* ▷ *q*   = *MkOut* (*ox* ++ *oy*, *y*)
>   **where** *MkOut* (*ox*, *x*) = *p*
>   *MkOut* (*oy*, *y*) = *q x*

First, we simplify the left-hand side:

>   (*p* ▷ *q*) ▷ *r*
> =   {definition of ▷ in the output monad}

$$MkOut\ (ox +\!\!+ oy, y)$$
$$\textbf{where } MkOut\ (ox, x)\ =\ p \triangleright q$$
$$\qquad\qquad MkOut\ (oy, y)\ =\ r\,x$$

$=\quad$ {definition of $\triangleright$}

$$MkOut\ (ox +\!\!+ oy, y)$$
$$\textbf{where } MkOut\ (ox, x)\ =\ MkOut\ (ou +\!\!+ ov, v)$$
$$\qquad\qquad\qquad\qquad \textbf{where } MkOut\ (ou, u)\ =\ p$$
$$\qquad\qquad\qquad\qquad\qquad MkOut\ (ov, v)\ =\ q\,u$$
$$\qquad\qquad MkOut\ (oy, y)\ =\ r\,x$$

$=\quad$ {simplification}

$$MkOut\ ((ou +\!\!+ ov) +\!\!+ oy, y)$$
$$\textbf{where } MkOut\ (ou, u)\ =\ p$$
$$\qquad\qquad MkOut\ (ov, v)\ =\ q\,u$$
$$\qquad\qquad MkOut\ (oy, y)\ =\ r\,v$$

Similarly, we simplify the right-hand side:

$$p \triangleright s \ \textbf{where } s\,x = q\,x \triangleright r$$

$=\quad$ {definition of $\triangleright$, twice}

$$MkOut\ (ou +\!\!+ (ov +\!\!+ oy), y)$$
$$\textbf{where } MkOut\ (ou, u)\ =\ p$$
$$\qquad\qquad MkOut\ (ov, v)\ =\ q\,u$$
$$\qquad\qquad MkOut\ (oy, y)\ =\ r\,v$$

The result then follows from the associativity of $+\!\!+$. Furthermore, the left and right unit laws for the output monad follow from the left and right unit laws for $+\!\!+$, respectively.

10.3.1 Laws of do notation

We can also state the laws in terms of **do** notation. They read:

$$\textbf{do } \{B;\ x \leftarrow p;\ return\ x\}\ =\ \textbf{do } \{B;\ p\}$$
$$\textbf{do } \{B;\ x \leftarrow return\ e;\ C;\ r\}\ =\ \textbf{do } \{B;\ C[x := e];\ r[x := e]\}$$
$$\textbf{do } \{B;\ x \leftarrow \textbf{do } \{C;\ p\};\ D;\ r\}\ =\ \textbf{do } \{B;\ C;\ x \leftarrow p;\ D;\ r\}$$

Here, B, C, D range over sequences of commands and $C[x := e]$ means the sequence C with all free occurrences of x replaced by e. We will leave as an exercise the proofs that these three laws are equivalent to the ones stated earlier.

There is also one additional rule, called the *collapse* law, which is a consequence of the definition of **do** notation:

$$\textbf{do } \{C;\ \textbf{do } \{D;\ r\}\}\ =\ \textbf{do } \{C;\ D;\ r\}$$

To demonstrate these versions of the monad laws, consider a variant of the evaluator of the previous section, based on addition rather than division:

$$
\begin{aligned}
&\textbf{data } \textit{Term} &&=&& \textit{Con Int} \ \mid\ \textit{Add Term Term} \\
&\textit{eval} &&:: && \textit{Monad m} \Rightarrow \textit{Term} \rightarrow \textit{m Int} \\
&\textit{eval (Con x)} &&= && \textit{return x} \\
&\textit{eval (Add t u)} &&= && \textbf{do } \{x \leftarrow \textit{eval t};\ \ y \leftarrow \textit{eval u};\ \ \textit{return } (x + y)\}
\end{aligned}
$$

The aim is to show that evaluation of

$$\textit{Add t (Add u v)}\quad \text{and}\quad \textit{Add (Add t u) v}$$

both compute the same result. First, we simplify the left term:

$$\textit{eval (Add t (Add u v))}$$

$=$ {definition of *eval*}

$$\textbf{do } \{x \leftarrow \textit{eval t};\ \ w \leftarrow \textit{eval (Add u v)};\ \ \textit{return } (x + w)\}$$

$=$ {definition of *eval*}

$$
\begin{aligned}
&\textbf{do } x \leftarrow \textit{eval t} \\
&\quad w \leftarrow \textbf{do } \{y \leftarrow \textit{eval u};\ z \leftarrow \textit{eval v};\ \textit{return } (y + z)\}; \\
&\quad \textit{return } (x + w)
\end{aligned}
$$

$=$ {associative law}

$$
\begin{aligned}
&\textbf{do } x \leftarrow \textit{eval t} \\
&\quad y \leftarrow \textit{eval u} \\
&\quad z \leftarrow \textit{eval v} \\
&\quad w \leftarrow \textit{return } (y + z) \\
&\quad \textit{return } (x + w)
\end{aligned}
$$

$=$ {left unit law}

$$\textbf{do } \{x \leftarrow \textit{eval t};\ \ y \leftarrow \textit{eval u};\ \ z \leftarrow \textit{eval v};\ \ \textit{return } (x + (y + z))\}$$

Simplification of the right term is similar:

$$\textit{eval (Add (Add t u) v)}$$

$=$ {as before}

$$\textbf{do } \{x \leftarrow \textit{eval t};\ \ y \leftarrow \textit{eval u};\ \ z \leftarrow \textit{eval v};\ \ \textit{return } ((x + y) + z)\}$$

The result follows by the associativity of addition.

Note carefully that the proof works in *any* monad, provided the program is as above. In Section 10.2, we modified the program by adding calls to *tick* in the case of the state monad. However, associativity still holds, as can be demonstrated using the law

$$\textbf{do} \{tick;\ x \leftarrow p;\ return\ x\} \quad = \quad \textbf{do} \{x \leftarrow p;\ tick;\ return\ x\}$$

This law holds provided *tick* is the only action on state within *m*. Similarly, in the case of the output monad, we modified the program by adding calls to *line*. In this case, the two terms are no longer equivalent, because the traces will be different. Of course, the two computations will still yield the same final value.

10.3.2 Laws of monad composition

Perhaps the best way to remember the monad laws is to restate them in terms of a monad *composition* operator. The operator ($\diamond$) is defined by

$$
\begin{aligned}
(\diamond) \quad &::\quad (\alpha \to m\,\beta) \to (\beta \to m\,\gamma) \to (\alpha \to m\,\gamma) \\
(f \diamond g)\,x \quad &=\quad f\,x \triangleright g
\end{aligned}
$$

Equivalently, using a section,

$$f \diamond g \quad = \quad (\triangleright g) \cdot f$$

The operator ($\diamond$) is like function composition ($\cdot$), except that the component functions each have type $\alpha \to m\,\beta$ for appropriate α and β, and the order in which functions are composed is reversed. In fact, ($\diamond$) can be used to define $\triangleright$:

$$(\triangleright g) \quad = \quad id \diamond g$$

Note also that ($\diamond$) and ($\cdot$) are related by the useful law

$$(f \diamond g) \cdot h \quad = \quad (f \cdot h) \diamond g$$

The proof follows immediately from the definition of ($\diamond$). We will refer to this law as the *leapfrog* law.

Now, reformulated, the first two monad laws state that *return* is a left and right unit of ($\diamond$):

$$p \diamond return = p \quad \text{and} \quad return \diamond q = q$$

And, reformulated, the third law states that ($\diamond$) is associative:

$$(f \diamond g) \diamond h \quad = \quad f \diamond (g \diamond h)$$

Proof of the equivalence of the two sets of laws is left as an exercise.

So a monad is, after all, a monoid. Although the monad laws are easier to state in terms of ($\diamond$), monadic programs are easier to state in terms of **do** notation, which is based on $\triangleright$.

10.3.3 Map and concat

There is yet another, and very revealing, way we can describe the fundamental laws of a monad. First of all, consider the following definitions:

$$mapm \qquad :: \quad Monad\ m \Rightarrow (\alpha \to \beta) \to (m\ \alpha \to m\ \beta)$$
$$mapm\ f\ p \quad = \quad \textbf{do}\ \{x \leftarrow p;\ return\ (f\ x)\}$$

$$concatm \qquad :: \quad Monad\ m \Rightarrow m\ (m\ \alpha) \to m\ \alpha$$
$$concatm\ ps \quad = \quad \textbf{do}\ \{p \leftarrow ps;\ p\}$$

The function *mapm* applies a function to the result yielded by a computation. To compute *mapm f p*, first compute p, bind x to the result, and then return $f\ x$. In the definition of *concatm ps*, the variable *ps* denotes a computation that, when performed, *itself* yields a computation. Thus, *concatm* flattens a mind-boggling double layer of computation into a run-of-the-mill single layer of computation.

We can also express *mapm* and *concatm* using the monad composition operator $\diamond$. First, we have

$$mapm\ f\ p$$
$$= \quad \{\text{definition}\}$$
$$\textbf{do}\ \{x \leftarrow p;\ return\ (f\ x)\}$$
$$= \quad \{\text{translating } \textbf{do} \text{ notation into } \triangleright\}$$
$$p \triangleright (return \cdot f)$$
$$= \quad \{\text{definition of } \diamond, \text{ using the identity function } id\}$$
$$(id \diamond (return \cdot f))\ p$$

Hence *mapm f* = $id \diamond (return \cdot f)$. Second,

$$concatm\ ps$$
$$= \quad \{\text{definition}\}$$
$$\textbf{do}\ \{p \leftarrow ps;\ p\}$$
$$= \quad \{\text{translating } \textbf{do} \text{ notation into } \triangleright\}$$
$$ps \triangleright id$$
$$= \quad \{\text{definition of } \diamond\}$$

$$(id \diamond id)\, ps$$

Hence $concatm = id \diamond id$. The first id has type $id :: m\,(m\,\alpha) \to m\,(m\,\alpha)$, while the second id has type $id :: m\,\alpha \to m\,\alpha$.

There are seven laws that characterise $mapm$ and $concatm$, all of which have a familiar ring:

$$
\begin{aligned}
mapm\ id &= id \\
mapm\ (f \cdot g) &= mapm\ f \cdot mapm\ g
\end{aligned}
$$

$$
\begin{aligned}
mapm\ f \cdot return &= return \cdot f \\
mapm\ f \cdot concatm &= concatm \cdot mapm\ (mapm\ f)
\end{aligned}
$$

$$
\begin{aligned}
concatm \cdot return &= id \\
concatm \cdot mapm\ return &= id \\
concatm \cdot mapm\ concatm &= concatm \cdot concatm
\end{aligned}
$$

The first two laws state that $mapm$ is a *functor*, just as map over lists is a functor (see Section 4.3). The third and fourth laws are *naturality* conditions on *return* and *concatm*, just as the laws

$$
\begin{aligned}
map\ f \cdot wrap &= wrap \cdot f \\
map\ f \cdot concat &= concat \cdot map\ (map\ f)
\end{aligned}
$$

are naturality conditions on the list-processing functions *wrap* and *concat* (again, see Section 4.3). And the final three laws are generalisations of similar laws for *wrap* and *concat*.

These seven laws are equivalent to the three monad laws. For example, we will prove the law

$$mapm\ f \cdot concatm \quad = \quad concatm \cdot mapm\ (mapm\ f)$$

We will need the fact that

$$(return \cdot h) \diamond g \quad = \quad g \cdot h$$

The proof is

$$
\begin{aligned}
& (return \cdot h) \diamond g \\
= \quad & \{\text{leapfrog law} - (f \cdot h) \diamond g = (f \diamond g) \cdot h\} \\
& (return \diamond g) \cdot h \\
= \quad & \{\text{left unit}\} \\
& g \cdot h
\end{aligned}
$$

For the main proof, we simplify the left-hand side:

$$mapm\ f \cdot concatm$$
$$= \quad \{\text{definitions of } mapm \text{ and } concatm \text{ in terms of } (\diamond)\}$$
$$(id \diamond (return \cdot f)) \cdot (id \diamond id)$$
$$= \quad \{\text{leapfrog}\}$$
$$(id \diamond id) \diamond (return \cdot f)$$

Similarly, we simplify the right-hand side:

$$concatm \cdot mapm\ (mapm\ f)$$
$$= \quad \{\text{definitions of } mapm \text{ and } concatm \text{ in terms of } (\diamond)\}$$
$$(id \diamond id) \cdot (id \diamond (return \cdot (id \diamond (return \cdot f))))$$
$$= \quad \{\text{leapfrog}\}$$
$$(id \diamond (return \cdot (id \diamond (return \cdot f)))) \diamond id$$
$$= \quad \{\text{associativity}\}$$
$$id \diamond (return \cdot (id \diamond (return \cdot f))) \diamond id$$
$$= \quad \{\text{above, and } id \cdot h = h\}$$
$$id \diamond (id \diamond (return \cdot f))$$

The two results are the same since $\diamond$ is associative. We will leave the other proofs to the diligent reader.

10.3.4 Summary

We have now seen four different ways of expressing the laws of a monad. Each has its advantages. The laws of $\triangleright$, and its equivalent in terms of **do** notation, are most useful when reasoning about programs written in **do** notation. The laws of $(\diamond)$ are the simplest to remember, and show that monads are examples of monoids. The laws of $mapm$ and $concatm$, which are the way category theorists introduce monads, are the most revealing in that they suggest that monads may be found in all kinds of places.

Exercises

10.3.1 Writing $List\ \alpha$ for $[\alpha]$, install $List$ as a member of $Monad$.

10.3.2 Let M be a monoid with unit e and operation $\oplus$. Install Mon as a member of $Monad$, where

$$\textbf{data } Mon\ \alpha \quad = \quad MkMon\ (M, \alpha)$$

The output monad is a special case of this monad, as is the counting monad implicit in Exercise 10.2.2.

10.3.3 Prove the law *concatm · mapm concatm = concatm · concatm*.

10.4 Combining monads

Sometimes we want to combine monads. For instance, we may want to modify the evaluator of Section 10.2 to use both exception handling and state. One possibility is to construct yet another monad, combining aspects of both exceptions and state. But it would be preferable if, having separately done the work to define exception and state monads, we could combine them simply in some way.

It would be delightful if there were a single, uniform rule that could be used to combine any two monads. Unfortunately, no such rule exists. Indeed, as we will see, there are sometimes two distinct ways in which two monads can be combined. However, it is usually possible to define a uniform rule for combining one monad with another. The basic idea is to define an operation τ, taking type constructors into type constructors, such that if *m* is a monad, then τ *m* is also a monad. Such an operation is called a *monad transformer*.

Each operation to be defined will be used in several different monads, so we form a type class for each operation. Recall that we already have a type class for the two basic monad operations:

> **class** *Monad m* **where**
> $return \quad :: \quad \alpha \to m\,\alpha$
> $(\triangleright) \qquad :: \quad m\,\alpha \to (\alpha \to m\,\beta) \to m\,\beta$

By definition, an *exception monad* is one with an operation to raise an exception:

> **class** *Monad m* $\Rightarrow$ *ExMonad m* **where**
> $raise \quad :: \quad Exception \to m\,\alpha$

Similarly, a *state monad* is one with an operation to increment the state:

> **class** *Monad m* $\Rightarrow$ *StMonad m* **where**
> $tick \quad :: \quad m\,()$

Finally, a *show monad* is one with an operation to display an appropriate value:

> **class** *Monad m* $\Rightarrow$ *ShowMonad m* **where**
> $showMonad \quad :: \quad m\,String \to String$

Whereas the usual *Show* class takes a type as its argument, this version takes a type constructor.

By definition, a *monad transformer* is an operation τ, taking monads to monads, with the property that it is possible to promote computations from the underlying monad into the transformed monad:

> **class** *Transformer* τ **where**
> *promote* :: *Monad* $m \Rightarrow m\,\alpha \to \tau\,m\,\alpha$

Here α varies over types, m varies over type constructors, which act like functions from types to types, and τ varies over functions from type constructors to type constructors.

Here is a version of the evaluator from Section 10.2 that both raises an exception on division by zero, and counts the number of division operations. The type indicates that it uses a monad that has both exceptions and state:

> $$\begin{array}{lcl} eval & :: & (ExcMonad\ m,\ StMonad\ m) \Rightarrow Term \to m\,Int \\ eval\ (Con\ x) & = & return\ x \\ eval\ (Div\ t\ u) & = & \textbf{do}\ x \leftarrow eval\ u \\ & & \quad\ \ y \leftarrow eval\ t \\ & & \quad\ \ tick \\ & & \quad\ \ \textbf{if}\ y == 0 \\ & & \quad\quad\ \ \textbf{then}\quad raise\ \text{``divide by zero''} \\ & & \quad\quad\ \ \textbf{else}\quad return\ (x\ \textbf{div}\ y) \end{array}$$

10.4.1 Combining exceptions

Our first monad transformer combines an arbitrary monad m with the exception monad. We will follow a convention of giving monad transformers names that are all upper case.

> $$\begin{array}{lcl} \textbf{newtype}\ EXC\ m\ \alpha & = & MkEXC\ (m\ (Exc\ \alpha)) \\ \textbf{data}\ Exc\ \alpha & = & Raise\ Exception\ \mid\ Return\ \alpha \\ \textbf{type}\ Exception & = & String \end{array}$$

Here, *Exc* and *Exception* are exactly as in Section 10.2. Why have we chosen to write $m\,(Exc\ \alpha)$ rather than, say, $Exc\,(m\ \alpha)$? The answer is: because it works. It appears impossible to write a suitable definition of $\triangleright$ for the other variant.

We will need an auxiliary function *recover* to recover the underlying type from the new type:

> $$\begin{array}{lcl} recover & :: & EXC\ m\ \alpha \to m\ (Exc\ \alpha) \\ recover\ (MkEXC\ g) & = & g \end{array}$$

The next step is to install *EXC m* as a monad, using the assumption that *m* is a monad:

> **instance** *Monad m* ⇒ *Monad* (*EXC m*) **where**
> *return x* = *MkEXC* (*return* (*Return x*))
> *p* ▷ *q*   = *MkEXC* (*recover p* ▷ *r*)
>   **where** *r* (*Raise e*)   = *return* (*Raise e*)
>   *r* (*Return x*) = *recover* (*q x*)

Here, *return* and ▷ in the monad *EXC m* (those on the left-hand side of the equations) are defined in terms of *return* and ▷ in the underlying monad *m* (those on the right-hand side of the equations). It is a useful exercise to check the types:

> $x :: \alpha$
> ⇒   {definition of *Exc*}
> *Return x* :: *Exc* α
> ⇒   {definition of *return* in monad *m*}
> *return* (*Return x*) :: *m* (*Exc* α)
> ⇒   {definition of *EXC*}
> *MkEXC* (*return* (*Return x*)) :: *EXC m* α

Similarly,

> $p :: EXC\ m\ \alpha$ and $q :: \alpha \to EXC\ m\ \beta$
> ⇒   {definition of *recover* and ▷ in monad *m*}
> *recover p* :: *m* (*Exc* α) and *r* :: *Exc* $\alpha \to m$ (*Exc* β)
> ⇒   {definition of *EXC*}
> *MkEXC* (*recover p* ▷ *r*) :: *EXC m* β

It is also necessary to show that if *return* and ▷ in the underlying monad *m* satisfy the three monad laws, then so do *return* and ▷ in the new monad *EXC m*. Here is the proof of the right unit law:

> *p* ▷ *return*
> =   {definition of *return* and ▷ for monad *EXC m*}
> *MkEXC* (*recover p* ▷ *r*)
> **where** *r* (*Raise e*)   = *return* (*Raise e*)
>   *r* (*Return x*) = *return* (*Return x*)
> =   {since, by extensionality, *r* = *return*}

$$MkEXC \ (recover \ p \rhd return)$$

= {right unit law for monad m}

$$MkEXC \ (recover \ p)$$

= {definition of $recover$}

$$p$$

The other two proofs are similar.

We have now installed *EXC m* as a monad, and the next step is to install *EXC* as a monad transformer:

instance *Transformer EXC* **where**
   $promote \ g \ = \ MkEXC \ (\textbf{do} \ \{x \leftarrow g; \ return \ (Return \ x)\})$

This is similar to the definition of *return* on *Exc*, with an added bind and *return* on m to get the types right.

The monad *EXC m* is an exception monad for any monad m:

instance *Monad m* $\Rightarrow$ *ExMonad (EXC m)* **where**
   $raise \ e \ = \ MkEXC \ (return \ (Raise \ e))$

The monad *EXC m* is a state monad, whenever m is a state monad:

instance *StMonad m* $\Rightarrow$ *StMonad (EXC m)* **where**
   $tick \ = \ promote \ tick$

Here *tick* in the monad *EXC m* (on the left) is defined in terms of *tick* in the monad m (on the right).

The monad *EXC m* is a show monad, whenever m is a show monad:

instance *ShowMonad m* $\Rightarrow$ *ShowMonad (EXC m)* **where**
   $showMonad \ p \ = \ showMonad \ (recover \ p \rhd q)$
        where
        $q \ (Raise \ e) \ \ = \ return \ (\text{"exception: "} + e)$
        $q \ (Return \ cs) \ = \ return \ cs$

On the left, *showMonad* :: *EXC m String* $\rightarrow$ *String*. On the right, *showMonad* :: *m String* $\rightarrow$ *String*. We can use *showMonad* to install *EXC m* α as a member of *Show*:

instance *(ShowMonad m, Show* α*)* $\Rightarrow$ *Show (EXC m* α*)* **where**
   $show \ = \ showMonad \cdot mapMonad \ show$

The function *mapMonad* is as defined in Section 10.3, where it was called *mapm*.

10.4.2 Combining state

Our second monad transformer combines an arbitrary monad m with the state monad:

$$\textbf{newtype } STT\ m\ \alpha\ =\ MkSTT\ (State \to m\ (\alpha, State))$$
$$\textbf{type } State\ \qquad =\ Int$$

Note this follows a slightly different pattern than the previous definition. The underlying monad m is wrapped around the pair formed from the value and the final state. Compare this with other possible variations, such as $m\ (State \to (\alpha, State))$ or $State \to (m\ \alpha, State)$. Again, this definition is chosen because it works. It appears impossible to write a suitable definition of $\triangleright$ for the other variants.

We need an auxiliary function to apply a computation to an initial state:

$$apply \qquad\qquad ::\quad STT\ m\ \alpha \to State \to m\ (\alpha, State)$$
$$apply\ (MkSTT\ f)\ =\ f$$

The next step is to install $STT\ m$ as a monad, using the assumption that m is a monad:

$$\textbf{instance } Monad\ m \Rightarrow Monad\ (STT\ m)\ \textbf{where}$$
$$return\ x\ =\ MkSTT\ f\quad\textbf{where}\ f\ s = return\ (x, s)$$
$$p \triangleright q\qquad =\ MkSTT\ f$$
$$\qquad\qquad\quad \textbf{where}$$
$$\qquad\qquad\quad f\ s\ =\ \textbf{do}\ (x, s') \leftarrow apply\ p\ s$$
$$\qquad\qquad\qquad\qquad\qquad apply\ (q\ x)\ s'$$

Again it is useful to check the types, a task we leave as an exercise.

It is also necessary to show that if *return* and $\triangleright$ in the underlying monad m satisfy the three monad laws, then so do *return* and $\triangleright$ in the new monad $STT\ m$. Here is the proof of the right unit law:

$$apply\ (p \triangleright return)\ s$$
$$=\quad \{\text{definition of } \triangleright \text{ for monad } STT\ m\}$$
$$\textbf{do}\ \{(x, s') \leftarrow apply\ p\ s;\ apply\ (return\ x)\ s'\}$$
$$=\quad \{\text{definition of } return \text{ and } apply\}$$
$$\textbf{do}\ \{(x, s') \leftarrow apply\ p\ s;\ return\ (x, s')\}$$
$$=\quad \{\text{right unit law for monad } m\}$$
$$apply\ p\ s$$

We have now installed *STT m* as a monad, and the next step is to install *STT* as a monad transformer:

> **instance** *Transformer STT* **where**
>   *promote g* = *MkSTT f*
>   **where**
>   *f s* = **do** $\{x \leftarrow g;\ return\,(x, s)\}$

This is similar to the definition of *return* on *St*, with an added bind and *return* on *m* to get the types right.

The monad *STT m* is a state monad for any monad *m*:

> **instance** *Monad m* ⇒ *StMonad (STT m)* **where**
>   *tick* = *MkSTT f* **where** $f\,s = return\,((), s + 1)$

This is similar to the definition of *raise* on *St*, with an added *return* on *m* to get the types right.

The monad *STT m* is an exception monad if *m* is an exception monad:

> **instance** *ExMonad m* ⇒ *ExMonad (STT m)* **where**
>   *raise e* = *promote (raise e)*

The monad *STT m* is a show monad if *m* is a show monad:

> **instance** *ShowMonad m* ⇒ *ShowMonad (STT m)* **where**
>   *showMonad p*
> = *showMonad q*
>   **where**
> $q = $ **do** $(x, s) \leftarrow apply\,p\,0$
>   *return* ("value: " ++ x ++ ", count: " ++ *show s*)

We can use *showMonad* to install *STT m α* as a member of *Show*:

> **instance** *(ShowMonad m, Show α)* ⇒ *Show (STT m α)* **where**
>   *show* = *showMonad · mapMonad show*

10.4.3 Putting it all together

Having carefully sown the seeds, we may now reap the benefits. The monad transformers *EXC* and *STT* each take a monad into a monad. We need some monad to start with, and the identity monad *Id* defined in Section 10.2 fills the bill nicely. Recall that

> **newtype** *Id α* = *MkId α*

> **instance** *Monad Id* **where**
>   *return x*   =   *MkId x*
>   *(MkId x) ▷ q* =   *q x*

We have to install *Id* as a show monad:

> **instance** *ShowMonad Id* **where**
>   *showMonad (MkId cs)* =   *cs*

Observe that the monad *EXC Id* is equivalent to the monad *Exc* and that the monad *STT Id* is equivalent to the monad *St*.

    There are two different ways in which we can build up a monad that supports both exceptions and state, depending on the order in which we apply our monad transformers:

> *evalStEx* :: *Term → STT (EXC Id) Int*
> *evalStEx* =   *eval*
>
> *evalExSt* :: *Term → EXC (STT Id) Int*
> *evalExSt* =   *eval*

Either way around, the result seems to be the same. Given

> *answer* =   *Div (Div (Con 1972) (Con 2)) (Con 23)*

we have

? *evalStEx answer*
value: 42, count: 2

?*evalExSt answer*
value: 42, count: 2

However, the similarity is only skin deep: the answers look the same, but they have different types and different structure. In the first case, evaluation yielded the computation

> *MkSTT f* **where** *f s = MkEXC (MkId (Return (42, s + 2)))*

whereas in the second case, evaluation yielded the computation

> *MkEXC (MkSTT f)* **where** *f s = (MkId (Return 42), s + 2)*

This difference becomes apparent when we consider evaluating a term that raises an exception. Recall that

> *wrong* =   *Div (Con 2) (Div (Con 1) (Con 0))*

We have

? *evalStEx wrong*
exception: division by zero

? *evalExSt wrong*
value: exception: division by zero, count: 1

In the first case, evaluation yielded the computation

$$MkSTT\ f\ \ \textbf{where}\ f\ s = MkEXC\ (MkId\ (Raise\ \text{"divide by zero"}))$$

indicating only that an error occurred, whereas in the second case, evaluation yielded the computation

$$MkEXC\ (MkSTT\ f)\ \ \textbf{where}\ f\ s = (MkId\ (Raise\ \text{"divide by zero"}), s + 1)$$

indicating that one tick was counted before the exception was raised.

The second of these two combinations corresponds more closely to the way state is normally implemented, namely with a global variable. With a global variable, the value of the state can always be recovered from the variable, even after an exception is raised. The first combination is akin to the case where raising an exception causes a state to be 'rolled back' to its value at the point where the exception handler is invoked, and can be considerably more expensive to implement.

The moral is clear: complex features may interact in complex ways. There is no fixed rule for combining monads because there is no fixed rule for combining features. But monads do offer some help in structuring this complexity, as here, where they reveal two alternative ways of combining state with exceptions.

Exercises

10.4.1 A transformer *OUT* that adds output to a given monad is given by

$$\textbf{data}\ OUT\ m\ \alpha\ \ =\ \ m\ (\alpha, Output)$$

Define suitable instances of the classes *Monad*, *ShowMonad*, and *Transformer*, and define a class *OutMonad* with a suitable instance. Also, define instances to ensure that if *m* is an exception or state monad then so is *OUT m*, and that if *m* is an output monad then so are *ST m* and *EXC m*.

10.4.2 Build an evaluator that uses both *EXC* and *OUT* (from Exercise 10.4.1), and show that the two ways of composing the transformers yield different results. Which composition corresponds best to the usual implementation of output? Repeat for *ST* and *OUT*.

10.4.3 The function *promote* should be a *monad morphism*, in that it should preserve the monad structure:

$$
\begin{aligned}
promote\,(return\,x) &= return\,x \\
promote\,(p \rhd q) &= (promote\,p) \rhd (promote \cdot q)
\end{aligned}
$$

Here, *return* and $\rhd$ on the left are in the monad *m*, and on the right are in the monad $\tau\,m$. Show that the *promote* operations defined on *ST* and *EXC* are indeed monad morphisms.

10.5 Chapter notes

Moggi (1989, 1991) introduced monads to computing science as a way of structuring denotational semantics. Independently, Spivey (1990) noted that monads provided a useful way of structuring exception handling in functional programs. Subsequently, Wadler (1990a, 1995) proposed monads as a general technique for structuring functional programs.

Monads are used to structure the Glasgow Haskell compiler, which itself is written in Haskell; see Hall, Hammond, Partain, Jones, and Wadler (1992). Each phase of the compiler uses a monad for bookkeeping information. For instance, the type checker uses a monad that combines state (to maintain a current substitution), a name supply (for fresh type variable names), and exceptions. Monads for interaction have been extended to include concurrency; see Jones, Gordon, and Finne (1996). Monad transformers are discussed in Liang, Hudak, and Jones (1995).

The program for the game of Hangman was adapted from a similar program in Hutton and Meijer (1996).

The special **do** notation was suggested by Launchbury (1993) and was first implemented by Jones (1993) in a version of Gofer. Subsequently, it was adopted in Haskell.

Parsing

A *parser* is a program that analyses a piece of text to determine its logical structure. For example, the text may describe an arithmetic expression, a computer program, or a database of information. The output of a parser is usually a tree of some kind; for instance, a parser for arithmetic expressions might return a tree with constants in the leaves, and operators at internal nodes. In this chapter we will describe a monadic approach to designing parsers. The material will be used in the following chapter.

11.1 Sequencing

Let us start by thinking of a parser as a function that takes a string as input and returns a tree as output:

newtype *Parser* = *MkP* (*String* → *Tree*)

The type *Parser* is declared as a new type, distinct from but isomorphic to the underlying type of functions from strings to trees.

What is inadequate about this definition is that it provides no obvious way for *sequencing* parsers. For instance, in a parser for arithmetic expressions one may want to look for, in sequence, a numeral, an operator, and another numeral. The first parser for a numeral will consume some initial portion of the input string, the parser for an operator some more of the input, and the second parser for a numeral the remaining portion. It follows that a better idea is to refine the type *Parser* to return the unconsumed suffix of the input string as part of the result:

newtype *Parser* = *MkP* (*String* → (*Tree*, *String*))

Before considering how to combine two parsers in sequence, let us first look at another aspect of parsing. It can happen that a parser may *fail* on some input. It is not a mistake to construct parsers that may fail. For example, in a parser for arithmetic expressions, we may want to look for either an operator symbol or an opening bracket. One or either of these subsidiary parsers will certainly fail. More generally, a parser may find a number of different ways that some initial portion of the input can be structured as a tree. Failure then corresponds to the particular case that there are no parses. In order to handle these various possibilities, we refine the type *Parser* to return a list of pairs:

$$\textbf{newtype } Parser \;=\; MkP \; (String \rightarrow [(\,Tree, String)\,])$$

Under this scheme a parser fails by returning the empty sequence. By definition, a parser is *deterministic* if it returns an empty or singleton list in all possible cases.

The final refinement comes from the observation that different parsers are likely to return different kinds of trees. To deal with this point, we abstract from any specific datatype *Tree* and define a parser as an element of type

$$\textbf{newtype } Parser \; \alpha \;=\; MkP \; (String \rightarrow [(\alpha, String)\,])$$

At this point, it begins to look like a parser is equivalent to *STT List*, where *STT* is the state transformer of the previous chapter, with the state being a string rather than an integer. As in the previous chapter, we define a function *apply* for applying a parser:

$$
\begin{aligned}
apply & \quad :: \quad Parser \; \alpha \rightarrow String \rightarrow [(\alpha, String)] \\
apply \; (MkP \; f) \; s & \quad = \quad f \; s
\end{aligned}
$$

Using *apply*, we can define a function *applyParser* for returning one result of a parse:

$$
\begin{aligned}
applyParser & \quad :: \quad Parser \; \alpha \rightarrow String \rightarrow \alpha \\
applyParser \; p & \quad = \quad fst \cdot head \cdot apply \; p
\end{aligned}
$$

The function *applyParser* returns the first component of the first element in a list of parses.

Using *apply*, we can now install *Parser* as an instance of a monad:

$$
\begin{aligned}
&\textbf{instance } Monad \; Parser \; \textbf{where} \\
&\quad return \; x \;=\; MkP \; f \quad \textbf{where } f \; s = [(x, s)] \\
&\quad p \triangleright q \;\;=\; MkP \; f \\
&\qquad \textbf{where } f \; s = [(y, s'') \mid (x, s') \leftarrow apply \; p \; s, \; (y, s'') \leftarrow apply \; (q \; x) \; s']
\end{aligned}
$$

In the definition of $p \triangleright q$, the parser p is applied to an input string s, producing a list of possible parses, each paired with the corresponding remaining input; the parser q is then applied to each parse and corresponding input to produce, in turn, a list of results whose concatenation provides the final answer. One must also show that the three monad laws hold, a task we will leave as an exercise.

Having installed *Parser* as a monad, we can combine parsers in sequence using **do** notation. We will need some basic parsers to start with, one of which is

$$
\begin{array}{lll}
item & :: & Parser\ Char \\
item & = & MkP\ f \\
& & \textbf{where}\ f\ [\,] & = & [\,] \\
& & \quad\quad f\ (c:cs) & = & [(c,cs)]
\end{array}
$$

The parser *item* returns the first character of the input, and fails if the input is exhausted. Thus *item* plays the same role for parsers as *getChar* does for the input-output monad of the previous chapter.

The second basic parser is one that always fails:

$$
\begin{array}{lll}
zero & :: & Parser\ \alpha \\
zero & = & MkP\ f \quad \textbf{where}\ f\ s = [\,]
\end{array}
$$

The parser is called *zero* because it returns zero parses. Also, we have

$$
\begin{array}{lll}
zero \triangleright p & = & zero \\
p \triangleright (const\ zero) & = & zero
\end{array}
$$

Hence *zero* is the zero element of $\triangleright$, just as 0 is the zero element of $\times$.

To illustrate the use of *item* and *zero*, here is a parser for recognising a character that satisfies a given property:

$$
\begin{array}{lll}
sat & :: & (Char \rightarrow Bool) \rightarrow Parser\ Char \\
sat\ p & = & \textbf{do}\ \{c \leftarrow item;\ \textbf{if}\ p\ c\ \textbf{then}\ return\ c\ \textbf{else}\ zero\}
\end{array}
$$

Using *sat* we can define a number of other parsers:

$$
\begin{array}{lll}
char & :: & Char \rightarrow Parser\ () \\
char\ x & = & \textbf{do}\ \{c \leftarrow sat\ (== x);\ return\ ()\}
\end{array}
$$

$$
\begin{array}{lll}
string & :: & String \rightarrow Parser\ () \\
string\ [\,] & = & return\ () \\
string\ (x:xs) & = & \textbf{do}\ \{char\ x;\ string\ xs;\ return\ ()\}
\end{array}
$$

$$
\begin{array}{lll}
lower & :: & Parser\ Char \\
lower & = & sat\ isLower
\end{array}
$$

$$digit \quad :: \quad Parser\ Int$$
$$digit \quad = \quad \textbf{do}\ \{d \leftarrow sat\ isDigit;\quad return\ (ord\ d - ord\ \text{‘0’})\}$$

The parser *char x* looks for the specific character *x* as the next item in the input string, while *string xs* looks for a specific string *xs*; both parsers return () if successful. The parser *lower* looks for a lower-case letter, and *digit* looks for a digit, returning the associated numeric value if successful.

Exercises

11.1.1 Show that the monad laws hold for the monad *Parser*.

11.1.2 Modify *applyParser* to return a suitable error message on parsers that fail.

11.1.3 Prove that *zero* is the zero element of $\diamond$, where $\diamond$ is the composition operator associated with the monad *Parser*.

11.1.4 Define a parser *upper* that recognises an upper-case letter.

11.1.5 Define a parser that recognises an upper-case letter followed by a lower-case letter.

11.2 Alternation

In order to be able to build more sophisticated parsers, we need an operator for combining *alternative* parses. One such operator is

$$(\textbf{plus}) \quad :: \quad Parser\ \alpha \rightarrow Parser\ \alpha \rightarrow Parser\ \alpha$$
$$p\ \textbf{plus}\ q \quad = \quad MkP\ f \quad \textbf{where}\ f\ s = apply\ p\ s \mathbin{+\mkern-10mu+} apply\ q\ s$$

The parser *p* **plus** *q* takes an input string *s* and returns all parses of *p* applied to *s*, followed by all parses of *q* applied to *s*.

The operator **plus** satisfies a number of useful laws. Firstly, it forms a monoid with *zero* as the unit element:

$$\begin{aligned}
zero\ \textbf{plus}\ p \quad &= \quad p \\
p\ \textbf{plus}\ zero \quad &= \quad p \\
p\ \textbf{plus}\ (q\ \textbf{plus}\ r) \quad &= \quad (p\ \textbf{plus}\ q)\ \textbf{plus}\ r
\end{aligned}$$

Secondly, we have the distributive law

$$(p\ \textbf{plus}\ q) \triangleright r \quad = \quad (p \triangleright r)\ \textbf{plus}\ (q \triangleright r)$$

This law, like the others, is an easy consequence of the definitions.

To illustrate the use of **plus,** here is a parser for recognising a sequence of lower-case letters:

> *lowers* :: *Parser String*
> *lowers* = **do** {*c* ← *lower*; *cs* ← *lowers*; *return* (*c* : *cs*)} **plus** *return* ""

In order to see how this parser works, suppose the input is the string "Upper". In this case the parser on the left of **plus** fails, because 'U' is not a lower-case letter. However, the parser on the right succeeds, so

> *lowers* "Upper" = [("", "Upper")]

With input string "sUpper", the left-hand parser succeeds, and so does the right-hand parser. Hence

> *lowers* "sUpper" = [("s", "Upper"), ("", "sUpper")]

Finally, applied to the input string "isUpper", *lowers* returns three parses:

> [("is", "Upper"), ("i", "sUpper"), ("", "isUpper")]

Each parse in this list consumes a smaller portion of the input string than its predecessors.

Normally, we are interested only in that parse which consumes the longest initial portion of the input. One solution is to return only the first parse in a list of possible results, taking care to ensure that parses are produced in an appropriate order. A superior alternative is to introduce another choice combinator **orelse,** defined by

> (**orelse**) :: *Parser α* → *Parser α* → *Parser α*
> *p* **orelse** *q* = *MkP f*
> > **where** *f s* = **if** *null ps* **then** *apply q s* **else** *ps*
> > *ps* = *apply p s*

In words, *p* **orelse** *q* returns the same parses as *p* unless *p* fails, in which case the parses of *q* are returned. If *p* and *q* are deterministic parsers, then so is *p* **orelse** *q*. The operator **orelse** satisfies the same laws as **plus,** as the reader can check.

To illustrate the use of **orelse,** suppose that **plus** is replaced by **orelse** in the definition of *lowers.* Then we have

> *lowers* "isUpper" = [("is", "Upper")]

Only the longest parse is returned, so *lowers* is a deterministic parser.

Use of **orelse** rather than **plus** requires care. For example, consider a very simple form of arithmetic expression that consists of either a single digit or a digit followed by a plus sign followed by another digit. Consider the two parsers:

> *right* :: *Parser Int*
> *right* = *digit* **plus** *addition*

> *wrong* :: *Parser Int*
> *wrong* = *digit* **orelse** *addition*

> *addition* :: *Parser Int*
> *addition* = **do** {*m* ← *digit*; *char* '+'; *n* ← *digit*; *return* (*m* + *n*)}

Applied to the input string "1 + 2", the parser *right* yields two parses:

> [(1, "+2"), (3, "")]

However, *wrong* yields only the first of these parses. The parser *digit* succeeds, so the parser *addition* is not invoked.

One way to correct *wrong* is to rewrite it in the form

> *better* :: *Parser Int*
> *better* = *addition* **orelse** *digit*

Applied to the input "1 + 2", the parser *better* yields [(3, "")]. What is wrong with *better* is that it is inefficient: applied to the input "1", it parses the digit but fails to find a subsequent plus sign, so the left-hand argument to **orelse** fails. As a result, the input is reparsed from scratch to find a digit. This is not so much a problem with this little example, but it would be if *digit* were replaced by a parser that recognised a sequence of digits. Such a sequence would be parsed again when the left-hand parser failed.

The best solution is to *factor* the parser for digits out of the two component parsers, writing

> *best*   :: *Parser Int*
> *best*   = **do** {*m* ← *digit*; *rest m*}
> *rest m* = **do** {*char* '+'; *n* ← *digit*; *return* (*m* + *n*)} **orelse** *return m*

The parser *rest* handles the rest of the input, if any. It takes an argument *m* whose value is the digit parsed so far. We will return to the subject of efficiency in Section 11.4 but the lesson to be learned here is that it is sensible to factorise parsers to avoid repeating unnecessary work.

Exercises

11.2.1 Is the operator **plus** commutative?

11.2.2 Define a variant of *lowers* that produces a list of parses in which each parse consumes a larger portion of the input string than its predecessors.

11.2.3 Show that **orelse** satisfies the same four laws as **plus**.

11.3 Repetition

Generalising from the definition of *lowers* in the previous section, we can define a parser combinator that repeats a parser zero or more times:

> *many*   ::   *Parser α → Parser* [α]
> *many p* = **do** {x ← p; xs ← *many p*; *return* (x : xs)} **orelse** *return* [ ]

For example, we now have *lowers = many lower*.

The following parser recognises an identifier, which by definition is a string of letters and digits beginning with a lower-case letter:

> *ident*   ::   *Parser String*
> *ident*   =   **do** {c ← *lower*; cs ← *many alphanum*; *return* (c : cs)}

The definition of *alphanum* is left as an exercise.

Sometimes we want to repeat a parser *p* one or more times, rather than zero or more times. This can be done by a combinator *some*, defined by

> *some*   ::   *Parser α → Parser* [α]
> *some p* = **do** {x ← p; xs ← *many p*; *return* (x : xs)}

For example, here is a parser for natural numbers:

> *nat*   ::   *Parser Int*
> *nat*   =   **do** {ds ← *some digit*; *return* (foldl1 (⊕) ds)}
>   **where** $m ⊕ n = 10 × m + n$

The parser *digit* was defined in Section 11.1.

Consider now how to define a parser for an integer numeral, which by definition is a nonempty string of digits possibly prefixed by a minus sign. One approach is to define

> *int*   ::   *Parser Int*
> *int*   =   **do** {char '-'; n ← *nat*; *return* (−n)} **orelse** *nat*

Another, rather more sophisticated, definition is

$$int \quad = \quad \textbf{do } \{f \leftarrow op; \ n \leftarrow nat; \ return \ (f \ n)\}$$
$$\textbf{where } op = \textbf{do } \{char \ \text{`-'}; \ return \ negate\} \textbf{ orelse } return \ id$$

The parser *op* returns a function, which is either *negate* if the next character is a minus sign, or the identity function otherwise.

11.3.1   Repetition with separators

Consider the problem of parsing a nonempty list of integers, separated by commas and enclosed in square brackets. Such a parser can be defined by

$$ints \quad :: \quad Parser \ [Int]$$
$$ints \quad = \quad \textbf{do } char \ \text{`['}$$
$$n \leftarrow int$$
$$ns \leftarrow many \ (\textbf{do } \{char \ \text{`,'}; \ int\})$$
$$char \ \text{`]'}$$
$$return \ (n : ns)$$

It is useful to abstract on this fairly common pattern of repetition by defining a special combinator *somewith* that acts like *some* but differs in that the instances of the parser are separated by another parser whose results are ignored. The definition is

$$somewith \qquad :: \quad Parser \ \beta \rightarrow Parser \ \alpha \rightarrow Parser \ [\alpha]$$
$$somewith \ q \ p \quad = \quad \textbf{do } x \leftarrow p$$
$$xs \leftarrow many \ (\textbf{do } \{q; \ p\})$$
$$return \ (x : xs)$$

For possibly empty sequences we can define

$$manywith \qquad :: \quad Parser \ \beta \rightarrow Parser \ \alpha \rightarrow Parser \ [\alpha]$$
$$manywith \ q \ p \quad = \quad somewith \ q \ p \textbf{ orelse } return \ [\,]$$

11.3.2   Skipping white-space

In most applications, *white-space* (sequences of space, newline and tab characters) can appear between *tokens* (identifiers, numbers, and so on) to make the text easier to read. The parser *space* recognises white-space:

$$space \quad :: \quad Parser \ ()$$
$$space \quad = \quad many \ (sat \ isSpace) \ \triangleright \ return \ ()$$

A suitable definition of *isSpace* is left as an exercise. To take account of white-space, we can define a parser combinator that skips white-space around a parser:

> *token*   ::   *Parser* α → *Parser* α
> *token p*   =   **do** {*space*; *x* ← *p*; *space*; *return x*}

For example, the parser

> *symbol*   ::   *String* → *Parser* ()
> *symbol xs*   =   *token* (*string xs*)

looks for the string *xs* in the input, ignoring white-space before and after the string.

Exercises

11.3.1 The bracketing of pars rs by other parsers, whose results are ignored, can be formulated as a parse ombinator. Give details.

11.3.2 Redo the text-processing functions described in Section 5.5 as monadic parsers.

11.4   Efficiency

The combinators described so far are sufficiently powerful for us to be able to translate a natural structural description of what is required directly into a functional program. However, unless one takes care, the result can be a parser with unexpected time and space performance. In this section we will describe some simple techniques for improving the efficiency of parsers.

11.4.1   Left recursion

Let us start by building a parser for the type *Expr*, defined by

> **data** *Expr*   =   *Con Int* | *Bin Op Expr Expr*
> **data** *Op*   =   *Plus* | *Minus*

Here is a grammar for fully parenthesised expressions, expressed in what is known as *Backus-Naur* form, or BNF for short:

> *expr*   ::=   *const* | '(' *expr addop expr* ')'
> *addop*   ::=   '+' | '-'

Such a grammar provides a 'natural structural description' of what is required. Each identifier in this grammar describes a *syntactic category*, while symbols enclosed in quotation marks denote *terminal* symbols, symbols that actually appear in the text. It is implicitly understood in the description that white-space is ignored between terminal symbols where appropriate. The particular grammar for *expr* states that an expression is either an (integer) constant or else a compound expression consisting of an opening parenthesis, followed by an expression, followed by either a plus or minus sign, followed by another expression, and finally followed by a closing parenthesis. The grammar translates directly into a parser for expressions:

expr :: *Parser Expr*
expr = *token const* **orelse**
      do {*symbol* "("; *t* ← *term*; *symbol* ")"; *return t*}

const = **do** {*n* ← *int*; *return* (*Con n*)}
term = **do** {*t* ← *expr*; *op* ← *addop*; *u* ← *expr*; *return* (*Bin op t u*)}
addop = **do** {*symbol* "+"; *return Plus*} **orelse**
      do {*symbol* "-"; *return Minus*}

Now suppose we want a parser that also works for expressions that are not fully parenthesised. In such a case, (+) and (−) should associate to the left in expressions. The usual way to express such a grammar in BNF is to write

expr ::= *expr addop factor* | *factor*
factor ::= *const* | '(' *expr* ')'

This grammar also translates directly into a parser:

expr = *term* **orelse** *factor*
term = **do** {*t* ← *expr*; *op* ← *addop*; *u* ← *factor*; *return* (*Bin op t u*)}
factor = *token const* **orelse**
      do {*symbol* "("; *e* ← *expr*; *symbol* ")"; *return e*}

However, this parser is inefficient – so inefficient, in fact, that it fails to deliver any result. The problem is that the first action of the parser *expr* is to invoke the parser *term*, whose first action is to invoke the parser *expr* again, leading to an infinite loop. Furthermore, as we have seen in Section 11.2, it isn't correct to rewrite *expr* as

expr = *factor* **orelse** *expr*

because the result parses only a factor, ignoring the rest of the expression. Replacing **orelse** in the definition of *expr* by **plus** doesn't work either: the parser will find the first factor, but then go into an infinite loop trying to complete the remaining parses. The problem is called the *left recursion* problem and is a difficulty with all recursive parsers, functional or otherwise.

The solution is to rewrite the grammar for *expr* in the following equivalent form:

$$expr \quad ::= \quad factor\ rest$$
$$rest \quad = \quad addop\ factor\ rest \mid nothing$$

The new syntactic category *rest* handles the rest of an expression, if any, and *nothing* denotes the category that describes the empty sequence of terminal symbols. The new parser for *expr* takes the form

$$expr \quad = \quad \textbf{do}\ \{t \leftarrow factor;\ rest\ t\}$$
$$rest\ t \quad = \quad \textbf{do}\ \{op \leftarrow addop;\ u \leftarrow factor;\ rest\ (Bin\ op\ t\ u)\}$$
$$\textbf{orelse}\ return\ t$$

The parser *rest* takes an argument corresponding to the expression parsed so far, and acts as an accumulating parameter.

11.4.2 Improving laziness

A typical lazy functional program from lists to list works by reading its input on demand, computing the first part of the output after only a portion of the input is read. For example, the standard functions *map* and *filter* have this behaviour. It is unreasonable to expect similar behaviour from a parser since, in general, it cannot be known that the input will be parsed successfully until all of it is read. However, in some cases one may hope to do better.

Consider, for example, the parser *many p*, whose definition was

$$many\ p \quad = \quad some\ p\ \textbf{orelse}\ return\ [\ ]$$
$$some\ p \quad = \quad \textbf{do}\ \{x \leftarrow p;\ xs \leftarrow many\ p;\ return\ (x : xs)\}$$

Applying *as = many (char* 'a') to the input "aab" gives the output [("aa", "b")]. Under lazy evaluation, one might might hope that each letter 'a' in the output becomes available after each corresponding letter in the input is processed. After all, *as* is guaranteed to succeed, producing the longest possible sequence of 'a's. But this is not what happens: *as* reads the entire input before any output is generated. One can verify that

$$apply\ as\ \bot \qquad\qquad = \quad \bot$$
$$apply\ as\ (\text{`a'} : \bot) \qquad = \quad \bot$$
$$apply\ as\ (\text{`a'} : \text{`a'} : \bot) \qquad = \quad \bot$$
$$apply\ as\ (\text{`a'} : \text{`a'} : \text{`b'} : \bot) \quad = \quad [(\text{``aa''}, \text{`b'} : \bot)]$$

Only when the letter 'b' is read is the output produced. What is wanted is some way to encode the fact that, for any p, the parser *many p* always succeeds. This is the purpose of the combinator *force*, defined by

$$
\begin{array}{lll}
force & :: & Parser\ \alpha \rightarrow Parser\ \alpha \\
force\ p & = & MkP\ f \\
& & \textbf{where}\ f\ cs\ =\ (fst\ (head\ rs), snd\ (head\ rs)) : tail\ rs \\
& & \qquad\qquad \textbf{where}\ rs = apply\ p\ cs
\end{array}
$$

Here is the new definition of *many* with added *force*:

$$
\begin{array}{lll}
many\ p & = & force\ (some\ p\ \textbf{orelse}\ return\ [\,]) \\
some\ p & = & \textbf{do}\ \{x \leftarrow p;\ xs \leftarrow many\ p;\ return\ (x : xs)\}
\end{array}
$$

Now one can verify that with $as = many\ (char\ `a")$ we have

$$
\begin{array}{lll}
apply\ as\ \bot & = & (\bot, \bot) : \bot \\
apply\ as\ (`a" : \bot) & = & (`a" : \bot, \bot) : \bot \\
apply\ as\ (`a" : `a" : \bot) & = & (`a" : `a" : \bot, \bot) : \bot \\
apply\ as\ (`a" : `a" : `b" : \bot) & = & [(\text{``aa"}, `b" : \bot)]
\end{array}
$$

Other parsers can also benefit from judicious use of *force*.

11.4.3 Limiting the number of results

One crucial difference between the choice combinators **plus** and **orelse** is that if p and q are deterministic, then so is $p\ \textbf{orelse}\ q$, while $p\ \textbf{plus}\ q$ is deterministic only if either p or q is *zero*. There is a more general way to limit the number of results. The idea is to provide a way of making explicit that we are interested only in the first result returned by certain parsers. The combinator *limit* is defined by

$$
\begin{array}{lll}
limit & :: & Parser\ \alpha \rightarrow Parser\ \alpha \\
limit\ p & = & MkP\ (first \cdot apply\ p)
\end{array}
$$

$$
\begin{array}{lll}
first & :: & [\alpha] \rightarrow [\alpha] \\
first\ [\,] & = & [\,] \\
first\ (r : rs) & = & [r]
\end{array}
$$

Now, for deterministic parsers p and q we have

$$
p\ \textbf{orelse}\ q\ =\ limit\ (p\ \textbf{plus}\ q)
$$

On the other hand, *limit* $(p\ \textbf{plus}\ q)$ is deterministic even if p and q are not.

The reader may wonder why a function *first* was defined, when it is clearly equivalent to *take* 1. The answer has to do with space efficiency. We have

$$take\,1\;(r:rs)\quad=\quad r:take\,0\;rs$$

Although *take* 0 *rs* evaluates to [ ], this evaluation is not performed until the value is actually required. The effect is that a pointer to the remaining results *rs* is retained, thereby causing a potential space leak. By defining *first* explicitly, we avoid the problem.

Exercises

11.4.1 Prove that *p* **orelse** *q* = *limit* (*p* **plus** *q*).

11.5   Chapter notes

For a general introduction to practical parsing techniques, and their application in compiler design, consult Aho, Sethi, and Ullman (1986). The design of functional parsers has been a favourite application of functional programming for many years, e.g. Burge (1975), Wadler (1985). Modern treatments include Fokker (1995), Hutton (1992), and Hutton and Meijer (1996), on which this chapter is closely based.

The converse problem to parsing is *pretty printing*, the laying out of a structured document in an aesthetically pleasing manner. See Hughes (1995) for a design for a pretty-printing library.

Chapter 12

An automatic calculator

The final chapter is devoted to a single programming project: the design and implementation of a functional calculator for doing certain kinds of proof automatically. It is based fairly closely on a theorem prover written by Mike Spivey. Although the calculator provides only a small subset of the facilities one might want in an automatic proof assistant, and is restrictive in a number of other ways, it will nevertheless be powerful enough to prove many of the point-free laws described in previous chapters.

12.1 Basic considerations

The idea is to construct a function *calculate* with type

$$calculate \quad :: \quad [Law] \rightarrow Expr \rightarrow Calculation$$

The first argument to *calculate* is a list of laws that may be applied. Each law has a name and takes the form of an equation. The second argument is the starting expression, and the result is a calculation. A calculation consists of a sequence of steps; each step is generated by applying the left-hand side of one of the given laws to the current expression. The calculation ends when no more laws can be applied. The entire process is automatic, requiring no intervention on the part of the human theorem prover. Example calculations produced by *calculate* are given below and in Section 12.5.

Laws, expressions, and calculations are each elements of appropriate datatypes to be defined in the following section. In order to be able to describe and print elements of these datatypes in a readable form, we will need four conversion functions:

$$\begin{array}{lll} parseLaw & :: & String \rightarrow Law \\ parseExpr & :: & String \rightarrow Expr \\ printExpr & :: & Expr \rightarrow String \\ printCalc & :: & Calculation \rightarrow String \end{array}$$

For example, we can use *parseLaw* to set up a list of laws about pairs:

```
pairs
  = map parseLaw [
    "definition fst:      fst.pair(f, g) = f",
    "definition snd:      snd.pair(f, g) = g",
    "definition cross:    cross(f, g) = pair(f.fst, g.snd)",
    "pair absorption:     pair(f, g).h = pair(f.h, g.h)"]
```

Each law consists of a name and an equation. The name of the law is terminated by a colon sign, and the equation consists of two expressions separated by an equals sign. Expressions are built from constants, like *fst* and *pair*, and variables, like *f* and *g*. The precise syntax allowed for expressions is given in the following section.

Using *parseExpr* and *printCalc*, we can define a command *simplify* that carries out a calculation:

$$\begin{array}{lll} simplify & :: & [Law] \rightarrow String \rightarrow IO\,() \\ simplify\ laws & = & putStr \cdot printCalc \cdot calculate\ laws \cdot parseExpr \end{array}$$

The command *simplify* uses *parseExpr* to interpret the given string as an expression, then uses *calculate* to produce a calculation, then uses *printCalc* to turn the result into a string, and finally causes the string to be printed. For example,

```
? simplify pairs "cross(f, g).pair(h, k)"

  cross(f, g).pair(h, k)
=    {definition cross}
  pair(f.fst, g.snd).pair(h, k)
=    {pair absorption}
  pair(f.fst.pair(h, k), g.snd.pair(h, k))
=    {definition fst}
  pair(f.h, g.snd.pair(h, k))
=    {definition snd}
  pair(f.h, g.k)
```

The steps of the calculation are displayed in the conventional format; the name of the law used at each step is printed in curly brackets between the two expressions to which it applies.

At each step of a calculation some subexpression of the current expression is *matched* against the left-hand side of some law. The process results in a *substitution* for the variables occurring in the law. For example, in the second step of the calculation above, the expression

$$pair\ (f \cdot fst, g \cdot snd) \cdot pair\ (h, k)$$

is successfully matched against the left-hand side of the pair absorption law, resulting in a substitution in which the variable f of the pair absorption law is bound to the expression $f \cdot fst$, variable g is bound to $g \cdot snd$, and h is bound to $pair\ (h, k)$. The result of the step is the instance of the right-hand side of the pair absorption law in which each variable is replaced by the expression to which it is bound. Notice that, although the expressions being manipulated also contain variables, such variables are not changed by the steps of a calculation. Substitutions are performed only for the variables appearing in laws.

A crucial aspect in the design of *calculate* is that laws are applied only from left to right. This is to prevent calculations from looping. If laws could be applied in both directions, then an automatic calculator could always oscillate by applying a law in one direction and then immediately applying it in the reverse direction. A related argument holds for a law such as

$$iterate\ f \quad = \quad cons \cdot pair\,(id, iterate\ f \cdot f)$$

This is the definition of *iterate* expressed in point-free form. The appearance of the term *iterate f* on both sides of the law means that it is possible for an automatic calculator to apply the law infinitely often, and so never reach a conclusion.

Sometimes we do want to apply laws in both directions, and sometimes we do want to make use of laws like that of *iterate*. Potential infinite loops are avoided either by phrasing a law in a more generalised form than necessary, or by prioritising the application of laws in some way.

12.1.1 Proofs

Sometimes we want to prove equations rather than just calculate alternative forms for expressions. One method is to consider each side of the equation separately and to simplify them to the same result. The two calculations can then be pasted together by reversing the steps of the second one. To illustrate, suppose we set up the following list of laws:

```
laws = filters ++ ifs ++ others

filters
 = map parseLaw [
   "definition filter:  filter p = concat.map(box p)",
   "definition box:     box p = if(p, wrap, nil)"]

ifs
 = map parseLaw [
   "if over composition:  if(p,f,g).h = if(p.h, f.h, g.h)",
   "composition over if:  h.if(p,f,g) = if(p, h.f, h.g)"]

others
 = map parseLaw [
   "nil constant:     nil.f = nil",
   "nil natural:      map f.nil = nil",
   "wrap natural:     map f.wrap = wrap.f",
   "concat natural:   map f.concat = concat.map(map f)",
   "map functor:      map f.map g = map(f.g)"]
```

Given a function *prove*, described below, we have

```
? prove laws "filter p.map f = map f.filter(p.f)"

  filter p.map f
=   {definition filter}
  concat.map(box p).map f
=   {map functor}
  concat.map(box p.f)
=   {definition box}
  concat.map(if(p, wrap, nil).f)
=   {if over composition}
  concat.map(if(p.f, wrap.f, nil.f))
=   {nil constant}
  concat.map(if(p.f, wrap.f, nil))
=   {wrap natural}
  concat.map(if(p.f, map f.wrap, nil))
=   {nil natural}
  concat.map(if(p.f, map f.wrap, map f.nil))
=   {composition over if}
  concat.map(map f.if(p.f, wrap, nil))
=   {definition box}
  concat.map(map f.box(p.f))
=   {map functor}
```

```
  concat.map(map f).map(box(p.f))
=   {concat natural}
  map f.concat.map(box(p.f))
=   {definition filter}
  map f.filter(p.f)
```

Although the calculation is laid out as a single sequence of steps, it proceeds in two distinct phases. First, the left-hand expression *filter p · map f* is simplified, yielding the result *concat · map (if (p · f, wrap · f, nil))*. Second, the right-hand expression *map f · filter (p · f)* is simplified, yielding the same result. The two parts of the calculation are then pasted together by reversing the steps of the second half. The main advantage of this scheme is simplicity; we do not have to invent another proof format, and we do not have to apply laws from right to left in order to reach the desired goal.

There are two obvious disadvantages. One is stylistic, in that one half of the calculation has to be read backwards. The other is that the method may fail. It is not always the case that an equation holds because both sides can be simplified to the same result (see Exercise 12.1.3).

The function *prove* can be defined as follows:

$$prove \qquad :: \quad [Law] \rightarrow String \rightarrow IO\ ()$$
$$prove\ laws \quad = \quad putStr \cdot printCalc \cdot proveEqn\ laws \cdot parseEqn$$

$$proveEqn :: [Law] \rightarrow (Expr, Expr) \rightarrow Calculation$$
$$proveEqn\ laws\ (lhs, rhs)$$
$$= \quad paste\ (calculate\ laws\ lhs)\ (calculate\ laws\ rhs)$$

The remaining functions

$$parseEqn \quad :: \quad String \rightarrow (Expr, Expr)$$
$$paste \qquad :: \quad Calculation \rightarrow Calculation \rightarrow Calculation$$

will be defined in the following section.

12.1.2 Further considerations

It is unlikely that any automatic calculator can match the skill of a human one. Over a range of examples, a human calculator is likely to find shorter calculations, or calculations involving smaller intermediate expressions, than a machine could hope to achieve. Unlike a machine, a human calculator will happily apply laws in either direction without falling into a black hole.

In the scheme of automatic calculation that we are envisaging, there are only two degrees of freedom: the choice of law to apply, and the choice of subexpression to be changed. The first degree of freedom can be resolved by the order in which laws are presented to the calculator: if two different laws are applicable, then the one earlier in the list can be chosen. The second degree of freedom is represented by the order in which the subexpressions of a given expression are presented as candidates for instances of laws: if laws are applicable to two different subexpressions, then the subexpression coming earlier in the enumeration can be chosen. This still leaves open the decision whether to give preference to laws or subexpressions in proofs. In other words, is a calculation dominated at each step by the desire to apply a particular law or to change a particular subexpression?

In the main, the focus of a step in a calculation is usually at a particular place in the expression, rather than in a law one might want to apply. However, certain kinds of law are often applied between the major steps; these are laws that reduce the complexity of intermediate expressions. A good example is the law $f \cdot id = f$ (and also $id \cdot f = f$). It is unlikely to be a mistake to apply this law as soon as the opportunity arises. Similarly, early application of laws like $nil \cdot f = nil$ and $fst \cdot pair\,(f,g) = f$ can help to reduce the sizes of intermediate expressions. For the sake of a word, let us call these *basic* laws. It therefore seems a sensible idea to divide the given list of laws into two kinds, basic laws and others, and to give priority to the basic laws in the steps of a calculation.

Bearing this aspect in mind, we will change the definition of *simplify* and *calculate* slightly:

> *simplify laws*
> = *putStr* · *printCalc* · *calculate* (*basic, others*) · *parseExpr*
> **where** (*basic, others*) = *partition basicLaw laws*

The function *partition p* partitions the elements of a list into two sublists, those satisfying p and the others. The function *basicLaw* :: *Law* → *Bool* is defined in the following section. The type of *calculate* is changed to

> *calculate* :: ([*Law*], [*Law*]) → *Expr* → *Calculation*

and *prove* is changed in a similar manner. The example calculations recorded above were produced with the modified definitions.

Exercises

12.1.1 Some of the laws one might wish to use in calculations depend on certain subsidiary conditions being satisfied. Give an example of such a law. Such laws can only be used in the proposed scheme by assuming that the subsidiary conditions hold.

12.1.2 Suggest an appropriate description of a basic law.

12.1.3 Can the law *zipp · pair (map f, map g) = map (pair (f, g))* be proved by simplifying both sides to the same result? It can be proved by simplifying the expression *zipp · unzip · map (pair (f, g))* in essentially two different ways; one is to use the law *zipp · unzip = id*, and the other is to use the definition of *unzip*. Give details.

12.1.4 The two functor laws for *map* are important in many proofs. Which orientation of these laws is likely to be the most useful? Using the *zipp* law of the previous exercise, prove *zipp · pair (id, map g) = map (pair (id, g))*. Did your proof use the functor laws in the preferred direction?

12.1.5 There are many ways in which the design of the calculator can be improved. For example, the laws could be read in from one or more files, the idea of splitting laws into two kinds can be generalised into a more abstract notion of a proof strategy, and the calculator could be made interactive. Give a list of other features or improvements that you would like to see in an automatic calculator.

12.2   Expressions, laws, and calculations

At the heart of the calculator is the datatype *Expr* of expressions; most of the components of the calculator are concerned with recognising, manipulating, or printing expressions. In the proposed framework, every expression describes a function. Expressions are built from (function) variables and constants, using functional composition as the basic combining form. Variables take no arguments, but constant functions can take any number of arguments, which themselves are expressions. We therefore will adopt the following definition of *Expr*:

```
data Expr
   =   Var VarName   |   Con ConName [Expr]   |   Compose [Expr]
       deriving (Eq)

type VarName   =   Char
type ConName   =   String
```

For simplicity, we suppose that single-letter names denote variables and multi-letter names denote constants. We will avoid special symbols in the names of constants, for example by writing *plus* for (+) and *zero* for 0. Thus the names of constants are sequences of at least two alphanumeric characters beginning with a letter. Variables and constants are referred to collectively as *terms*.

The type *Expr* is declared to be an instance of *Eq* because we will need to test expressions for equality.

Here are some examples of expressions:

$$
\begin{array}{lcl}
\textit{fst} & \Rightarrow & \textit{Con} \text{ ``fst''} [\,] \\
\textit{fst} \cdot f & \Rightarrow & \textit{Compose} [\textit{Con} \text{ ``fst''} [\,], \textit{Var} \text{ `f'}] \\
\textit{map } f & \Rightarrow & \textit{Con} \text{ ``map''} [\textit{Var} \text{ `f'}] \\
\textit{cross} (f, g) & \Rightarrow & \textit{Con} \text{ ``cross''} [\textit{Var} \text{ `f'}, \textit{Var} \text{ `g'}]
\end{array}
$$

Each constant takes a tuple of arguments, which may be the empty tuple (as in the case of *fst*), a singleton tuple (as with *map*), a pair, and so on. The scheme is very simple and does not allow us to represent expressions, such as *foldr f e*, that make use of currying. But we can always represent *foldr f e* by the term *foldr* (f, e). The two equations defining *foldr* can be expressed in the functional form

$$
\begin{array}{lcl}
\textit{foldr } (f, e) \cdot \textit{nil} & = & e \\
\textit{foldr } (f, e) \cdot \textit{cons} & = & f \cdot \textit{cross} (\textit{id}, \textit{foldr} (f, e))
\end{array}
$$

In these equations both *f* and *cons* are noncurried functions taking a pair as argument.

It is the intention of the design that the associativity of functional composition is built-in. Thus, both $(f \cdot g) \cdot h$ and $f \cdot (g \cdot h)$ will be represented by the same expression

$$
\textit{Compose} [\textit{Var} \text{ `f'}, \textit{Var} \text{ `g'}, \textit{Var} \text{ `h'}]
$$

As a result, *Expr* has two datatype invariants: (i) the expression *Compose xs* is valid only if the length of *xs* is at least two; (ii) no expression of the form *Compose xs* contains an element of *xs* that is itself of the form *Compose ys*. To maintain these invariants, compositions of expressions are constructed by the function *compose*:

$$
\begin{array}{lcl}
\textit{compose} & :: & [\textit{Expr}] \rightarrow \textit{Expr} \\
\textit{compose xs} & = & \textbf{if } \textit{singleton xs} \\
& & \textbf{then } \textit{head xs} \\
& & \textbf{else } \textit{Compose} (\textit{concat} (\textit{map decompose xs}))
\end{array}
$$

$$
\begin{array}{lcl}
\textit{decompose} & :: & \textit{Expr} \rightarrow [\textit{Expr}] \\
\textit{decompose} (\textit{Var } v) & = & [\textit{Var } v] \\
\textit{decompose} (\textit{Con } f \textit{ xs}) & = & [\textit{Con } f \textit{ xs}] \\
\textit{decompose} (\textit{Compose xs}) & = & \textit{xs}
\end{array}
$$

The function *compose* will be applied only to nonempty lists.

The complexity of an expression is defined to be its number of terms:

$$
\begin{array}{lll}
complexity & :: & Expr \rightarrow Int \\
complexity \ (Var \ v) & = & 1 \\
complexity \ (Con \ f \ xs) & = & 1 \\
complexity \ (Compose \ xs) & = & length \ xs
\end{array}
$$

It is possible to give a more refined definition of *complexity*, but the given one suffices in practice.

In printing an expression, we put parentheses only around tuples of size at least two, or around single arguments that are not simple terms:

$$
\begin{array}{lll}
printExpr & :: & Expr \rightarrow String \\
printExpr \ (Var \ v) & = & [v]
\end{array}
$$

$$
printExpr \ (Con \ f \ xs)
$$
$$
\begin{array}{lll}
\quad \mid \ null \ xs & = & f \\
\quad \mid \ simple \ xs & = & f \ +\!\!+ \ \text{“}\sqcup\text{”} \ +\!\!+ \ printExpr \ (head \ xs) \\
\quad \mid \ otherwise & = & f \ +\!\!+ \ \text{“(”} \ +\!\!+ \\
& & joinWith \ \text{“,}\sqcup\text{”} \ (map \ printExpr \ xs) \ +\!\!+ \ \text{“)”}
\end{array}
$$

$$
printExpr \ (Compose \ xs) \quad = \quad joinWith \ \text{“.”} \ (map \ printExpr \ xs)
$$

$$
\begin{array}{lll}
simple & :: & [Expr] \rightarrow Bool \\
simple \ xs & = & singleton \ xs \wedge simpleton \ (head \ xs)
\end{array}
$$

$$
\begin{array}{lll}
simpleton & :: & Expr \rightarrow Bool \\
simpleton \ (Var \ v) & = & True \\
simpleton \ (Con \ f \ xs) & = & null \ xs \\
simpleton \ (Compose \ xs) & = & False
\end{array}
$$

The function *joinWith* was defined in Section 5.5. A more sophisticated definition of *printExpr* should arrange to break an expression attractively across lines if it is too large to fit on one line. This refinement is left as an exercise.

12.2.1 Parsing expressions

It remains to define *parseExpr*. Naturally, we will use the combinators described in the previous chapter. The definition is

$$
\begin{array}{lll}
parseExpr & :: & String \rightarrow Expr \\
parseExpr & = & applyParser \ expr
\end{array}
$$

The parser *expr* recognises a nonempty sequence of terms separated by composition signs:

> *expr* :: *Parser Expr*
> *expr* = **do** {*xs* ← *somewith* (*symbol* ".") *term*; *return* (*compose xs*)}

The parser *term* recognises a variable or constant:

> *term* :: *Parser Expr*
> *term* = **do** *space*
>   *c* ← *letter*
>   *cs* ← *many alphanum*
>   **if** *null cs*
>   **then** *return* (*Var c*)
>   **else** **do** *xs* ← *argument*
>   *return* (*Con* (*c* : *cs*) *xs*)

The parser *argument* recognises the argument of a constant function, if any:

> *argument* :: *Parser* [*Expr*]
> *argument* = *tuple* **orelse** (*notuple* **orelse** *return* [ ])

The parser *tuple* recognises an expression in parentheses:

> *tuple* :: *Parser* [*Expr*]
> *tuple* = **do** *symbol* "("
>   *xs* ← *somewith* (*symbol* ",") *expr*
>   *symbol* ")"
>   *return xs*

The parser *notuple* recognises a variable or a constant with no arguments:

> *notuple* :: *Parser Expr*
> *notuple* = **do** *space*
>   *c* ← *letter*
>   *cs* ← *many alphanum*
>   **if** *null cs*
>   **then** *return* [*Var c*]
>   **else** *return* [*Con* (*c* : *cs*) [ ]]

This completes the definition of *parseExpr*. The function *parseEqn* is similar but simpler:

> *parseEqn* :: *String* → (*Expr*, *Expr*)
> *parseEqn* = *applyParser eqn*

$$eqn \quad :: \quad Parser\ (Expr, Expr)$$
$$eqn \quad = \quad \textbf{do}\ space$$
$$x \leftarrow expr$$
$$symbol\ \text{"="}$$
$$y \leftarrow expr$$
$$return\ (x, y)$$

12.2.2 Laws

A law consists of three logical components: a name and two expressions:

$$\textbf{type}\ Law \qquad = \quad (LawName, Expr, Expr)$$
$$\textbf{type}\ LawName \ = \quad String$$

By definition, a law is a *basic* law if the complexity of its left-hand expression is greater than its right-hand one:

$$basicLaw \qquad\qquad\qquad :: \quad Law \rightarrow Bool$$
$$basicLaw\ (name, lhs, rhs) \quad = \quad (complexity\ lhs > complexity\ rhs)$$

Other definitions of a basic law are possible, but this one works well enough in most situations.

The remaining function on laws is *parseLaw*:

$$parseLaw \quad :: \quad String \rightarrow Law$$
$$parseLaw \quad = \quad applyParser\ law$$

$$law \quad :: \quad Parser\ Law$$
$$law \quad = \quad \textbf{do}\ space$$
$$name \leftarrow some\ (sat\ (\neq\ \text{':'}))$$
$$symbol\ \text{":"}$$
$$(x, y) \leftarrow eqn$$
$$return\ (name, x, y)$$

12.2.3 Calculations

A calculation consists of a starting expression together with a sequence of steps. Each step consists of the name of the law being applied and the resulting expression. Hence we can define

$$\textbf{type}\ Calculation \ = \quad (Expr, [Step])$$
$$\textbf{type}\ Step \qquad\quad = \quad (LawName, Expr)$$

The conclusion of a calculation is the last expression in it:

$$\begin{aligned}
conclusion &\quad :: \quad Calculation \rightarrow Expr \\
conclusion\ (x, steps) &\quad = \quad \textbf{if}\ null\ steps\ \textbf{then}\ x\ \textbf{else}\ snd\ (last\ steps)
\end{aligned}$$

The function *paste* for pasting two calculations together can now be defined by

$$\begin{aligned}
paste &\quad :: \quad Calculation \rightarrow Calculation \rightarrow Calculation \\
paste\ lhc\ rhc &\quad = \quad (fst\ lhc, snd\ lhc \mathbin{+\!\!+} link\ x\ y \mathbin{+\!\!+} shuffle\ rhc) \\
&\quad \textbf{where}\ x \quad = \quad conclusion\ lhc \\
&\qquad\qquad\ \ y \quad = \quad conclusion\ rhc
\end{aligned}$$

The function *link* inserts an indication of failure if the two conclusions are not the same:

$$\begin{aligned}
link &\quad :: \quad Expr \rightarrow Expr \rightarrow [Step] \\
link\ x\ y &\quad = \quad \textbf{if}\ x == y\ \textbf{then}\ [\ ]\ \textbf{else}\ [(\text{``... ??? ...''}, y)]
\end{aligned}$$

The function *shuffle* reverses the steps of a calculation, taking

$$(x, [(r_1, y_1), \ldots, (r_n, y_n)]) \quad \text{to} \quad [(r_n, y_{n-1}), \ldots, (r_2, y_1), (r_1, x)]$$

The definition is

$$\begin{aligned}
shuffle &\quad :: \quad Calculation \rightarrow [Step] \\
shuffle(x, ss) &\quad = \quad snd\ (foldl\ shunt\ (x, [\ ])\ ss) \\
&\quad \textbf{where}\ shunt\ (x, rs)\ (r, y) = (y, (r, x) : rs)
\end{aligned}$$

The function *printCalc* is defined by

$$\begin{aligned}
printCalc &\quad :: \quad Calculation \rightarrow String \\
printCalc\ (x, ss) &\quad = \quad \text{``}\bar{\mathbf{t}}\text{\textvisiblespace\textvisiblespace''} \mathbin{+\!\!+} printExpr\ x \mathbin{+\!\!+} \\
&\qquad \text{``}\bar{\mathbf{t}}\text{''} \mathbin{+\!\!+} concat\ (map\ printStep\ ss)
\end{aligned}$$

$$\begin{aligned}
printStep &\quad :: \quad Step \rightarrow String \\
printStep\ (why, x) &\quad = \quad \text{``=\textvisiblespace\textvisiblespace\{''} \mathbin{+\!\!+} why \mathbin{+\!\!+} \text{``\}}\bar{\mathbf{t}}\text{''} \mathbin{+\!\!+} \\
&\qquad \text{``\textvisiblespace\textvisiblespace''} \mathbin{+\!\!+} printExpr\ x \mathbin{+\!\!+} \text{``}\bar{\mathbf{t}}\text{''}
\end{aligned}$$

Exercises

12.2.1 Various alternative definitions of *Expr* are possible. One is to say that an expression is either a variable, or a constant (with no arguments), or the application of one expression to another. Formalise the associated datatype and give the representation of *fst · fold f e* as an element. What are the advantages and disadvantages of this representation?

12.2.2 A useful generalisation of the proposed type for *Expr* is to replace the constructor *Compose* by a more general constructor *Ass ConName*. Constructions *Ass f xs* are allowed when *f* is any associative operation on functions. Give an example where this generalisation might be useful.

12.2.3 Give an improved definition of *printExpr* that handles line breaks in a reasonable manner.

12.2.4 As an alternative to providing a function *printExpr* explicitly, *Expr* can be made an instance of the class *Show*. Give details. Show how to handle the printing of calculations in a similar fashion.

12.3 Matchings and substitutions

Let us now show how to match one expression *x* against another expression *y*. Matching is used in the calculator when *x* is the left-hand side of some law, and *y* is some subexpression of the current expression in a partially completed calculation. The result of matching is a *set* of possible substitutions. A substitution associates each variable of *x* with an expression in such a way that when the substitution is applied to *x*, the result is *y*. We also say that *y* is an *instance* of *x* under the substitution.

A match may fail, yielding the empty set of substitutions, or it may succeed in one or more ways. For example, matching

$$foo\,(f \cdot g, f \cdot g) \quad \text{against} \quad foo\,(a \cdot b \cdot c, a \cdot b \cdot c)$$

succeeds in two different ways, either by binding *f* to $a \cdot b$ and *g* to *c*, or by binding *f* to *a* and *g* to $b \cdot c$. Although the automatic calculator will select a single substitution for use at each step of a calculation, it is important to take account of multiple matchings in the process of determining the valid substitutions. As we will see, the general scheme is to match expressions by matching corresponding subexpressions and combining the results. For example, in matching

$$foo\,(f \cdot g, bar\,g) \quad \text{against} \quad foo\,(a \cdot b \cdot c, bar\,c)$$

the subexpression $f \cdot g$ is matched against $a \cdot b \cdot c$, resulting in two possible substitutions. Only when the subexpression *bar g* is matched with *bar c* is one of the substitutions rejected. A premature commitment to a single substitution for the first pair of subexpressions may result in a successful substitution being missed.

12.3.1   Substitutions

We will implement substitutions as elements of the type *Subst*, where

> **type** *Subst*   = $[(VarName, Expr)]$

In words, a substitution is represented as a list of bindings. An empty list does not represent the undefined substitution, but rather the substitution in which each variable *v* is associated with *Var v*. Thus an empty list represents the identity substitution.

The function *binding* returns the expression associated with a given variable in a substitution:

> | *binding* | :: | *Subst* → *VarName* → *Expr* |
> |---|---|---|
> | *binding* [ ] *v* | = | *Var v* |
> | *binding* $((u, x) : s)$ *v* | = | **if** *u* == *v* **then** *x* **else** *binding s v* |

We will also want to apply a substitution to an expression:

> | *applySub* | :: | *Subst* → *Expr* → *Expr* |
> |---|---|---|
> | *applySub s* (*Var v*) | = | *binding s v* |
> | *applySub s* (*Con f xs*) *s* | = | *Con f* (*map* (*applySub s*) *xs*) |
> | *applySub s* (*Compose xs*) | = | *compose* (*map* (*applySub s*) *xs*) |

Finally, we will want to extend a substitution with an additional binding:

> *extend* :: *Subst* → (*VarName*, *Expr*) → [*Subst*]
> *extend s* (*v*, *x*)
> | *y* == *x*   =   [*s*]
> | *y* == *Var v* =   [(*v*, *x*) : *s*]
> | *otherwise*   =   [ ]
>   **where** *y* = *binding s v*

The function *extend* returns a list of substitutions; this list is empty if the additional binding is incompatible with the given substitution, and is a singleton list otherwise.

12.3.2   Matching

The function *match* takes a pair of expressions and returns a set of substitutions. For reasons of efficiency, *match* is defined in terms of a generalised function *xmatch*:

> | *match* | :: | (*Expr*, *Expr*) → [*Subst*] |
> |---|---|---|
> | *match* (*x*, *y*) | = | *xmatch* [ ] (*x*, *y*) |

The first argument to *xmatch* is an accumulating parameter of type *Subst*. The following definition of *xmatch* will be derived formally in Section 12.5 from a direct definition of *match*; for now, we will simply explain the definition clause by clause. First,

$$
\begin{array}{lll}
xmatch & :: & Subst \rightarrow (Expr, Expr) \rightarrow [Subst] \\
xmatch\ s\ (Var\ v, x) & = & extend\ s\ (v, x)
\end{array}
$$

Matching a variable *v* against an arbitrary expression *x* always succeeds. However, extending the substitution *s* with (v, x) may yield an empty list of substitutions. Next,

$$
\begin{array}{lll}
xmatch\ s\ (Con\ f\ xs, Var\ v) & = & [\,] \\
xmatch\ s\ (Con\ f\ xs, Compose\ ys) & = & [\,]
\end{array}
$$

$$
\begin{array}{l}
xmatch\ s\ (Con\ f\ xs, Con\ g\ ys) \\
\quad = \ \textbf{if}\ f == g\ \textbf{then}\ xmatchlist\ s\ (zip\ xs\ ys)\ \textbf{else}\ [\,]
\end{array}
$$

Matching a constant against a variable or composition always fails. On the other hand, matching a constant against the same constant succeeds if corresponding elements in the two argument lists can be matched. The function *xmatchlist* is defined by

$$
\begin{array}{lll}
xmatchlist & :: & Subst \rightarrow [(Expr, Expr)] \rightarrow [Subst] \\
xmatchlist\ s\ [\,] & = & [s] \\
xmatchlist\ s\ (xy : xys) & = & concat\ [xmatchlist\ t\ xys\ |\ t \leftarrow xmatch\ s\ xy]
\end{array}
$$

Matching an empty list always succeeds; matching a list $(xy : xys)$ involves first computing *xmatch s xy* to produce a list of possible substitutions, and then refining each substitution *t* in this list by computing *xmatchlist t xys*. The result is a list of lists of substitutions, which is flattened by *concat*.

The remaining three clauses of *xmatch* are

$$
\begin{array}{lll}
xmatch\ s\ (Compose\ xs, Var\ v) & = & [\,] \\
xmatch\ s\ (Compose\ xs, Con\ g\ ys) & = & [\,]
\end{array}
$$

$$
\begin{array}{l}
xmatch\ s\ (Compose\ xs, Compose\ ys) \\
\quad = \ concat\ (map\ (xmatchlist\ s)\ (align\ xs\ ys))
\end{array}
$$

Matching a composition against a variable or constant fails because *Compose xs* is a valid expression only when *length xs* ≥ 2. Matching two sequences of compositions succeeds if matching appropriately aligned segments does. The function *align* is defined below. For each list *xys* of appropriately aligned segments, the value of *xmatchlist s xys* is computed and the results are concatenated.

To define *align xs ys* suppose *length xs* = *m* and *length ys* = *n*. If *m* > *n*, then *xs* cannot be matched to *ys* as there are not enough elements of *ys* to go round. If *m* ≤ *n*, then each element of *xs* has to be matched with some segment of *ys*. In other words, if $ys_1, ys_2, \ldots, ys_m$ is a partition of *ys* into nonempty contiguous segments, then the first element of *xs* has to be matched to ys_1, the second element to ys_2, and so on. We will therefore need to make use of a function *parts m* that returns a list of all partitions of a sequence into a list of *m* components. Given *parts*, we can define

$$align \qquad :: \quad [Expr] \to [Expr] \to [[(Expr, Expr)]]$$
$$align\ xs\ ys \quad = \quad [zip\ xs\ (map\ compose\ zs)\ |\ zs \leftarrow parts\ (length\ xs)\ ys]$$

The definition of *parts* is

$$parts \qquad\qquad :: \quad Int \to [\alpha] \to [[[\alpha]]]$$
$$parts\ 0\ [\,] \qquad\quad = \quad [[\,]]$$
$$parts\ 0\ (x:xs) \qquad = \quad [\,]$$
$$parts\ (n+1)\ [\,] \qquad = \quad [\,]$$
$$parts\ (n+1)\ (x:xs) \quad = \quad map\ (new\ x)\ (parts\ n\ xs) +\!\!+$$
$$\qquad\qquad\qquad\qquad\qquad map\ (glue\ x)\ (parts\ (n+1)\ xs)$$

The first equation says that there is just one partition of the empty sequence into a list of zero components, namely the empty partition. The second equation says that there are no partitions of a nonempty sequence into zero components. The third equation says that there are no partitions of the empty sequence into *m* components if *m* > 0. Finally, the fourth equation says that every partition of *x : xs* into *n* + 1 components is obtained either by generating a partition *yss* of *xs* of length *n* and then adding in [*x*] as a new first component, or else by generating a partition *ys : yss* of *xs* of length *n* + 1 and then 'gluing' *x* to the first component *ys*. The functions *new* and *glue* are defined by

$$new \qquad\qquad :: \quad \alpha \to [[\alpha]] \to [[\alpha]]$$
$$new\ x\ yss \qquad\ = \quad [x] : yss$$
$$glue \qquad\qquad :: \quad \alpha \to [[\alpha]] \to [[\alpha]]$$
$$glue\ x\ (ys:yss) \quad = \quad (x:ys):yss$$

Exercises

12.3.1 Prove that *applySub* [ ] = *id*.

12.3.2 The function *match* can be defined directly. Two of the clauses are

> *match* (*Con f xs, Con g ys*)
> $\quad$ = $\;$ **if** $f == g$ **then** *matchlist* (*zip xs ys*) **else** [ ]
> *match* (*Compose xs, Compose ys*)
> $\quad$ = $\;$ *concat* (*map matchlist* (*align xs ys*))

Fill in the remaining clauses. (This exercise is answered in Section 12.5.)

12.3.3 The function *matchlist* of the previous exercise is defined by

> *matchlist* $\quad$ :: $\quad$ [(*Expr, Expr*)] $\rightarrow$ [*Subst*]
> *matchlist* $\quad$ = $\quad$ *concat* $\cdot$ *map unify* $\cdot$ *cplist* $\cdot$ *map match*

This definition reads: first compute the list of lists of partial substitutions (via *map match*), then combine all partial substitutions into a list of candidate substitutions (via *cplist*), then unify each candidate (via *unify*), and finally collect the valid substitutions (via *concat*).

The function *cplist* (short for 'cartesian product over lists') is defined informally by

$$cplist\ [xs_1, \ldots, xs_n] \quad = \quad [[x_1, \ldots, x_n] \mid x_1 \leftarrow xs_1, \ldots, x_n \leftarrow xs_n]$$

Give a formal definition of *cplist*. (This exercise is answered in Section 12.5.)

12.3.4 The function *unify* :: [*Subst*] $\rightarrow$ [*Subst*] takes a list of partial substitutions and combines them into a single complete substitution. Thus, *unify* returns either an empty list, if the partial substitutions cannot be combined, or a singleton list containing the unified substitution. It can be defined by

> *unify* $\quad\quad$ :: $\quad$ [*Subst*] $\rightarrow$ [*Subst*]
> *unify* [ ] $\quad\quad$ = $\quad$ [[ ]]
> *unify* (*s* : *ss*) $\quad$ = $\quad$ *concat* [*union s t* $\mid$ *t* $\leftarrow$ *unify ss*]

The function *union* :: *Subst* $\rightarrow$ *Subst* $\rightarrow$ [*Subst*] takes two substitutions and, provided they are compatible, merges them into a single substitution. Give a definition of *union*. (This exercise is answered in Section 12.5.)

12.4 Subexpressions and rewriting

In the previous section we saw how to match one expression (the left-hand side of a law) against another expression. Now we want to match an expression against a subexpression of a given expression. If the matching succeeds, then the appropriate instance of the right-hand side of the law replaces the subexpression. To carry out this replacement, it is necessary to locate subexpressions in their parent expression. Hence we define

type *SubExpr* = (*Location, Expr*)

A subexpression of an expression *x* may be *all* of *x*, or a *segment* of *x* (if *x* is a composition of terms), or a subexpression of some term of *x*. This leads to the following declaration of *Location*:

data *Location* = *All* | *Seg Int Int* | *Pos Int Location*

The location *Seg j k* denotes a segment beginning at position *j* and extending for $k \geq 2$ terms; a location *Pos j loc* denotes the subexpression located at *loc* of the expression located at position *j*.

Let us see how this scheme works out on the expression

fst · pair (f · fst, g · snd) · zip

Here is a complete list of the subexpressions of the above expression and the locations at which each subexpression appears:

fst · pair (f · fst, g · snd) · zip	at	*All*
fst · pair (f · fst, g · snd)	at	*Seg 0 2*
pair (f · fst, g · snd) · zip	at	*Seg 1 2*
fst	at	*Pos 0 All*
pair (f · fst, g · snd)	at	*Pos 1 All*
f · fst	at	*Pos 1 (Pos 0 All)*
f	at	*Pos 1 (Pos 0 (Pos 0 All))*
fst	at	*Pos 1 (Pos 0 (Pos 1 All))*
g · snd	at	*Pos 1 (Pos 1 All)*
g	at	*Pos 1 (Pos 1 (Pos 0 All))*
snd	at	*Pos 1 (Pos 1 (Pos 1 All))*
zip	at	*Pos 2 All*

The above subexpressions are listed in the order in which they are generated by the function *subexprs*:

subexprs	::	*Expr* → [*SubExpr*]
subexprs (Var v)	=	[(*All, Var v*)]
subexprs (Con f xs)	=	[(*All, Con f xs*)] ++ *subterms xs*
subexprs (Compose xs)	=	[(*All, Compose xs*)] ++ *segments xs* ++
		subterms xs

$subterms :: [Expr] \rightarrow [SubExpr]$
$subterms\ xs$
  $=\ [(Pos\ j\ loc, y) \mid j \leftarrow [0 .. n - 1], (loc, y) \leftarrow subexprs\ (xs \mathbin{!!} j)]$
  where $n = length\ xs$

$segments :: [Expr] \rightarrow [SubExpr]$
$segments\ xs$
  $=\ [(Seg\ j\ k, Compose\ (take\ k\ (drop\ j\ xs))) \mid k \leftarrow [2 .. n - 1],$
  $\qquad\qquad\qquad\qquad\qquad\qquad\qquad j \leftarrow [0 .. n - k]]$

  where $n = length\ xs$

The function *subexprs* produces segments before subterms; this is probably
sensible, though more sophisticated generation orders are possible. Again,
subterms are generated from left to right; in practice, manipulations usually
proceed right to left. Another option is to have *subexprs* take an additional argument, the location at which the current expression was last changed, and then
to generate subexpressions around that location first. All these refinements are
left as exercises.

Finally, we need a function for replacing subexpressions by other expressions:

$replace \qquad\quad :: \quad Expr \rightarrow Location \rightarrow Expr \rightarrow Expr$
$replace\ x\ All\ y \ = \ y$

$replace\ (Con\ f\ xs)\ (Pos\ j\ loc)\ y$
  $=\ Con\ f\ (take\ j\ xs \mathbin{+\!\!+} [replace\ (xs \mathbin{!!} j)\ loc\ y] \mathbin{+\!\!+} drop\ (j + 1)\ xs)$
$replace\ (Compose\ xs)\ (Pos\ j\ loc)\ y$
  $=\ compose\ (take\ j\ xs \mathbin{+\!\!+} [replace\ (xs \mathbin{!!} j)\ loc\ y] \mathbin{+\!\!+} drop\ (j + 1)\ xs)$
$replace\ (Compose\ xs)\ (Seg\ j\ k)\ y$
  $=\ compose\ (take\ j\ xs \mathbin{+\!\!+} [y] \mathbin{+\!\!+} drop\ (j + k)\ xs)$

12.4.1 Rewriting

We are at last in a position to define the function *calculate*. To calculate with
an expression means using the laws repeatedly to rewrite the expression until
no more steps are possible. Hence we can define

$calculate \qquad :: \quad ([Law], [Law]) \rightarrow Expr \rightarrow Calculation$
$calculate\ pls\ x \ = \ (x, repeatedly\ (rewrites\ pls)x)$

Recall that the list of laws is split into two sublists, the basic laws that are
always tried first, and the others.

The function *rewrites* produces all possible ways of rewriting an expression:

$$rewrites \quad :: \quad ([Law], [Law]) \rightarrow Expr \rightarrow [Step]$$
$$rewrites \; (llaws, rlaws) \; x$$
$$= \quad concat \; ([rewrite \; law \; sx \; x \mid law \leftarrow llaws, \; sx \leftarrow subexprs \; x]$$
$$+\!\!\!+ [rewrite \; law \; sx \; x \mid sx \leftarrow subexprs \; x, \; law \leftarrow rlaws])$$

The two kinds of law are treated differently. Basic laws are tried first, each law being tried in sequence with all possible subexpressions. In the case of the other laws, the rule is different: each subexpression is tried in sequence with all possible laws.

The function *rewrite* produces all possible ways of rewriting a single expression with a single law:

$$rewrite :: Law \rightarrow SubExpr \rightarrow Expr \rightarrow [Step]$$
$$rewrite \; (name, lhs, rhs) \; (loc, y) \; x$$
$$= \quad [(name, replace \; x \; loc \; (applySub \; s \; rhs)) \mid s \leftarrow match \; (lhs, y)]$$

Finally, *repeatedly* applies the first rewrite at each step:

$$repeatedly :: (Expr \rightarrow [Step]) \rightarrow Expr \rightarrow [Step]$$
$$repeatedly \; rws \; x$$
$$= \quad \textbf{if} \; null \; steps \; \textbf{then} \; [\,] \; \textbf{else} \; (n, y) : repeatedly \; rws \; y$$
$$\quad \textbf{where} \; steps \quad = \quad rws \; x$$
$$\quad\quad\quad (n, y) \quad = \quad head \; steps$$

Nondeterminism is resolved simply by choosing the first among many possible steps. Other schemes are, of course, possible. For instance, in an interactive setting the choice could be offered to the user. Another possibility is to explore the complete tree of feasible calculations and return a shortest one.

Exercises

12.4.1 Modify the definition of *subexprs* so that one can install different generation orders in a simple way. This will involve adding an extra argument to *calculate* to indicate which of the orderings should be chosen.

12.4.2 Rewrite the calculator to implement the idea that *subexprs* should take an additional argument, namely the location of the last replacement.

12.4.3 Explore the idea of making the calculator interactive, so that a choice of steps can be offered to the user.

12.5 Testing the calculator

How useful is the calculator in practice? The only way to answer the question is to try it out on a nontrivial example. In this section we are going to use the calculator to generate part of the definition of *xmatch* given in Section 12.3 from a direct definition of *match*. The part we have chosen to automate is the most difficult one; the rest of the synthesis is sufficiently easy not to warrant automation.

The direct definition of *match* (see Exercise 12.3.2) is as follows:

$$
\begin{array}{lcl}
match & :: & (Expr, Expr) \rightarrow [Subst] \\
match\,(Var\;v, x) & = & [[(v, x)]] \\
match\,(Con\,f\;xs, Var\;v) & = & [\,] \\
match\,(Con\,f\;xs, Compose\;ys) & = & [\,]
\end{array}
$$

$$
\begin{array}{l}
match\,(Con\,f\;xs, Con\,g\;ys) \\
\quad = \quad \textbf{if } f == g \textbf{ then } matchlist\,(zip\;xs\;ys) \textbf{ else } [\,]
\end{array}
$$

$$
\begin{array}{lcl}
match\,(Compose\;xs, Var\;v) & = & [\,] \\
match\,(Compose\;xs, Con\,g\;ys) & = & [\,]
\end{array}
$$

$$
\begin{array}{l}
match\,(Compose\;xs, Compose\;ys) \\
\quad = \quad concat\,(map\;matchlist\,(align\;xs\;ys))
\end{array}
$$

The function *matchlist* (see Exercise 12.3.3) is defined by

$$
\begin{array}{lcl}
matchlist & :: & [(Expr, Expr)] \rightarrow [Subst] \\
matchlist & = & concat \cdot map\;unify \cdot cplist \cdot map\;match
\end{array}
$$

The function *matchlist* computes the substitutions for each pair of expressions, collects all combinations, and unifies each combination.

The function *cplist* is defined by

$$
\begin{array}{lcl}
cplist & :: & [[\alpha]] \rightarrow [[\alpha]] \\
cplist\,[\,] & = & [[\,]] \\
cplist\,(xs : xss) & = & [y : ys \mid y \leftarrow xs,\; ys \leftarrow cplist\;xss]
\end{array}
$$

The function *unify* is defined by

$$
\begin{array}{lcl}
unify & :: & [Subst] \rightarrow [Subst] \\
unify\,[\,] & = & [[\,]] \\
unify\,(s : ss) & = & concat\,[union\;s\;t \mid t \leftarrow unify\;ss]
\end{array}
$$

The function *union* can be defined by

$$union \quad :: \quad Subst \rightarrow Subst \rightarrow [Subst]$$
$$union\ s\ t \quad = \quad \textbf{if}\ compatible\ s\ t\ \textbf{then}\ [merge\ s\ t]\ \textbf{else}\ [\ ]$$

Two substitutions are compatible if and only if they agree on the variables in their common domain. The function *merge* can be implemented by (++), or by merging the two lists of bindings, removing duplicates. We will not go into details. Not only is *union* complicated to define, it is also expensive to compute. A better idea, and one that motivates the efficient definition of *xmatch*, is to compute the union of two substitutions only when one of them is a substitution involving a single binding. This is the point of the function *extend*, which is specified by

$$extend\ s\ (v, x) \quad = \quad union\ s\ [(Var\ v, x)]$$

The definition of *extend* given in Section 12.3 implements this specification in an obvious way.

However it is implemented, we will need two assumptions about *union*. First, *union* [ ] *s* = [*s*] for all *s*. In words, the empty substitution is compatible with every substitution and is the unit of *merge*. Second, define *cup* by

$$cup \quad :: \quad [Subst] \rightarrow [Subst] \rightarrow [Subst]$$
$$cup\ ss\ ts \quad = \quad concat\ [union\ s\ t \mid s \leftarrow ss,\ t \leftarrow ts]$$

The assumption is that *cup* is associative:

$$cup\ ss\ (cup\ ts\ us) \quad = \quad cup\ (cup\ ss\ ts)\ us$$

It follows from the first assumption that [[ ]] is the unit of *cup*.

12.5.1 The generalisations

The function *xmatch* is specified by

$$xmatch \quad :: \quad Subst \rightarrow (Expr, Expr) \rightarrow [Subst]$$
$$xmatch\ s\ xy \quad = \quad concat\ [union\ s\ t \mid t \leftarrow match\ xy]$$

Since *union* [ ] *t* = [*t*], we obtain *match* = *xmatch* [ ].

It is very easy to use the definition of *match* to derive the following equations for *xmatch*:

$$
\begin{aligned}
xmatch\ s\ (Var\ v, x) & = & extend\ s\ (v, x) \\
xmatch\ s\ (Con\ f\ xs, Var\ v) & = & [\ ] \\
xmatch\ s\ (Con\ f\ xs, Compose\ ys) & = & [\ ] \\
xmatch\ s\ (Compose\ xs, Var\ v) & = & [\ ] \\
xmatch\ s\ (Compose\ xs, Con\ g\ ys) & = & [\ ]
\end{aligned}
$$

$xmatch\ s\ (Con\ f\ xs, Con\ g\ ys)$
$= $ **if** $f == g$ **then** $concat\ [union\ s\ t\ |\ t \leftarrow matchlist\ (zip\ xs\ ys)]$ **else** $[\ ]$
$xmatch\ s\ (Compose\ xs, Compose\ ys)$
$= \ concat\ [union\ s\ t\ |\ t \leftarrow concat\ (map\ matchlist\ (align\ xs\ ys))]$

The last two equations can be simplified by introducing

$xmatchlist \qquad :: \quad Subst \rightarrow [(Expr, Expr)] \rightarrow [Subst]$
$xmatchlist\ s\ xys \quad = \quad concat\ [union\ s\ t\ |\ t \leftarrow matchlist\ xys]$

Then we have

$xmatch\ s\ (Con\ f\ xs, Con\ g\ ys)$
$= \ $ **if** $f == g$ **then** $xmatchlist\ s\ (zip\ xs\ ys)$ **else** $[\ ]$

$xmatch\ s\ (Compose\ xs, Compose\ ys)$
$= \ concat\ (map\ (xmatchlist\ s)\ (align\ xs\ ys))$

The first equation is immediate, and the second is left as an easy exercise.

At this point we have derived the required definition of *xmatch*, except for the crucial fact that *xmatchlist* is defined as above, and not in the form given in Section 12.3, namely

$xmatchlist\ s\ [\ ] \qquad\qquad = \quad [s]$
$xmatchlist\ s\ (xy : xys) \quad = \quad concat\ [xmatchlist\ t\ xys\ |\ t \leftarrow xmatch\ s\ xy]$

This definition does not involve the function *union*, which is the whole point of phrasing matching in terms of *xmatch*.

In order to prove that the two definitions of *xmatchlist* are equivalent, we have to pass through an intermediate stage. Both *xmatch* and *xmatchlist* take a single substitution as an accumulating parameter, while the functions *gmatch* and *gmatchlist* each take a *list* of substitutions:

$gmatch \qquad\qquad :: \quad [Subst] \rightarrow (Expr, Expr) \rightarrow [Subst]$
$gmatch\ ss\ xy \quad = \quad concat\ [union\ s\ t\ |\ s \leftarrow ss, t \leftarrow match\ xy]$

$gmatchlist \qquad\qquad :: \quad [Subst] \rightarrow [(Expr, Expr)] \rightarrow [Subst]$
$gmatchlist\ ss\ xys \quad = \quad concat\ [union\ s\ t\ |\ s \leftarrow ss, t \leftarrow matchlist\ xys]$

It is clear that $xmatch\ s = gmatch\ [s]$ and $xmatchlist\ s = gmatchlist\ [s]$. In fact, except at one point, we will use these definitions of *xmatch* and *xmatchlist* rather than the previous ones. It is also clear that $match = gmatch\ [[\ ]]$. In fact, one way of viewing the derivation of an efficient program for *match* is first to express the program in terms of *gmatch*, and then refine the result to use *xmatch*.

12.5.2   The combinators

The first task is to recast all the previous equations in functional, noncurried form. For this purpose we will need a number of special combinators.

First, the combinator *star* is defined by

$$star \quad :: \quad (\alpha \rightarrow [\beta]) \rightarrow [\alpha] \rightarrow [\beta]$$
$$star\ f \quad = \quad concat \cdot map\ f$$

Use of *star* is not absolutely necessary, but it will help to shorten expressions.

The next group of combinators are *cpp*, *cpr*, and *cpl*:

$$cpp \qquad\qquad :: \quad ([\alpha], [\beta]) \rightarrow [(\alpha, \beta)]$$
$$cpp\ (xs, ys) \quad = \quad [(x, y) \mid x \leftarrow xs,\ y \leftarrow ys]$$

$$cpr \qquad\qquad :: \quad (\alpha, [\beta]) \rightarrow [(\alpha, \beta)]$$
$$cpr\ (x, ys) \quad = \quad [(x, y) \mid y \leftarrow ys]$$

$$cpl \qquad\qquad :: \quad ([\alpha], \beta) \rightarrow [(\alpha, \beta)]$$
$$cpl\ (xs, y) \quad = \quad [(x, y) \mid x \leftarrow xs]$$

Use of *cpp* is convenient but not necessary, because *cpp = star cpr · cpl*, as the reader can check from the laws of list comprehensions.

Finally, we will need the combinator *assl* (short for 'associate left'), defined by

$$assl \qquad\qquad :: \quad (\alpha, (\beta, \gamma)) \rightarrow ((\alpha, \beta), \gamma)$$
$$assl\ (x, (y, z)) \quad = \quad ((x, y), z)$$

Here are the definitions we will use:

```
matchs
 = map parseLaw [
   "def matchlist:  matchlist  = star unify.cplist.map match",
   "def unify:    unify.nil   = wrap.nil",
   "def unify:    unify.cons  = star union.cpr.cross(id,unify)",
   "def cplist:   cplist.nil  = wrap.nil",
   "def cplist:   cplist.cons = map cons.cpp.cross(id,cplist)"]

gmatchs
 = map parseLaw [
   "def gmatchlist: gmatchlist = star union.cpp.cross(id,matchlist)",
   "def gmatch:      gmatch     = star union.cpp.cross(id,match)"]

xmatchs
 = map parseLaw [
   "def xmatchlist: xmatchlist = gmatchlist.cross(wrap,id)",
   "def xmatch:      xmatch     = gmatch.cross(wrap,id)"]
```

The above definitions are straightforward translations of the previous ones into functional form. Note that there is no definition of *match* because it is not needed in the proof.

For the proof we will need a number of laws, including the following:

```
laws1 = stars ++ cps ++ ids ++ functors

stars
= map parseLaw [
   "star after map:     star f.map g = star(f.g)",
   "star after concat: star f.concat = star(star f)",
   "star after wrap:    star f.wrap = f",
   "star after nil:     star f.nil = nil",
   "star after star:    star(star f.g) = star f.star g"]
```

The "star after star" law is an easy consequence of "star after concat" and "star after map". One can use the calculator to prove these laws, a task we leave as an exercise.

```
cps = cpps ++ cpls ++ cprs

cpps
 = map parseLaw [
   "def cpp:           cpp = star cpr.cpl"]

cpls
 = map parseLaw [
   "cpl after nil:     cpl.cross(nil,id) = nil",
   "cpl after wrap:    cpl.cross(wrap,id) = wrap",
   "cpl after map:     cpl.cross(map f,id) = map(cross(f,id)).cpl",
   "cpl after concat: cpl.cross(concat,id) = star cpl.cpl",
   "cpl after id:      cpl.cross(id,g) = map(cross(id,g)).cpl",
   "cpl after star:    cpl.cross(star f,g) = star(cpl.cross(f,g)).cpl"]

cprs
 = map parseLaw [
   "cpr after nil:     cpr.cross(id,nil) = nil",
   "cpr after wrap:    cpr.cross(id,wrap) = wrap",
   "cpr after map:     cpr.cross(id,map g) = map(cross(id,g)).cpr",
   "cpr after concat: cpr.cross(id,concat) = star cpr.cpr",
   "cpr after id:      cpr.cross(f,id) = map(cross(f,id)).cpr",
   "cpr after star:    cpr.cross(f,star g) = star(cpr.cross(f,g)).cpr"]
```

The "cpl after star" and "cpr after star" laws are easy consequences of the associated "after concat" and "after map" laws. The "after id" laws are instances of the corresponding "after map" laws, introduced simply to avoid use of the law *id = map id*. The remaining laws are

```
ids
 = map parseLaw [
   "id left unit:        id.f = f",
   "id right unit:       f.id = f"]
```

```
functors
 = map parseLaw [
   "cross functor:  cross(f,g).cross(h,k) = cross(f.h, g.k)",
   "cross functor:  cross(id,id) = id",
   "map functor:    map f.map g = map(f.g)",
   "map functor:    map id = id",
   "map after nil:  map f.nil = nil",
   "map after cons: map f.cons = cons.cross(f,map f)"]
```

We will also need some additional laws, to be described in due course.

It is a fair question to ask why we have chosen the above laws and not others. The answer is simply that we have recorded all the laws of *star*, *cpr*, and so on, that might prove useful. In fact, many of the laws listed above are not used in the proof.

12.5.3   The calculations

Our eventual objective is to show

```
xmatchlist.cross(id,nil)  = wrap.fst
xmatchlist.cross(id,cons) = star xmatchlist.cpl.cross(xmatch,id).assl
```

At the point level, these equations read:

$$xmatchlist\,(s, [\,]) \quad = \quad [s]$$
$$xmatchlist\,(s, xy : xys)$$
$$= \quad concat\,[xmatchlist\,(t, xys) \mid t \leftarrow xmatch\,(s, xy)]$$

Apart from the fact that *xmatchlist* is a noncurried function, this is a faithful transcription of the definition in Section 12.3.

It would be nice to just press a button and have the calculation unfold, but life is not like that and we have to proceed more slowly. In outline, the proof is in three stages:

- Obtain a recursive definition of *matchlist*.

- Use the result to obtain a recursive definition of *gmatchlist*.

- Use the result to obtain the required definition of *xmatchlist*.

For the first stage we will need a claim:

```
claims
 = map parseLaw [
    "claim: star(cpr.cross(id,g)).cpp = cpp.cross(id,star g)"]

? prove laws1 "star(cpr.cross(id,g)).cpp = cpp.cross(id,star g)"

   star(cpr.cross(id, g)).cpp
=    {def cpp}
   star(cpr.cross(id, g)).star cpr.cpl
=    {star after star}
   star(star(cpr.cross(id, g)).cpr).cpl
=    {cpr after star}
   star(cpr.cross(id, star g)).cpl
=    {star after map}
   star cpr.map(cross(id, star g)).cpl
=    {cpl after id}
   star cpr.cpl.cross(id, star g)
=    {def cpp}
   cpp.cross(id, star g)
```

Having established the claim, we can proceed with the task of obtaining a recursive definition of *matchlist*:

```
laws2 = matchs ++ laws1 ++ claims

? prove laws2 "matchlist.nil  = wrap.nil"

   matchlist.nil
=    {def matchlist}
   star unify.cplist.map match.nil
=    {map after nil}
   star unify.cplist.nil
=    {def cplist}
   star unify.wrap.nil
=    {star after wrap}
   unify.nil
=    {def unify}
   wrap.nil
```

The second proof is as follows:

```
? prove laws2 "matchlist.cons = star union.cpp.cross(match,matchlist)"

   matchlist.cons
=    {def matchlist}
   star unify.cplist.map match.cons
=    {map after cons}
   star unify.cplist.cons.cross(match, map match)
=    {def cplist}
   star unify.map cons.cpp.cross(id, cplist).cross(match, map match)
```

```
 =    {star after map}
    star(unify.cons).cpp.cross(id, cplist).cross(match, map match)
 =    {cross functor}
    star(unify.cons).cpp.cross(id.match, cplist.map match)
 =    {id left unit}
    star(unify.cons).cpp.cross(match, cplist.map match)
 =    {def unify}
    star(star union.cpr.cross(id, unify)).cpp.cross(match, cplist.map match)
 =    {star after star}
    star union.star(cpr.cross(id, unify)).cpp.cross(match, cplist.map match)
 =    {claim}
    star union.cpp.cross(id, star unify).cross(match, cplist.map match)
 =    {cross functor}
    star union.cpp.cross(id.match, star unify.cplist.map match)
 =    {id left unit}
    star union.cpp.cross(match, star unify.cplist.map match)
 =    {def cpp}
    star union.star cpr.cpl.cross(match, star unify.cplist.map match)
 =    {def matchlist}
    star union.star cpr.cpl.cross(match, matchlist)
 =    {def cpp}
    star union.cpp.cross(match, matchlist)
```

We install the results as new definitions, replacing the previous ones:

```
newmatchs
 = map parseLaw [
   "matchlist-1:  matchlist.nil  = wrap.nil",
   "matchlist-2:  matchlist.cons = star union.cpp.cross(match,matchlist)"]
```

The next stage is to use these new definitions to express *gmatchlist* recursively as well. It is here that we will need the fact that *cup*, where *cup* = *star union · cpp*, is associative and has [[ ]] as unit:

```
cups
 = map parseLaw [
   "cup intro: star union.cpp = cup",
   "cup assoc: cup.cross(id,cup.f) = cup.cross(cup,id).assl.cross(id,f)",
   "iden cup:  cup.cross(id,wrap.nil) = fst"]
```

The associative law for *cup* is really

$$\texttt{cup.cross(id,cup) = cup.cross(cup,id).assl}$$

The form above is needed to avoid using the cross functor law in the backwards direction, thereby invoking a loop in calculations. The laws of *assl* are

```
assls
 = map parseLaw [
```

```
"assl natural: assl.cross(f,cross(g,h)) = cross(cross(f,g),h).assl",
"assl help:    assl.cross(f,id) = cross(cross(f,id),id).assl"]
```

The second law is introduced to avoid using *cross* (*id*, *id*) = *id* in the reverse direction.

We are ready for the proof:

```
laws3 = newmatchs ++ gmatchs ++ cups ++ assls ++ laws1

? prove laws3 "gmatchlist.cross(id,nil) = fst"

  gmatchlist.cross(id, nil)
=   {def gmatchlist}
  star union.cpp.cross(id, matchlist).cross(id, nil)
=   {cup intro}
  cup.cross(id, matchlist).cross(id, nil)
=   {cross functor}
  cup.cross(id.id, matchlist.nil)
=   {id left unit}
  cup.cross(id, matchlist.nil)
=   {matchlist-1}
  cup.cross(id, wrap.nil)
=   {iden cup}
  fst

? prove laws3 "gmatchlist.cross(id,cons) = gmatchlist.cross(gmatch,id).assl"

  gmatchlist.cross(id, cons)
=   {def gmatchlist}
  star union.cpp.cross(id, matchlist).cross(id, cons)
=   {cup intro}
  cup.cross(id, matchlist).cross(id, cons)
=   {cross functor}
  cup.cross(id.id, matchlist.cons)
=   {id left unit}
  cup.cross(id, matchlist.cons)
=   {matchlist-2}
  cup.cross(id, star union.cpp.cross(match, matchlist))
=   {cup intro}
  cup.cross(id, cup.cross(match, matchlist))
=   {cup assoc}
  cup.cross(cup, id).assl.cross(id, cross(match, matchlist))
=   {assl natural}
  cup.cross(cup, id).cross(cross(id, match), matchlist).assl
=   {cross functor}
  cup.cross(cup.cross(id, match), id.matchlist).assl
=   {id left unit}
  cup.cross(cup.cross(id, match), matchlist).assl
=   {cup intro}
  cup.cross(star union.cpp.cross(id, match), matchlist).assl
```

```
=   {def gmatch}
  cup.cross(gmatch, matchlist).assl
=   {id right unit}
  cup.cross(gmatch, matchlist.id).assl
=   {id left unit}
  cup.cross(id.gmatch, matchlist.id).assl
=   {cross functor}
  cup.cross(id, matchlist).cross(gmatch, id).assl
=   {cup intro}
  star union.cpp.cross(id, matchlist).cross(gmatch, id).assl
=   {def gmatchlist}
  gmatchlist.cross(gmatch, id).assl
```

At the point level, we have shown

$$gmatchlist\,(ss, [\,]) \qquad = \quad ss$$
$$gmatchlist\,(ss, xy : xys) \quad = \quad gmatchlist\,(gmatch\,(ss, xy), xys)$$

Hence we have shown that *curry gmatchlist = foldl (curry gmatch)*.

In a sense, we have achieved the main objective of the optimisation of *match*, namely to derive a computation in which the function *union* does not appear. It is easy to use the definition of *match* to get a definition of *gmatch* that does not mention *union*, so why bother with the extra refinement of replacing *gmatch* by *xmatch*? The answer has to do with efficiency. If *xmatch (s, xy)* fails, returning the empty list, then *xmatchlist (s, xy : xys)* fails at once; but if *gmatch (ss, xy)* fails, then *gmatchlist (ss, xy : xys)* does not fail until all the remaining pairs *xys* have been processed. In this context, see Exercise 12.5.4.

To continue, we install the recursive definition of *gmatchlist* as a replacement for the previous one:

```
newgmatchs
 = map parseLaw [
   "gmatchlist-1: gmatchlist.cross(f,nil) = f.fst",
   "gmatchlist-2: gmatchlist.cross(f,cons)
                    = gmatchlist.cross(gmatch,id).assl.cross(f,id)"]
```

The forms of these equations are made necessary in order to avoid appeal to the law *cross (f, g) = cross (id, g) · cross(f, id)*. The right-hand side of the first equation is equal to *fst · cross (f, id)*.

We can now use the recursive definition of *gmatchlist* to get close to the result we are after:

```
laws4 = newgmatchs ++ xmatchs ++ assls ++ laws1

? prove laws4 "xmatchlist.cross(id,nil) = wrap.fst"
```

```
  xmatchlist.cross(id, nil)
=   {def xmatchlist}
  gmatchlist.cross(wrap, id).cross(id, nil)
=   {cross functor}
  gmatchlist.cross(wrap.id, id.nil)
=   {id left unit}
  gmatchlist.cross(wrap.id, nil)
=   {id right unit}
  gmatchlist.cross(wrap, nil)
=   {gmatchlist-1}
  wrap.fst
```

? prove laws4 "xmatchlist.cross(id,cons) = gmatchlist.cross(xmatch,id).assl"

```
  xmatchlist.cross(id, cons)
=   {def xmatchlist}
  gmatchlist.cross(wrap, id).cross(id, cons)
=   {cross functor}
  gmatchlist.cross(wrap.id, id.cons)
=   {id left unit}
  gmatchlist.cross(wrap.id, cons)
=   {id right unit}
  gmatchlist.cross(wrap, cons)
=   {gmatchlist-2}
  gmatchlist.cross(gmatch, id).assl.cross(wrap, id)
=   {assl help}
  gmatchlist.cross(gmatch, id).cross(cross(wrap, id), id).assl
=   {cross functor}
  gmatchlist.cross(gmatch.cross(wrap, id), id.id).assl
=   {id left unit}
  gmatchlist.cross(gmatch.cross(wrap, id), id).assl
=   {def xmatch}
  gmatchlist.cross(xmatch, id).assl
```

Comparison of the last result with the one we are after shows that we need a final fact, namely that *gmatchlist = star xmatchlist · cpl*. In order to prove this equation, we have to go back to the original definitions of *xmatchlist* and *gmatchlist*:

```
originals
 = map parseLaw [
   "xmatchlist: xmatchlist = star union.cpr.cross(id,matchlist)",
   "gmatchlist: gmatchlist = star union.cpp.cross(id,matchlist)"]

laws5 = originals ++ laws1

? prove laws5 "gmatchlist = star xmatchlist.cpl"

  gmatchlist
```

```
=   {gmatchlist}
    star union.cpp.cross(id, matchlist)
=   {def cpp}
    star union.star cpr.cpl.cross(id, matchlist)
=   {cpl after id}
    star union.star cpr.map(cross(id, matchlist)).cpl
=   {star after map}
    star union.star(cpr.cross(id, matchlist)).cpl
=   {star after star}
    star(star union.cpr.cross(id, matchlist)).cpl
=   {xmatchlist}
    star xmatchlist.cpl
```

12.5.4 Conclusions

The positive conclusion from the exercise is that one indeed can get the calculator to assist in the construction of detailed proofs. However, there remains a need for human input to the process, to set up appropriate laws, to identify subsidiary claims, and to control the order in which calculations are carried out. The major negative conclusion is that some laws have to be installed in a more complicated form than is desired, in order to avoid having to invoke other laws in a right to left, as well as left to right, direction. The functor laws cause particular trouble in this respect.

Perhaps the most interesting conclusion of the experiment is that it does seem a viable approach to express all laws as equations between functions, and to use a simple equational logic for proving results.

Exercises

12.5.1 Use the calculator to prove the laws of *star*.

12.5.2 Use the definition of *match* to get a program for *gmatch* that does not mention *union*.

12.5.3 The proof that *matchlist* can be expressed recursively in effect shows that *matchlist* = *foldr* (*cup*, [[ ]]). Apply the first duality theorem to obtain another expression for *matchlist*.

12.5.4 Consider evaluation of $foldl(\oplus) e$. Say that z is a *left zero* of $\oplus$ if $z \oplus x = z$ for all x. Prove that

$$foldl(\oplus) z\ xs\ =\ z$$

for all finite lists xs whenever z is a left zero of $\oplus$. How many steps does it take to reduce the left-hand side to z?

Since

$$foldl\ (\oplus)\ e\ (xs + ys)\quad =\quad foldl\ (\oplus)\ (foldl\ (\oplus)\ e\ xs)\ ys$$

it is clear that if $foldl\ (\oplus)\ e\ xs$ is a left zero of $\oplus$, then

$$foldl\ (\oplus)\ e\ (xs + ys)\quad =\quad foldl\ (\oplus)\ xs$$

In words, evaluation of *foldl* can be truncated as soon as a left zero is encountered. Define a function

$$doWhile\quad ::\quad (\beta \rightarrow Bool) \rightarrow (\beta \rightarrow \alpha \rightarrow \beta) \rightarrow \beta \rightarrow [\alpha] \rightarrow \beta$$

so that if p is an effective test for left zeros of $\oplus$, then $doWhile\ p\ (\oplus) = foldl\ (\oplus)$. Using *doWhile* in the definition of *gmatchlist* leads to a program with the same efficiency as *matchlist*.

12.6 Chapter notes

Mike Spivey's original calculator was written in Orwell, a predecessor of Haskell; although the program hasn't been documented in the literature, Spivey (1990) contains a discussion on matching and rewriting expressions. Another interactive equational reasoning assistant for Orwell, called ERA, is described in Wilson (1993).

Mechanical theorem proving and interactive proof assistance form a large and buoyant subject, and dozens of systems are available to the interested user. We will not attempt to enumerate them, but the references in Chapter 4 give some pointers. For an easily accessible reference, consult Paulson (1996). This text describes the implementation in ML of a tactical theorem prover called Hal.

The hidden agenda of this chapter has been to demonstrate the advantages of phrasing laws and proofs as equations between functional expressions. The mathematical foundations of this approach is the subject matter of category theory (see the references cited in Chapter 2). However, for a truly viable method of specification and proof, one needs to replace functional expressions by *relational* ones, and equational reasoning by *inequational* reasoning. See Bird and de Moor (1997) for details.

Appendix: Some standard functions

Below, arranged in alphabetical order, is a summary of the most commonly used functions, together with their definitions. In some cases, these definitions differ slightly from those found in the Haskell Standard Prelude.

1. $(\cdot)$. Functional composition:

$$(\cdot) \quad :: \quad (\beta \to \gamma) \to (\alpha \to \beta) \to (\alpha \to \gamma)$$
$$(f \cdot g)\, x \quad = \quad f\, (g\, x)$$

2. $(+\!\!+)$. Concatenates two lists:

$$(+\!\!+) \quad :: \quad [\alpha] \to [\alpha] \to [\alpha]$$
$$[\,]\, +\!\!+\, ys \quad = \quad ys$$
$$(x : xs)\, +\!\!+\, ys \quad = \quad x : (xs\, +\!\!+\, ys)$$

3. $(\wedge)$. Conjunction:

$$(\wedge) \quad :: \quad Bool \to Bool \to Bool$$
$$True \wedge x \quad = \quad x$$
$$False \wedge x \quad = \quad False$$

4. $(\vee)$. Disjunction:

$$(\vee) \quad :: \quad Bool \to Bool \to Bool$$
$$True \vee x \quad = \quad True$$
$$False \vee x \quad = \quad x$$

5. (!!). List indexing:

$$
\begin{array}{lcl}
(!!) & :: & [\alpha] \rightarrow \mathit{Int} \rightarrow \alpha \\
[\,]\ !!\ n & = & \mathit{error}\ \text{``(!!): index too large''} \\
(x:xs)\ !!\ 0 & = & x \\
(x:xs)\ !!\ (n+1) & = & xs\ !!\ n
\end{array}
$$

6. *and*. Returns the logical conjunction of a list of booleans:

$$
\begin{array}{lcl}
\mathit{and} & :: & [\mathit{Bool}] \rightarrow \mathit{Bool} \\
\mathit{and} & = & \mathit{foldr}\ (\wedge)\ \mathit{True}
\end{array}
$$

7. *concat*. Concatenates a list of lists:

$$
\begin{array}{lcl}
\mathit{concat} & :: & [[\alpha]] \rightarrow [\alpha] \\
\mathit{concat} & = & \mathit{foldr}\ (+\!\!+)\ [\,]
\end{array}
$$

8. *const*. Creates a constant-valued function:

$$
\begin{array}{lcl}
\mathit{const} & :: & \alpha \rightarrow \beta \rightarrow \alpha \\
\mathit{const}\ x\ y & = & x
\end{array}
$$

9. *cross*. Applies a pair of functions to corresponding elements of a pair:

$$
\begin{array}{lcl}
\mathit{cross} & :: & (\alpha \rightarrow \gamma, \beta \rightarrow \delta) \rightarrow (\alpha, \beta) \rightarrow (\gamma, \delta) \\
\mathit{cross}\ (f,g) & = & \mathit{pair}\ (f \cdot \mathit{fst}, g \cdot \mathit{snd})
\end{array}
$$

10. *curry*. Converts a noncurried function into a curried one:

$$
\begin{array}{lcl}
\mathit{curry} & :: & ((\alpha, \beta) \rightarrow \gamma) \rightarrow (\alpha \rightarrow \beta \rightarrow \gamma) \\
\mathit{curry}\ f\ x\ y & = & f\ (x, y)
\end{array}
$$

11. *drop*. Selects a final segment of a list:

$$
\begin{array}{lcl}
\mathit{drop} & :: & \mathit{Int} \rightarrow [\alpha] \rightarrow [\alpha] \\
\mathit{drop}\ 0\ xs & = & xs \\
\mathit{drop}\ (n+1)\ [\,] & = & [\,] \\
\mathit{drop}\ (n+1)\ (x:xs) & = & \mathit{drop}\ n\ xs
\end{array}
$$

12. *dropWhile*. Removes the longest initial segment of a list all of whose elements satisfy a given predicate:

$$
\begin{array}{lcl}
\mathit{dropWhile} & :: & (\alpha \rightarrow \mathit{Bool}) \rightarrow [\alpha] \rightarrow [\alpha] \\
\mathit{dropWhile}\ p\ [\,] & = & [\,] \\
\mathit{dropWhile}\ p\ (x:xs) & = & \textbf{if}\ p\ x\ \textbf{then}\ \mathit{dropWhile}\ p\ xs\ \textbf{else}\ x:xs
\end{array}
$$

13. *filter*. Filters a list with a predicate:

$$filter \quad :: \quad (\alpha \rightarrow Bool) \rightarrow [\alpha] \rightarrow [\alpha]$$
$$filter\ p\ [\ ] \quad = \quad [\ ]$$
$$filter\ p\ (x:xs) \quad = \quad \textbf{if}\ p\ x\ \textbf{then}\ x:filter\ p\ xs\ \textbf{else}\ filter\ p\ xs$$

14. *flip*. Flips the arguments to a function:

$$flip \quad :: \quad (\beta \rightarrow \alpha \rightarrow \gamma) \rightarrow \alpha \rightarrow \beta \rightarrow \gamma$$
$$flip\ f\ x\ y \quad = \quad f\ y\ x$$

15. *foldl*. Fold-left:

$$foldl \quad :: \quad (\beta \rightarrow \alpha \rightarrow \beta) \rightarrow \beta \rightarrow [\alpha] \rightarrow \beta$$
$$foldl\ f\ e\ [\ ] \quad = \quad e$$
$$foldl\ f\ e\ (x:xs) \quad = \quad strict\ (foldl\ f)\ (f\ e\ x)\ xs$$

16. *foldl1*. Fold-left over nonempty lists:

$$foldl1 \quad :: \quad (\alpha \rightarrow \alpha \rightarrow \alpha) \rightarrow [\alpha] \rightarrow \alpha$$
$$foldl1\ f\ [\ ] \quad = \quad error\ \text{``}foldl1\text{: empty list''}$$
$$foldl1\ f\ (x:xs) \quad = \quad foldl\ f\ x\ xs$$

17. *foldr*. Fold-right:

$$foldr \quad :: \quad (\alpha \rightarrow \beta \rightarrow \beta) \rightarrow \beta \rightarrow [\alpha] \rightarrow \beta$$
$$foldr\ f\ e\ [\ ] \quad = \quad e$$
$$foldr\ f\ e\ (x:xs) \quad = \quad f\ x\ (foldr\ f\ e\ xs)$$

18. *foldr1*. Fold-right over nonempty lists:

$$foldr1 \quad :: \quad (\alpha \rightarrow \alpha \rightarrow \alpha) \rightarrow [\alpha] \rightarrow \alpha$$
$$foldr1\ f\ [\ ] \quad = \quad error\ \text{``}foldr1\text{: empty list''}$$
$$foldr1\ f\ [x] \quad = \quad x$$
$$foldr1\ f\ (x:xs) \quad = \quad f\ x\ (foldr1\ f\ xs)$$

19. *fst*. Selects the first component of a pair:

$$fst \quad :: \quad (\alpha, \beta) \rightarrow \alpha$$
$$fst\ (x, y) \quad = \quad x$$

20. *head*. Returns the first element of a nonempty list:

$$head \quad :: \quad [\alpha] \rightarrow \alpha$$
$$head\ [\ ] \quad = \quad error\ \text{``}head\text{: empty list''}$$
$$head\ (x:xs) \quad = \quad xs$$

21. *id*. The identity function:

$$id \quad :: \quad \alpha \to \alpha$$
$$id\ x \ = \ x$$

22. *init*. Returns a list without its last element:

$$
\begin{aligned}
init \qquad &:: \quad [\alpha] \to [\alpha] \\
init\ [\,] \qquad &= \quad error\ \text{"}init\text{: empty list"} \\
init\ [x] \qquad &= \quad [\,] \\
init\ (x:y:xs) \qquad &= \quad x:init\ (y:xs)
\end{aligned}
$$

23. *iterate*. Produces an infinite list of iterated applications of a function to a value:

$$
\begin{aligned}
iterate \qquad &:: \quad (\alpha \to \alpha) \to \alpha \to [\alpha] \\
iterate\ f\ x \qquad &= \quad x:iterate\ f\ (f\ x)
\end{aligned}
$$

24. *last*. Returns the last element of a nonempty list:

$$
\begin{aligned}
last \qquad &:: \quad [\alpha] \to \alpha \\
last\ [\,] \qquad &= \quad error\ \text{"}last\text{: empty list"} \\
last\ [x] \qquad &= \quad x \\
last\ (x:y:xs) \qquad &= \quad last\ (y:xs)
\end{aligned}
$$

25. *length*. Returns the length of a list:

$$
\begin{aligned}
length \qquad &:: \quad [\alpha] \to Int \\
length\ [\,] \qquad &= \quad 0 \\
length\ (x:xs) \qquad &= \quad 1 + length\ xs
\end{aligned}
$$

26. *map*. Applies a function to every element of a list:

$$
\begin{aligned}
map \qquad &:: \quad (\alpha \to \beta) \to [\alpha] \to [\beta] \\
map\ f\ [\,] \qquad &= \quad [\,] \\
map\ f\ (x:xs) \qquad &= \quad f\ x:map\ f\ xs
\end{aligned}
$$

27. *not*. Negation:

$$
\begin{aligned}
not \qquad &:: \quad Bool \to Bool \\
not\ True \qquad &= \quad False \\
not\ False \qquad &= \quad True
\end{aligned}
$$

28. *null*. Tests a list for being empty:

$$
\begin{aligned}
null \qquad &:: \quad [\alpha] \to Bool \\
null\ [\,] \qquad &= \quad True \\
null\ (x:xs) \qquad &= \quad False
\end{aligned}
$$

29. *or*. Returns the logical disjunction of a list of booleans:

$$or \quad :: \quad [Bool] \rightarrow Bool$$
$$or \quad = \quad foldr \ (\lor) \ False$$

30. *pair*. Applies a pair of functions to an argument:

$$pair \qquad :: \quad (\alpha \rightarrow \beta, \alpha \rightarrow \gamma) \rightarrow \alpha \rightarrow (\beta, \gamma)$$
$$pair \ (f, g) \ x \quad = \quad (f \ x, g \ x)$$

31. *partition*. Partitions a list according to a given test (compare *span* and *splitAt*):

$$partition \qquad :: \quad (\alpha \rightarrow Bool) \rightarrow [\alpha] \rightarrow ([\alpha], [\alpha])$$
$$partition \ p \ [\ ] \qquad = \quad ([\ ], [\ ])$$
$$partition \ p \ (x : xs) \quad = \quad \textbf{if} \ p \ x \ \textbf{then} \ (x : ys, zs) \ \textbf{else} \ (ys, x : zs)$$
$$\textbf{where} \ (ys, zs) = partition \ p \ xs$$

32. *reverse*. Reverses a finite list:

$$reverse \quad :: \quad [\alpha] \rightarrow [\alpha]$$
$$reverse \quad = \quad foldl \ (flip \ (:)) \ [\ ]$$

33. *scanl*. Applies *foldl* to every initial segment of a list:

$$scanl \qquad :: \quad (\beta \rightarrow \alpha \rightarrow \beta) \rightarrow \beta \rightarrow [\alpha] \rightarrow [\beta]$$
$$scanl \ f \ e \ xs \quad = \quad e : scanl' \ f \ e \ xs$$
$$\textbf{where} \ scanl' \ f \ a \ [\ ] \qquad = \quad [\ ]$$
$$scanl' \ f \ a \ (y : ys) \quad = \quad scanl \ f \ (f \ a \ y) \ ys$$

34. *scanl1*. Applies *foldl1* to every nonempty initial segment of a nonempty list:

$$scanl1 \qquad :: \quad (\alpha \rightarrow \alpha \rightarrow \alpha) \rightarrow [\alpha] \rightarrow [\alpha]$$
$$scanl1 \ f \ [\ ] \qquad = \quad error \ \text{``scanl1: empty list''}$$
$$scanl1 \ f \ (x : xs) \quad = \quad scanl \ f \ x \ xs$$

35. *scanr*. Applies *foldr* to every tail segment of a list:

$$scanr \qquad :: \quad (\alpha \rightarrow \beta \rightarrow \beta) \rightarrow \beta \rightarrow [\alpha] \rightarrow [\beta]$$
$$scanr \ f \ e \ [\ ] \qquad = \quad [e]$$
$$scanr \ f \ e \ (x : xs) \quad = \quad f \ x \ (head \ ys) : ys$$
$$\textbf{where} \ ys = scanr \ f \ e \ xs$$

36. *scanr1*. Applies *foldr1* to every nonempty tail segment of a nonempty list:

$$
\begin{array}{lll}
scanr1 & :: & (\alpha \to \alpha \to \alpha) \to [\alpha] \to [\alpha] \\
scanr1\ f\ [\,] & = & error\ \text{``}scanr1\text{: empty list''} \\
scanr1\ f\ [x] & = & [x] \\
scanr1\ f\ (x:y:xs) & = & f\ x\ (head\ zs) : zs \\
& & \textbf{where}\ zs = scanr1\ f\ (y:xs)
\end{array}
$$

37. *singleton*. Tests a list for being a singleton list:

$$
\begin{array}{lll}
singleton & :: & [\alpha] \to Bool \\
singleton\ xs & = & not\ (null\ xs) \wedge null\ (tail\ xs)
\end{array}
$$

38. *span*. Splits a list into two parts:

$$
\begin{array}{lll}
span & :: & (\alpha \to Bool) \to [\alpha] \to ([\alpha],[\alpha]) \\
span\ p\ [\,] & = & ([\,],[\,]) \\
span\ p\ (x:xs) & = & \textbf{if}\ p\ x\ \textbf{then}\ (x:ys,zs)\ \textbf{else}\ ([\,],x:xs) \\
& & \textbf{where}\ (ys,zs) = span\ p\ xs
\end{array}
$$

39. *splitAt*. Splits a list into two parts of given length:

$$
\begin{array}{lll}
splitAt & :: & Int \to [\alpha] \to ([\alpha],[\alpha]) \\
splitAt\ 0\ xs & = & ([\,],xs) \\
splitAt\ (n+1)\ [\,] & = & ([\,],[\,]) \\
splitAt\ (n+1)\ (x:xs) & = & (x:ys,zs) \\
& & \textbf{where}\ (ys,zs) = splitAt\ n\ xs
\end{array}
$$

40. *snd*. Selects the second component of a pair:

$$
\begin{array}{lll}
snd & :: & (\alpha,\beta) \to \beta \\
snd\ (x,y) & = & y
\end{array}
$$

41. *tail*. Removes the first element of a nonempty list:

$$
\begin{array}{lll}
tail & :: & [\alpha] \to [\alpha] \\
tail\ [\,] & = & error\ \text{``}tail\text{: empty list''} \\
tail\ (x:xs) & = & xs
\end{array}
$$

42. *take*. Selects an initial segment of a list:

$$
\begin{array}{lll}
take & :: & Int \to [\alpha] \to [\alpha] \\
take\ 0\ xs & = & [\,] \\
take\ (n+1)\ [\,] & = & [\,] \\
take\ (n+1)\ (x:xs) & = & x:take\ n\ xs
\end{array}
$$

43. *takeWhile*. Selects the longest initial segment of a list all of whose elements satisfy a given predicate:

$$takeWhile \qquad :: \quad (\alpha \to Bool) \to [\alpha] \to [\alpha]$$
$$takeWhile\ p\ [\ ] \qquad = \quad [\ ]$$
$$takeWhile\ p\ (x : xs) \quad = \quad \textbf{if}\ p\ x\ \textbf{then}\ x : takeWhile\ p\ xs\ \textbf{else}\ [\ ]$$

44. *uncurry*. Converts a curried function to noncurried form:

$$uncurry \qquad :: \quad (\alpha \to \beta \to \gamma) \to (\alpha, \beta) \to \gamma$$
$$uncurry\ f\ xy \quad = \quad f\ (fst\ xy)\ (snd\ xy)$$

45. *until*. Applied to a predicate, a function, and a value, returns the result of applying the function to the value the smallest number of times in order to satisfy the predicate:

$$until \qquad :: \quad (\alpha \to Bool) \to (\alpha \to \alpha) \to \alpha \to \alpha$$
$$until\ p\ f\ x \quad = \quad \textbf{if}\ p\ x\ \textbf{then}\ x\ \textbf{else}\ until\ p\ f\ (f\ x)$$

46. *unzip*. Unzips a list of pairs:

$$unzip \quad :: \quad [(\alpha, \beta)] \to ([\alpha], [\beta])$$
$$unzip \quad = \quad foldr\ f\ ([\ ], [\ ])$$
$$\qquad\qquad \textbf{where}\ f\ (x, y) = cross\ ((x :), (y :))$$

47. *wrap*. Converts a value into a singleton list:

$$wrap \quad :: \quad \alpha \to [\alpha]$$
$$wrap\ x \quad = \quad [x]$$

48. *zip*. Zips two lists:

$$zip \qquad\qquad :: \quad [\alpha] \to [\beta] \to [(\alpha, \beta)]$$
$$zip\ [\ ]\ ys \qquad\quad = \quad [\ ]$$
$$zip\ (x : xs)\ [\ ] \qquad = \quad [\ ]$$
$$zip\ (x : xs)\ (y : ys) \quad = \quad (x, y) : zip\ xs\ ys$$

49. *zipp*. The uncurried version of *zip*:

$$zipp \quad :: \quad ([\alpha], [\beta]) \to [(\alpha, \beta)]$$
$$zipp \quad = \quad uncurry\ zip$$

Bibliography

Adelson-Velski, G. M. and Landis, E. M. (1962). An algorithm for the organisation of information. *Soviet Mathematics - Doklady*, *3*(5), 1259–1263. English translation in *Doklady Akademia Nauk SSSR*, *146*, 263–266.

Aho, A., Sethi, R., and Ullman, J. (1986). *Compilers – Principles, Techniques and Tools*. Addison-Wesley, Reading, Mass., USA.

Andersson, A. (1993). Binary trees made simple. In Dehne, F., Sack, J.-R., Santoro, N., and Whitesides, S., editors, *Workshop on Algorithm Design and Data Structures*, Volume 709 of *Lecture Notes in Computer Science*. Springer-Verlag.

Barr, M. and Wells, C. (1995). *Category Theory for Computing Science* (second edition). Prentice Hall International, Hemel Hempstead, Herts, UK.

Bellman, R. E. (1957). *Dynamic Programming*. Princeton University Press, Princeton, USA.

Ben-Ari, M. (1993). *Mathematical Logic for Computing Science*. Prentice Hall International, Hemel Hempstead, Herts, UK.

Bentley, J. R. (1987). *Programming Pearls*. Addison-Wesley, Reading, Mass., USA.

Bird, R. and de Moor, O. (1997). *The Algebra of Programming*. Prentice Hall International, Hemel Hempstead, Herts, UK.

Bird, R. S. (1980). Tabulation techniques for recursive programs. *ACM Computing Surveys*, *12*(4), 403–417.

Bird, R. S. (1984). The promotion and accumulation strategies in functional programming. *ACM Transactions on Programming Languages and Systems*, *6*(4), 487–504.

Bird, R. S. (1986). Transformational programming and the paragraph problem. *Science of Computer Programming, 6*(2), 159–189.

Bird, R. S. (1989). Algebraic identities for program calculation. *Computer Journal, 32*(2), 122–126.

Bird, R. S. (1991). Meertens' number. In Jeuring, J., editor, *Lambert Meertens, Liber Amicorum,* pages 4–10 Amsterdam, The Netherlands. CWI.

Bjerner, B. and Holmström, S. (1989). A compositional approach to time analysis of first order lazy functional programs. In *Conference on Functional Programming Languages and Computer Architecture,* pages 157–165. ACM.

Boole, G. (1847). *The Mathematical Analysis of Logic.* Cambridge. Reprinted, 1948, by Basil Blackwell, Oxford, UK.

Boyer, R. S. and Moore, J. S. (1979). *A Computational Logic.* Academic Press, London, UK.

Burge, W. H. (1975). *Recursive Programming Techniques.* Addison-Wesley, Reading, Mass., USA.

Burke, E. and Foxley, E. (1996). *Logic and its Applications.* Prentice Hall International, Hemel Hempstead, Herts, UK.

Burstall, R. M. and Darlington, J. (1977). A transformational system for developing recursive programs. *Journal of the ACM, 24*(1), 44–67.

Church, A. (1941). *The Calculi of Lamda Conversion,* Volume 6 of *Annals of Mathematical Studies.* Princeton University Press, Princeton, USA.

Clack, C., Myers, C., and Poon, E. (1995). *Programming with Miranda.* Prentice Hall International, Hemel Hempstead, Herts, UK.

Cormen, T. H., Leiserson, C. E., and Rivest, R. L. (1990). *Introduction to Algorithms.* MIT Press, Cambridge, Mass., USA.

Davey, B. and Priestley, H. (1990). *Introduction to Lattices and Order.* Cambridge University Press, Cambridge, UK.

de Moor, O. (1994). Categories, relations and dynamic programming. *Mathematical Structures in Computer Science, 4,* 33–69.

Dielissen, V. J. and Kaldewaij, A. (1995). A simple, efficient, and flexible implementation of flexible arrays. In Möller, B., editor, *Third International Conference on the Mathematics of Program Construction,* Volume 947 of *Lecture Notes in Computer Science,* pages 232–241. Springer-Verlag.

Fokker, J. (1995). Functional parsers. In Jeuring, J. and Meijer, E., editors, *Advanced Functional Programming,* Volume 925 of *Lecture Notes in Computer Science,* pages 1–23. Springer-Verlag.

Fokkinga, M. M. (1992). *Law and Order in Algorithmics*. Ph.D. thesis, Technical University of Twente, The Netherlands.

Gibbons, J. (1991). *Algebras for Tree Algorithms*. Ph.D. thesis, Programming Research Group, Oxford University, UK. Technical Monograph PRG-94.

Gödel, K. (1990). *Kurt Gödel, Collected Works*, Volume I. Oxford University Press, Oxford, UK. Edited by S. Feferman *et al*.

Gordon, A. (1993). *Functional Programming and Input/Output*. Ph.D. thesis, Computing Laboratory, Cambridge, UK. Published as a Distinguished Dissertation by Cambridge University Press.

Gordon, M. J., Milner, R., and Wadsworth, C. P. (1979). *Edinburgh LCF*, Volume 78 of *Lecture Notes in Computer Science*. Springer-Verlag.

Gordon, M. J. C. (1979). *The Denotational Description of Programming Languages, An Introduction*. Springer-Verlag.

Gordon, M. J. C. (1994). *Programming Language Theory and its Implementation*. Prentice Hall International, Hemel Hempstead, Herts, UK.

Graham, R. L., Knuth, D. E., and Patashnik, O. (1990). *Concrete Mathematics: A Foundation for Computer Science*. Addison-Wesley, Reading, Mass., USA.

Gries, D. and Schneider, F. B. (1995). *A Logical Approach to Discrete Math*. Texts and Monographs in Computer Science. Springer-Verlag.

Gunter, C. (1992). *Semantics of Programming Languages*. Foundations of Computing. MIT Press, Cambridge, Mass., USA.

Guttag, J. V. and Horning, J. J. (1978). The algebraic specification of abstract data types. *Acta Informatica*, *10*(1), 27–52.

Hall, C., Hammond, K., Partain, W., Jones, S. P., and Wadler, P. (1992). The Glasgow Haskell compiler: a retrospective. In *Proceedings of the 1992 Glasgow Workshop in Functional Programming*, Springer-Verlag Workshops in Computing, pages 134–143. Springer-Verlag.

Harrison, R. (1989). *Abstract Data Types in Modula-2*. John Wiley and Sons, Chichester, UK.

Hoare, C. A. R. (1962). Quicksort. *Computer Journal*, *5*(1), 10–15.

Hofstadter, D. R. (1979). *Gödel, Escher, Bach: An Eternal Golden Braid*. Harvester Press, Hassocks, Essex, UK.

Hoogerwoord, R. (1991). A logarithmic implementation of flexible arrays. In Bird, R. S., Morgan, C. C., and Woodcock, J. P. C., editors, *Second International Conference on the Mathematics of Program Construction*, Volume 669 of *Lecture Notes in Computer Science*, pages 191–207. Springer-Verlag.

Hu, T. C. (1982). *Combinatorial Algorithms.* Addison-Wesley, Reading, Mass., USA.

Hudak, P., Fasel, J., and Peterson, J. (1996). A gentle introduction to Haskell. Technical Report YALEU/DCS/RR-901, Yale University, USA.

Huffman, D. A. (1952). A method for the construction of minimum redundancy codes. *Proceedings of the IRE, 40,* 1098–1101.

Hughes, R. J. M. (1984). *The Design and Implementation of Programming Languages.* Ph.D. thesis, Programming Research Group, Oxford University, Oxford, UK.

Hughes, R. J. M. (1995). The design of a pretty-printing library. In Jeuring, J. and Meijer, E., editors, *Advanced Functional Programming,* Volume 925 of *Lecture Notes in Computer Science,* pages 53–96. Springer-Verlag.

Hutton, G. (1992). Higher-order functions for parsing. *Journal of Functional Programming, 2,* 323–343.

Hutton, G. and Meijer, E. (1996). Monadic parser combinators. Draft manuscript.

ISO (1989). A character set for Western European languages. ISO Standard 8859-1.

Jeuring, J. (1993). *Theories for Algorithm Calculation.* Ph.D. thesis, University of Utrecht, The Netherlands.

Jones, M. P. (1992). *Qualified Types: Theory and Practice.* Ph.D. thesis, Programming Research Group, Oxford University, Oxford, UK.

Jones, M. P. (1993). Release notes for Gofer 2.28. User manual for Gofer.

Jones, M. P. (1995). A system of constructor classes: overloading and implicit higher-order polymorphism. *Journal of Functional Programming, 5*(1), 1–35.

Jones, S. P., Gordon, A., and Finne, S. (1996). Concurrent Haskell. In *23rd ACM Symposium on Principles of Programming Languages, St. Petersburg, Florida.* ACM.

Kaldewaij, A. (1990). *Programming: The Derivation of Algorithms.* Prentice Hall International, Hemel Hempstead, Herts, UK.

Knuth, D. E. (1973a). *The Art of Computer Programming: Fundamental Algorithms* (second edition)., Volume 1. Addison-Wesley, Reading, Mass., USA.

Knuth, D. E. (1973b). *The Art of Computer Programming: Sorting and Searching,* Volume 3. Addison-Wesley, Reading, Mass., USA.

Knuth, D. E. (1981). *The Art of Computer Programming: Seminumerical Algorithms* (second edition)., Volume 2. Addison-Wesley, Reading, Mass., USA.

Knuth, D. E. and Plass, M. F. (1981). Breaking paragraphs into lines. *Software, Practice and Experience, 11,* 1119-1184.

Launchbury, J. (1993). Lazy imperative programming. In *Proceedings of the ACM SigPlan Workshop on State in Programming Languages.* Also University of Yale Research Report, YALEU/DCS/RR-968, New Haven, USA.

Liang, S., Hudak, P., and Jones, M. (1995). Monad transfomers and modular interpreters. In *Proceedings of the 22nd ACM Conference on Principles of Programming Languages.*

Malcolm, G. R. (1990). *Algebraic Data Types and Program Transformation.* Ph.D. thesis, University of Groningen, Groningen, The Netherlands.

Martin, J. J. (1986). *Data Types and Data Structures.* Prentice Hall International, Hemel Hempstead, Herts. UK.

Martin, U. and Nipkow, T. (1990). Automating squiggol. In Broy, M. and Jones, C. B., editors, *Programming Concepts and Methods*, pages 223-236 Amsterdam, The Netherlands. North-Holland.

Meertens, L. G. L. T. (1987). First steps towards the theory of rose trees. Draft Report, CWI, Amsterdam, The Netherlands.

Meijer, E. (1992). *Calculating Compilers.* Ph.D. thesis, University of Nijmegen, The Netherlands.

Moggi, E. (1989). Computational lambda-calculus and monads. In *IEEE Symposium on Logic in Computer Science* Asilomar, Calif., USA.

Moggi, E. (1991). Notions of computation and monads. *Information and Control, 93,* 55-92.

Morgan, C. (1996). *Programming from Specifications* (Second edition). Prentice Hall International, Hemel Hempstead, Herts, UK.

Okasaki, C. (1995). Simple and efficient purely functional queues and deques. *Journal of Functional Programming, 5*(4), 583-592.

Okasaki, C. (1996). *Purely Functional Data Structures.* Ph.D. thesis, School of Computer Science, Carnegie Mellon University, Pittsburgh, USA.

Paulson, L. C. (1983). Rewriting in Cambridge LCF. *Science of Computer Programming, 3*(2), 119-149.

Paulson, L. C. (1996). *ML for the Working Programmer* (second edition). Cambridge University Press, Cambridge, UK.

Penrose, R. (1994). *Shadows of the Mind.* Oxford University Press, Oxford, UK.

Pettorossi, A. (1984). *Methodologies for transformations and memoing in applicative languages.* Ph.D. thesis, University of Edinburgh, Edinburgh, UK.

Peyton Jones, S. (1987). *The Implementation of Functional Programming Languages.* Prentice Hall International, Hemel Hempstead, Herts, UK.

Peyton Jones, S. and Lester, D. (1991). *Implementing Functional Languages.* Prentice Hall International, Hemel Hempstead, Herts, UK.

Pierce, B. C. (1991). *Basic Category Theory for Computer Scientists.* Foundations of Computing. MIT Press, Cambridge, Mass., USA.

Pitts, A. and Dyber, P., editors (1997). *Semantics and Logics of Computation.* Publications of the Newton Institute, Cambridge University Press, Cambridge, UK.

Runciman, C. and Röjemo, N. (1996). New dimensions in heap profiling. *Journal of Functional Programming, 6*(4), 587-620.

Sands, D. (1995). A naive time analysis and its theory of cost equivalence. *Journal of Logic and Computation, 5*(4), 495-541.

Schoenmakers, B. (1992). *Data Structures and Amortized Complexity in a Functional Setting.* Ph.D. thesis, Eindhoven University of Technology, Eindhoven, The Netherlands.

Scott, D. (1976). Data types as lattices. *SIAM Journal of Computing, 5*, 522-587.

Scott, D. (1982). Domains for denotational semantics. In *International Colloquium on Automata, Languages and Programming,* Volume 140 of *Lecture Notes in Computer Science,* pages 577-613. Springer-Verlag.

Sijtsma, B. (1988). *Verification and Derivation of Infinite-list Programs.* Ph.D. thesis, University of Groningen, The Netherlands.

Spivey, M. (1990). A functional theory of exceptions. *Science of Computer Programming, 14*, 25-42.

Stoy, J. (1977). *Denotational Semantics: The Scott-Strachey Approach to Programming Language Theory.* MIT Press, Cambridge, Mass., USA.

Thompson, S. (1995). *Miranda: The Craft of Functional Programming.* Addison-Wesley, London, UK.

Thompson, S. (1996). *Haskell: The Craft of Functional Programming.* Addison-Wesley, London, UK.

Wadler, P. (1984). *Listlessness is better than Laziness.* Ph.D. thesis, School of Computer Science, Carnegie Mellon University, Pittsburgh, USA.

Wadler, P. (1985). How to replace failure by a list of successes. In *Second International Conference on Functional Programming Languages and Computer Architecture,,* Volume 201 of *Lecture Notes in Computer Science.* Springer-Verlag.

Wadler, P. (1987). Strictness analysis aids time analysis. In *Proceedings of the 14th ACM Symposium on the Principles of Programming Languages,* pages 307–313.

Wadler, P. (1989). Theorems for free!. In *Proceedings of the 16th ACM Symposium on Principles of Programming Languages,* pages 347–359.

Wadler, P. (1990a). Comprehending monads. In *Proceedings of the ACM Symposium on Lisp and Functional Programming,* pages 347–359. Also in *Mathematical Structures in Computer Science,* 2, 461–493, 1992.

Wadler, P. (1990b). Deforestation: transforming programs to eliminate trees. *Theoretical Computer Science,* 73, 231–248.

Wadler, P. (1995). Monads for functional programming. In Jeuring, J. and Meijer, E., editors, *Advanced Functional Programming,* Volume 925 of *Lecture Notes in Computer Science.* Springer-Verlag.

Wadler, P. and Blott, S. (1989). How to make *ad hoc* polymorphism less *ad hoc.* In *Proceedings of the 16th ACM Symposium on Principles of Programming Languages,* pages 60–76.

Wilson, S. P. (1993). Equational reasoning support for Orwell. Technical Report PRG Monographs, PRG-104, Oxford University Computing Laboratory, Oxford, UK.

Index

(), 44
(++), 53, 95, 228, 409
(→), 15, 24
(·), 44, 228, 347, 409
(:), 92
(<), 32, 57, 152
(≤), 32, 45, 55, 152
(=), 11, 31
(>), 32
(≥), 32, 55
(‼), 107, 141, 304, 410
(▷), 327
(⊥), 42
(==), 9, 18, 31, 49, 93
(◇), 347
(≠), 31
(≫), 326
(∨), 30, 55, 409
(∧), 30, 55, 409
[..], 110
⊥, 8, 30, 61, 72, 95, 243, 253, 299
⌈ ⌉, 182
≡, 69
⌊ ⌋, 77, 81, 158
[ ], 91, 92
π, 298

above, 164

abs, 21, 81, 82
abstract datatypes, x, 251, 325
abstraction barriers, 252, 263
abstraction functions, 254
accumulating parameters, 160,
            199, 228, 246, 289, 371,
            389, 397
actions, 325
addition, 14, 58, 76, 88, 153
algebraic laws, ix, 110
algebraic specifications, 252, 293
algorithm design, xi, 236
amortised complexity, 293
amortised costs, 258, 267
and, 117, 410
approx, 300, 304
approximation ordering, 299
approximations, 298
arbitrary-precision integers, *see*
            Integer
arguments of functions, 10
arithmetic expressions, 334
arrays, 251, 281
ascending order, *see*
            nondecreasing order
association, 12, 15, 128
associativity, 15, 16, 31, 66, 69, 96,
            120, 164, 176, 343, 348

SPIVEY, J.M., *An Introduction to Logic Programming through Prolog*
SPIVEY, J.M., *The Z Notation: A reference manual (2nd edn)*
TENNENT, R.D., *Semantics of Programming Languages*
WATT, D.A., *Programming Language Concepts and Paradigms*
WATT, D.A., *Programming Language Processors*
WATT, D.A., *Programming Language Syntax and Semantics*
WATT, D.A., WICHMANN, B.A. and FINDLAY, W., *ADA: Language and methodology*
WELSH, J. and ELDER, J., *Introduction to Pascal (3rd edn)*
WOODCOCK, J. and DAVIES, J., *Using Z: Specification, refinement and proof*

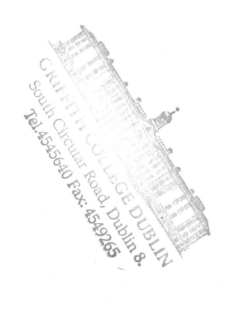